D0414679

The Globalization of Musics in Transit

This book traces the particularities of music migration and tourism in different global settings, and provides current, even new perspectives for ethnomusicological research on globalizing musics in transit. The dual focus on tourism and migration is central to debates on globalization, and their examination—separately or combined—offers a useful lens on many key questions about where globalization is taking us: questions about identity and heritage, commoditization, historical and cultural representation, hybridity, authenticity and ownership, neoliberalism, inequality, diasporization, the relocation of allegiances, and more. Moreover, for the first time, these two key phenomena—tourism and migration—are studied conjointly, as well as interdisciplinary, in order to derive both parallels and contrasts. While taking diverse perspectives in embracing the contemporary musical landscape, the collection offers a range of research methods and theoretical approaches from ethnomusicology, anthropology, cultural geography, sociology, popular music studies, and media and communication. In so doing, *Musics in Transit* provides a rich exemplification of the ways that all forms of musical culture are becoming transnational under post-global conditions, sustained by both global markets and musics in transit, and to which both tourists and diasporic cosmopolitans make an important contribution.

Simone Krüger is a Programme Leader in Popular Music Studies at Liverpool John Moores University, UK.

Ruxandra Trandafoiu is Reader in Communication at Edge Hill University, UK.

Routledge Studies in Ethnomusicology

The Globalization of Musics in Transit

Music Migration and Tourism

Edited by Simone Krüger and Ruxandra Trandafoiu

Routledge
Taylor & Francis Group
NEW YORK   LONDON

First published 2014
by Routledge
711 Third Avenue, New York, NY 10017

and by Routledge
2 Park Square, Milton Park, Abingdon, Oxon OX14 4RN

*Routledge is an imprint of the Taylor & Francis Group,
an informa business*

Library of Congress Cataloging-in-Publication Data
   The globalization of musics in transit : music migration and tourism /
edited by Simone Krüger and Ruxandra Trandafoiu.
      pages cm. — (Routledge studies in ethnomusicology ; 4)
   Includes bibliographical references and index.
   1. Music and globalization.   2. Emigration and immigration.
3. Music and tourism.   4. Ethnomusicology.   I. Krüger, Simone, editor
of compilation.   II. Trandafoiu, Ruxandra, editor of compilation.
   ML3916.G56 2013
   780.9—dc23
   2013014867

ISBN13: 978-0-415-64007-7 (hbk)
ISBN13: 978-0-203-08291-1 (ebk)

Typeset in Sabon
by IBT Global.

To Lorcan and Ezra,
who have taken us onto new journeys.

Contents

Figures

Acknowledgments

We would like to thank Routledge, particularly Liz Levine, commissioning editor, and Emily Ross, acting commissioning editor, as well as the four anonymous reviewers, who have provided useful insights and comments on the initial book proposal and sample chapters. The editors are particularly grateful for the time, effort, and expertise imparted by the following external reviewers, who were subsequently invited to offer additional feedback and suggestions to individual chapters: Margaret H. Beissinger, Tim Cooley, Peter Dunbar-Hall, Byron Dueck, Mark F. DeWitt, Hillegonda Rietveld, Trevor Wiggins, and Abigail Wood. We are also indebted to Timothy D. Taylor for his support for the project and the survey of the final manuscript, which provided a much needed overview and emphasis of common themes in the afterword.

We dedicate this book to our sons, Lorcan and Ezra, who were born while this book was in the making, and thus provided us with much joy and motivation.

Introduction
Touristic and Migrating Musics in Transit

Simone Krüger and Ruxandra Trandafoiu

Music travels, especially in the age of globalization. Marked by human movement—voluntary or forced, temporary or permanent—musical experience around the world is being shaped in often diverse and complex ways. For some, music travels through migratory movements, the mass movement of people without intended permanent return, while accompanying migrating peoples to new locations, but also when people use music to migrate symbolically in search of new horizons. For others, music travels through touristic movements, undertaken temporarily and voluntarily by people to places away from home in search for new musicultural experiences.

Both tourism and migration resignify our sense of place and rewrite the relationship between place and identity. Like the tourist, the migrant is in place, but not 'of the place' (Bauman 1996, 29). Mobility not only threatens our sense of place (Frith 1996, 110), but it also highlights the importance of the 'journey', since the road is often more important than the destination (Bauman 1996, 20). This identity journey 'enables us to place ourselves in imaginative cultural narratives' (Frith 1996, 124), which, as Timothy D. Taylor reiterates in the afterword to this volume, are occasionally fabricated, often contested, and certainly overlapping.

Both migration and tourism are bound together by the practice of traveling and transiting—both actual and symbolic. And both migration and tourism may exist side by side or indeed be closely intertwined in certain contexts.[1] Migrant culture may, for instance, feature in various representations in official or promotional materials that serve place-branding projects to boost tourism (see Krüger in this volume), or migrant culture may deliberately be silenced in efforts to promote an 'official' culture that is based on a selected music heritage (see Cohen and Roberts in this volume). Meanwhile, migrants' musical choices may pivot around certain styles of 'world music', thereby engaging in virtual tourism that reconnects them with a constructed version of their homeland, one that is highly idealized, commercialized, and capitalist (see Muir, Silverman, and Trandafoiu in this volume). Moreover, migrants may actively promote their own musical traditions in touristic contexts to which they have been granted access (see Amico in this volume, where 'migrant' may also take on a broader meaning). And yet both migration and tourism stand in stark contrast to one another, one often (although not always) related to poverty and the subaltern, the other often related to capitalism and Western hegemony and thus often overlooked within ethnomusicology.

Indeed, music tourism has only gained momentum in ethnomusicology since the late 1980s, while music tourism is still often seen as an 'Other' of ethnographic fieldwork (Cooley 1999, 32; Nettl 2005, 195). This theme is taken up by some authors here in a self-critical, reflexive attempt to grasp the impact of their 'role play' between tourist and ethnographer, which, as one author writes, can lead to 'productive misunderstanding,' the result of a 'game of reciprocal gazes' played out between tourists and locals, while 'the ethnographer takes part in the tourist encounter, managing an ambiguous third role' (Amico in this volume). In touristic contexts, researchers may initially set out in the role as tourist (or at least being perceived as such), yet they do gradually move into the role of ethnographer, as noted by another author (McIntosh) in a study of child performers in Balinese touristic events. Interestingly, a shared underlying desire to be 'the' ethnographer, not a music tourist, in tourist contexts shines through these writings, which may be born out of some of the negative assumptions surrounding tourism: colonialism, commodification, cultural loss, staged authenticity, capitalism, and so forth. To focus on tourist events and their perceived hypo-reality somehow implies to miss 'the real thing' that in-depth ethnographic fieldwork promises instead. Moreover, tourism is often regarded as a form of neocolonialism that postmodern approaches to ethnography sought to challenge. That tourism bears (implicitly) negative connotations is also evident in recent discussions on World Music and 'audio tourism', a form of imaginary travel associated with hyper-consumerism and Orientalism (Kassabian 2004). Here, a recent lecture by Keith Howard (2009) shows how binary divisions between ethnographically rooted music of authentic traditions versus commercialized (familiar/Other) world music; music studied by ethnomusicologists versus music made for consumption; diversity (local music) versus standardization (the 'great melt'); thorough appreciation versus audio tourism are still well and alive in the ethnomusicological imagination.[2] In this context, we remember the 2009 Annual Conference of the British Forum for Ethnomusicology in Liverpool,[3] when conference attendees, most of them ethnomusicologists, participated in the Magical Mystery Tour as part of the social events program, many enthusiastically, some rather reluctantly proclaiming: 'I would have *never* thought to see ethnomusicologists on a tourist tour of the Beatles!'

Migration resembles a somewhat equally 'uncomfortable' phenomenon to some ethnomusicologists and, like tourism, has only fairly recently been taken up in ethnomusicological enquiry (Slobin 1994, 2012). This may be so since migration is similarly an 'Other' of ethnography, one associated with movement, convergence, and diaspora, which stands directly opposed to (earlier) ethnographic concerns with place, homogeneity, and authenticity (Cooley 1999, 38; Reyes 2009, 178), although since the latter part of the 20th century, ethnomusicology has no longer been framed by certain subject matters regardless of their place of origin (commonly called the 'approach to subject matter'), also evident in the shift toward studying migrant, diasporic musics in urban contexts (Barfield 1997, 163). As a result of postcolonial awareness, postmodernism, and globalization, the emphasis of ethnomusicological research began to shift also to acknowledge the dynamics of musics transculturally and, indeed, globally, a shift marked by the introduction of subfields like 'urban ethnomusicology' or 'ethnomusicology at home' to denote the new fieldsites where ethnomusicologists study musics today (Nettl 2005, 184–96; Stock 2008, 199–204). It is specifically within 'urban ethnomusicology' where ethnomusicologists study processes surrounding human migration and, with it, the fluidity, hybridity, and multiplicity that mark contemporary urban musical expressions and phenomena (Reyes 2009). In turn, ethnomusicology studies have also naturally come to engage with diasporization (see Brubaker 2005 for a useful conceptualization of 'diaspora') as an obligatory part of the migratory process (see, e.g., Campbell 2010; Gopinath 1995; Manuel 1997/1998; Slobin 1994; Zheng 2010). Authors present in this volume use the terms migrant music and diasporic music equally to describe the outcome of music migration and inherent diasporization. Musics in transit take musical forms, themes, sounds, and voices, as well as instruments from the homelands, but these are transformed by the new experiences of journeying and resettlement. Musics in migratory transit establish new connections and adopt new 'traditions', marked by multiplicity and multimodality, while also creating cosmopolitan tastes. The result can be equally described as migrant and/or diasporic.

This special combination of migration and tourism represents the unique contribution of this book with its focus on the way musics are produced, circulated, and consumed in relation to multiple journeys and transits, as expressed by both migration and tourism. This dual focus allows us to explore the juxtaposition of phenomena like cosmopolitan empathy, advocacy, and responsibility versus the commoditization of the Other, authenticity, and capitalism. In doing so, the book shows how both individual and group musical biographies do away with traditional understandings of 'mainstream' and 'marginality', and how old hierarchies of power are dismantled (or not) by post-Western frameworks. While the book aims to deconstruct elements of classic globalization theory, it is in no way attempting to rewrite it. It attempts, however, to engage with post-globalization phenomena that have already led to new identities, new musical practices, and new ways of being in the world. We are now living through a period, which Bauman (2009) evocatively calls 'interregnum':

the old is dying; the new is just beginning to be born among uncertainty. This book captures the 'new dawn', the much needed new additions in both theory and research practice to the discipline of ethnomusicology. The book's interdisciplinary perspective through case studies that cover a number of continents and musical styles allows us to deconstruct established theories and propose new methodological solutions by looking at audiences animated by cosmopolitan imagination, who challenge global capitalism's commodification of the exotic.

MUSIC TOURISM

Tourism is an important human activity. Indeed, pilgrimage and other forms of travel for noncommercial purposes existed in most societies well before the mass tourism and leisure industry began to develop in the 19th century. Musical styles like flamenco, for instance, are closely associated with the rise of early French and British international tourism fueled by European romanticism toward Spanish gypsies, which rendered flamenco an exotic expression of Oriental mysticism and, in turn, transformed flamenco art into an export commodity long before the emergence of modern cultural tourism (Aoyama 2007, 105–6). Ever since, tourism has become one of the fastest-growing and largest industries in the world. Tourism is practically universal, and touristic practices pervade many areas of social life. Tourism has transformed host communities: their social and cultural life, environment, economies, politics, and their music. Tourism may be defined as the temporary leisure-based travel and activities undertaken voluntarily by persons outside their 'usual' home environments (World Tourism Organization 2013). Unlike other tangible goods, tourism is not produced, packaged, shipped, or received, but is nonetheless a product for sale. As such, tourism is intrinsic to 'our' lifestyles—most of us have been tourists or fantasize about visiting new places. Tourism is generally categorized into domestic; inbound and outbound; internal (a combination of the previous two); and national and international tourism (ibid.), although clear definitions in analytically useful ways pose a significant challenge (Cohen 2003, 382). Tourism is a global industry of considerable economic importance and social benefits for local communities,[4] alongside its apparent potential to promote international peace and goodwill through cultural appreciation, and has therefore gained significant attention by governments, regional and local authorities, policy makers, business investors, academics, and others. Thus while global tourism was historically more important for developing countries, it has become of increasing importance for developed, industrialized countries.

The tourism industry gained momentum during the 1950s and witnessed a global boom during the 1980s and 1990s, which is mirrored in academic circles, where it became established in the 1980s as an interdisciplinary field of study, often considered from economic, geographical, historical, political, psychological, or sociological perspectives. Tourism is nowadays built on the post-Fordist global capitalist structures by focusing also on specialization and niche tourism, rather than standard, packaged tours. Here it is specifically the attractions that entice tourists to visit the locations in the first place, which are usually studied and understood within the context of 'cultural tourism'. Cultural attractions include a broad range of activities and cultural forms like handicrafts, food, religion, language, architecture, sports, and the arts, while music—classical, traditional, popular—plays a pivotal, if not even central, role in cultural tourism. Indeed, as expression and reflection of culture, music provides an incredibly emotional narrative for tourists, which is nowadays packaged in the form of 'niche music tourism' (Figure I.1). With its emotional and personal appeal, music tourism has developed into a major tourism branch in countries like the US and the UK where tourism is mature and music industries are strong.

Given that tourism is one of the fastest-growing industries in the world, music and cultural tourism is an increasingly vibrant arena for academic study. Yet ethnomusicological discourse on tourism and travel is still rare (see Post 2011 for a handful of examples), even while ethnomusicologists have recognized that types of travel coalesce into a central

Figure I.1   Screenshot of 'Songlines Music Travel'.

Note: 'Songlines Music Travel' is a branch of British world music magazine *Songlines* in partnership with the Tailor-Made Groups Company, offering a range of world music tours to bring customers 'close to the music of your destination: through evenings listening to live bands, time spent at festivals, dropping in on instrument makers or enjoying sessions with local musicians. The music is the focal point for these journeys' (Songlines 2013).

feature of people's contemporary lives. Where ethnomusicologists reflect on their associations with tourists and tourism, much focus has been placed on the infrastructures and impact of musical tourism culturally, socially, economically, and environmentally (Post 2006, 5). This includes, for example, ethnomusicological collections on the themes of traditional music and tourism (Kaeppler and Lewin 1988); performance, tourism, and ethnicity (Burckhardt Qureshi 1998); and music, travel, and tourism (DeWitt 1999). Important and often overlooked research on the theme of music tourism also includes Wolfgang Suppan's (1991) *Schladminger Gespräche zum Thema Musik und Tourismus* and Max Peter Baumann's (1995) *Music in the Dialogue of Cultures: Traditional Music and Cultural Policy*. More recently, the journal the *World of Music* also issued a volume on *Folk Music in Public Performance* (Baumann 2001), which includes some well-developed theoretical approaches on music tourism.

While ethnomusicologists may still often focus on traditional and folk musics in these studies, the focus on contemporary, popularized musics occurs more frequently in studies by popular music scholars, anthropologists, sociologists, and cultural geographers. Here, research often focuses on the significance of specific geographic locations for music tourism, most notably Liverpool as the birthplace of the Beatles (Cohen 1997, 2001, 2007); Graceland, the Memphis home of Elvis Presley and birthplace of the blues (Gibson and Connell 2007); or New Orleans as the city of jazz (Atkinson 1996, 1997), to name only three examples. More eclectic collections on tourism are frequent, most notably Simone Abram, Jacqueline Waldren, and Donald V. L. Macleod's *Tourists and Tourism: Identifying with People and Places* (1997), with chapters written by social anthropologists, geographers, sociologists, and popular music scholars. Here, tourism studies often seek to understand the ways in which museums and other cultural heritage sites are sites for the transmission and negotiation of particular cultural values and visions, or how tourism constructs cultural imagery and social stereotypes by staging authenticity and providing spectacles aimed at the tourist gaze (see Urry 1990), among other themes. Meanwhile, from cultural geography, Chris Gibson and John Connell's *Music and Tourism: On the Road Again* (2005) is usually regarded as a key title that addresses popular music and tourism from a broad perspective, ranging from virtual tourism, hula sounds to musical landscapes, tourism as theater, and the issue of travel. Their book *Sound Tracks: Popular Music, Identity and Place* (Connell and Gibson 2002) also contains important discussions on music tourism, among other cultural themes. The fact that music tourism is becoming an important area for research in its own right is also demonstrated by a conference held at the University of Liverpool in 2012, which was dedicated entirely to the theme of 'Soundtracks: Music, Tourism and Travel' (ICRETH 2012).

CURRENT PERSPECTIVES ON MUSIC TOURISM

While tourism has become an increasingly vibrant arena for ethnomusicological and anthropological study, the chapters presented here extend this body of theory by exploring the relationships between tourism, tourists, and musics across cultures. In the context of global mobility, some of the key research and debates in the field of music tourism are examined, while drawing on case studies and field observations in the countries or cultural spaces studied by ethnographic researchers and/or visitors as tourists, and thereby presenting different contemporary forms of music tourism. The authors take us on a journey to sites in the UK, Bali, Mali, Australia, and Liverpool, and onto cruise ships and imaginary voyages around the world, and present encounters with pop, traditional, world, classical, rock, and dance musics. The chapters also highlight in broader terms how the study of music tourism and tourist practices enhances our understanding of identity and heritage, interethnic interactions, neocolonialism, neoliberalism, media and representation, the staging and marketing of music, commoditization, and notions of ownership, authenticity, and desire. Certain subthemes emerge, such as the construction of tourist discourses, narratives, and memories through material culture (Cohen and Roberts); empowering the Other through representation and inclusion (McIntosh); the role of authenticity in the marketing of people and places (Amico); music tourism at sea and the fantasy island phenomenon (Cashman and Hayward); festival tourism for rural transformation (Connell and Gibson); place-branding and cultural mega-event tourism (Krüger); and music, travel, and touristic diasporas (St John), and each will be introduced and duly contextualized here.

Constructing Tourism Narratives:
Material Cultures of Music Tourism

One important theme in the anthropological study of music tourism concerns the ways in which (verbal and material) narratives construct images of tourist destinations, and how subtle messages are embedded in tourism materials. How do such narratives contribute to the shaping of tourists' perceptions and experiences of destinations and of the peoples residing in those destinations? What is the role of material culture in defining tourist destinations? How do local residents construct ideas about 'their' places? Relevant here is the way in which states use tourism for national agendas and/or place-branding, and what role cultural heritage sites such as national museums and exhibits play in this process for the transmission and negotiation of particular cultural values and visions for both citizens and visitors.

Sara Cohen and Les Roberts make an important contribution here in their chapter 'Heritage Rocks! Mapping Spaces of Popular Music Tourism,' in which they focus their analytic and ethnographic attention on different kinds of maps as markers of UK popular music heritage sites. For example, the chapter illustrates how 'official' maps like those constructed by Visit Britain and the British Music Experience are part of a wider national marketing campaign designed predominantly for place-branding and urban regeneration purposes and for boosting domestic and national tourism. In doing so, however, these official narratives tend to provide a highly selective and predominantly 'white, male, rock' representation of UK popular music heritage, and only a superficial, arbitrary engagement with local music geographies. By contrast, nonprofessional music heritage maps and trails (available online and as smartphone apps) represent more localized narratives of British popular music histories, heritages, and musical memories, and are thus different in terms of scale and cartographic precision. Drawing users 'into the map' by appropriating new, locative media technologies, these maps reflect a desire (by individuals and organizations) toward a more direct engagement with local musicscapes, thereby challenging dominant and official discourses of music heritage. Finally, Cohen and Roberts also illustrate user-based, 'unofficial' mapping practices (used by the authors as tools for research) as these have grown out of vernacular memory or 'heritage-as-praxis'. Representing more dynamic and inclusive narratives of local musical heritage, culture, and identity, local maps of vernacular musical memory also provide a stark contrast to more 'official' tourist maps and discourses used to brand and symbolize 'the nation', as they are more closely reflexive of personal musical memory, cultural experience, and locally specific identity. By comparing and contrasting official tourist narratives ('official' maps), localized material culture (localized maps), and narratives of local vernacular memory (user-based mapping as research tool), Cohen and Roberts highlight the complex connections between popular music, place, and tourism, while raising important questions about musical heritage: what it is, what it is for, and why it matters.

Empowering the Other: Representation and Inclusion in Music Tourism

One important theme in the anthropological study of tourism concerns the ways in which local stakeholders' perceptions and concerns are respected and included in music tourism, a focus still often rare in anthropology, where the trend has been to address the perspective of the 'guest' over that of the 'host' (Guerrón Montero 2011a, 2). If, as some tourism critics suggest, tourism is a form of neocolonialism, how can this dynamic be altered or avoided in destinations under development for tourism? And if music tourism can also benefit the 'host', given that much tourist activity around the world continues to be managed in a way that directs investment away from local facilities and infrastructures, how can 'hosts' be more directly involved in the management of tourist activities? This focus is based on the reality that tourism often transforms sensibilities about identity, ethnic and gendered hierarchies, and class in touristic settings, which raises questions about 'whose cultural capital' and, with it, issues surrounding local agency and power (Cheong and Miller 2000). Relevant in this context are tourism studies that acknowledge the fact that 'those subjected to the ethnographic/ touristic gaze gaze back [and that] the ethnomusicological viewpoint is just one among many others' (Stokes 1999, 143).

Jonathan McIntosh's study on 'Negotiating Musical Boundaries and Frontiers: Tourism, Child Performers, and the Tourist-Ethnographer in Bali, Indonesia' makes a significant contribution to understanding how participants themselves perceive the ways in which they are represented, photographed, and 'taken back home', and how they themselves choose to represent 'their' culture in particular ways and not in others. In doing so, this chapter addresses the recent critique that 'we very seldom hear about reflections from relevant participants themselves (musicians, audiences, others)' (Stokes 1999, 144). Moreover, a book on music tourism that does not include a chapter on Bali must simply be incomplete, clearly evident in the exuberant body of academic writing on this topic. And yet it is McIntosh's unique ethnographic focus on child dancers and the ways in which they interact with visitors to their island (ethnographers, tourists) that marks the chapter's contribution to the large body of literature on music tourism in Bali. The child performers have little or no cultural authority of their own and are accorded little power over their dance performances because of their ambiguous status as culture bearers. Moreover, they receive little remuneration for participation in tourist performances, while being expected to be highly proficient and professional in set choreographed (secular) dance productions to meet touristic expectations. Even so, McIntosh found that the children displayed a worldly approach that showed them to be culture bearers and creatively active indeed, while the children also made informed choices about what they deemed to be taboo performances for tourists. In doing so, McIntosh allows these children to speak out for themselves, for their voices to be heard among those of adults, culture bearers, tourists, and ethnographers, and so to be represented, visible, included, empowered.

Tourism, Authenticity, and the Marketing of People and Places

An important theme in ethnomusicological and anthropological writings on music tourism is concerned with authenticity (Urry 1990) and related ideas like 'staged authenticity' (MacCannell 1976), or post-tourism and McDisneyization (Ritzer and Liska 1997).[5] Indeed, tourism—like ethnography—is marked historically by a quest for authenticity (Cooley 1999, 39). These writings often consider the economic dimensions of tourism and, with it, cultural and musical commoditization, where the authentic is usually entangled with nostalgia, folklore, heritage, and exoticism. Such debates have circulated at times around the (mis)representations of 'traditional' music cultures, or folklore's manufactured-ness that can lead to 'fakelore' (DeWitt 1999, 6), while more recent thinking regards authenticity as a discursive construct (Stokes 1999, 143–45). For example, Timothy J. Cooley describes folk festivals in the Polish Tatra Mountains as mediators of a kind of 'heritage' that combine *both*, preservation and invention, history and fantasy, old and new, folklore and fakelore, authentic and spurious (1999, 40, 43).

How difference and authenticity are constructed and managed in festival tourism is a focus shared by Marta Amico in her chapter on 'The Staged Desert: Tourist and Nomad Encounters at the Festival au Désert,' which illustrates cultural tourism in Mali as being constructed around the mythical image of the Sahara desert and its inhabitants, the Tuaregs. The festival has become an important means for boosting the economy nationally and promoting a Malian place brand that is based on the imagined notion of reconciliation with Tuaregs (see, e.g., Worley 2012). To this end, 'authenticity' is rigorously exploited by the Malian tourism industry in promoting the festival as a means to journey through an authentic landscape (the desert) and encounter its traditional peoples (the nomads), and thus to create a 'desert desire' in Western tourists. Here, the desert, turbans, camels, tents, and 'Malian music' all play pivotal roles for authenticating tourists' experiences who willingly tap into the narratives of 'desert life' and 'nomad otherness'. That these encounters are far from being authentic but constructed spaces and narratives is revealed through Amico's ethnographic insights into the careful preparation of the festival site and scenery, the staging of international and globally known 'Tuareg music' alongside more locally based musical styles, and the musical exchanges between global and local musics that the festival facilitates. In doing so, the festival resembles a social space where musical preservation and innovation, authenticity and spuriousness intersect.

Tourism at Sea: Cruise Ship Tourism and the Fantasy Island Phenomenon

The cruise ship industry represents a paradigmatic case of globalization, often raising questions about issues surrounding ethnic hierarchies at sea, the fate of cruise ship-dependent ports, the fantasy island phenomenon, or environmental issues pertaining to cruise ships and their ramifications for local communities, among other themes (see also Patullo 2009; Wood 2000). David Cashman and Philip Hayward's chapter 'The Golden Fleece: Music and Cruise Ship Tourism,' contributes pivotal insights to this theme, but with specific focus on the onboard experience in situations of extreme musical commodification during cruising, with the ship resembling a 'floating pleasure palace' that not only transits tourists between set points, but also provides 'a bounded, monopolistic touristic environment' that taps into the 'experience economy' concept. Cashman and Hayward's ethnographic insights reveal how music is a quintessential means during sea days to create congenial ambiance in order to encourage consumption of 'experience enhancements' (like gambling, dancing, or drinking) and boost onboard revenue, especially through live music performance of various types and levels of interaction, whereby performer–audience interaction and participation play an increasingly important role in the onboard consumption of touristic music. While much of this music is drawn from familiar, predictable Western culture, some performances readily tap into tourists' expectations of journeying to and encountering the exotic Other, even if presented as part of their onboard experiences. Such touristic musical performances, which stereotypically include 'Caribbean bands' performing calypso classics, Harry Belafonte and Bob Marley numbers, and tropicalist Western pop songs, are usually promoted as authentic extensions of the culture from which they originate, even though in reality 'any sense of specific place and culture of origin is effaced in favor of a vague Caribbeanistic groove and sense of sun-drenched hedonism' (in this volume).

The onboard experience of an authentic (banalized) musical Other is typically extended onshore in cruise ship–dependent port areas, like the Island Village in Ocho Rios, North Jamaica, a market area that exists exclusively for and because of the cruise ships that stop there, or the restricted, 'safe' port areas in Tahiti, which are similarly used to stage (here, government-approved) versions of Tahitian culture, music, and dance to their consumer guests, and thereby promote a particular place brand around the concept 'Tahiti'. Clearly, these port experiences tap into the tourism industry's careful constructions of 'islandness' and 'island paradise,' as discussed, for instance, in anthropological analyses of island tourism, even if these studies often lack a focus on music (e.g., Guerrón Montero 2011b). To this end, Cashman and Hayward's study of music and cruise ship tourism provides important insights into situations of extreme commodification that have not only transformed some of the most secluded locations into commercially viable tourist destinations, but have turned transport facilities themselves into hyper-commercialized locales of touristic consumption.

Festival Tourism for Rural Transformation

Festivals are events of a broadly celebratory nature that usually feature a series of musical performances, which represent an important attraction for music tourists in search for new musical and cultural experiences. Festivals proliferated in the Northern Hemisphere since the 1960s as engineered revivals and/or reinventions of older (rural) traditions that declined because of industrialization and urbanization (marked by urban-to-rural mobility), while more recently, music festivals resemble the practice of more popular cultural phenomena that encourage contemporary creativity and/or the safeguarding of vanishing traditions, also to address economic goals like income generation and economic regeneration through positive cultural transformation. Authors in the tourism part of the book all address festival contexts to some extent, yet only few center on festivals, asking questions about the impact of festivals culturally, socially, and economically.

John Connell and Chris Gibson's chapter, 'Mobilizing Music Festivals for Rural Transformation: Opportunities and Ambiguities,' makes a significant contribution about the opportunities and ambiguities afforded by music festivals in the contexts of attempts to stimulate rural tourism, mobility, and regional development in Australian country towns. Regional music festivals exist around the world, as do proliferations to celebrate individual musicians, different musical styles, and music instruments, among other reasons. In Australia alone, 'every town and even most small villages now host a music festival of some sort' (Connell and Gibson in this volume), characterized by increased specialization of the music festival scene. In turn, festivals—however small or regional—can generate significant social and economic returns for primary and secondary, local and supra-local beneficiaries, ranging from hotels and restaurants, stores and portable toilet hire companies, tent providers, transport companies, and charities to lawyers, printers, furniture shops, and undertakers, and enhance creative industries outside major cities. Festivals have thus begun to play a critical role in 'post-productivist' Australia. More specifically, the Four Winds Festival near Bermagui on the south coast of New South Wales provides a striking case in point here, a biannual festival initially focusing on 'high-quality classic and classical music,' but gradually also featuring other, eclectic forms of musical expression, initially conceived for cultural objectives but later becoming a source for economic development. Here, we gain detailed ethnographic insight into the history, organization, running, and impact of the festival through the voices of some locals and Sheila Boughen, chair of the festival's board. The festival's attraction for nonlocals came specifically from the branding of Bermagui as 'paradise', while locals feel attracted by the sense of community that the event facilitates, whereby the regional cuisine plays a huge role in promoting place beyond music.

The growing emphasis on community involvement and engagement, involving Aboriginal artists, nonprofit groups, and choirs (among others) by the festival committee is particularly stressed here, a trend also reflexive elsewhere (see, e.g., Krüger in this volume). Even so, 'this does not thwart the criticism that such events contribute to upwardly-mobile gentrification of the place, but it does provide a more sophisticated view of mobilities of migrants, tourists, and musicians, beyond simplistic "us and them" dichotomies' (Connell and Gibson in this volume). Indeed, the success of festivals in addressing rural decay and transformation depends on a complex web of inside and outside factors and particularities. On balance, then, festivals provide spaces in which the commercial and 'local' intersect, where hopes and tensions, opportunities and ambiguities coexist, an understanding to which locally specific, empirical enquiry can make a significant contribution.

Place Branding and Mega-Event Tourism

That festivals have become important events for positive transformation in certain regions is further illustrated by research that focuses on the use of festive time strategies for urban revitalization since the 1990s. Here, temporal festive celebrations are 'mined' for their touristic potential to support the practice of place-branding or city 'imagineering' (Hughes 2010, 119). These developments must be contextualized within the emergence of the postindustrial city in the US, the UK, Australia, or elsewhere in an effort to tackle the aesthetic, economic, and social problems of decline so as to make cities more attractive to entrepreneurs, tourists, and shoppers. Today, most cities in the West actively and self-consciously engage in forms of city image building, a trend that

> evolved from the institutional and discursive changes forced upon city administrators in the previous decade. . . . Thus cities began to jockey for public attention. . . . The spectacular lays claim to ever larger audiences in a bid to be the world's biggest party and the annual calendar seems now to be saturated with an orgy of competing entertainment. (Hughes 2010, 123–24)

The European Capital of Culture (ECOC) event provides a striking example in this context, an initiative created by the European Union in 1985 to encourage city administrators to promote the city, its region and characteristics, people, culture, and identity. Simone Krüger's chapter, 'Branding the City: Music Tourism and the European Capital of Culture Event,' contributes to this growing discourse with its specific focus on the functions and impacts of mega-events for constructing the place brand 'Liverpool' so as to boost the city's economy through music tourism. Prior to 2008, Liverpool already had a relatively well-established music tourism industry that packaged and sold 'the Beatles' as nostalgia and heritage, enticing tourists to embark on a pilgrimage to the City of Pop's sites of musical production, performance, memory, and so forth. Music tourism in locations like Liverpool is thus often conceptualized as constituting a kind of sacred or ritual experience, 'a modern form of mass religion' (Stokes 1999, 148). Yet in the context of Liverpool ECOC, the city became branded under the theme 'The World in One City' in celebration of its apparent multiculturalism, which the city sought to achieve by staging events of differing scale, varied musical styles, and of multicultural nature, thereby emphasizing both the economic *and* cultural objectives of the ECOC event. To this end, economic objectives were officially underpinned by more democratic concerns with building community access and participation, an initiative that portrays a new urbanity that is carnivalesque and festive. On the other hand, however, the ECOC event also tended toward a certain place brand that reflected and promoted (at least at an international level) an official culture, as local culture did not feature for the gazes of the world tourist.

Dance Culture, Audio Culture, and the Psychedelic Diaspora

An important, yet perhaps still overlooked theme in ethnomusicological and anthropological writings concerns imaginary tourism and travel, which thus far can be found in discourses surrounding World Music and audio tourism (see earlier discussions), or house music and dance culture, of which World Music 2.0 is also a relevant example (see Burkhalter 2012). Here, the transitory nature of the dance music experience is understood in terms of the temporal aspect of the musical experience as an impermanent form of escapism and the concept of movement, both involving the impermanence of place and the alteration of dance spaces. The notion of a temporal journey is often deconstructed as a type of musical tourism, as seeking a brief escape from reality, a fleeting form of escapism that is grounded in the safety of returning home. House music and dance culture thus contains a 'nomadic' aspect that positions listeners in the social imaginary and entails movement to imaginary places, whether to mythologized spaces of 'house music origin' like Chicago (Rietveld 1998) or an idealized space of 'authentic' consumption such as Ibiza (Bennett 2004), Koh Samui, or Anjuna (Connell and Gibson 2002, 230), or Goa (St John in this volume) as 'mythologized sites of music consumption with "mystical resonance"' (Connell and Gibson 2002, 230). These 'cartographies of sound' (ibid., 17–18) describe the mobile and unfixed nature of sound and musical experiences in these musical contexts, alongside a form of travel that takes place through listening to and participating in music *without* physical movement.

It is within this context that Graham St John presents his chapter, 'Goatrance Travelers: Psychedelic Trance and Its Seasoned Progeny,' with its special focus on tribalism, Orientalism, festivals, and travelers as it is centered on and around the Goatrance (an electronic dance music genre) experience, and informed by the author's long-term multimodal research conducted on psychedelic trance history, culture, and music—Psyculture. By focusing on nomadic, psychedelic, and visionary sensibilities associated with events related to Goatrance music, St John offers an original approach to the notion of global and transnational music tourism and travel. Here 'diaspora' acquires a new meaning. The 'psychedelic diaspora,' as St John terms it, provides a shared space for the dispersed psychedelic Goatrance scene, and is marked by notions of counterculture, neo-nomadism, Orientalism, escapism, existentialist hedonism, and translocal imagination. Diasporism is a state of mind, a sense of 'being-in-transit.' St John alludes thus to a key question in this book: Who or what is a diaspora, and what constitutes migration?

MUSIC MIGRATION

Migration is not a new phenomenon, but it has become one of the defining experiences of the 20th century and a key trait of globalization. Migration thus features heavily in globalization theory, if we were just to mention Appadurai's (1990) 'ethnoscapes', which represent an early attempt to define migration as a life-enhancing and culturally relevant event. Migration is also a prolific theme in sociology, often challenging academics to find its triggers and patterns (Massey et al. 1998); political theory, where the focus is typically on policy and human rights implications (Hollifield 2004); and postcolonial and cultural studies, which often attempt to explain the implications of migratory movements for both the collective consciousness and the individual (Gilroy 1993). More recently, the light has been shone on the transitions and adaptations sparked by migration and settlement. These experiences produce new ways of existing in the world for both individuals and groups, which are now at the heart of a thriving corpus of diasporic studies (Brubaker 2005; Tsagarousianou 2004). Fewer texts in ethnomusicology follow the tendencies exhibited by these disciplines. A certain delay in acknowledging the impact of migration on music production, circulation, and its audiences—while key authors like Alan Merriam and Bruno Nettl talked about change and transformation already in the 1960s and 1970s, a focus on music migration only emerged since the 1990s—has meant a slimmer but still illuminating body of work (for collections of representative research in this area, see Clausen et al. 2009; Levi and Scheding 2010; Lornell and Rasmussen 1997; Ramnarine 2008; Raussert and Miller Jones 2009; Toynbee and Dueck 2011b; Turino and Lea 2004). Migration has compelled ethnomusicologists to re-assess music's role in shaping identities, but most importantly to investigate how migration destabilizes meanings, how it racializes and hybridizes music, how it provides a critique of authenticity and changes our understanding of place, while also erasing the artificial boundary between the West and its 'Others'. Such texts consider music to be the ideal vehicle for capturing movement and an essential tool for asserting identity (see, e.g., Baily and Collyer 2006; Zheng 2010). So, for example, the musics that the Chinese listen to in the US can, according to a recent text by Su Zheng (2010), tell us a lot about the experiences that first-generation Chinese migrants have in comparison to subsequent generations. Similarly, studies of bhangra bring an understanding of the way 'home' is redefined and repositioned by music-producing diasporas (Gopinath 1995). In terms of affirming or reaffirming identity through music, we now take for granted that both individual and collective identities (the 'self' and 'Others') are performed through music, which offers us the opportunity to experience the 'self-in-process' (Frith 1996, 109). At a collective level, migrating music also helps construct spaces for the articulation of identity politics (Lipsitz 1994, 28). Music becomes the conduit through which difference begins to be articulated and hybridity begins to be accepted. This is an important shift in ethnomusicology.

Music also tells the story of shared painful experiences induced by displacement (initially through colonialism and post-colonialism, more recently by a myriad of complex factors). However, it does so '*through* rather than outside of existing structures' (Lipsitz 1994, 34; emphasis in the original). Lipsitz's reference to hip-hop, but also other forms of diasporic African music, as well as the example of bhangra (Gopinath 1995) or burger highlife (Carl in this volume), show that musics often traverse the racial or ethnic divide and allow the subaltern to colonize in its turn through hybridized forms (Radano and Bohlman 2000). This happens through established (and yes, commercial) networks of music production, circulation, and consumption. It is an example of how music can support the formation of a global consciousness (Lipsitz 1994, 33) that dismantles the artificial boundary between Western and non-Western musical phenomena once common in ethnomusicology (Frith 1996).

CURRENT PERSPECTIVES ON MUSIC MIGRATION

The phenomena mentioned above are produced by musics in transit, musics that pass through and across, that move and migrate, causing important changes, which we aim to capture in this volume. We aim to capture change in the new geometries, the new configuration of networks and flows, the translations that result in hybridization and enrichment, the adaptations that signal new ways of branching out and making new connections. Identity is redefined, borders reconfigured, new spaces created. Movement and change result thus in diasporization and re-diasporization, often experienced symbolically through mental migration (see Sabry 2005), and the new 'world order' that rearticulates the relationship between the local and the global, places and spaces, homeland and hostland. Diasporization is a trigger for musical creativity. Migrants do not just take music along, like Desert Island Discs, but they reach out, appropriating, mixing and matching, and ultimately producing something anew. Migrants can therefore be placed at the heart of musical innovation, not just appropriation or repetition (Baily and Collyer 2006, 171). In this sense, migration, the bureaucratic and institutionalized practice of exclusion, containment, and marginalization, is pitted against the freedom to dream, with music winning the day.

So what does this new world that emerges as a result of migratory experiences look like? First of all, it exemplifies the transition from the old nationalism theory, with its emphasis on groups, ethnos, national culture, and borders, which produces a 'spiral of silence' that mutes ethnic minority groups and makes them largely invisible, to a theory that uses the terminological arsenal of postcolonialism, diasporism, and globalization to talk about 'third' space (Bhabha 1994), nonplaces, networks and flows (Castells 1996),[6] and 'liquid life' (Bauman 2005). It might be therefore useful to borrow Martin Stokes's term 'relocations' (1994, 3) to describe the journeys encapsulated in any musical experience that is anchored in multiple spaces, both real and imagined.[7] We argue that music is the means by which people experience alterity, access the 'pick and mix' of identities on offer (see also Taylor's afterword in this volume), and invent new spaces of expression and interaction that give contemporary encounters a sense of freedom, playfulness, and fluidity. In this sense, any 'relocation' tells the story of finding new flexible homes (through, for example, playing samba in Toronto, as Pravaz's study shows in this volume), erecting hybrid cultural spaces under the radar of nation-state attempts to restrict and channel culture (as in Oldfield's examination of bardic oral culture in the Caucasus in this volume), or tapping into a choice of roots to construct different images of the past and legitimize new musical practices that are global in nature (as Muir's research with Jewish choirs in Cape Town showcases in this volume). As some of the following chapters show, certain genres or musical tastes can only result from the experience of relocation (see Carl, Silverman, and Trandafoiu in this volume).

The chapters in the migration part of the book are organized according to the evolution of certain concepts and themes, but also in accordance to the diasporic age of the groups studied. This chronological organization takes the reader through the experiences of 'old' diasporas (the Roma, the Jews, the people of the Caucasus region) to arrive at more recent cases of settlement and diasporization (the Brazilians, the Ghanaians, and the Romanians). On this journey, we get to listen to brass, choral, and gospel music, as well as *dastan*, samba, folklore, and pop, in a true global experience of the mind and senses.

The following chapters often engage with a lesser-studied issue in ethnomusicology: the role of music in creating and expressing a new diasporic reflexivity as a result of migration. This reflexive diasporic condition is an edifice built in various stages. Firstly, it is built through imagining and preparing the migratory act. Pre-migrants acquire a migratory state of mind and basic language skills, start to tap into transnational and diasporic networks of support, and most importantly begin to inhabit symbolically the hostland, and embody and act out their new identities (Culic 2010). This is often achieved through symbolic emigration supported by music (consumed, appropriated, owned). Secondly, it is built through the engagement with diasporic structures *en route* and at destination, and by gaining the ability to participate in micropolitical debate and action (often through mobile technologies) designed to improve the success of the migratory project (Castells et al. 2007; Trandafoiu 2013). Thirdly, it is built through the growth in the number of itinerant migrants, capable to move from one country to another, who display the ability to rationalize their losses and gains, and deploy appropriate strategies to maximize the latter. Finally, it is built through the return/s to the homeland that help the circulation of the acquired transnational capital and reapplied diasporic reflexivity. Again, music can be the conduit for expressing these various stages of the migratory project, often through the musical choices made and the tastes displayed. These journeys allow migrants to become diasporans by performing the diasporic condition. This performance takes place within multiple transnational spaces: DJs playing Gypsy music in dance clubs all over the world, American musicals encountering Jewish congregations in Cape Town, burger and gospel highlife transiting between Ghana and Germany, Brazilian samba creating new musical spaces in Canada, or Romanians consuming turbo folk online from Italy.

The chapters included here exemplify the freedom to re-elaborate music, which results from migration and diasporization. For example, the construction of the 'fantasy Gypsy' through the appropriation and consumption of Balkan music (Silverman); the shifting symbolic geographies expressed in the music of South African Jews, between invented tradition and global cosmopolitanism (Muir); the role of music and oral narratives in the creation of transborder flexible communities in the Caucasus (Oldfield); the establishment of new social imaginaries and thus musical genres by Ghanaians in Germany (Carl); the reterritorialization of samba and the creation of new diasporic audiotopias by non-Brazilians in Toronto (Pravaz); Romanian migrants in Italy, Spain, and the United Kingdom reflecting on their diasporic condition through a dialogical critique of both tradition and modernity (Trandafoiu). All of these contributions bring new perspectives on music migration, which deserve a closer look.

Music Appropriation, Authenticity, and Auto-Exoticization

The formation of new music geometries and the phenomenon of diasporization are both reflected in Carol Silverman's chapter, 'Global Balkan Gypsy Music: Issues of Migration, Appropriation, and Representation,' via the theme of music appropriation. As more non-Roma play, consume, or appropriate Gypsy music, the Roma are displaced from musical 'ownership' (a difficult concept anyway, in the case of an oral-based culture growing out of a multicultural and multimusical environment). The Roma suffer multiple diasporizations in their transit from India to Europe and from Europe onto the world stage, a journey during which the 'fantasy Gypsy' is constructed and reproduced. Gypsy music is displaced, hybridized, and resold as 'authentic' since in typical globalization style, the paradoxical shift from 'authenticity-as-pure to authenticity-as-hybrid' (Taylor 2007, 143–44) takes place. The Roma lose control over their historical and cultural narratives, and their identity begins to be brokered by others, as their music is appropriated by known musicians, Western impresarios, and dance club DJs. The music of Balkan brass bands and the marketing strategies that aim to bring this music to global audiences prove that even the Roma have come to internalize historical stereotypes—in a process of auto-exoticization—driven by branding, hybridization, and appropriation. Silverman warns that although an 'aura of equality' surrounds such exhibition, music appropriation does not provide an adequate answer to discrimination, nor is it proof of democratization. As a result, both 'anxious' and 'celebratory' narratives of World Music appropriation need to be critically interrogated. This can be achieved by focusing on the new power relations exhibited by migrating musics.

In their introduction to *Music and the Racial Imagination*, Radano and Bohlman (2000) address one relative absence in ethnomusicology: the impact of the 'racial imagination' on music. Although Silverman does not dwell at length on the importance of racial differences, these are still inferred in the way she describes the marketization of Gypsy brass bands. Radano and Bohlman talk about the 'ideological constructions of difference associated with body type and color' (2000, 5), an idea strongly purported by cultural theorist Stuart Hall (1997), which they observe in the American context, and we can also see at work in the way the Gypsy body is constructed and performed on stage at various European festivals, according to Silverman. Racial differences also seep into the way rhythmical patterns are perceived, for example, through what Radano and Bohlman call a process of racialization. When Gypsy music migrates, musical continuity is challenged and sonic meanings are rearticulated and rewritten from the point of view of those who appropriate it, as Silverman describes with reference in particular to Goran Bregović.

Tradition and Modernity: Overlapping Symbolic Geographies

For Jews in South Africa, the past also lends itself to partial appropriations and re-elaborations. According to Stephen Muir's chapter, 'From the *Shtetl* to the Gardens and Beyond: Identity and Symbolic Geography in Cape Town's Synagogue Choirs,' the choral musical repertoire is key to the strategy of recruiting new church members into Cape Town's Jewish synagogues. This is accomplished though simultaneously remembering and forgetting, reworking and repositioning collective memories, but also inventing traditions that echo global trends (Hobsbawm and Ranger 1983), whereby the 'old ' and the 'new' become redefined by migration (see also Reyes 1999). The Jews of Cape Town use elements of identity and heritage to engage with global phenomena, and they negotiate both tradition and modernity in a game of identity politics. The result is a complex kaleidoscope of overlapping symbolic geographies (inhabited according to circumstance) that sees the neo-Hasidic, the reinvented Lithuanian, and the global coexisting side by side. A similar phenomenon is described by Trandafoiu (in this volume), who analyzes the identity negotiations of the Romanian diaspora, between tradition and modernity, among various models now available in the global identity market. Yet while the Romanian diaspora still tries to come to terms with Westernization, Jewish communities in South Africa are in dialogue with a global repertoire that comprises both music that is described as traditionally Jewish but still global in its geographical spread and music that belongs to the phenomenon of Americanization and globalization through popular culture tropes. In both examples, 'tradition' and 'authenticity' are interrogated as a result of diasporization and multiple positionings.

Muir's chapter also engages with the way memory is negotiated, which can differ from group to group and from generation to generation, a focus shared with previous, seminal research on music, collective history, and memory (e.g., Bohlman 2002, 2008; Shelemay 1998, 2006). Another recent study on the way memories of migration and displacement are reflected focuses on Irish-English rock music, with particular reference to The Smiths, and describes the way music can convey the image of a home imagined in the abstract, a life lived between spaces, between two cultures in tension, that create in second-generation Irish in England the 'trope of ambivalence' (Campbell 2010, 95). Muir's research reveals an equally interesting appropriation or rejection of the past based on the need to reconcile ambivalence. Jews in South Africa use their musical repertoire to strategically silence, reduce, or emphasize certain memories and cultural affiliations. This phenomenon shows that communities are no longer defined by the doubleness of departure and arrival, but express a fluid network with multiple anchorings (a suggestion also made by Kiwan and Meinhof 2011, 1), geography bypassed by fluid music imaginaries that articulate 'a state of mind rather than a specific locale' (Manuel 1997/1998, 31). Instead of focusing on 'origin,' the homeland from which diaspora was dispersed, it is important to recognize that 'the connections between the "outlying" points of the diaspora are as important, or more so, than the connections between the outliers and the origin' (Wade 2008, 41). So, for example, as Muir's chapter explains, the musical repertoire of Cape Town's Jewish synagogues may be determined to a certain extent by a remotely remembered European past, but ultimately the key determinant is the contemporary repertoire of Jewish choirs around the world and the desire to tap into the global popular culture matrix.

Escaping the Predicament of the 'Imagined Community'

The chapters mentioned above propose new examples of being in the world, away from the impositions of nation-state cultural politics. Anna Oldfield's chapter, 'Reimagining the Caucasus: Music and Community in the Azerbaijani *Aşıq* Tradition,' provides a further critique of staple concepts of nationalism theory (notably Anderson 1983) that privilege the grand narratives of nation-state creationism. The author proposes instead a reevaluation of local hybridized identities, as expressed by *Aşıq* bards in the Caucasus region. Like previous chapters, the research here speaks compellingly about the fluid and adaptable nature of Azerbaijani identities forged within multicultural areas under and after the Soviet occupation. The symbolic geographies of the 'imagined community' portrayed here are rooted in the geographies of vernacular musical practices, through which standardization and interchangeability are being rejected in favor of the small and the unique. This process helps ensure a culture of resistance in the face of historical events that bring cultural earthquakes and long transition periods (e.g., Soviet occupation and communist values, the fall of the Soviet Union and commercialization, among the most significant). It also ensures survival and adaptability, since the music is rooted in local communities of musical practice and dissemination. Oldfield's chapter proposes the local as the site of complex negotiations between the old and the new, oral and commodified cultures, gender roles and power, cultural and identity politics.

Like the work of St John, Pravaz, or Trandafoiu in this volume, Oldfield's chapter also engages with the complexity of diasporic experiences in (in this case) an ethnically 'complicated' region of the world. As has been argued before, 'ethnicity', 'mobility', or 'displacement' are 'not sufficient parameters to allow us to make sense of diasporic phenomena and to retain the critical edge of the concept' (Tsagarousianou 2004, 64). Instead, 'the concept of diaspora inhabits the "transnational" and refers to complex multidirectional flows of human beings, ideas, products—cultural and physical and to forms of interaction, negotiation and exchange, processes of acculturation and cultural creativity, webs of exclusion and struggles to overcome it' (ibid.). In this view, 'diasporas' make the transition from groups defined by ethnicity, protective of boundaries, and perpetually locked into a world system of nation-states and national cultures, to groups set apart by transformation, interactivity, and claim staking. The bards and the *dastans* that Oldfield vividly evokes in her chapter are a clear illustration of this important shift that subverts (but not dismantles) the nation-state system.

Music as Cosmopolitan Accumulation

Florian Carl's chapter, 'From Burger Highlife to Gospel Highlife: Music, Migration, and the Ghanaian Diaspora,' describes how capital accumulation (financial, symbolic, and above all cosmopolitan) through migration has produced important social shifts that tell the story of well-being and empowerment, expressed particularly in the lifestyle, gospel worship, and the aesthetic of liveliness performed within the space of the Pentecostal-Charismatic Churches. This chapter builds on the theory of music 'repositioning' (Stokes 1994), but with reference to the multiple social imaginaries associated with black music (Gilroy 1993). As Carl compellingly explains, both gospel and burger highlife have emerged as a result of musical style negotiations produced by the emergence of new diasporic identities, as well as changes in the social status of Ghanaians living in Germany. Music in the diaspora, often blending older forms of guitar-band highlife and newer styles of synthesized pop, becomes the conduit for expressing diasporic experiences and communicating a diasporic 'state of mind'. Through burger highlife, Ghanaians in Germany aim to participate in the world as cosmopolitans, displaying thus the post-globalization experience of being, which encompasses various types of capital accumulated through transit and migration. At the same time, gospel highlife anchors diasporic and religious experiences and provides a means of empowerment (Dueck 2011).

Meanwhile, in an article explaining the evolution of bhangra music in Britain, Gopinath observes that any musical genre evolving as a result of diasporic experiences, 'displaces the "home" country from its privileged position as originary site and redeploys it as but one of many diasporic locations' (1995, 304). Carl's chapter similarly describes how the diasporic experiences of Ghanaians in Germany produce new styles of music defined not only by African memories, but primarily by the experience of the transit and settlement into a new home. The homeland that is recalled, therefore, in music is a mythical home imbued with diasporic reflection. Similarly, Trandafoiu's research (in this volume) reveals the emergence of a new diasporic imagination that frames musical choices. By moving diasporic groups and their musical practices at the core of contemporary experiences, the contributions in this volume avoid thus the fetishization of marginality (as described by Connell and Gibson 2004, 354).

Reterritorializing Music

Older diasporic theories spoke of separation, deterritorialization, and alienation. However, as Carl's research has shown, music migration does not need to lead to distancing and isolation. Rather than talking about deterritorialization (with its negative connotations), it is more useful to look at processes of reterritorialization that lead to the emergence of new diasporic musicscapes or audiotopias. Natasha Pravaz's chapter, 'Transnational Samba and the Construction of Diasporic Musicscapes,' shows how these musicscapes are actualized through symbolic or physical connections to real or imagined homelands. Pravaz describes such strategies of homing and re-homing through music by exploring samba ensembles in Toronto. Her chapter interrogates what 'home' means, and she redefines our understanding of diaspora to include those who feel an affinity with Brazilianness, though they may be born in Canada or elsewhere. As she points out, once lifted from the original home, samba decouples itself from the constricting worship of tradition, and North American samba ensembles open the door to cosmopolitan encounters of re-homing. Her research thus describes new ways of socialization through music and renationalization at a distance. In this sense, her work recalls the concept of 'mental migration' (Sabry 2005), which here subverts the much talked about issue of 'authenticity' in music by proposing a fresh look at the relationship between the local and the global, and the way they are imagined through musical appropriation and performance.

Pravaz's chapter also seems to suggest that we can rewrite the definition of diasporas to encompass 'members' for whom identity and belonging are a matter of selection. In this sense, long-term settlement, over generations, is not a requirement anymore. Dispersion because of poverty, war, or discrimination is not a necessary prerequisite. The continuous attachment to the homeland is a choice in a world defined by the ready availability of identities to be appropriated and performed.[8] What counts is the ability to build a (diasporic) identity, which is a 'sociopolitical process, involving dialogue, negotiation and debate as to "who we are" and, moreover, what it means to be "who we are"' (Tsagarousianou 2004, 60). While it is generally true that the 'free' movement of people and musics tends to be 'tightly channelled and controlled' (Toynbee and Dueck 2011a, 5) by the political economy, Pravaz's research proves that there are now new ways of escaping the traditional channeling of musical practices. There are now new opportunities for cosmopolitan accumulation, reterritorialization, or re-homing, often aided by new technologies, new opportunities to travel, and new spaces of interaction and experience. Will the new opportunities, the new spaces, and the new practices lead to the establishment of a new cosmopolitan vision? Can music make us more understanding of the 'Other'? The implicit answers that Pravaz's chapter gives are indeed affirmative.

Re-Homing

In the introduction to a special issue on music published by the *Diaspora* journal, Mark Slobin places music at the center of diasporic experiences, which get to 'the heart of what it means to live a multifocal life' (1994, 245). Trandafoiu's chapter, 'Music in Cyberspace. Transitions, Translations, and Adaptations on Romanian Diasporic Websites,' provides the opportunity to document the role music plays in the problematic re-elaboration of Romanianness, conducted from a diasporic position. The chapter describes how Romanian diasporans elaborate a critique of 'national culture' and 'national taste', and begin to elaborate a new spiritual *Heimat* anchored in the liquidity of migratory experiences through the consumption of a diverse musical repertoire that includes folklore, rock, and pop, from Romania and elsewhere. Romanians therefore use music as the conduit that helps them elaborate an identity discourse to express their diasporic condition and newly acquired cosmopolitan tastes. Diasporic musical tastes thus exemplify a symbolic decoupling from national/homeland culture and the emergence of new spaces of reflections on the diasporic condition. Once more, the issue of Westernization or re-elaboration for a global market appears, and once more it helps interrogate 'authenticity' claims. The example of *manele* or turbo folk, the postcommunist Balkan-based genre already born as a hybrid and transnational offering is thus a valid object of investigation.

This genre undermines from the onset the classic understanding of traditional national culture, but it lacks the relabeling resources that would make it an 'exotic' enough proposal in the 'world music' market (see Taylor 2007). *Manele* becomes thus an interesting point of contention for modernizers and traditionalists alike.

Mark Slobin (2012) has recently provided a comprehensive historical journey of the term 'diaspora' in ethnomusicology that culminates with a recent definition, which describes diaspora as an analytical category, a type of awareness, and a vehicle for oppositional politics (Zheng 2010; also cited in Slobin 2012). Zheng, supported by Slobin, thus adds some interesting qualifications, mainly the importance of diasporic awareness and also political reflexivity, which echo Tsagarousianou, to a certain extent, and also Rogers Brubaker (2005). Brubaker also saw the diaspora as 'a category of practice', one that makes 'claims', 'articulates projects', and mobilizes (2005, 12). It is within this context of a clear recent shift of the term 'diaspora' and its theoretical arsenal that Trandafoiu's chapter aims to focus on the new diasporic condition that might give us a better understanding of the way music travels, adapts, is translated, and begins to define processes of reflexivity, identity mobilization, and exchange through music migration.

The Technological Articulation of Migratory Music Experiences

Finally, we could not talk about contemporary migratory experiences without also observing that technology increasingly emerges as a key mediator of migratory phenomena. Returning to Muir's research (in this volume), he illustrates that the success of maintaining 'traditions' lies not just in plugging relevant or 'invented' aspects of tradition into the global matrix, but also deploying social networking as a means of re-socializing people back into the traditional community. For Carl, meanwhile, the sounds of burger highlife are defined by modern technology, as sound technology mediates everyday experiences. Furthermore, the migratory consumption of music naturally moves online, with its ready availability and rich offering. The diasporans' access to technology becomes thus central for constituting a social imaginary of the migrant group. A similar experience is replicated by the Romanian diaspora, as Trandafoiu points out, where diasporic websites enable a reflexive conversation on the nature of migratory experiences and the relevance of maintaining (or not) the umbilical cord of the homeland.

MUSICAL IDENTITIES AND TOURISMS IN TRANSIT

This collection of essays traces the particularities of music migration and tourism in different global settings and provides current, even new, perspectives for ethnomusicological research on globalizing musics in transit. The dual focus on tourism and migration is central to debates on globalization, and their examination—separately or combined—offers a useful lens on many key questions about where globalization is taking us: questions about identity and heritage, commoditization, historical and cultural representation, hybridity, authenticity and ownership, neo-liberalism, inequality, diasporization, the relocation of allegiances, and more. In this respect, *Musics in Transit* represents a unique contribution to the field of music and globalization. For the first time, these two key phenomena—tourism and migration—are studied conjointly, as well as interdisciplinary, in order to derive both parallels and contrasts. This approach allows us to study and configure for the first time in relation to music the new fluid spaces that take shape as people and musics travel, migrate and transit, as well as the new configurations sparked by the new networks of interactions.

In doing so, this collection illustrates a range of different, heterogeneous forms of travel—music tourisms and migrations—as these occur in different cultural and sociopolitical contexts. One emergent theme here concerns people's multiple and various identities as these are constantly negotiated, reinforced, subverted, and renegotiated in current touristic and migratory contexts. Timothy D. Taylor's afterword provides an understanding of our fascination with identity, stemming, to a certain extent, from the ability we have to choose, construct, consume, and even perfect identities. As Taylor observes, the contributions in this volume examine both instances of commonality and divisiveness through identity, but above all they comment on the power identity has to liberate us, through change, from the fixities of inherited structures.

Meanwhile, an important issue not yet elaborated concerns the methods of research used for studying music tourisms and migrations. Capturing musics in transit is an endeavor that poses certain methodological challenges, all the more so since recent approaches to the study of world musics place equal value on real or imagined, face-to-face or virtual/symbolic musical encounters (White 2012, 11). It is perhaps safe to say that ethnography alone no longer suffices for studying and understanding musics in transit under post-global conditions. Historical research alongside ethnography can serve as the methodological tools of choice in this case, yet these may also be complemented by cartography, semiotic analysis, performer-observations, statistical analysis, virtual observation, and social media monitoring, in short, multimodal research, as is demonstrated in this collection. Multimodal ethnomusicological enquiry would suit us well in studying musics in situations of local and global, micro and macro scale. In this process, some authors adopt unique positions as ethnographer/tourist and ethnographer/migrant; the doubling of those *in situ*, who are both tourist and researcher, migrant and researcher, gives the research a certain, even useful advantage in that it provides context and entry into a reality that is often fraught with discrepancies. These multiple approaches and roles allow the ethnomusicological researcher to capture phenomena that are symbolic, virtual, or 'of the mind', and thus of significant relevance to musics in transit. The mobile, the fleeting, the dynamic, the imagined all play an equal part, together with the historical, the durable, or the recurrent.

The musics and musical practices analyzed here can be described as 'accented', to use a term originally applied to diasporic film (Naficy 2001). In other words, they are defined and brought together by the experience of movement, transit, or displacement, by their multiple anchorings in various and variable geographies, real or imagined. Moreover, the phenomena exemplified here, while unbounded, are not decontextualized; they speak of replacement and repositioning, rather than displacement. Today, the musics that fall between genres, spaces, and ethnicities are 'quite deliberately and self-consciously about transgressing traditionally defined borders and about creating new artistic and cultural spaces' (Hernández Pacini 2003, 30), and are therefore self-referential, strategic, and reflexive. Identity, history, and cultural politics still matter, but they are constantly being reassessed through the lens of new cosmopolitan experiences. The contributions present in this volume thus provide a rich exemplification of how all forms of musical culture are becoming transnational under post-global conditions, sustained by both global markets and musics in transit, and to which both tourists and diasporic cosmopolitans make an important contribution.

NOTES

1. The fact that migration and tourism may exist side by side in some contexts is shown in this book, yet this area of inquiry is still critically absent in ethnomusicological discourses.
2. An updated version of the paper cited here was published in 2010, featuring some of the blog discussions on Charlie Gillett's former site that appeared in response to Keith Howard's 2009 lecture (see Howard 2010).
3. The conference was organized and hosted by coeditor Simone Krüger on the theme of 'Music, Culture and Globalisation', where the idea for this edited collection was conceived. See http://www.bfe.org.uk/resources/DelegateHandbook$2428FINAL$2429.pdf (accessed March 16, 2013).
4. For instance, tourism creates a positive multiplier effect on economic growth via the creation of employment, enhancement of education and professionalism, heightened public pride, public revenue, foreign direct investment, foreign exchange earnings, and so forth. International tourism thus provides a powerful stimulus for economic development in the tourist-receiving country so that international tourism is regarded to be a top priority for governments' policy making worldwide (World Travel and Tourism Council 2013) and has grown to become one of the world's largest industries (World Tourism Organization 2013). Meanwhile, tourism also brings about a range of social benefits for local communities, for example, improvements in education, libraries, and health and social spaces, such as Internet cafés.
5. See also Cohen and Roberts (in this volume) for a useful overview of literatures on music tourism and authenticity.
6. Or the shift from 'space of places to space of flows', according to Castells (1996).

7. Which Stokes himself derives from Giddens.
8. We are, of course, using here the criteria of 'classic' diasporas (see Cohen 2008; Clifford 1994; Safran 1991).

REFERENCES

Abram, Simone, Jacqueline Waldren, and Donald V.L. Macleod, eds. 1997. *Tourists and Tourism: Identifying with People and Places*. Oxford: Berg.

Anderson, Benedict. 1983. *Imagined Communities: Reflections on the Origin and Spread of Nationalism*. London: Verso.

Aoyama, Yuko. 2007. 'The Role of Consumption and Globalization in a Cultural Industry: The Case of Flamenco.' *Geoforum* 38:103–13.

Appadurai, Arjun. 1990. 'Disjuncture and Difference in the Global Cultural Economy.' *Public Culture* 2(2):1–24.

Atkinson, Connie. 1996. '"Shakin' Your Butt for the Tourist": Music's Role in the Identification and Selling of New Orleans.' In *Dixie Debates: Perspectives on Southern Cultures*, edited by Richard H. King, and Helen Taylor, 150–64. New York: New York University Press.

Atkinson, Connie. 1997. 'New Orleans: Popular Music and the Social, Cultural, and Economic Production of Locality.' In *Tourists and Tourism: Identifying with People and Places*, edited by Simone Abram, Jacqueline Waldren, and Donald V.L. Macleod, 91–106. Oxford: Berg.

Baily, John, and Michael Collyer. 2006. 'Introduction: Music and Migration.' *Journal of Ethnic and Migration Studies Special Issue* 32(2):167–82.

Barfield, Thomas. 1997. *The Dictionary of Anthropology*. Malden: Blackwell.

Bauman, Zygmunt. 1996. 'From Pilgrim to Tourist—or a Short History of Identity.' In *Questions of Cultural Identity*, edited by Stuart Hall and Paul du Gay, 18–36. London: Sage.

Bauman, Zygmund. 2005. *Liquid Life*. Cambridge: Polity Press.

Bauman, Zygmund. 2009. 'Europe and the Rest. A Dialogue between Étienne Balibar and Zygmund Bauman.' *Leeds Institute for Colonial and Postcolonial Studies*, May 13.

Baumann, Max Peter, ed. 1995. *Music in the Dialogue of Cultures: Traditional Music and Cultural Policy*. Wilhelmshaven: Florian Noetzel Verlag.

Baumann, Max Peter, ed. 2001. *Folk Music in Public Performance*. Special Issue of *The World of Music* 43(2/3).

Bennett, Andy. 2004. '"Chilled Ibiza": Dance Tourism and the Neo-Tribal Island Community.' In *Island Musics*, edited by Kevin Dawe, 123–36. Oxford: Berg.

Bhabha, Homi K. 1994. *The Location of Culture*. Routledge: London.

Bohlman, Philip V. 2008. 'Returning to the Ethnomusicological Past.' In *Shadows in the Field. New Perspectives for Fieldwork in Ethnomusicology*, edited by Gregory Barz and Timothy J. Cooley, 246–70. Oxford: Oxford University Press.

Bohlman, Philip V. 2002. 'Ethnic Musics/Religious Identities: Toward a Historiography of German-American Sacred Music.' In *Land Without Nightingales: Music in the Making of German-America*, edited by Philip V. Bohlman and Otto Holzapfel, 127–57. Madison: University of Wisconsin Press.

Brubaker, Rogers. 2005. 'The "Diaspora" Diaspora.' *Ethnic and Racial Studies* 28(1):1–19.

Burckhardt Qureshi, Regula, ed. 1998. *Identity and Adaptation in Musical Performance: Interactions between Tradition and Tourism in East and Southeast Asia*. Special Issue of *Journal of Musicological Research* 17(2).

Burkhalter, Thomas. 2012. 'Weltmusik 2.0—Musikalische Positionen zwischen Spass- und Protestkultur [World Music 2.0—Musical Positions between Fun and Protest Cultures].' In *Out of the Absurdity of Life: Globale Musik*, edited by Theresa Beyer and Thomas Burkhalter, 28–46. Bern, Switzerland: Norient.

Campbell, Sean. 2010. 'Displaced Sounds: Popular Music-Making among the Irish Diaspora in England.' In *Music and Displacement: Diasporas, Mobilities, and Dislocations in Europe and Beyond*, edited by Erik Levi and Florian Scheding, 89–103. Lanham, MD: Scarecrow Press.

Castells, Manuel. 1996. *The Rise of the Network Society*. Oxford: Blackwell.

Castells, Manuel, Fernández-Ardèvol, Mireia, Linchuan Qiu, Jack and Araba Sey. 2007. *Mobile Communication and Society. A Global Perspective*. Cambridge, MA: MIT Press.

Cheong, Do-Min, and M. Miller. 2000. 'Power and Tourism: A Foucaldian Approach.' *Annals of Tourism Research* 27(2):371–90.

Clausen, Bernd, Ursula Hemetek, Eva Saether, and European Music Council, eds. 2009. *Music in Motion: Diversity and Dialogue in Europe*. Bielefeld, Germany: Transcript Verlag.

Clifford, James. 1994. 'Diaspora.' *Cultural Anthropology* 9(3):302–38.

Cohen, Robin. 2008. *Global Diasporas: An Introduction*. London: Routledge.

Cohen, Sara. 1997. 'Popular Music, Tourism, and Urban Regeneration.' In *Tourists and Tourism: Identifying with People and Places*, edited by Simone Abram, Jacqueline Waldren, and Donald V.L. Macleod, 71–90. Oxford: Berg.

Cohen, Sara. 2001. 'Popular Culture in Liverpool.' In *Liverpool at the Millennium: Living in the City,* edited by R. Meegan and M. Maddon. Liverpool: Liverpool University Press.

Cohen, Sara. 2003. 'Tourism.' In *Continuum Encyclopedia of Popular Music of the World*. Volume 1. *Media, Industry and Society*, edited by David Horn, Dave Laing, Paul Oliver, and Peter Wicke, 382–85. London: Continuum.

Cohen, Sara. 2007. *Decline, Renewal and the City in Popular Music Culture: Beyond the Beatles*. Aldershot: Ashgate.

Connell, John, and Chris Gibson. 2002. *Sound Tracks. Popular Music, Identity and Place*. London: Routledge.

Connell, John, and Chris Gibson. 2004. 'World Music: Deterritorializating Place and Identity.' *Progress in Human Geography* 28(3):342–61.

Cooley, Timothy J. 1999. 'Folk Festival as Modern Ritual in the Polish Tatra Mountains.' Special Issue (Music, Travel, and Tourism) of *The World of Music* 41(3):31–55.

Culic, Irina. 2010. 'State of Imagination: Embodiments of Immigration Canada.' *Sociological Review* 58(3):343–60.

DeWitt, Mark F., ed. 1999. *Music, Travel, and Tourism*, Special Issue of *The World of Music* 41(3).

Dueck, Byron. 2011. 'Part1: Migrants—Introduction.' In *Migrating Music*, edited by Jason Toynbee and Byron Dueck, 21–27. London: Routledge.

Frith, Simon. 1996. 'Music and Identity.' In *Questions of Cultural Identity*, edited by Stuart Hall and Paul du Gay, 108–27. London: Sage.

Gibson, Chris, and John Connell. 2005. *Music and Tourism: On the Road Again*. Clevedon: Channel View Publications.

Gibson, Chris, and John Connell. 2007. 'Music, Tourism and the Transformation of Memphis.' *Tourism Geographies: An International Journal of Tourism Space, Place and Environment* 9(2):160–90.

Gilroy, Paul. 1993. *The Black Atlantic. Modernity and Double Consciousness*. London: Verso.

Gopinath, Gayatri. 1995. '"Bombay, UK, Yuba City": Bhangra Music and the Engendering of Diaspora.' *Diaspora* 4(3):303–21.

Guerrón Montero, Carla. 2011a. 'Heritage, Identity and Globalization: The Case of Island Tourism in the Caribbean.' *Bulletin of Latin American Research* 30(1):1–6.

Guerrón Montero, Carla, ed. 2011b. *Island Tourism in the Americas*. Special Issue of *Bulletin of Latin American Research* 30(1).

Hall, Stuart. 1997. *Race, The Floating Signifier*. Northampton, MA: Media Education Foundation. Accessed March 16, 2013. http://www.mediaed.org/assets/products/407/transcript_407.pdf.

Hernández Pacini, Deborah. 2003. 'Amalgamating Musics. Popular Music and Cultural Hybridity in the America.' In *Musical Migrations. Transnationalism and Cultural Hybridity in Latin/o America*, vol. 1, edited by Frances R. Aparicio and Càndida F. Jàquez, 13–32. Basingstoke: Palgrave.

Hobsbawm, Eric, and Terence Ranger. 1983. *The Invention of Tradition*. Cambridge: Cambridge University Press.

Hollifield, James F. 2004. 'The Emerging Migration State.' *International Migration Review* 38(3):885–911.

Howard, Keith. 2009. 'Live Music vs. Audio Tourism: World Music and the Changing Music Industry.' An Inaugural Lecture given on November 11, 2008. London: SOAS, University of London. Accessed March 16, 2013. https://eprints.soas.ac.uk/7151/.

Howard, Keith. 2010. 'World Music: Whose Music and Whose World?' *OMNES— The Journal of Multicultural Society* 1(2):1–34.

Hughes, George. 2010. 'Urban Revitalization: The Use of Festive Time Strategies.' *Leisure Studies* 18(2):119–35.

ICRETH. 2012. 'Soundtracks: Music, Tourism and Travel.' Conference proceedings. Leeds Metropolitan University. Accessed February 10, 2013. https://sites.google.com/site/soundtracksconference/home.

Kaeppler, Adrienne, and Oliver Lewin, eds. 1988. *Come mek me hol' yu han': The Impact of Tourism on Traditional Music. ICTM Colloquium, 1986*. Kingston: Jamaica Memory Bank.

Kassabian, Annahid. 2004. 'Would You Like Some World Music with Your Latte? Starbucks, Putumayo, and Distributed Tourism.' *Twentieth Century Music* 2(1):209–23.

Kiwan, Nadia, and Ulrike Hanna Meinhof. 2011. *Cultural Globalization and Music: African Artists in Transnational Networks*. Basingstoke: Palgrave Macmillan.

Levi, Erik, and Florian Scheding, eds. 2010. *Music and Displacement: Diasporas, Mobilities, and Dislocations in Europe and Beyond*. Lanham, Maryland: Scarecrow.

Lipsitz, George. 1994. *Dangerous Crossroads: Popular Music, Postmodernism and the Poetics of Place*. London: Verso.

Lornell, Kip, and Anne Rasmussen, eds. 1997. *Musics of Multicultural America: A Study of Twelve Musical Communities*. New York: Schirmer.

MacCannell, Dean. 1976. *The Tourist: A New Theory of the Leisure Class*. New York: Schocken.

Manuel, Peter. 1997/1998. 'Music, Identity, and Images of India in the Indo-Caribbean Diaspora.' *Asian Music* 29(1):17–35.

Massey, Douglas, Arango, Joaquin, Hugo, Graeme, Kouaouci, Ali, Pellegrino, Adela and J. Edward Taylor. 1998. *Worlds in Motion. Understanding International Migration at the End of the Millennium*. Oxford: Clarendon Press.

Naficy, Hamid. 2001. *An Accented Cinema: Exilic and Diasporic Filmmaking*. Princeton, NJ: Princeton University Press.

Nettl, Bruno. 2005. *The Study of Ethnomusicology: Thirty-One Issues and Concepts*. 2nd ed. Urbana: University of Illinois Press.

Patullo, Polly. 2009. 'Sailing into the Sunset: The Cruise Ship Industry.' In *Tourists and Tourism: A Reader*, 2nd ed., edited by Sharon Gmelch, 399–418. Long Grove, IL: Waveland.

Post, Jennifer C. 2006. 'Introduction.' In *Ethnomusicology: A Contemporary Reader*, edited by Jennifer C. Post, 1–13. New York: Routledge.

Post, Jennifer. 2011. *Ethnomusicology: A Research and Information Guide*. 2nd ed. New York: Routledge.

Radano, Ronald, and Philip Bohlman. 2000. 'Introduction: Music and Race, Their Past, Their Presence.' In *Music and the Racial Imagination*, edited by Ronald Radano, and Philip Bohlman, 1–53. Chicago: University of Chicago Press.

Ramnarine, Tina K., ed. 2008. *Musical Performance in the Diaspora*. New York: Routledge.

Raussert, Wilfried and John Miller Jones, eds. 2009. *Traveling Sounds: Music, Migration, and Identity in the U.S. and Beyond (Transnational and Transatlantic American Studies)*. Berlin: Lit Verlag.

Reyes, Adelaida. 1999. *Songs of the Caged, Songs of the Free: Music and the Vietnamese Refugee Experience*. Philadelphia: Temple University Press.

Reyes, Adelaida. 2009. 'Urban Ethnomusicology: Past and Present.' In *Music in Motion: Diversity and Dialogue in Europe*, edited by Bernd Clausen, Ursula Hemetek, Eva Saether, and European Music Council, 173–90. Bielefeld, Germany: Transcript Verlag.

Rietveld, Hillegonda. 1998. *This Is Our House: House Music, Cultural Spaces, And Technologies*. Aldershot: Ashgate.

Ritzer, George, and Allan Liska. 1997. 'McDisneyization and Post-Tourism: Complementary Perspectives on Contemporary Tourism.' In *Touring Cultures: Transformations of Travel and Theory*, edited by Chris Rojek and John Urry, 96–112. London: Routledge.

Sabry, Tarik. 2005, 'The Day Moroccans Gave up Couscous for Satellites: Global TV, Structures of Feeling, and Mental Migration.' *Transnational Broadcasting Studies* 14. Accessed February 2, 2006. www.tbsjournal.com/Archives/Spring05/sabry.html.

Safran, William. 1991. 'Diasporas in Modern Societies: Myths of Homeland and Return.' *Diaspora* 1(1):83–99.

Shelemay, Kay Kaufman. 2006. 'Music, Memory and History.' Special Issue (The Past in Music) of *Ethnomusicology Forum* 15(1):17–37.

Shelemay, Kay Kaufman. 1998. *Let Jasmine Rain Down: Song and Remembrance Among Syrian Jews*. Chicago: University of Chicago Press.

Slobin, Mark. 1994. 'Music in Diaspora: The View from Euro-America.' *Diaspora* 3(3):243–51.

Slobin, Mark. 2012. 'The Destiny of "Diaspora" in Ethnomusicology.' In *The Cultural Study of Music: A Critical Introduction*, edited by Martin Clayton, Trevor Herbert, and Richard Middleton, 96–106. Routledge: London.

Songlines. 2013. 'Songlines Music Travel.' Accessed January 13, 2013. http://www.songlines.co.uk/music-travel/info/tours.php.

Stock, Jonathan P.J. 2008. 'New Directions in Ethnomusicology: Seven Themes Toward Disciplinary Renewal.' In *The New (Ethno)Musicologies*, edited by Henry Stobart, 188–206. Lanham, MD: Scarecrow Press.

Stokes, Martin. 1994. 'Introduction: Ethnicity, Identity and Music.' In *Ethnicity, Identity and Music. The Musical Construction of Place*, edited by Martin Stokes, 1–27. Oxford: Berg.

Stokes, Martin. 1999. 'Music, Travel and Tourism: An Afterword.' *World of Music* 41(3):141–56.

Suppan, Wolfgang. 1991. *Schladminger Gespräche zum Thema Musik und Tourismus* [Schladminger Debates on the Theme of Music and Tourism]. Tutzing: Hans Schneider Verlag.

Taylor, Timothy. 2007. *Beyond Exoticism: Western Music and the World*. Durham, NC: Duke University Press.

Toynbee, Jason, and Byron Dueck. 2011a. 'Migrating Music. Introduction.' In *Migrating Music*, edited by Jason Toynbee, and Byron Dueck, 1–17. London: Routledge.

Toynbee, Jason, and Byron Dueck, eds. 2011b. *Migrating Music*. New York: Routledge.

Trandafoiu, Ruxandra. 2013. *Diaspora Online: Identity Politics and Romanian Migrants*. Oxford: Berghahn Books.

Tsagarousianou, Roza. 2004. 'Rethinking the Concept of Diaspora: Mobility, Connectivity and Communication in a Globalised World.' *Westminster Papers in Communication and Culture* 1(1):52–65.

Turino, Thomas, and James Lea, eds. 2004. *Identity and the Arts in Diaspora Communities*. Michigan: Harmonie Park Press.

Urry, John. 1990. *The Tourist Gaze: Leisure and Travel in Contemporary Societies*. London: Sage.

Wade, Peter. 2008. 'African Diaspora and Colombian Popular Music in the Twentieth Century.' *Black Music Research Journal* 28(2):41–56.

White, Bob W. 2012. 'Introduction: Rethinking Globalization through Music.' In *Music and Globalization: Critical Encounters*, edited by Bob W. White, 1–14. Bloomington: Indiana University Press.

Wood, Robert. 2000. 'Caribbean Cruise Tourism: Globalization at Sea.' *Annals of Tourism Research* 27(2):345–70.

World Tourism Organization. 2013. Accessed January 14, 2013. http://www2.unwto.org/.

World Travel and Tourism Council. 2013. Accessed January 14, 2013. http://www.wttc.org/.

Worley, Barbara A. 2012. 'The 2012 Tuareg Revolt: Regional Identities and Barriers to Reconciliation.' *Tuareg Culture and News*, July 30. Accessed February 22, 2013. http://tuaregcultureandnews.blogspot.com/2012_07_30_archive.html.

Zheng, Su. 2010. *Claiming Diaspora. Music, Transnationalism, and Cultural Politics in Asian/Chinese America*. Oxford: Oxford University Press.

Part I
Music and Tourism

1 Heritage Rocks!

Mapping Spaces of Popular Music Tourism

Sara Cohen and Les Roberts

The online blog of the UK travel company Thompson Holidays includes an interactive map entitled 'How Music Travels: The Evolution of Western Dance Music' (Khan 2011). The map features styles of electronic dance music and draws on information from Wikipedia and other sources to show when and where these styles emerged and how they interacted and developed. The blog is headed by the following statement:

> Music tourism (visiting a city or town to see a gig or festival) is on the rise. But why stop at gigs and festivals? Why not visit the birthplace of your favourite genre and follow the actual journey various music genres have taken as one style developed into another. (Khan 2011)

Comments posted on the blog show that the map prompted discussion and debate, but it also provided a marketing device for the company, which has specialized in package holidays to Ibiza and other Mediterranean locations targeted at young adults. The map suggests that music is a perfect example of a global 'traveling culture' (Clifford 1992), and that one of the UK's leading travel companies has recognized the commercial appeal of mapping the flows, routes, and mobilities of popular music cultures, which is testament to the growing importance attached to music geographies and 'musicscapes',[1] whether locally, nationally, or, as with the Thompson example, as a feature of global and transnational tourism mobilities.

Drawing on the twofold mobilities tied up with the recognition that 'people tour cultures; and that cultures and objects themselves travel' (Rojek and Urry 1997, 1), the Thompson map provides a salient point of entry into the subject of music and tourism not just on account of its making explicit the ties between popular musicscapes and the tourism industry. More importantly for the purposes of this chapter, its significance also lies in the fact that these ties are presented in the form of a map. This chapter explores the relationship between popular music, place, and tourism through a focus on maps, which, in their different ways, mark sites of UK popular music heritage. The maps that we discuss were produced or planned by businesses and organizations concerned with music, heritage, and tourism in the UK, and were referred to or discussed during interviews we conducted in 2011 with some of the people involved. These interviews were conducted as part of an ongoing international and collaborative research project on popular music heritage, cultural memory, and cultural identity.[2]

Using the maps to explore broader issues surrounding popular music heritage in the UK, methodologically and critically our attention is drawn to the ways in which maps 'do' different things, and work or 'perform' in different ways (Wood 2012). In particular, we discuss how maps work and function across various discursive and institutional contexts; perform different notions of music, place, and heritage; and offer different forms of spatial engagement. Insofar as they conform to a loosely defined spatial logic, and in terms of the trajectory of our analysis, the maps we discuss are compared and contrasted according to the degree to which they enable users to 'zoom in' to significant aspects of ethnographic or cartographic detail. Reflecting on this, we consider how the maps might contribute to or inhibit fine-grained understandings of music, tourism, and place. The first of the chapter's three sections focuses on 'official' maps that are interactive but designed largely for symbolic and place-branding purposes rather than to provide users with much detail of particular musical sites and localities (whether regions, cities, or neighborhoods). The second section discusses more localized maps of popular music heritage. It begins with maps designed to be not just interactive but used in situ, and as part of journeys around, and experiences of, the various sites involved. It then moves on to consider maps created by users that chart vernacular spaces of memory, lived and everyday musical pathways, and which exemplify what we have elsewhere described as 'heritage-as-praxis' (Roberts and Cohen 2012). The third and final section of the chapter draws together some of the threads of discussion and reflects on the role and significance of maps for research on music, place, and tourism.

BRITAIN ROCKS! MUSIC, TOURISM, AND PLACE MARKETING

Music tourism is defined in various ways and related to a broad range of music practices. It is nevertheless commonly associated with visits to live music performance events, such as concerts, festivals, and carnivals, or to sites of music heritage, such as places associated with well-known musicians and music scenes and sounds. These events and sites have been studied in various parts of the world and across many academic disciplines, and they involve diverse music genres and styles, including classical art musics and traditional, folk, and world musics. The focus here is on Anglo-American popular music and tourism and heritage in the UK. Over the past three decades, official and commercial interests in popular music heritage and tourism has grown in the UK and beyond, evident in the proliferation of monuments and plaque schemes, tours and trails, maps and museums connected to a broad range of styles, from jazz to techno (Gibson and Connell 2005; Cohen 2012b; Roberts and Cohen 2012). European rock and pop museums, for example, include the Beatles Story museum in Liverpool, the ill-fated National Centre for Popular Music in Sheffield, and the more recent British Music Experience (BME) in London, as well as the museum Rockart in Hoek Van Holland, the Irish Music Hall of Fame in Dublin, the Rockheim museum in Trondheim, and the Beatles museum in Hamburg. Similar initiatives have emerged in places that are not so widely known for popular music, such as the small coastal town of Karvana, now officially branded 'the rock capital of Bulgaria'.

This turn to popular music heritage has been prompted by various developments, including the marketing of popular music history and nostalgia by the music industries as a response to a decline in record sales from the mid-1980s, and the use of culture and the cultural or creative industries as a tool for remodeling cities and regions as part of a wider process of restructuring, governed by the politics and economics of neoliberalism.[3] It has involved, among other things, the development of cultural tourism and the use of cultural heritage for place marketing and urban regeneration, and it is illustrated in this first section of the chapter by two examples of 'official' cartographies and discourses of popular music as national heritage: a 2007 tourist marketing campaign conducted by Visit Britain, and the BME, an interactive museum of popular music heritage that opened in London in 2009.

Visit Britain

Over the last two decades, Visit Britain, a government-funded national tourism agency, has established a reputation as a leading player in film-related tourist marketing initiatives, working alongside major film companies to exploit the iconographic potential of UK film locations. These locations are promoted in Britain and overseas through the publication of movie maps, web-based marketing campaigns, and related tie-in products designed to market Britain as a visitor attraction, as well as the films in which these locations are represented (Roberts 2010, 2012a). Over recent years, similar initiatives have sought to exploit the economic potential of music-related tourism, such as the British Tourist Authority's music tourism guide 'One Nation Under a Groove: The Rock & Pop Map of Britain.' This free pocket-size map unfolded into a poster featuring Britain in the shape of an electric guitar and nearby Ireland as an amplifier. It was launched by a government minister at Madam Tussaud's Rock Circus in London in 1998. It was part of the so-called Cool Britannia marketing initiative of a new Labour government keen to develop 'the creative industries' for the purposes of national economic development, and to associate itself and the nation with images of vibrant, youthful, commercially successful creativity.[4]

Visit Britain also produced printed and online maps featuring a selection of sites marking Britain's rock music heritage as part of the more recent marketing campaigns Britain Rocks! and England Rocks! (2007). These maps were produced in collaboration with the British music company EMI and incorporated information on British artists, highlighting places linked to those artists. The England Rocks! campaign, for example, was aimed at achieving maximum impact within a specified timeframe but also involved an online interactive map of 'English' music landmarks that could be accessed via Enjoy England's website until 2011. Users were presented with a pale green map of England surrounded by blue, and featuring colorful dots to mark locations across the various regions. The map was positioned against a backdrop that had been designed to look like an urban brick wall, which was adorned with graffiti and colorful posters, featuring information about the musical landmarks of various cities and regions marked on the map. Clicking on some of these sites enabled access to a larger poster that provided a list of relevant facts and information. Across the top of the map was the map logo with the words 'England Rocks!' picked out in red, white, and blue using a font similar to that associated with British mod culture of the 1960s and 1970s and the rock band The Who, and a white plectrum featuring the Enjoy England logo in red. Underneath was a banner proclaiming 'From the Animals to the Zutons and every place in between.'

The director of marketing at Visit Britain showed us a series of annotated sketches that had been produced by the marketing company hired to design the map. They featured various black ink doodles created during the initial brainstorming exercise, and illustrating efforts to come up with a logo (or 'scamps') using generic items of rock and pop iconography. On the notes, these images were supplemented by scribbled phrases such as 'coat of arms', 'heritage of rock', 'band typefaces', 'resonates across all target audiences'. The words 'urban' and 'distressed' also appeared, suggesting, along with the brick wall, an effort to relate English music heritage to notions of 'the street' as opposed to the museum. There was also a list of decades and associated artists that could provide a semiotic trigger to evoke them: 1950s—Cliff R[ichard], 1960s—Stones/Beatles, 1970s—Queen, 1980s—Joy Division, 1990s—Robbie [Williams].' In view of the range of performers that could have been chosen, it is a somewhat arbitrary selection that reflected the personal tastes and memories of the marketing staff involved. As we have discussed elsewhere (Roberts and Cohen 2012), the influence, habitus, and personal background of those motivated to establish forms of popular music heritage, or lobby for their 'official' recognition, plays an influential role in shaping dominant ideas of what music is categorized as heritage, and whose memories and identities are represented.

When we interviewed the marketing director of Visit Britain about the England Rocks! and Britain Rocks! campaign and maps, he referred to the National Brand Index,[5] which showed that a high percentage of international audiences associated the UK with music (telephone interview with Lawrence

Bresh, conducted by Les Roberts, March 25, 2011). The director explained that the maps were primarily a PR exercise aimed at rebranding Britain as an exciting country with a rich and diverse music heritage 'from heavy metal to pop and everything in between.' The maps were thus intended to be broad in their coverage but the emphasis was, the director continued, on performers that 'have stood the test of time, bands that have had a huge following rather than more ephemeral pop acts,' and on tangible sites, such as plaques erected as a tribute to particular performers and places that could be visited. This involved sites largely associated with white, male, rock musicians; hence, the map promoted an image of England and Englishness that strikes a somewhat dissonant chord with a sense of national cultural identity that reflects the social, cultural, and ethnic diversity of England's popular music heritage. The marketing team at Visit Britain compiled an initial list of music landmarks and edited it down to provide a short list of locations that were, in the first instance, conducive to sightseeing, touristic consumption practices, and the exploitation of established tourism and heritage resources. They included locations represented through songs, album covers, and existing tourist attractions, such as museum exhibits. London and Liverpool featured prominently on both maps, partly because of their density of music tourism sites, their appeal to overseas visitors, and the fact that the maps were produced in association with regional and national music tour operators, as well as EMI. Other familiar visitor attractions featured on the maps included Ely Cathedral, which appears on the cover of Pink Floyd's 1994 progressive rock album *The Division Bell*, and Hatfield House, a stately home where the post-punk band Adam and the Ants filmed their 'Stand and Deliver' video (Liverpool 08 2007).

The hard copy and online versions of the England Rocks! map were distributed widely. One BBC radio program promoted the maps as 'website of the week', while the British tabloid newspaper the *Sun* declared: 'This week, tourism bosses launch England Rocks!, a campaign showing how you can discover our rich musical heritage on holiday' (*Sun* 2007). According to Visit Britain, the maps were successful in boosting domestic or national tourism, and in generating interest from Europe, parts of Asia, and particularly the US. According to the *New York Times*:

> Everyone knows that Jim Morrison's grave is in Paris, but who knew that Dusty Springfield's grave, above right, is in Henley-on-Thames or that the grave of the former Rolling Stone Brian Jones, above left, is in Cheltenham? Now, thanks to a free downloadable England Rocks map . . . music fans can learn everything there is to know about more than 100 English sites associated with rock 'n' roll and then make a pilgrimage that goes far beyond the average visit to the Abbey Road Studios. (2007)

England Rocks! thus had an instrumental function as a tourist marketing tool but was also a publicly accessible resource that provided information about popular music heritage. It did so on a very selective basis, however, and by shaping and reinforcing a dominant historical narrative about English popular music that was largely based around white, male, rock music, and deemed likely to have widespread and international appeal in terms of potential tourist consumption patterns and mobilities.

British Music Experience

The BME provides the second example of an 'official' cartography and discourse of popular music heritage. It is a permanent exhibition dedicated to the history of popular music in Britain that opened in 2009 as part of London's O2 complex. Situated on the Greenwich Peninsula in southeast London, the O2 is a commercial development made up of restaurants and bars; the music and performance venue, the O2 Arena; and the O2 Bubble, an exhibition space that houses the BME. The US-owned global live sports and entertainment company AEG provided the initial funding, but the exhibition is administered as a charitable foundation and managed by an independent board of trustees chaired by the music promoter Harvey Goldsmith. It is also sponsored by several major corporations, including two world-leading music instrument and technology manufacturers, the Performing Right Society of Great Britain and BBC Worldwide, which disseminates BBC content nationally and internationally via magazines, DVDs, live events, and merchandise. The BME website describes the exhibition as 'Britain's only interactive museum of popular music' (BME 2012a) and invites visitors to 'relive the glorious history of British popular music' (BME 2012b), while its curator states, 'The emphasis is on experience, not museum' (Hayes 2009).

The experience, which we visited in February and October 2011, begins and ends in the BME shop. From here, visitors are directed toward the main exhibition space and an introduction from the broadcaster Lauren Laverne, who, projected onto a huge screen (the first of many screen interactive experiences), extends a welcome and provides instructions on the use of the Smarticket, which, as the BME website points out, 'allows you to create your own personal musical journey as you go around the exhibition and to continue your experience [online] when you get home'(BME 2012d).[6] The main exhibition space consists of The Core, Edge Zones, Gibson Interactive Studio, and The Finale. The Edge Zones are a series of galleries that each covers a specific period of Britain's postwar popular music history. Much of their content consists of a 'Rock 'n' Roll Years'–style collection of music videos, archive footage and clips, and some items of memorabilia (guitars, T-shirts, costumes, album sleeves, and such).[7]

Gibson Interactive Studio offers visitors the opportunity to play a range of different musical instruments, including guitars, bass, keyboards, and drums, with the option of step-by-step video tuition from rock musicians such as Blur, KT Tunstall, and others. The Finale, as its name suggests, is the final attraction in the exhibition and represents by far the most insubstantial aspect of the BME 'experience', not least on account of its attempt to somehow evoke the atmosphere or experience (it is difficult to avoid using this particular word as it is at the core of what the exhibition purports to offer) of live music performance (BME 2012c). On both occasions we visited the exhibition, we experienced The Finale with a handful of bemused-looking fellow visitors, who, like us, appeared uncertain as to how to respond or perform to this rather unconvincing simulacrum of a live music experience. The Core of the exhibition features the interactive Dance the Decades (in which a virtual dance instructor performs a range of dance moves, which visitors are invited to follow, essentially the same concept as the popular Nintendo Wii home video game 'Just Dance'); Hey DJ!, a virtual collection of dance music records; interactive exhibits on the history of music broadcasting and playback technology; and an interactive music map Where It's At (Figure 1.1).

This map—a large horizontal representation of the UK—occupies a central position within The Core. Arranged around it are three user interfaces where museumgoers can navigate their way around Britain and Northern Ireland by operating a trackball device and clicking on location icons representing variously: videos, gigs and venues, facts, hometowns, festivals,

Figure 1.1 'Where It's At' interactive map, British Music Experience, O2 London.

album covers. Yet when zooming in at the local level, the map reveals little if any cartographic detail, making it difficult to explore or navigate particular localities and cityscapes. Facing the map users is a large vertical screen, which displays a random selection of facts that appear independently of their interactions and of the geographical content extracted from the map. On our second visit to the BME, there was a sheet of white A4 paper affixed to the side of the screen, consisting of a word-processed statement informing visitors that the map content has been sourced from a book by the music journalist and rock genealogist Pete Frame entitled *Rockin' around Britain: Rock and Roll Landmarks of the UK and Ireland* (1999).

The reliance on information drawn from Frame's book prompts the question as to what the BME map does that would not be done more efficiently and effectively by the book itself. The map illustrates a cursory, almost arbitrary engagement with local music geographies and a performative emphasis on the national 'geo-body' (Thongchai Winichakul 1994, in Wood 2012, 297)—that is, '[performing] *the shape of statehood*' (ibid.; emphasis in original). It lacks more clearly defined 'local' geographical detail that would enable engagement with the specificities of place and locality at a smaller (more locally specific) geographical scale. This suggests that although the main functional imperative of the BME map is a focus on the spatial iconography of the local, the map provides instead an instrumental reminder of the overarching national symbolic context within which the local or regional is (and, implicitly, should be) framed. Like the Visit Britain maps, the BME map thus performs an idea of music and place in which the 'local' is metonymically expressive of, in the first instance, 'British' or English geographies of consumption and spectacle, a reification of an explicitly national spatial imaginary that is efficacious in the touristic branding of Britain's popular music heritage.

The map, in other words, performs the nation; interpolating the map user (or consumer), by corollary, in what the critical cartographer Denis Wood describes as the 'great map ritual of the state' (2012, 300). As with The Finale, the Where It's At map is of interest as much for what it doesn't do as for what it does. In the same way that The Finale falls short of conveying 'the intensity of intimate gigs [or the] spine tingling euphoria of massive stadium concerts and festivals'(BME 2012d) the map's lack of cartographic detail, or anything other than a vague claim to locality or region, restricts its ability to meaningfully convey 'where it's at' (whatever 'it' is). Users are presented instead with a scatter of musical miscellany whose function appears, if anything, to be to signify the map rather than the other way around. Having shuffled our way back into the BME shop, we were also left wondering what it is that is specifically British about the BME, as well as, more pointedly, just how possible is it to talk of, in the singular, the British music 'experience'. By extension, we found ourselves reflecting on the question of who it is, in fact, for. While this is not a question we address here, for Harvey Goldsmith, according to one newspaper article, the aim of the BME is to enthuse young people about music (*Telegraph* 2009). It is nevertheless clear that what might be mapped on official cartographies of national music heritage does not tell us how these symbolic landscapes resonate with other 'dissonant' (Tunbridge and Ashworth 1996) narratives of British music heritage, and with the everyday vernacular music experiences and landscapes of the maps' users, however young, old, or socially and ethnically diverse they might be.

LOCALIZING POPULAR MUSICSCAPES

The BME map illustrates a growing interest in local music geographies, as does the book it is sourced from, which is one of several published guides to Britain's popular music sites, locations, and landmarks that have emerged over the past decade or so (Frame 1999; Perry and Glinert 1998; Roberts 2011; Wooldridge 2010). There is now also a plethora of nonprofessional websites and online resources featuring music heritage maps and trails, as well as smartphone map-based apps. These map apps do not necessarily represent a better, more representative or 'authentic' engagement with local musicscapes than the Visit Britain and BME music heritage maps. Many of them are connected to (and often appropriated by) official discourses and produced as part of, or in association with, national bodies linked to the tourist and cultural industries, and they are used in similarly instrumental ways to encourage consumers to visit tourist destinations or purchase music downloads. They differ, however, in terms of scale and cartographic precision, enabling users to zoom in and explore places and sites in more detail and also in situ, thus allowing for a more embodied and embedded engagement with musical practices and 'pathways' (Finnegan 1989) and with musical geographies or 'musicscapes' of everyday life. They therefore illustrate alternative ways in which individuals and organizations have mapped Britain's popular music histories, heritages, and musical memories, shifting the focus away from more abstract cartographic representations of the nation and enabling a more localized storytelling about British culture and identity.

Music Heritage Map Apps

In August 2010, the British Prime Minister David Cameron delivered a speech in which he emphasized the importance of tourism for the nation, describing it as 'an often overlooked giant within the UK economy' (Department for Culture, Media and Sport [DCMS] 2011, 6).[8] According to DCMS:

> Devoting an entire speech to Tourism within the first 100 days of a new Government's time in office is unprecedented—DCMS officials have been unable to find any examples of previous Prime Ministers giving the industry this level of priority, ever—and underlines the industry's enormous potential for the UK's economic and cultural future. (Ibid.)[9]

In response to this speech, UK Music, the main representative body for the UK's commercial music industry, commissioned a report on music tourism entitled *Destination Music*. Based on research conducted by Bournemouth University's International Centre for Tourism and Hospitality Research, the report was promoted as 'the most comprehensive study ever undertaken on the power of music as a tourist draw, and to give this a value in economic terms' (UK Music 2011, 4). It highlighted the economic contribution of live music to the tourism economy, emphasizing that this stemmed from 'the musical talent of the artists—and the investment in that talent—that attracts so many music tourists in the first place' (UK Music 2011, 11),[10] and it focused on live music tourism and festivals and concerts involving audiences of over 5,000 people. This provided a basis for an online map of 'Great British Festivals' launched by UK Music in 2012 in collaboration with Visit Britain. At the same time, however, the *Destination Music* report also presented 'a snapshot' of popular music heritage attractions across the UK, such as the Salford Lads Club, a mecca for fans of The Smiths, despite a commonly shared ambivalence to the notion of popular music heritage on the part of many working in the music industries (see Cohen 2007; Roberts and Cohen 2012).When we visited its offices in London, UK Music's head of communications explained to us the organization's interest in the contemporary music industries and initiatives that help to support and develop them, and made a distinction between heritage as something associated with the musical past, and 'the contemporary scene', which involves 'making your own heritage all the time.' As he spoke, the CEO of the organization nodded in agreement and stressed the importance of fostering an environment where a vibrant and cutting-edge UK music culture can thrive, and nurturing and supporting the next Tinie Tempah or Adele, rather than raking over the relics of a dead musical past.

Among the various recommendations of *Destination Music* was the production of a mobile phone music tourism map app, 'which can help potential tourists to design their own musical tour to cater for every musical taste, incorporating iconic places, histories, and opportunities to attend live music events' (UK Music 2011, 54). The organization planned to develop the app in collaboration with a music journalist who was about to publish a book of UK music landmarks. Plans to develop digital maps of UK music heritage had also been mentioned to us by representatives we spoke to from various other music organizations. PRS for Music (formerly known as the Performing Right Society), for example, had used music heritage to help create a brand for the organization, as illustrated by its Heritage Award plaque scheme. The organization's head of PR explained that they planned to develop an archive of music heritage materials and a related map and emphasized the importance of music heritage for the identity of the industry as a whole. The CEO of another organization, Music Heritage UK, explained that his organization also planned a digital map that would pull together and consolidate information and materials on music heritage that currently existed online, and provide a 'living and breathing resource' and 'one-stop shop' to music heritage. The map app recommended by *Destination Music* differed from these examples, however, inasmuch as its aim was not just to allow users flexibility in terms of how they navigated it, but also to enable access for users while they were on the move and in situ, rather than sitting in front of a computer exploring web-based cartographies of music or standing around a museum exhibit. By the time of the publication of the *Destination Music* report, and thus signaling a wider uptake of interest in locative media technologies, other UK music map apps had already been launched, including the Belfast Music iPhone app, billed as 'a way to discover the rich musical heritage of a world-renowned city, through a mixture of historical anecdotes and street level music info' (Culture Northern Ireland 2010),[11] and 'Soundtrack to London'.

The 'Soundtrack to London' smartphone app developed through a partnership between the Museum of London and Nokia and launched in 2011. The app provides users with a map of London and enables them to zoom in to particular sites in order to explore them in more detail and search for music landmarks via 200 locations or 160 artists or find the sites nearest to them (Nokia UK 2011).[12] Some of the locations are featured in song lyrics and clicking on them reveals information about the song and a link to Nokia's Ovi store from which it can be downloaded, while a promotional video for the app shows the presenter, a young woman dressed in the style of many UK university students (with black leggings, a pink woolly hat, long dyed black hair, and bright red lipstick), searching for the UK hip-hop artist Plan B and heading off to the Heygate Estate in South London where a recent Plan B video was shot. 'The good thing about this map,' the presenter explains, 'is that it doesn't just take you to the most obvious landmarks or locations but surprises you with some quite unknown spots that you can impress even your most geekiest of friends' (Nokia UK 2011).[13] The app (also referred to in the press as a 'music trivia' app) follows the success of the Museum of London 'Streetmuseum' app, which provides over 200 images of London from the museum's art and photographic collections and allows users to explore them in situ in order to compare past and present views.

The use of locative media technologies (Farman 2012) such as map apps to connect and engage users (whether tourists, music pilgrims, 'street museum' visitors, and so on) with popular musicscapes mirrors the much wider appropriation of new media and social networking sites as marketing and consumer tools in the tourism, heritage, and cultural industries. By way of illustration, the marketing director of Visit Britain informed us that 'We [now] tend to use social media . . . getting things out via Facebook, Twitter, blogging sites. Then it's more of a conversation with customers' (interview with Lawrence Bresh, March 25, 2010). Conversely, the take-up of locative media devices and map apps reflects wider trends that operate independently of, or in parallel with, more 'official' tourism and heritage initiatives that have been informed by a growth of interest in community mapping or vernacular mapping projects (Clifford and King 1996; Harzinski 2010; Leslie

2006; Roberts 2012b; Wood 2010). In the case of popular music heritage, such trends signal the desire to explore and engage more directly with local musicscapes and sites of vernacular musical memory. These 'unofficial' or DIY cultural mappings often invoke a markedly different sense of place than that typically framed in official spatial histories and narratives of music heritage, and by drawing them into dialogue with national music geographies we can examine the different ways in which maps work and perform.

Mapping Vernacular Musical Memory

The Museum of London plans to build on the 'Soundtrack to London' app and develop maps for future music exhibitions. Similarly, as Andy Linehan, curator of Popular Music at the British Library Sound Archive, informed us, the British Library (BL) has plans to build on its existing UK sound maps and extend them to popular music by exploring the possibilities of geo-referencing popular music archival materials held within the archive.[14] Distinguishing the products of the 'heritage industry' from a notion of cultural heritage-as-praxis, curators and archivists such as Linehan and the music historian Mykaell Riley were keen to stress the importance of challenging dominant and official discourses of music heritage, particularly insofar as these typically focus on a narrow lineage of popular musicians (referred to by both Riley and Linehan as 'the usual suspects'). They envisaged a more dynamic and inclusive model of musical mapping that involved users in the mapping process, enabling them to upload materials, trace their own personal musical pathways and influences, listen to related interviews with musicians, and create their own map of music heritage. As Linehan explained:

> I like the idea that we [the Sound Archive] have collected over the years all the kind of musical influences that have filtered through to what's happening now and you can go back and trace the path, and you can make you own . . . you work out your own way of doing it [. . .]; build your own picture. And so I kind of see it as . . . you can come here and construct your history and your heritage, if you like. We hopefully are providing the building blocks for you to construct your [own] ideas. The notion of heritage is generally 'the usual suspects' and we are a lot more than that I think is what I try to get across. (Interview with Andy Linehan, March 11, 2011).

Riley was keen to explore possibilities for a dynamic, three-dimensional model of mapping Britain's 'black' music heritage, and in describing this model to us he gave the kind of map envisaged by Music Heritage UK as a 'living breathing resource' a more tangible and expressive form:

> [Firstly,] it's got to be time-stamped. Every decade that map, that narrative actually changes. [. . .] Then there's location. And we have to be specific

because we tend to generalize. So if you say 'the UK,' that's one thing, if you say 'Britain' or 'British', that's another. If you say 'London' that's one thing. But then you might say 'Hackney'. [. . .] So location is absolutely critical. And then lastly, the third element is community or people. Because within that you find a culture within which—or around which—these genres or musics specifically were conceived and lived through.

While the maps envisaged here had not yet been created, the notion of maps that enable audiences to build their own music heritage resonates with the ways in which we have used maps as part of our own research on music and film (Cohen 2012a; Roberts 2012a). Cohen conducted ethnographic research with rock, pop, and hip-hop musicians in Liverpool for a project on music and urban landscape (entitled Popular Musicscapes). This involved tracing the everyday routes of these musicians as they engaged in music-making activities; exploring real and imagined sites connected to their music making, including buildings and neighborhoods; and considering how musicians inhabit and experience such sites and how they interpret them, associating them with particular ideas, emotions, and memories. It also involved making use of maps as a research tool, which included asking musicians to create their own hand-drawn maps illustrating their experiences and memories of music making in the city and the journeys and places involved, including sites of music performance, rehearsal, and recording. These kinds of hand-drawn maps (also commonly referred to as cognitive, conceptual, or sketch maps) have long been used by human geographers, social anthropologists, and others to study how people describe places and remember what is where, their subjective sense of space and place, and differences between people in terms of their spatial knowledge and understanding.[15]

For the purposes of this particular project, the act of mapping helped to prompt memories and conversation about music making and urban landscape, and the patterns that emerged from these maps prompted reflection on what mattered to musicians and why, what made places distinctive and valuable for them, and how those places might have changed. In general, the maps of the rock musicians tended to focus on public music performance venues in Liverpool city center, and the mapping process was accompanied by stories about these venues. Many of them had closed or been demolished, and some had been so significant for these musicians and their music-making activities and careers that they were described as 'my heritage'. In contrast, the maps of the hip-hop musicians tended to focus on neighborhoods outside the city centre, and on the private and domestic homes in which the musicians composed and recorded their music. Comparison between the rock and hip-hop maps helped to highlight the influence of music genre on local musical pathways and geographies or musicscapes. At the same time, however, the maps of all of these musicians provided a contrast with official maps of Liverpool's music heritage, such as maps produced to celebrate the city's year as European Capital of Culture (ECOC), and maps distributed to tourists and visiting Beatles fans (Lashua, Cohen, and Schofield 2010).

Figure 1.2   Music memory map, female, late 30s, Liverpool (July 2012). Reproduced with permission.

These differences encouraged us to explore a similar approach to mapping as part of our current research on popular music heritage, cultural memory, and cultural identity in England. The project involves face-to-face interviews with music audiences, with individual interviewees selected on the basis of their response to a project questionnaire. We have asked these individuals to tell us how music relates to their memories of the past, or to how they remember the past. We have also invited them to create a 'map' of their musical memories. The map can take any form and trace journeys and influences, feature significant landmarks and milestones, and focus on a small and specific place or time, or on events much broader in scope and scale. Our focus is on the stories told through and about these maps, and how they help to explore vernacular musical memories and geographies. Some of the maps we have collected are hand-drawn, but others have been created using computer software. Figure 1.2, for example, shows a map produced for us by a Liverpool-based medical researcher in her late 30s. She explained this map as follows:

> Participating in the research made me think about what music I had been listening to at different times of my life. When I started writing it down I realized how this grouped into stages beginning in my childhood, developing when I was a student and especially in my 20s when a lot of my friends were in bands and my social life largely revolved around gigs and festivals. I noticed that I am listening to less new stuff now, I'm more likely to put something on I know and love. It will take going to a music festival such as ATP [All Tomorrow's Parties] or a friend's recommendation that I will listen to something different. Or Jarvis Cocker's Sunday Service on 6 music (I never had much time for Pulp but Jarvis is legend). There are some things I won't think about for years but then something will remind me and I'll dig out a CD or get it from Amazon or Fopp. I think the music I listen to does say a lot about me and has been a central part of my social life and had a big influence on my friends and family. I like how music can bring people together to share experiences like festivals or just agree they like something on the radio. Or that because I am from Liverpool people recognize that as a place associated with music and creativity. I guess music can create a sense of belonging and familiarity which is reassuring. People like to be reassured. (Institute of Popular Music 2012)

Figure 1.3 shows another 'map' produced by a music industry professional in his late 50s. Consisting of, in collage form, a selection of ticket stubs from particularly memorable concerts he has attended over the years, the map provides a means by which he can evoke very specific memories and associated details linked to a lifetime of attending rock concerts. He provided the following description to accompany the map:

Figure 1.3 Music memory map, male, late 50s, London (October 2012). Reproduced with permission.

If memory is the process by which information is encoded, stored, and retrieved then ticket stubs represent a great (and no doubt lazy) way for me to recall my musical journey. More often than not the tickets have the time, the date, the place, and the principle reason of what I'm trying to remember all there right in front of me and therefore the hard work of recollection is all pretty much done. And yet, I find that once I start to put these random components together to form a memory map, the names and dates on the actual tickets themselves stay still and what is laying seemingly dormant beneath the surface starts to come to life. The different shapes, sizes and colours, the logos, the fonts, the quality of the paper all start to trigger more thoughts. The escalating price of tickets over the years. The venues: the dives that remained and the palaces that were closed. The ticket stubs that are conspicuous by their absence—I never got to see The Jam or Talk Talk. I've seen Primal Scream dozens of times but I've never actually owned any of their albums. I have a T-shirt that was the entry ticket for one gig (Lemon Jelly), I have a ticket stub for one gig ('Add N to (X)') and arrived late, just as the band were leaving the stage (forever). I have been present at the birth of some amazing careers and been partly responsible for prolonging some careers that should have been politely cut short. A few of the gigs I have tickets for

I can't even remember, a lot of the gigs I have tickets for I will never ever forget. (Institute of Popular Music 2012)

With the first example, the map and accompanying interview illustrate how for this particular individual the process of remembering involved connecting musicians, most of them from the UK or US and internationally known, to specific times and places in which their music was listened to. Above all, however, the music is connected to social experience and belonging. The second example illustrates the way material cultures of musical memory can themselves be used to map or 'locate' music cultures and histories in very specific places and environments. The kind of DIY music mapping these examples represent can be contrasted with the more 'official' maps produced by institutions such as Visit Britain and BME, and are more closely related to personal musical memory and to heritage-as-praxis, rather than to a more public memory based on notions of national music heritage. The individuals concerned have used their maps to tell stories about the past and the role and significance of music in their lives, and about their musical practices and pathways. Like the map apps, these maps enable a detailed focus on local music geographies and histories, but unlike those apps the emphasis here is on the maps and perspectives of audiences. The final section of the chapter will draw together the threads of discussion on all of these maps in order to consider their wider implications for the study of popular music, place, and heritage tourism.

TOWARD A SPATIAL HISTORIOGRAPHY OF MUSIC HERITAGE TOURISM

Our focus in this chapter has been on the practice of mapping music and comparison between different approaches to that practice, different ways in which maps are put into use, and the different notions of music, place, and heritage that they perform. In particular, we have compared maps of popular music heritage used to symbolize and brand the nation with maps that focus in more detail on specific places and sites and attend to the pathways and journeys linked to individual musical heritages. This provides a basis for three general concluding points about the relationship between popular music, place, and tourism.

The first point is that music tourism is a fragmented and wide-ranging field of practice involving a diversity of people and institutions. Thus the UK maps were targeted at various user groups both in and outside the UK, and produced or planned through collaboration between organizations and businesses involved with heritage and tourism, music and media, and media technologies. They were therefore related to different interests in music and tourism, and in the relationship between music and place. As we have seen, central and local governments have turned to popular music heritage as another tool (alongside film) for the development of niche tourism and for branding cities and nations in order to boost local economies; music organizations anxious to create jobs and stimulate growth within the industries have promoted music heritage and tourism in order to raise the profile of the music industries; and organizations keen to explore ways of taking museums and archives into the streets have focused on music heritage as a means of engaging and informing audiences (including tourists), and as something audiences can create for themselves.

The Visit Britain maps were made available in print and also online, where users could navigate their way through them, clicking on the various music sites to access related musical sounds and information, while the BME map was situated within the more interactive and performative environment of the BME exhibition. These maps were connected to some of the more 'official' institutions and discourses of cultural heritage and tourism. They provided a largely instrumental device for imagining the nation, serving policy agendas that have increasingly used culture and cultural heritage as resource for place marketing and the promotion of local distinctiveness, and for economic development and urban regeneration. In fact, they show how music geographies can be drawn on to perform the nation and to rehearse or in some way characterize the 'state of the nation', a purposefully ambiguous term by which we mean both a reification of the national body politic (popular music geographies as metonyms of national-cultural identity and its associative institutions); and the (loosely defined) 'well-being' of the nation in terms of an index or yardstick by which the nation's creativity and cultural 'iconicity' can be spotlighted, branded, and promoted. The emphasis was not on encouraging the map users to explore particular locations and the spatial histories and narratives they represent, but enabling them to imagine the nation as a whole and enact a particular (and partial) narrative of it, pressing local music geographies into service of an ideology of nationhood and collective identity that primarily celebrated white, English, male rock.

These maps show, from a marketing perspective at least, that official government organizations are keen to exploit the idea of music as heritage in collaboration with music and tourism industries, attaching particular musical sounds, styles, and icons to places in order to brand the nation and boost niche forms of cultural tourism. The Visit Britain maps in particular were informed by a sense of 'contagious magic': the idea that the symbolic or nostalgic value of the musical styles, the emotional resonance of the sounds, or the celebrity of the musicians can 'rub off' on associated places and be tapped into and exploited for economic gain, however tenuous the link between musician and place actually is (Roberts, forthcoming). Unlike the Visit Britain and BME maps, the Museum of London map app focuses on one particular city and enables users to interact with the map in situ whenever and however they choose, and to engage in a more embodied, immersive, and localized exploration of music and place. Although map apps may reinforce the dominant spatial narratives of the 'usual suspects', the shift toward material and site-specific engagement with local musics-capes allows scope for the production and mapping of alternative music geographies. Geographically more detailed and 'hands-on', and allowing for the possibility of serendipitous musical journeys, this bricolage model of spatio-cultural practice finds a logical extension in the production and elicitation of hand-drawn or DIY maps. These maps demonstrate the ways in which maps and mapping practices can inform the development of new historiographical perspectives on popular music history and heritage, as well as new critical insights into the inherent spatiality of popular music cultures. They also provide different perspectives on place and musical memory and highlight shifting and contested meanings surrounding ideas and sites/spaces of popular music as 'heritage'.

Following on from this, the second point is that despite the diverse and fragmented nature of music tourism, it is nevertheless characterized by common tensions and contradictions. Stokes (1999), for example, argues that cultural tourism is typified by certain debates (such as debates about whether cultural events aimed at tourists are genuine and authentic or contrived and artificial and merely a show staged for profit) that enable people to identify it and inform their understanding of what it is.[16] Similarly, the UK maps point to contested notions of music heritage and how it is used and conceptualized as tourist object and spectacle for visitors and for place marketing and branding, but also as a more embodied practice and experience, and as a pathway in and through life. At stake are not simply debates about whose music and heritage is represented on the map and whose is not, but fundamental notions of what music heritage is, what it is for, and why it matters. Further ethnographic research could explore what users actually do with these maps, enabling a richer and more nuanced account of how people relate music maps and music tourism to their own vernacular music practices and experiences, and the various and often conflicting ways in which music and music heritage are valued and interpreted.

The third and final point is that maps can provide a productive and insightful tool for research on music, place, and tourism. The literary scholar Franco Moretti argues that the critical value of maps lies in the extent to which they function 'as analytical tools . . . [that bring] to light relations that would otherwise remain hidden' (1998, 3). Similarly, as Hanna and Del Casino suggest: 'tourism maps . . . are key sites through which we can construct a critical study of the relationships among space, identity and representation' (2003, xi). The value of maps can also be attributed to their capacity to rethink and reinvigorate mapping cultures and practices in terms of a spatial historiography of music, place, and cultural memory. Maps can reveal, for example, what might count as personal and/or collective music heritage and how it is 'located'—whether spatially or temporally—in material and symbolic landscapes. As suggested above, the discursive and instrumental specificities that define 'popular music tourism' are often at variance with, or in tension with, concerns that might underpin local memory and heritage practices as they relate to popular music cultures. Nevertheless by framing the relationship between music, place, and identity in terms of wayfinding (Ingold 2007) and 'mapping cultures' (Roberts 2012b), we can explore in more detail, and more critically, the material sites, contours, and journeys, which, in all their complexity and color, define the spaces and landscapes of popular music memory.

NOTES

1. The term 'musicscape' has been used by scholars working in different areas of music studies, such as sound studies (Schafer 1977, 4), ethnomusicology (Slobin 1993), music marketing (Oakes 2000), media studies (Lundberg, Malm, and Ronström 2003), and popular music studies (Cohen 2012c). We use it here to refer to landscapes created and imagined through music, and through the practices and journeys of music makers.
2. The research was conducted as part of a three-year international project, 'Popular Music Heritage, Cultural Memory and Cultural Identity', based on a collaboration between Erasmus University Rotterdam, the Universities of Liverpool and Ljubljana, and Mediacult, Vienna, and we would like to thank HERA (Humanities in the Research Area) for supporting that project.
3. See, for example, Harvey (2001), Yudice (2003), Corner and Harvey (1991), Cronin and Hetherington (2008).
4. The map featured not only obvious sites of music heritage (e.g., Ray Davies's Waterloo from The Kinks song 'Waterloo Sunset') but also the more obscure, such as TJ's nightclub in Newport, South Wales, where Kurt Cobain from the Seattle rock band Nirvana proposed to Courtney Love; the Francis Service Station in Stratford, East London, where in 1965 three of the Rolling Stones chose to urinate on the wall, having been refused entry to the garage's toilets (magistrates fined them £5 each); or a slaughterhouse in Digbeth, Birmingham, where Black Sabbath's Ozzy Osbourne once dispatched at least 250 cattle a day (see http://www.independent.co.uk/news/legends-of-rock-put-britain-on-the-map-1144098.html; see also Connell and Gibson 2003, 236).
5. The annual Nation Brand Index survey is based on interviews with 20,000 people worldwide, and the UK is ranked fourth in the world for being an 'interesting and exciting place for contemporary culture such as music, films, art and literature,' with music listed at the top.
6. It does this by storing information linked to specific exhibition content (using touch sensor technology), which is then retrievable online using the Smarticket. This is now a commonplace feature in many museums. What is not clear is the extent to which visitors do in fact continue their experience online, or whether the novelty factor of using the Smarticket as part of the museum experience is its main appeal (although on one of the two occasions we visited the BME as part of our research the Smarticket technology did not appear to be working so this part of the experience remained off-limits anyway).
7. 'Rock 'n' Roll Years' was a BBC music nostalgia program, which cut archive news and documentary footage to the contemporary soundtrack of well-known pop songs associated with the era and events depicted on screen. Each program focused on a different year from 1956 to 1989. The series ran from 1985 to 1994. Much of the footage used in the Edge Zones exhibits can in all likelihood be found on YouTube in much greater variety, although a 'Table

Talk' interactive in each gallery does include original video content in the form of oral history interviews with musicians and music industry talking heads.

8. See http://www.culture.gov.uk/images/publications/Government2_Tourism_ Policy_2011.pdf p6 (accessed June 15, 2012).

9. See http://www.culture.gov.uk/images/publications/Government2_Tourism_ Policy_2011.pdf (accessed March 26, 2012).

10. In the report an overseas music tourist is defined as 'someone who booked a ticket to a live music event in the UK from their own country, prior to travelling', and a domestic music tourist as 'someone who booked a ticket to a live music event in advance, and who travelled outside their home region to attend the event (or outside their home nation in the case of Scotland, Wales and N. Ireland)' (UK Music 2011, 4).

11. See http://www.culturenorthernireland.org/article/3135/belfast-music- iphone-app (accessed March 10, 2011). The app was produced by Belfast City Council in partnership with Northern Ireland Tourism Board, Filmtrip (a Belfast-based cross-platform media production company), Belfast's OhYeah music center, and Culture Northern Ireland (a web-based organization funded mainly by the Arts Council of Northern Ireland).

12. See http://www.youtube.com/watch?v=r16k5_JdQ7I (accessed March 27, 2012).

13. See http://www.youtube.com/watch?v=B3XVwK50aYg (accessed March 27, 2012).

14. The BL website hosts a number of interactive sound maps. These include maps of local dialects and accents, wildlife, and environmental sounds, as well as selected World Music and traditional musics in England. See http:// sounds.bl.uk/sound-maps (accessed April 16, 2012).

15. See, for example, Lynch (1960), Tuan (1975), and Ben-Ze'ev (2012).

16. Cultural tourism has been seen, for example, to involve a quest for authenticity (MacCannell 1976), or an acceptance that 'there is no authentic tourist experience' (Urry 1990, 11). Similarly, cultural heritage has been described, following Hobsbawm and Ranger (1983), as the 'invention of tradition' (Kong 1998; Kneafsey 2002), a conspiratorial 'false-history' (Hewison 1987; Boniface and Fowler 1993, 16), and a form of 'strategic inauthenticity' (Gibson and Connell 2005, 158, 267). It has been feared, for example, that tourism based around traditional and 'world' music would end up destroying local music traditions, staging authenticity and inventing tradition, but such tourism has also been welcomed as a means of preserving local music traditions, promoting local identity and pride, and contributing to local economies. In New Orleans, bars in the city's French Quarter hired bands to play in a Dixieland style that many traditional jazz fans considered to be hackneyed and clichéd (Atkinson 1997; Gibson and Connell 2005, 142). Likewise, for some the Liverpool Sound represented by the Beatles was a tourist cliché, while for others it was an authentic expression of 1960s Liverpool (Cohen 2007).

REFERENCES

Atkinson, Connie Zeanah. 1997. 'Whose New Orleans? Music's Place in the Packaging of New Orleans for Tourism.' In *Tourists and Tourism: Identifying People with Place*, edited by Simone Abram, Jackie D. Waldren, and Don V.L. MacLeod, 91–106. Oxford: Berg.

Ben-Ze'ev, Efrat. 2012.'Mental Maps and Spatial Perceptions: The Fragmentation of Israel-Palestine.' In *Mapping Cultures: Place, Practice, Performance*, edited by Les Roberts, 237–59. Basingstoke: Palgrave Macmillan.

Boniface, Priscilla, and Fowler, Peter J. 1993. *Heritage and Tourism: in 'The Global Village'*. Routledge: London.

British Music Experience. 2012a. 'About Us.' Accessed January 17, 2012. http://www.britishmusicexperience.com/about-us/.

British Music Experience. 2012b. 'The Experience.' Accessed January 17, 2012. http://www.britishmusicexperience.com/the-experience/.

British Music Experience. 2012c. 'The Finale.' Accessed January 17, 2012. http://www.britishmusicexperience.com/finale/.

British Music Experience. 2012d. 'Smartickets.' Accessed January 17, 2012. http://www.britishmusicexperience.com/smartickets/.

Clifford, James. 1992. 'Traveling Cultures.' In *Cultural Studies*, edited by L. Grossberg, C. Nelson, and P. Treichle, 96–116. New York: Routledge.

Clifford, Sue, and Angela King, eds. 1996. *From Place to Place: Maps and Parish Maps*. London: Common Ground.

Cohen, Sara. 2007. *Decline, Renewal and the City in Popular Music Culture: Beyond the Beatles*. Aldershot: Ashgate.

Cohen, Sara. 2012a. 'Bubbles, Tracks, Borders and Lines: Mapping Music and Urban Landscape.' *Journal of the Royal Musical Association* 137(1): 135–71.

Cohen, Sara. 2012b. 'Musical Memory, Heritage & Local Identity: Remembering the Popular Music Past in a European Capital of Culture.' *International Journal of Cultural Policy*. iFirst: 1–19.

Cohen, Sara. 2012c. 'Urban Musicscapes: Mapping Music-Making in Liverpool.' In *Mapping Cultures: Place, Practice, Performance*, edited by Les Roberts, 123–43. Basingstoke: Palgrave Macmillan.

Connell, John, and Chris Gibson. 2003. *Sound Tracks: Popular Music, Identity and Place*. London: Routledge.

Corner, John, and Sylvia Harvey, eds. 1991. *Enterprise and Heritage: Crosscurrents of National Culture*. London: Routledge.

Cronin, Ann, and Kevin Hetherington. 2008. *Consuming the Entrepreneurial City: Image, Memory, Spectacle*. London: Routledge.

Culture Northern Ireland. 2010. 'Belfast Music iPhone App.' Accessed March 10, 2011. http://www.culturenorthernireland.org/article/3135/belfast-music-iphone-app.

Department for Culture, Media and Sport. 2011. 'Government Tourism Policy.' Accessed June 1, 2012. http://www.culture.gov.uk/images/publications/Government2_Tourism_Policy_2011.pdf.

Farman, Jason. 2012. *Mobile Interface Theory: Embodied Space and Locative Media*. New York: Routledge.

Finnegan, Ruth. 1989. *The Hidden Musicians: Music-Making in an English Town*. Cambridge: Cambridge University Press.

Frame, Pete. 1999. *Rockin' around Britain: Rock and Roll Landmarks of the UK and Ireland*. London: Omnibus Press.

Gibson, Chris, and John Connell. 2005. *Music and Tourism: On the Road Again*. Clevedon: Channel View Publications.

Hanna, Stephen P., and Vincent J. Del Casino. 2003. 'Tourism Spaces, Mapped Representations, and the Practices of Identity.' In *Mapping Tourism*, edited by Stephen P Hanna and Vincent Del Casino, ix–xxvii. Minneapolis: University of Minnesota Press.

Harvey, David. 2001. *Spaces of Capital: Towards a Critical Geography*. Edinburgh: Edinburgh University Press.

Harzinski, Kris. 2010. *From Here to There: A Curious Collection from the Hand Drawn Map Association*. New York: Princeton Architectural Press.

Hayes, S. 2009. 'British Music Experience Will Rock Your World.' Accessed March 10, 2012. http://www.wharf.co.uk/2009/03/british-music-experience-will.html.

Hewison, Robert. 1987. *The Heritage Industry: Britain in a Climate of Decline*. London: Methuen.

Hobsbawm, Eric, and Terence Ranger. 1983. 'Introduction: Inventing Traditions.' In *The Invention of Tradition*, edited by Eric Hobsbawm and Terence Ranger, 1–14. Cambridge: Cambridge University Press.

Ingold, Tim. 2007. *Lines: A Brief History*. London: Routledge.

Institute of Popular Music. 2012. 'Music Memory Maps.' Accessed February 1, 2013. https://www.liv.ac.uk/music/research/popular-music/popular-music-heritage/music-map-examples/

Khan, Osman. 2011. 'How Music Travels—The Evolution of Western Dance Music.' Accessed June 1, 2012. http://www.thomson.co.uk/blog/2011/10/how-music-travels-infographic/#.T3mDWvCmiMW.

Kneafsey, Moya. 2002. 'Sessions and Gigs: Tourism and Traditional Music in North Mayo, Ireland.' *Cultural Geographies* 9:354–58.

Kong, Lily. 1998. 'The Invention of Heritage: Popular Music in Singapore.' In *Popular Music: Intercultural Interpretations*, edited by Toru Mitsui, 448–59. Kanazawa, Japan: Kanazawa University.

Lashua, Brett D., Sara Cohen, and John Schofield. 2010. 'Popular Music, Mapping, and the Characterisation of Liverpool.' *Popular Music History* 4(2):126–44.

Leslie, Kim C. 2006. *A Sense of Place: West Sussex Parish Maps*. Chichester: West Sussex County Council.

Liverpool 08. 2007. 'New Campaign Draws Brits to England's Rock and Pop Locations.' Accessed March 30, 2012. http://www.liverpool08.com/archive/index.asp?tcmuri=tcm:79–81776&y=07&m=Feb.

Lundberg, Dan, Krister Malm, and Owe Ronström. 2003. *Music, Media, Multiculture: Changing Musicscapes*. Sweden: Svenskt Visarkiv.

Lynch, Kevin. 1960. *The Image of the City*. Cambridge, MA: MIT Press.

MacCannell, Dean. 1976. *The Tourist: A New Theory of the Leisure Class*. New York: Schocken.

Moretti, Franco. 1998. *Atlas of the European Novel 1800–1900*. London: Verso.

New York Times. 2007. 'England Rocks, and a Map Now Proves It.' Accessed March 11, 2011. http://query.nytimes.com/gst/fullpage.html?res=9C04E3D814 31F932A25750C0A9619C8B63.

Nokia UK. 2011. 'Soundtrack to London Launched by the Museum of London.' Accessed March 27, 2012. http://www.youtube.com/watch?v=r16k5_JdQ7I.

Oakes, Stephen. 2000. 'The Influence of the Musicscape within Service Environments.' *Journal of Services Marketing* 14(7):539–56.

Perry, Tim, and Ed Glinert. 1998. *Rock and Roll Traveller Great Britain and Ireland: The Ultimate Guide to Famous Rock Hangouts Past and Present*. New York: Fodor.

Roberts, David. 2011. *The Rock Atlas: 650 Great Music Locations and the Fascinating Stories behind Them*. Kimbolton, Cambridgeshire: Ovolo.

Roberts, Les. 2010. 'Projecting Place: Location Mapping, Consumption, and Cinematographic Tourism.' In *The City and the Moving Image: Urban Projections*, edited by Richard Koeck and Les Roberts, 183–204. Basingstoke: Palgrave Macmillan.

Roberts, Les. 2012a. *Film, Mobility and Urban Space: A Cinematic Geography of Liverpool*. Liverpool: Liverpool University Press.

Roberts, Les. 2012b. 'Mapping Cultures—A Spatial Anthropology.' In *Mapping Cultures: Place, Practice, Performance*, edited by Les Roberts, 1–25. Basingstoke: Palgrave Macmillan.

Roberts, Les. Forthcoming. 'Marketing Musicscapes, or, the Political Economy of Contagious Magic.' *Tourist Studies, Special Issue on Music and Tourism* 14 (1).

Roberts, Les, and Sara Cohen. 2012. 'Unauthorizing Popular Music Heritage: Outline of a Critical Framework.' *International Journal of Heritage Studies* 20(3):1–21. DOI:10.1080/13527258.2012.750619.

Rojek, Chris, and John Urry. 1997. 'Transformations of Travel and Theory.' In *Touring Cultures: Transformations in Travel and Theory*, edited by Chris Rojek and John Urry, 1–19. London: Routledge.

Schafer, Murray R. 1977. *The Tuning of the World: Toward a Theory of Soundscape Design*. New York: Knopf.

Slobin, Mark. 1993. *Subcultural Sounds: Micromusics of the West*. Middletown, CT: Wesleyan University Press.

Stokes, Martin. 1999. 'Music, Travel and Tourism: An Afterword.' *World of Music* 41(3):141–56.

Sun, the. 2007. 'England Really Rocks.' Accessed November 10, 2011. http://www.thesun.co.uk/sol/homepage/travel/17461/England-really-rocks.html.

Telegraph, the. 2009. 'Profile: Harvey Goldsmith.' Accessed March 27, 2012. http://www.telegraph.co.uk/finance/newsbysector/mediatechnologyandtelecoms/4864198/Profile-Harvey-Goldsmith.html.

Tuan, Yi Fu. 1975. 'Images and Mental Maps.' *Annals of the Association of American Geographers* 65:205–13.

Tunbridge, J.E., and Gregory J. Ashworth. 1996. *Dissonant Heritage: The Management of the Past as a Resource in Conflict*. Chichester: Wiley.

UK Music. 2011. *Destination Music: The Contribution of Music Festivals and Major Concerts to Tourism in the UK*. London: UK Music. Accessed on May 17, 2011. www.ukmusic.org.

Urry, John. 1990. *The Tourist Gaze: Leisure and Travel in Contemporary Societies*. London: Sage.

Wood, Denis. 2010. *Rethinking the Power of Maps*. New York: Guilford Press.

Wood, Denis. 2012. 'The Anthropology of Cartography.' In *Mapping Cultures: Place, Practice, Performance,* edited by Les Roberts, 280–303. Basingstoke: Palgrave Macmillan.

Wooldridge, Max. 2010. *Never Mind the Bollards: A Road Trip around England's Rock 'n' Roll Landmarks*. Bristol: Footprint.

Yudice, George. 2003. *The Expediency of Culture*. Durham, NC: Duke University Press.

2 Negotiating Musical Boundaries and Frontiers

Tourism, Child Performers, and the Tourist-Ethnographer in Bali, Indonesia

Jonathan McIntosh

In the first decades of the 20th century, and set against a backdrop of political, economic, social, and cultural change, tourists began to arrive in Bali, Indonesia. It was not until the years following the First World War, however, that visitors chose to extend the amount of time they spent on the island beyond simply eating lunch, buying 'curios and [watching] hurried performances of bored "temple dancers"' (Covarrubias 1937/1973, 392). During the 1920s and 1930s, anthropologists, musicologists, and artists, most notably Margaret Mead, Gregory Bateson, Jane Belo, Colin McPhee, and Walter Spies, journeyed to Bali. Attracted to the island for various reasons, the above individuals as well as other tourists and ethnographers, have contributed to what Boon (1977) terms the 'anthropological romance of Bali.' Consequently, the academic literature pertaining to the development of tourism on this small island is well established (see Chappell 2011; Connell 1993; Cukier 1996; Cukier, Norris, and Wall 1996; Cukier and Wall 1994, 1995; Cukier-Snow and Wall 1993; Darma Putra and Hitchcock 2006, 2008; Hill 1994; Hitchcock 2001; Hitchcock and Darma Putra 2005, 2007; Hobart, Ramseyer, and Leemann 1996; Howe 2005; James 1999; Long and Kindon 1997; Long, Wall, and Conlin 1995; McCarthy 1994; McKean 1989; Rubinstein and Connor 1999; Tarplee 2008; Vickers 1989, 1994; Wall 1996; Wall and Long 1996; Warren 1995; Yamashita 2003). While some studies suggest that the Balinese are unwitting victims of tourism, ever dominated by Western notions concerning the commoditization, authentication, reinvention, or revitalization of traditional culture, others focus on the creative capacity of the Balinese to respond to the dilemmas and opportunities associated with tourism. Similarly, within ethnomusicology and anthropology, a number of important studies highlight the various strategies Balinese musicians and dancers employ as a means to respond to the influences of tourism, specifically utilizing the traditional performing arts as a means with which to engage or separate themselves from tourists (Bakan 1999; Bandem and deBoer 1981; Bowers 1956; Dibia 1996/2000; Dibia and Ballinger 2004; Dunbar-Hall 2001, 2003, 2007; Herbst 1981, 1997; Johnson 2002; McGraw 2009; Picard 1990a, 1990b, 1993, 1996a, 1996b, 1997, 1999, 2003, 2008a, 2008b; Racki 1998;

Ramstedt 1991; Sanger 1986, 1988; Spies and de Zoete 1938/2002; Sugriwa 2000; Talamantes 2004; Tenzer 1991/1998, 2000).

Among these studies, and with reference to his research pertaining to cultural tourism in Bali, Dunbar-Hall (2001, 173) asserts that traditional Balinese music and dance performances serve to establish 'boundaries and frontiers between culture bearers and tourists.' Elaborating on this statement, Dunbar-Hall (2001, 174) defines 'boundaries' and 'frontiers' as 'sites at which tourists are restricted from or allowed entry to levels of insider experience and potential knowledge.' Although not necessarily prohibited from attending 'boundary' sites, a lack of knowledge and understanding concerning the 'cultural matrices' (Dunbar-Hall 2001, 173) associated with the performance of traditional music and dance forms in such contexts can restrict tourists from gaining more meaningful insights into certain aspects of Balinese culture. In contrast, and given the need to translate Balinese music and dance pieces from 'cultural artefacts in their original contexts to cultural commodities in new (tourist) contexts' (Dunbar-Hall 2001, 174), 'frontier' sites require culture bearers and tourists to participate in a process that involves the negotiation of musical meaning. For example, the Balinese often provide contextual information such as program notes to facilitate greater tourist engagement with the performing arts in frontier sites (Dunbar-Hall 2001, 174). Nevertheless, and as Dunbar-Hall (2001, 174) notes, frontier sites can also serve to promote 'superficial' interactions between Balinese performers and non-Balinese audience members, with visitors often observing a compressed sampling of traditional music and dance pieces, many of which are curtailed to accommodate the limited attention span or busy schedules of tourists (see also Daniel 1996).

Dunbar-Hall's (2001) approach is helpful in illuminating the ways in which Balinese musicians and dancers interact with visitors to their island. However, it creates a 'binary scheme' (Stokes 1999, 142) that, perhaps unknowingly, does not take into account peripheral characters that occupy 'liminal' positions (after Turner 1967) between the dichotomy of culture bearers and tourists. Such characters include child performers in Bali who, although they may partake in music and dance performances in boundary and frontier sites, are often still caught up in the process of learning to become culture bearers. Consequently, child performers have little or no real cultural authority of their own. Boys and girls rarely perform gamelan music for tourists,[1] and therefore this chapter provides insights into the liminal position of Balinese child performers by examining how children participate as dancers in tourist presentations, expanding on Dunbar-Hall's (2001) schema of (adult) culture bearers versus tourists.[2] By drawing on the concept of the 'touristic borderzone', which Bruner (1996, 158) defines as 'an empty stage waiting for performance time, for the audience of tourists and for the native performers,' the chapter also examines how children simultaneously approach 'tourist performances' as 'sites of creative cultural production' (Rosaldo 1989, 208) and sometimes as 'sites of struggle' (Bruner 1996, 159). In order to demonstrate how boys and girls negotiate issues of creativity and struggle associated with such sites, the chapter compares and contrasts the willingness of children to participate in a tourist performance in the Balinese center of Ubud versus their reluctance to 'perform' in front of tourists at a cremation ceremony in their home village, situated outside the Balinese tourist 'triangle'.[3] In approaching the literature on tourism in this way, the chapter also considers the increasingly problematic commodification of 'the Other' while complementing existing anthropological and ethnomusicological research concerning the role of music and dance in cultural shows for tourists not only in Bali, but also in other cultural contexts (for example, Abram 1997; Desmond 1999; Lau 1998; Rees 1998; Sarkissian 1998, 2000; Xie 2003).

Throughout the chapter, and in order to provide insights into the ways in which boys and girls shaped my liminal position as the 'tourist-ethnographer' (after Bruner 1995), I reflect on my experiences of conducting research with the young Balinese (McIntosh 2006, 2010). By outlining how boys and girls accepted me as 'their' ethnographer, I demonstrate how such a process enabled me to move from 'front stage' to 'backstage' (MacCannell 1973, 1976), and from tourist to ethnographer (Bruner 1995; Nettl 2005, 187; Sarkissian 2000, 7). The present chapter, therefore, builds on and extends the work of Dunbar-Hall (2001) and Bruner (1996), but, written from the perspective of an ethnographer working with children behind and beyond the typical tourist performance contexts, the chapter also contributes new and exciting insights into the world of cultural tourism in Bali by problematizing the more usual tourist-ethnographer dichotomy. The following discussion begins, however, with some important contextual background on the development of tourism in Bali that serves to highlight the various roles played by culture bearers, Westerners, tourists, and the Indonesian government in the reinvention and revitalization of Balinese culture. The evolution of these processes still resonates powerfully with contemporary 'culture bearers' (Dunbar-Hall 2001) as they position themselves within modern-day tourism, particularly the child performers in Bali who are the focus of this chapter and who leverage for themselves a certain position of resistance against the commoditization of cultural tourism.

THE EARLY DEVELOPMENT OF TOURISM IN BALI

The Dutch succeeded in taking control of north Bali in the mid-19th century, establishing a colonial administrative capital in the port of Singaraja. However, it was not until 1908, following the conquest of the last independent southern Balinese kingdom of Klungkung, that the Dutch exerted full jurisdiction over the island. Consequently, the influence of the once all-powerful Balinese royal courts, as well as their patronage of the performing arts, slowly seceded to village centers. Until this time, traditional music and dance performances tended to be associated with Balinese-Hindu religious festivities or royal court centers. Indeed, Dutch colonial scholars considered Bali, an island home to one of the last remaining Hindu cultures that were once widespread throughout island Southeast Asia, to be a 'living museum'. In light of this, the Dutch implemented a policy of Balinization (*Baliseering*), the aim of which was 'not so much to |preserve| the culture as they found it, |but rather to restore| it to its original integrity' (Picard 1996a, 21). Thus, by focusing on the use of culture to construct a traditional, primitive, and even exotic image of Bali—an island, for example, where 'everyone is an artist' (Covarrubias 1937/1973, 160)—Balinization succeeded in reifying stereotypes of an 'invented' culture that never existed (after Hobsbawm 1983/1991; see also Boon 1977, 1990; Picard 1992; Vickers 1989). Additionally, the colonial policy served to promote the impression that the Balinese and, in particular, the Balinese traditional performing arts (including music, dance, and drama), were somehow frozen in time. Expressing similar sentiments concerning the demise of traditional customs in light of 'good or bad |ideas| brought to their island by merchants, tourists, unsuitable education, and missionaries,' the Mexican artist Miguel Covarrubias (1937/1973, xxv) also predicted that Balinese culture was 'doomed to disappear under the merciless onslaught of modern commercialism and standardization.' Nevertheless, the political, economic, and social changes brought about as a result of colonialism facilitated exciting developments in the Balinese performing arts. The most important of these occurred circa 1915 in relation to the birth of a new style of gamelan music, *Gamelan Gong Kebyar*,[4] and its associated dance form, *Kebyar*. First introduced in north Bali, and unlike any other style, *Gamelan Gong Kebyar* quickly spread across the island to become the 'lingua franca' (Tenzer 1991/1998, 23) of Balinese music. Indeed, Colin McPhee (1900–1964), who had arrived in Bali to study the island's gamelan musics in their original context in 1931, set about transcribing the repertoires associated with older gamelan forms because in his opinion the enthusiasm the Balinese displayed towards *Gamelan Gong Kebyar* threatened the survival of some other, significant court ensembles (McPhee 1966, xiv).[5]

Despite such fears on the part of Westerners, the changes relating to the traditional Balinese performing arts brought about as a result of colonialism, globalization, modernization, and the gradual introduction of tourism at this time instead demonstrated the 'uncanny ability |of the Balinese] to assimilate . . . external, or global ideas and objects and localize them, infusing them with new and relevant local meanings' (Harnish 2005, 119). For example, the popularity of *Gamelan Gong Kebyar* and the development of tourism coalesced in the organization of early 'frontier' music and dance performances (after Dunbar-Hall 2001) outside the traditional confines of ritual contexts (Seebass 1996).[6] The Balinese also collaborated with Westerners to cocreate new music and dance genres based on traditional forms, an excellent example of which is the development of *Kecak* in the 1930s.

Bringing together the rhythmic vocal music used to accompany ritual trance dance (*Sanghyang*) and a dance performance involving well-known characters from the Indian Epic, the *Ramayana*, *Kecak* is the result of a collaborative project in the 'touristic borderzone' (Bruner 1996) between Balinese performers, the Russian-born German artist Walter Spies (1895–1942), and the American dance researcher Katharine Mershon (1885–1986) (Dibia 1996/2000; McKean 1979). As a secular form, the Balinese continue to perform *Kecak* for the entertainment of the gods of the Balinese-Hindu religion, themselves, and tourists. Although it has no formal ritual associations, *Kecak* 'retains the power to influence the spiritual state of its performers and to play a role in the religious consciousness of a community by who or for whom it is performed' (Dunbar-Hall 2001, 178).

During the Second World War, the Japanese invaded Bali and musical activity slowed. On August 17, 1945, following the surrender of the Japanese, Indonesia declared independence from the Netherlands, although the colonial power did not formally recognize Indonesian sovereignty until some years later. With the emergence of the newly independent Indonesia, the southern urban center of Denpasar replaced the northern colonial hub of Singaraja as the new capital of Bali. The transfer of administrative power from the north to the south of the island would also have great implications for the development of the Balinese performing arts and the expansion of tourism on the island in the second half of the 20th century. For instance, musicians in the south of the island, who tended to disparage the Singaraja style of gamelan playing, sought to refine and incorporate older performance styles and repertoires, most notably from *Gamelan Gambuh*,[7] *Gamelan Semar Pegulingan*,[8] and *Gamelan Gong Gede*,[9] into that of *Gamelan Gong Kebyar*.[10]

DEVELOPMENT OF TOURISM IN BALI AS A MANAGED NATIONALIZING PROCESS

Indonesia's first president, Sukarno (1901–1970), whose mother was Balinese, was also particularly fond of *Gamelan Gong Kebyar*. Consequently, Sukarno often invited Balinese music and dance troupes to perform at official government engagements in Jakarta, as well as at his retreat in the Balinese village of Tampaksiring (Tenzer 2000, 95). Following independence, and in an attempt to establish a new nationalist ideology for Indonesia, Sukarno also decided that the 'collective image of Balinese culture' would be used 'to further promote and symbolize Indonesia to the world' (Tenzer 2000, 94). In light of this, the Balinese performing arts (music, dance, and drama) were not only exploited as national cultural industries and texts, but they also provided a 'source of images and sounds for tourism promotion' (Gibson and Connell 2005, 14). In the early 1950s, and as part of this managed nationalizing process, John Coast—an Englishman who served as

Sukarno's press attaché—organized for a gamelan troupe from the Balinese village of Peliatan to undertake an international tour of Europe and North America (see Coast 1953/2004; Herbst 2006).[11] Presaging the active role that Balinese music and dance would play in the development and capitalization of Indonesia through tourism, Sukarno also encouraged musicians and dancers to curtail the duration of some performances, as well as to develop numerous abstract free dances (*Tari Lepas*) that could be performed outside the confines of lengthy traditional Balinese dance-dramas (Dibia and Ballinger 2004, 95; Ramstedt 1991, 112; Tenzer 2000, 95).[12] Gradually, these shortened and new forms gained popularity among village troupes, many of which embraced performing for tourists as a means of generating additional income. However, Sukarno's use of the Balinese traditional performing arts to promote Indonesia suffered a setback when, in 1965, an aborted communist coup in Jakarta resulted in the mass killing of communists across communities throughout the nation. In Bali alone, over 100,000 people, including many artists, musicians, and dancers died during this turbulent time (Hanna 1976/2004, 218). In 1967 and in the aftermath of the violence, President Suharto (1921–2008) took power with his New Order (*Orde Baru*) Government.

A key objective of the Suharto regime was to modernize Indonesia by means of attracting outside investment into the country, in particular through the development of tourism. Like Sukarno, Suharto used Balinese traditional culture as a means to develop Indonesian tourism (Picard 1997, 182). Following the opening of Bali's Ngurah Rai International Airport in 1969, the number of international visitors traveling to the island increased. During the 1970s, and as a result of the Indonesian government's instigation of a World Bank plan to develop regional tourism in Indonesia, the Balinese authorities implemented a policy of cultural tourism (*Pariwisata Budaya*). As part of this policy, Balinese authorities hoped that the 'revitalization of traditional Balinese culture' would 'also provide the means for the economic profit from tourism' (Ramstedt 1991, 115).

Concomitant with the use of cultural tourism to promote and revitalize the traditional performing arts, the growth of mass tourism resulted in mounting concerns among some Balinese officials, religious leaders, and performers pertaining to what forms of music and dance should be presented to tourists in this new climate of capitalization and commodification.[13] In 1971, and in order to provide advice concerning this issue, the Balinese Arts Council (LISTIBIYA) agreed on a 'three-tiered model of the spiritual contexts of performance in which spatial and functional considerations were prominent' (Herbst 1981, 47).[14] The three tiers of the model included: (1) sacred (*Wali*) music and dance pieces, normally performed in the inner courtyard (*Jeroan*) of a Balinese temple; (2) ceremonial (*Bebali*) music and dance pieces (that is, forms associated with, but not necessarily integral to, a religious ceremony), normally performed in the central courtyard (*Jaba Tengah*) of a Balinese temple; and, (3) secular (*Balih-Balihan*) music and dance pieces, normally performed in the outer courtyard (*Jaba*) of a temple or just outside a temple, as well as the repertoire performed specifically for tourists.[15] By categorizing music and dance pieces in this manner, the Balinese attempted to differentiate between forms for culture bearers and deities of the Balinese-Hindu religion (to be performed in 'boundary' sites) versus those suitable for presentation to tourists (to be performed in 'frontier' sites) (Dunbar-Hall 2001). Despite attempting to provide definitive guidance relating to this issue, 'in time, and over practice . . . slippage' (Bruner 1996, 167) has occurred concerning the music and dance repertoire performed for tourists. Nevertheless, such a process now means that the 'Balinese are used to coping with many levels of meaning and function, and the tourist dimension has been merged into the traditional framework, rather than permitted to destroy it' (Sanger 1988, 102).

Similarly, in the 1960s, the establishment of music and dance conservatories in Bali by the Indonesian government as 'an authentic product of the *orde baru*' (Tenzer 2000, 99) has also influenced the development of cultural tourism on the island. For instance, staff and students associated with these institutions have created numerous new music and dance pieces that, in turn, conservatory graduates have disseminated across the island (Bandem and deBoer 1981, 87). In light of this, some 'new' music and dance forms are not only established in the traditional canon, but are also regularly performed for tourists (Picard 1996b).[16] In addition to devising new forms, Balinese conservatories have played a vital role in preserving and reviving many older musical forms and their associated dance styles, including *Gamelan Gambuh* and *Gamelan Semar Pegulingan* (Ramstedt 1991, 114).[17] Likewise, the annual Bali Arts Festival (*Pesta Kesenian Bali*), which was first established in 1979 in association with the Balinese conservatories, not only contributes to the safeguarding of older music and dance practices, but also encourages the creation of new works (Foley and Sumandhi 1994; Hough 2000; Noszlopy 2002). Intended primarily for local Balinese audiences, few tourists attend the Bali Arts Festival, however. Thus, and following Dunbar-Hall (2001), it could be inferred that the Bali Arts Festival is more of a 'boundary' site.[18] This contrasts with practices in the village of Ubud, situated in the south-central administrative district of Gianyar, and a popular location in which tourists and ethnographers experience traditional Balinese music and dance performances. Such tourist-focused presentations and select ceremonial festivities, to which tourists are sometimes permitted, serve as the primary 'frontier' sites (Dunbar-Hall 2001) for visitors to Bali.

ARRIVING IN UBUD AS THE TOURIST-ETHNOGRAPHER

In contrast to the southern beach resorts of Kuta and Sanur, the village of Ubud is 'staged as being remote, or "non-touristic," in order to induce tourists to "discover"' (MacCannell 1973, 594) what is, in effect, a bustling and ever-expanding village heavily dependent on tourism (Bruner 1996, 158; Gibson and Connell 2005, 9). Styled as the cultural 'center' of Bali (Bakan 1999, 23; Hatchwell 1990, 435; MacRae 1999; Pendit in Vickers 1994, 205; Picard 1996a, 83–89), Ubud also attracts a substantial number of visitors (and ethnographers), many of whom choose to attend one or more of the numerous cultural performances staged every evening in and around the village. By means of observing the 'front stage' activities (Mac-Cannell 1973, 1976) at such events, tourist performances in Ubud reaffirm for many visitors a certain 'imagology . . . of traditional folk costumes, traditional musical instruments and forms of expression' (Baumann 2001, 16; see also Sarkissian 2000, 10). As 'frontier' sites (Dunbar-Hall 2001) in the Balinese 'touristic borderzone', Bruner (1996, 158) also notes that while tourists may view such settings as leisure contexts in which they can consume certain aspects of traditional culture, the Balinese associate such sites with 'work and cash'.

In 2003, when I first traveled to Bali to conduct ethnomusicological research with children, I chose to base myself in Ubud because the village was (in)famous as a 'frontier' site (Dunbar-Hall 2001) of musical activity. During this early stage in my fieldwork, I observed and documented several tourist performances in which children performed. In order to improve my proficiency in Indonesian and Balinese to be able to communicate with potential child informants, I also enrolled in language lessons at the Pondok Pekak Library and Learning Centre.[19] Built within the confines of a traditional Balinese family compound located on Monkey Forest Road (*Jalan Wanara Wana*), the 'Pondok Pekak' is a well-known haunt for tourists, ethnographers, expatriates, and local Balinese. As part of the organization's business model, the library provides educational programs for adults and children. These programs include language lessons and instruction in the Balinese arts, for example, traditional dance, gamelan music, or mask carving. The (tourist) income generated from these activities, as well as additional private donations, enables the Pondok Pekak to employ local teachers to provide Balinese children who live in the proximity of the library with access to free gamelan music and traditional dance lessons (see also Ramstedt 1991, 116).

One afternoon, I remained at the Pondok Pekak following the conclusion of a language lesson to watch a children's dance practice. After observing how the instructor sang aloud to reinforce the 'core melody' (*Pokok*) of the gamelan music accompaniment to the dances provided by a CD recording, I wished to understand what it was that the dance teacher was saying and why she sang the musical accompaniment to the various dances rehearsed by the children. To investigate this issue, I spent the next three months studying the solo male warrior dance, *Tari Baris Tunggal*, with the children's dance teacher, Ni Luh Happy Pariamini.[20] I remained at the Pondok Pekak after each lesson to observe the children's rehearsals; similarly intrigued by my study of traditional dance, some of the children started to arrive prior to the commencement of their own rehearsals in order to observe the conclusion of my dance lessons. Consequently, I—as the 'gazing' (after Urry 1990) tourist-ethnographer, struggling to execute nuanced Balinese dance movements—was subjected to what Stokes (1999, 142) terms the 'ethnographic/touristic gaze gaze back' (see also Cooley 1999). Despite this mutual gaze, the children at the Pondok Pekak still tended to regard me as a tourist and kept their distance from me. After discussing this setback during a break in one of my dance lessons, Happy invited me to visit her dance studio (*Sanggar Tari*), Sanggar Tari Mumbul Sari in Keramas, a village not far from Ubud, to meet not only her husband, I Wayan Suarta,[21] but also the 150 children that regularly attended twice-weekly dance lessons in her family compound.

FROM TOURIST TO ETHNOGRAPHER IN KERAMAS

Renowned as a center for folk opera (*Arja*) performance, Keramas is a 25-minute motorcycle ride from Ubud. During my first visit to observe a children's dance rehearsal at Sanggar Tari Mumbul Sari,[22] I was surprised when Happy instructed me to participate in the lesson whenever the boys took to the floor of the open pavilion (*Wantilan*) in which the rehearsal took place. According to Happy, I had to participate if I was to improve as a student of Balinese music and dance. At first, the sight of a tall, white man attempting to follow the movements of diminutive boy dancers caused much hilarity among all of those present. Parents who witnessed my participation in the children's rehearsals were also bemused as to why a tourist would wish to learn to dance in this manner. Moreover, not only is it highly unusual for Balinese adults to study dance without first having learned as a child, but also it would have been unimaginable for Balinese adults to participate with children in this way. Nevertheless, my participation in the children's lessons over the subsequent few weeks gradually paid off. Although the children were unaware of my complex but fluid evolution from tourist to ethnographer, the boys and girls at the *Sanggar* gradually perceived my transition from mere tourist to touristic 'Other', someone who looked like but did not necessarily behave like a tourist or other adults.[23]

In an effort to develop my relationship with the children at the *Sanggar*, I moved from Ubud to Keramas to live with Happy's family. Within days of relocating to Keramas, small groups of children began to visit the *Sanggar* to observe and indeed 'gaze back' (Stokes 1999, 143) at the 'tourist' outside the confines of their own dance lessons. So, for example, while I sat typing up field notes on my laptop, the children would wander in and out of my room to rummage through my belongings, open up my equipment bag, and stare at my field note journals (McIntosh 2006). Progressively, after many such visits during which the children spoke endlessly among themselves in Balinese but never to me, I started to initiate conversations with them. Despite the polite practice in Indonesia to address a man with whom one is not familiar as *Pak*, the Indonesian form for 'Mr.', during our initial conversations, the children simply referred to me as 'Jon'. Subsequently, and as a result of waiting for boys and girls to decide whether or not they would work with me as an ethnographer (after Corsaro 1985), the children assigned to me various roles that enabled me to further my research. For instance, in the confines of the *Sanggar*, I not only partook in the children's dance lessons, but boys and girls also invited me to participate in their play activities and song-games. However, because I rode a motorcycle and studied dances not taught to the children at the *Sanggar*, such as various forms of mask dance (for example, *Topeng*[24]), the children also chose to assign 'adult' roles to me. These roles included being someone who transported them to and from rehearsals and performances, as well as being an 'adult' apprentice to Happy's husband, Wayan, whenever I performed with him at various ceremonies in and around Keramas. In addition to being responsible for documenting the children's dance performances, I learned how to apply the boys' makeup and help dress them in their costumes, tasks in which not even the most skilled child dancers at the *Sanggar* are proficient (see McIntosh 2012, 203). In light of this, I gradually became privy to 'backstage' (MacCannell 1973, 1976) contexts and activities, to which tourists rarely have access. Upon reflection, the multiple roles that the teachers and students assigned to me clearly signify the complex position I occupied as 'their' tourist-ethnographer.

CHILDREN'S PARTICIPATION IN THE TOURIST PERFORMANCE AT THE PONDOK PEKAK, UBUD

Despite now living in Keramas, I frequently returned to the Pondok Pekak in Ubud not only to visit the children with whom I had become acquainted at the start of my fieldwork, but also to document the weekly tourist performance that took place at the library. Entitled '*Legong* and other Favourite Dances', this performance is similar to many of the other tourist shows presented in Ubud.[25] What differentiates the Pondok Pekak performance from others is that children perform most of the solo and ensemble dances included in the program.[26] As the dance teacher employed at the Pondok Pekak, Happy is responsible for training and sometimes recruiting children to perform in the organization's tourist presentation. Consequently, Happy sometimes arranges for boys and girls from Keramas to perform at the library. However, because of the professionalization of the Balinese performing arts,[27] a process influenced by the establishment of music and dance conservatories as well as the impact of tourism, only children with prodigious dance skills and substantial performance experience are invited to participate in such performances.[28] Despite receiving little remuneration, the nature of the disciple–student relationship in Bali ensures that boys and girls from Keramas almost always accept Happy's invitation to partake in the Pondok Pekak tourist performance. According to Bruner (1996), sites in the 'tourist borderzone' are 'creative,' and therefore Balinese boys and girls are creative when they perform for tourists. It could be argued, however, that by deciding which boys and girls will perform and what roles they will present, Happy, the Balinese tradition, and the expectations associated with tourist performances circumscribe the potential creativity of child dancers in the Pondok Pekak tourist presentations. It would be difficult for tourists to engage with inferior performances, thus implying that less proficient child dancers could turn a 'frontier' site into more of a 'boundary' site (after Dunbar-Hall 2001).

In August 2004, however, members of the Pondok Pekak music and dance studio, Sanggar Seni Pondok Pekak, decided to diversify the format of the library's weekly performance and produce a children's pantomime dance-drama (*Sendratari*) for tourists.[29] My participation in the *Sendratari* involved several activities, such as transporting two boy dancers from Keramas to Ubud, applying their makeup prior to the performance, and recording the event on behalf of the children. Being the children's ethnographer meant that although my 'front stage' actions (MacCannell 1973, 590) in documenting the performance may have appeared similar to those of 'other tourists,' the purpose and intention of my presence at the event was quite different. Indeed, being 'backstage' (MacCannell 1973, 590) with the children prior to the performance afforded me the opportunity to discuss with them aspects of their participation in the occasion. For instance, despite the intense rehearsal period leading up to the event, the three children from Keramas who were to participate in the *Sendratari* displayed few nerves about their immediate performance (see Figure 2.1). For them, performing for tourists at the Pondok Pekak was a 'fun activity'. 13-year-old Sadih spoke at length about how he had 'looked forward to the performance' because the opportunity to participate in the *Sendratari* was going to be 'a new experience' (personal communication, Ubud, August 15, 2004). Elaborating on this point, Sadih said that neither he, Tomi, nor Putu (the other two children from Keramas in the production), nor, for that matter, the other child dancers from Ubud had previously participated in a *Sendratari*. Sadih also mentioned how, at times, the rehearsals for the event had been 'difficult', primarily because the troupe of child dancers had not rehearsed together prior to the afternoon of the performance. Despite such difficulties, the pre-performance rehearsal had 'made things easier', and he was looking forward to the opportunity to improvise around the set choreographic sequences assigned to his character in the production.[30] It is significant to note that less professionally adept child dancers would have been unable to perform to this capacity and could have threatened the quality and subsequent touristic expectations of the performance. The children behaved instead like professional adult dancers who rarely rehearse

Figure 2.1   The principal child dancers in the Pondok Pekak *Sendratari* tourist performance. Note: Tomi is second from the left, Putu is in the center, and Sadih is standing on the right-hand side. Photograph by the author, and used with permission.

but have the facility to improvise within the stylistic (music/dance/drama) parameters of the performance genre. From Sadih's remarks it is clear that the *Sendratari* provided the child dancers involved in the project with an opportunity to further develop their skills—adhering to Rosaldo's (1989, 208) definition of a 'borderzone' as a site of 'creative cultural production'—and to gain recognition from not only their teacher but also tourists within the context of a professional, 'frontier' performance (after Dunbar-Hall 2001; McKean 1989, 131).

Keen also to gain insights into how children relate to the categorizations of Balinese music and dance, I asked Sadih, Tomi, and Putu if *Sendratari* was a secular or sacred form. Fixing me with a somewhat puzzled look, 12-year-old Tomi informed me that because the children's *Sendratari* would be presented 'for tourists', it was a 'secular performance' (personal communication, Ubud, August 15, 2004). Agreeing with Tomi, 9-year-old Putu (she is also Happy's daughter) told me that even when presented as part of a temple ceremony in Keramas, in which context it is performed as a means of entertainment for the 'gods and human beings', *Sendratari* is 'still secular' (personal communication, Ubud, August 15, 2004). The responses of Tomi and Putu concerning the categorization of *Sentratari* suggest that, despite their formative years, child dancers in Bali are cognizant of the spiritual and human audiences for which their performances are intended.

Therefore, while these child dancers at the Pondok Pekak tourist performance in Ubud have little authority and are accorded little power vis-à-vis their performance, their worldly approach to performing for tourists in 'tourist' contexts shows them to be both 'culture bearers' (after Dunbar-Hall 2001), though largely unrecognized, and creatively active within the Balinese 'touristic borderzone' (Bruner 1996).

CHILD PERFORMERS NEGOTIATING TOURISM AT A CREMATION CEREMONY IN KERAMAS

In addition to documenting children's participation in the Pondok Pekak tourist performance in Ubud, I also conducted research with child performers when they performed sacred forms in various ceremonial contexts in and around Keramas. For these events, and akin to my involvement in the Pondok Pekak *Sendratari* presentation, I applied children's makeup and helped them to dress in their costumes prior to performances, I escorted them to and from the performance venues, and I acted as the children's ethnographer/documentarian. My association with the *Sanggar* in Keramas also facilitated my attendance at village temple and regional festivals. At such events, those who did not know me referred to me using the Indonesian word *Tamu*, a term used to denote a foreigner. Upon hearing others referring to me in this manner, however, the children took great care to explain that I was not simply another tourist; according to them, I was 'Jon'; I lived at the *Sanggar* with Happy and Wayan; I studied traditional music and dance; and, most importantly, I was present at the ceremony to record their participation in the event.

In accordance with the Balinese model for categorizing traditional music and dance pieces, sacred forms should not be presented for tourists. Indeed, performances involving sacred forms could be characterized as 'boundary sites' (after Dunbar-Hall 2001) from which tourists (and ethnographers) may be excluded. Nevertheless, the Balinese sometimes permit tourists (and ethnographers) to observe sacred performances when presented in the context of a temple ceremony if, for example, such individuals wear temple or traditional clothes (*Pakaian Adat*) to attend the event and behave in an appropriate manner.[31] The children that I accompanied to such events were generally ambivalent to the presence of other tourists or ethnographers that attended such proceedings in Keramas. Nevertheless, on a few occasions boys from the *Sanggar* did express to me their dissatisfaction regarding the presence of tourists at sacred performance events in their village. In September 2004, the presence and behavior of tourists at a cremation (*Pengabenan* or *Ngaben*) in Keramas caused the children to become particularly upset.[32]

At 9:00 a.m. on the morning of the cremation, the boys arrived at the *Sanggar* for their makeup and costumes, after which we all traveled in the back of an open truck the short distance from the *Sanggar* to the family compound of the deceased. Not long after entering the compound, and as an offering to the ancestors associated with the household, the boys performed the group warrior dance *Tari Baris Gede*. Following, the children and I departed the compound and waited patiently at the side of the main road (*Jalan Raya*) until noon, the time when the funerary procession towards the village cremation ground would commence (see Figure 2.2). Opposite from us congregated hundreds of tourists, many of whom were not wearing temple clothes.[33] Dressed in their checkered fabric (*Kamben Poleng*) costumes, the boys suddenly found themselves the focus of the tourists' viewfinders. Yet, one entity spoiled this traditional scene: the presence of the white ethnographer in temple clothes talking to the children. After crossing the road to speak with me, one visitor asked if I could 'move out of the picture' to enable him to take a photograph of the children (personal communication, Keramas, September 21, 2004).[34] So that the boys could follow the conversation and discuss whether or not they wished to agree to such a request, I informed them that the man wished for me to move aside so that he could take their photograph. Looking a little perplexed, Tomi questioned why I 'should not be in the photograph' (personal communication, Keramas, September 21, 2004)? I responded that the man wanted to take a photograph of boys in their costumes, a request to which they begrudgingly agreed. Following, and seemingly agitated and irritated

Figure 2.2 Boy dancers from Sanggar Tari Mumbul Sari, dressed in *Tari Baris Gede* costumes awaiting the start of the funerary procession to the cremation ground in Keramas. Photograph by the author, and used with permission.

at the presence of so many tourists, the boys slowly turned their backs on the ever-growing crowd opposite, which by this time were confined behind metal barriers erected by the village security officers (*Pecalang*) who were in charge of keeping order at the event. After turning away from the tourists, the children spoke among themselves so quickly in Balinese that I found it difficult to follow what they were saying. After I inquired in Indonesian as to whether anything was wrong, several of the boys told me that they were 'unhappy' with the presence of tourists at the event because they considered the cremation to be a 'sacred occasion' (personal communication, Keramas, September 21, 2004).[35] The boys also made it clear to me that they thought it 'impolite' that so many of the tourists had not worn temple clothes to attend the event.

Interrupting our conversation, the crashing metallic sounds of a *Gamelan Beleganjur* ensemble signaled the start of the funerary procession to accompany the body of the deceased to the cremation ground.[36] Suddenly, there was much noise and animation among the villagers gathered in the street as the corpse, wrapped in a white shroud, was carried from the family compound and placed in the cremation tower.[37] A large group of men from the village then lifted the cremation tower up off the ground, and the procession—involving village priests (*Pemanku*), a visiting high priest (*Pedanda*), the gamelan orchestra, the boy dancers, members of the deceased's family, and other villagers—commenced its slow journey toward the cremation ground. The tourists followed the procession, some of them choosing to walk while others opted to ride in the back of cars and minivans.

Upon reaching the cremation ground, which is situated south of the village towards the sea,[38] the corpse was removed from the cremation tower and placed in a large wooden sarcophagus (*Pantulangan* or *Tulang*) constructed in the form of a white bull decorated with gold.[39] Surrounding the sarcophagus stood many of those who had participated in the procession, including the boy dancers and me. One of the priests instructed the boys to perform a shortened version of *Tari Baris Gede*, following which they proceeded to walk three times around the sarcophagus.[40] Having completed this task, and with their participation in the event complete, the boys and I clambered into the back of a truck to return to the *Sanggar*. Departing before the lighting of the funeral pyre, the truck had to negotiate its way through the throngs of tourists, who were by now positioned all around the edges of the cremation ground.[41]

While sitting on the floor of the truck, I took the opportunity to ask the boys about the presence of tourists at the cemetery. Ten-year-old Komang Joni was firm in his view that tourists should 'not have come to the cremation ground', a sentiment shared by many of the other boys (personal communication, Keramas, September 21, 2004). Thus, and in contrast to performing for tourists in Ubud, or exhibiting the dance *Tari Baris Gede* in the company of tourists in the context of other temple ceremonies, the children were uncomfortable with the presence of tourists at the cremation in Keramas, an occasion that according to them amounted to 'slippage' (Bruner 1996, 167) between 'boundary' and 'frontier' sites (Dunbar-Hall 2001). Moreover, as a 'boundary' site (Dunbar-Hall 2001), the boys also believed that tourists should have been restricted from attending the cremation ground. Taking this further, the children's remarks also affirm Bruner's (1996, 159) assertion that as an event performed in the 'touristic borderzone', the cremation was a 'site of struggle' where the children had 'little or no room for manoeuvre' (Bruner 1991, 241), for example, concerning the calls from the tourists to take photographs of them while they were awaiting the start of the funerary procession. This sense of struggle could also possibly be reflected in the noticeable change in mood among the children when they entered the 'tourist gaze' (Urry 1990) after having performed *Tari Baris Gede* in the family compound of the deceased, a context to which tourists were not permitted. Moreover, the children's remarks imply criticism of and a certain resistance toward the decision of the village elders to capitalize on a sacred event, buying into the very commercialist tourism that many researchers and commentators bemoan 'is responsible for the ongoing desacralization and detraditionalisation of pre-modern cultural space (Greenwood 1977)' (Stokes 1999, 147) in Bali. In relation to this point, 14-year-old Nomber reflected that on entering the street after performing in the compound of the deceased, he somehow felt more 'self-conscious' knowing that tourists were watching him (personal communication, Keramas, September 21, 2004). In light of this, the boys as 'culture bearers' (after Dunbar-Hall 2001) struggled to disentangle their roles or to even maintain an appropriate for-tourists performance mien while standing in the street, because the event was not framed in terms of the usual performance for tourists on a (Western) 'tourist stage' (as is the case for the Pondok Pekak tourist presentation). Consequently, my progression from tourist ('front stage') to the children's ethnographer, and my liminal position of not being a culture bearer but also not being a tourist, allowed me to be aware of the 'backstage' (after MacCannell 1973, 1976) ambivalence the children felt about this important sacred event, and the role they were expected to play in it. Again, my liminal role as the tourist-ethnographer put me in a unique position. Not only was I privy to the boys' critical evaluations of their elders as 'their' touristic other, but as an ethnographer I was aware of the ethical implications if I were to break confidence with the children regarding their thoughts relating to this matter. Obviously these were opinions they never would have said to a tourist, nor to any of the adults in their everyday lives. Consequently, they clearly trusted me with this information.

CONCLUDING REFLECTIONS ON BEING THE CHILDREN'S TOURIST-ETHNOGRAPHER

With reference to research pertaining to musical tourism, this chapter has focused on child dancers in Bali to illustrate how children perform for tourists in 'boundary' and 'frontier' sites (Dunbar-Hall 2011). In doing so, it examined how children who are cognizant of and competent within the touristic realities of life in Bali negotiate tourism in the 'liminal' (after Turner 1967) context of learning to become 'culture bearers' (Dunbar-Hall 2001). By highlighting how boys and girls shaped my development as their tourist-ethnographer, fellow dancer, and friend, the chapter has also outlined how I was privileged to behind-the-scenes activities to which tourists rarely, if ever, have access. While other researchers who investigate musical tourism discuss how they traverse from 'front stage' to 'backstage' (Mac-Cannell 1973, 1976) in various tourist performance contexts (for example, Rees 1998; Sarkissian 2000), scholars have tended not to focus on children's performances. Therefore, my success as an adult 'Other' whom children chose to welcome into their world (after Corsaro 1985) enabled me to critically reflect on the ethical implications that arise when conducting musical tourism research with children, as well as those that arose due to my complex role as a tourist-ethnographer. This unique access to a domain from which most Balinese adults are excluded essentially served to sublimate the 'tourist'/'culture bearer' dichotomy (Dunbar-Hall 2001).

In order to demonstrate how I came to occupy a liminal position as a tourist-ethnographer, the chapter first provided a contextual introduction to the cultural village of Ubud. It was in this site where I first commenced fieldwork in Bali and undertook research with the children who attended dance lessons at a 'frontier' site (Dunbar-Hall 2001), the Pondok Pekak Library. In order to better comprehend how children negotiate cultural tourism, and the ways in which they draw clear distinctions between tourist and 'nontourist' performances, I relocated to the nearby village of Keramas, where I successfully conducted child-focused research with approximately 150 children who facilitated the development of my skills as an ethnographer, while I was gradually becoming conscious of the myriad obligations of my research with child performers (McIntosh 2006). The chapter then contrasted how child dancers from Keramas approached with equanimity performing for tourists in Ubud vis-à-vis the dissatisfaction some children felt at having to perform in the presence of tourists at a cremation in their village. The juxtaposition of children's participation in the above two contexts outlines the liminal position of child dancers, as well as how the liminal roles offered to me by these same children enabled me to negotiate 'boundary' and 'frontier' music and dance performances (after Dunbar-Hall 2001), which, while occurring within the Balinese 'touristic borderzone,' were not only 'creative sites of expression' (Rosaldo 1989, 208) and but also 'sites of struggle' (Bruner 1996, 157). While it could be argued that Balinese child performers are the unwitting victims of musical tourism, ever powerless and dominated by their elders and the economic necessities of the 21st century, clearly these nascent 'culture bearers' inhabit the creative capacity and deep cultural understandings of their forebears. It is with these qualities and skills that they critically evaluate the persistent onslaught of modernization, commercialization, and tourism in contemporary Bali. Consequently, such research focusing specifically on minors is necessary and important because it provides scholars with a deeper understanding of how such issues affect the everyday lives of children and child performers within musical tourism contexts.

ACKNOWLEDGMENTS

I wish to thank Karen Elizabeth Schrieber, Simone Krüger, and Ruxandra Trandafoiu for their insightful comments pertaining to previous drafts of this chapter. I am also grateful to the two anonymous reviewers for their careful reading and constructive feedback.

NOTES

1. Synonymous with Indonesia, but particular to the islands of Java and Bali, a gamelan ensemble includes metallophones (large glockenspiel-like instruments), gongs, and drums. Through the interaction of players and instruments within an ensemble, gamelan music stresses notions of unity, community, and totality (see Keeler 1975).
2. In Bali, gamelan music always accompanies traditional dance, and to become a successful dancer, boys and girls must embody the requisite high-level musical skills required to lead, cue, and communicate with the members of a gamelan ensemble during a performance.
3. Dunbar-Hall (2001, 176) states that Ubud is located 'at the apex of a triangle' (that also incorporates the southern beach resorts of Kuta and Sanur). In the early years of tourism development in Bali, and so that the Balinese could profit from tourists but protect the rest of the island from outside influences, it was intended that visitors should be confined to this 'triangle' (see also McKean 1989, 132).
4. Although difficult to translate, the term Kebyar refers to a 'sudden outburst, "like the bursting open of a flower"' (McPhee 1966, 328). As an onomatopoeic term, Kebyar also denotes the 'explosive unison attack' (McPhee 1966, 328) with which all *Gamelan Gong Kebyar* compositions commence.
5. As a young composer living in New York, Colin McPhee first became aware of Balinese gamelan music via recordings produced in 1928 by the Odeon/Beka record company (Herbst 1999; Oja 1990, 63). McPhee was so fascinated by Balinese music that he lived in Bali almost continuously from 1931 until 1939 when the rumblings of the Second World War necessitated not just his departure but also that of many of the other Western scholars and expatriates living on the island at the time (McPhee 1944/2002; also see Oja 1990).
6. The 'link between culture and economy in Bali' (Yamashita 2003, 86) apropos the introduction of tourism to the island at this time was not necessarily new, however. Traditionally, Balinese performance troupes were paid a fee to present music, dance, and drama productions (see also Bowers 1956, 240).
7. *Gamelan Gambuh* is the oldest form of classical dance-drama in Bali. Almost all other Balinese music, dance, and drama forms originate from this genre.
8. A royal court ensemble, *Gamelan Semar Pegulingan* was traditionally performed outside the king's bedchamber.

9. *Gamelan Gong Gede* is a large ceremonial gamelan ensemble.
10. Prior to the island-wide craze for *Gamelan Gong Kebyar* in the early decades of the 20th century, ensembles including *Gamelan Gambuh*, *Gamelan Semar Pegulingan*, and *Gamelan Gong Gede* had been prevalent throughout south Bali.
11. New Gamelan Gong Kebyar compositions were created especially for this tour, including the Dance of the Bumblebees (*Tari Oleg Tamulilingan*). A duet presented by a female and male performer, *Tari Oleg Tamulilingan* has since been absorbed into the Balinese performance canon, with child dancers continuing to study and perform this dance.
12. Although performed outside the confines of traditional dance-drama productions, many *Tari Lepas* are still 'to some extent, programmatic' (Sanger 1991, 48).
13. Traditionally, performances of sacred music and dance were reserved for the gods of the Balinese-Hindu religion, with other forms presented for the enjoyment of spiritual deities as well as human beings. In the late 1960s, however, the inclusion of ritual forms of music and dance in some tourist performances led Balinese religious leaders, government officials, and performers to become anxious about the desacralization of the traditional performing arts through tourism.
14. For further discussion regarding the categorization of Balinese music and dance, see Dibia and Ballinger (2004), Gold (2005), Picard (1990a), and Sanger (1989).
15. In 1978, and because of confusion among some regional music and dance practitioners, the model relating to the categorization of traditional music and dance was revised to 'stress the function' (Picard 1990a, 67) and not necessarily the context in which music and dance pieces should be performed. It remains the case, however, that ritual forms intended for presentation to the gods of the Balinese-Hindu religion should not be performed for tourists.
16. This includes secular works, such as the welcome dance, *Tari Panyembrama*, and the Bird of Paradise Dance (*Tari Cendrawasi*), which are not only frequently included in tourist performances, but also integral to the repertoire studied by aspiring child dancers in Bali.
17. As a result of the preservation and revival activities of the Balinese music and dance conservatories, some older forms, including *Gamelan Gambuh*, are now presented for tourists. Consequently, tourism has also become 'a vital element in the survival and revival of cultural forms' (Sanger 1988, 100).
18. It should be noted, however, that performance troupes from the other parts of Indonesia, as well as gamelan ensembles from outside Indonesia (most notably the group Gamelan Sekar Jaya from California, US), sometimes perform at the Bali Arts Festival.
19. Established in 1995 by American expatriate Laurie Billington (1958–2009) and her Balinese husband, Made Sumendra, the Pondok Pekak Library and Learning Centre (Perpustakaan Pondok Pekak) is a private organization that offers library-lending services and educational classes to tourists and members of the expatriate community, as well as Balinese adults and children who live in and around Ubud.
20. Born in 1971 in Singaraja, situated in the northern administrative district of Buleleng, Ni Luh Happy Pariamini (known as 'Happy') is a graduate of the Balinese music and dance conservatory that is now known as the Indonesia Institute of Arts, Denpasar (Insitut Seni Indonesia, Denpasar).
21. Born in 1969 in Keramas, a village located in the south-central administrative district of Gianyar, I Wayan Suarta (known as 'Wayan' but also called 'Rawit') is also a graduate of the Balinese music and dance conservatory.

22. In the remainder of the chapter, I will refer to Sanggar Tari Mumbul Sari simply as the *Sanggar*.

23. Although I regularly took part in the children's dance rehearsals, I never attempted to behave in a childlike manner (see Laerke 1998). Instead, my willingness to participate in the children's lessons and acquire the necessary skills to be able to perform various dances in public served to communicate to the children that I was not simply a 'tourist', but an 'ethnographer' who wanted to learn from and with them. Having established this fact, the teachers at the *Sanggar* then discussed the various aspects of my research with the children's parents. Following, parents gave verbal consent for their son or daughter to participate in the research. Throughout the research process, I also always sought verbal permission from children to take photographs or videos during rehearsals and performances. For a detailed discussion pertaining to the ethical implications of my research with children in Bali, see McIntosh (2006).

24. *Topeng* is a traditional mask dance-drama, the plots for which are derived from Balinese historical chronicles (*Babad*).

25. The Pondok Pekak tourist performance comprises six or seven free dances (*Tari Lepas*) that follow an instrumental overture performed by the Sanggar Seni Pondok Pekak adult male gamelan ensemble. Not all tourist presentations follow this format, however, with some troupes choosing to perform Balinese dance-drama productions, including *Sendratari*, *Ramayana* Ballet, *Kecak*, and *Barong* (a masked, mythical beast performed by two male dancers). Like many other tourist performances in Ubud, the Pondok Pekak presentation also makes use of a Western-style stage (decorated to look like a Balinese temple setting) that faces the audience (*Panggung*) and not a traditional three-sided Balinese stage (*Kalangan*) (see Picard 1990a, 54).

26. These include a welcome dance (*Tari Panyembrama*), a solo male warrior dance (*Tari Baris Tunggal*), a cross-dressing seated dance (*Tari Kebyar Duduk*), a work for three girl dancers (*Tari Legong Kraton*), and occasionally the Dance of the Bumblebees (*Tari Oleg Tamulilingan*). Adult performers associated with Sanggar Seni Pondok Pekak may also present other dances, for example, the Bird of Paradise Dance (*Tari Cendrawasih*), which is performed by two female dancers, and a solo male mask dance depicting a demonlike figure (*Tari Jauk Manis*).

27. In relation to this point, Sanger (1988, 92–96) notes that Balinese musicians and dancers never compromise performance standards for tourist audiences, be they performers, children, or adults (see also McKean 1989, 123).

28. The decision to include less proficient child dancers in the Pondok Pekak production could potentially result in a lower standard of performance, thus serving to denigrate not only Happy's reputation as a renowned teacher, but also the standing of the library's presentation in the competitive Ubud tourist market.

29. *Sendratari* is a pantomime dance-drama, with the term being an acronym of the Indonesian words for art (*Seni*), drama (*Drama*), and dance (*Tari*). Devised by Javanese music and dance conservatories, *Sendratari* was first introduced to Bali in the early 1960s (Bandem and deBoer 1981, 86; deBoer 1996; Dibia and Ballinger 2004, 96). In a Balinese *Sendratari* performance, the dancers mime their roles, a gamelan ensemble accompanies the performance, and a male singer-cum-narrator (*Juru Tandak*) provides the commentary for the audience. Consequently, Dibia and Ballinger (2004, 96) note that 'it may be difficult for non-Balinese to understand the nuances of Sendratari due to the use of colloquial Balinese language.'

30. Similar to other Balinese dance-drama genres, *Sendratari* has a number of 'stock characters', the identities of which are based on specific 'movements, gestures and body-coded positions' (Rubin and Sedana 2007, 83).

31. To attend a Balinese temple ceremony, it is expected that men and women should cover their shoulders and knees. In particular, men wear a head covering (*Udeng*), a T-shirt or shirt (*Baju*), a sarong (*Kamben*), a piece of cloth worn over the sarong (*Saput*), and a sash (*Selendang*) worn around the waist; women wear a long-sleeved blouse (*Kebaya*), a sarong (*Kamben*), as well as a sash (*Selendang*) around the waist.

32. In common Balinese language, *Pengabenan* or *Ngaben* (*Palebonan* in high Balinese language) involves a series of rituals designed to release the soul of a corpse. The cremation is the 'the climax of *pengabenan*', following which a 'second, complementary series of ceremonies' ensures the return of the 'now-released soul . . . to God' (Eiseman 1990/2004, 116).

33. A week earlier, an announcement pertaining to the cremation in Keramas had appeared on the notice board in the Ubud tourist office. I had observed it when—as part of my ethnographic research—I had gone to the Ubud tourist office to collect promotional flyers for tourist performances! The announcement concluded with the words: 'To attend the cremation, tourists must wear temple clothes (pakaian adat). Ticketed transport will be available from outside the tourist office on the morning of the event.'

34. As a 'tourist object' (after Morris 1995) at the cremation in Keramas, my presence with the children did not conform to touristic expectations of the event.

35. The children's response to the presence of tourists at the cremation in Keramas contrasts with findings by Chappell (2011, 56) who, as a result of his research on cremations and tourism in Ubud, states that 'depending upon the social class and demeanor of the family or village, tourists are welcome to view cremations without experiencing a suppressed animosity on the part of the Balinese participating in the ceremony.'

36. A *Gamelan Beleganjur* ensemble consists of numerous sets of large crash cymbals (*Ceng-Ceng Kopyak*), several handheld kettle chimes of various sizes (*Bonang/Reyong* and *Ponggang*), a timekeeper flat gong (*Kajar*), two conical drums (*Kendang*), a gong with a sunken boss (*Bende*), a medium-size suspended gong with a raised boss (*Kempur*), and two large suspended gongs each with a raised boss (*Gong Ageng*). The *Bende*, *Kempur*, and the two *Gong Ageng* are suspended on separate long wooden poles, each of which is carried on the shoulders of two musicians. For a detailed discussion of *Gamelan Beleganjur*, see Bakan (1999).

37. In Bali, corpses are usually transported to the cremation ground in elaborate pagoda-like towers (*Bade*) constructed from wood and bamboo that are decorated with colorful ornaments. For a detailed discussion of Balinese funerary rites, see Connor (1995, 1996), Covarrubias (1937/1973, 359–88), Eiseman (1990/2004, 115–26), and Hobart (1978).

38. The connections among people, landscape, and the spirit world are integral to the way in which the Balinese conduct their everyday activities. In Bali, the concept of *Kaja*, meaning 'upstream' or 'towards the mountain,' denoting Bali's highest volcano, Mount Gunung (Gunung Agung, meaning 'Great Mountain'), is associated with benevolent spiritual deities. In contrast, *Kelod*, meaning 'downstream' or 'towards the sea', is associated with malevolent spirits (Hobart 1978; McIntosh n.d.; Stuart-Fox 2002, 4–5). Because of their association with destructive spiritual entities, cremation grounds and cemeteries tend to be located either 'downstream' or to the left of a village, spatial orientations associated with *Kelod*.

39. In Bali, the form of the sarcophagus in which a corpse is cremated varies depending on the status of the deceased. Traditionally, high-caste Balinese (*Brahmana*) are cremated in a sarcophagus in the form of bull (*Lembu*); the

second highest caste (*Kasatria*) use a winged lion (*Singa*); the third highest caste (*Wesia*) use a deer (*Kambing*); and low caste (*Sundra*) use a fish-elephant (*Gajah Mina*). Caste also determines the color of the sarcophagus (see Covarrubias 1937/1973, 373).

40. As if sensing my uncertainty as to what I was supposed to do at this point in the cremation ceremony, a priest held out his hand and indicated for me to come forward. For a split second, I froze to the spot, not knowing how to react. After beckoning me forward a second time, the priest motioned for me to join the boys as they circumnavigated the sarcophagus. Such an invitation to participate in the funerary rites at the cremation site also served to underline my unique liminal position as the children's ethnographer in Keramas.

41. Similarly, Chappell (2011, 56) notes that although tourists may be 'blocked from viewing a cremation closely . . . they are still welcomed to watch from a distance and are not totally extricated from the site.'

REFERENCES

Abram, Simone. 1997. 'Performing for Tourists in Rural France.' In *Tourists and Tourism: Identifying People with Place*, edited by Simone Abram, Jacqueline D. Waldren, and Donald V.L. MacLeod, 29–49. Oxford: Berghahn.

Bakan, Michael B. 1999. *Music of Death and New Creation: Experiences in the World of Balinese Gamelan Beleganjur*. Chicago: University of Chicago Press.

Bandem, I Made, and Fredrik E. deBoer. 1981. *Kaja and Kelod: Balinese Dance in Transition*. Kuala Lumpur: Oxford University Press.

Baumann, Max Peter. 2001. 'Festivals, Musical Actors and Mental Constructs in the Process of Globalization.' *World of Music* 43(2/3):9–29.

Boon, James A. 1977. *The Anthropological Romance of Bali 1597–1972: Dynamics Perspectives in Marriage and Caste, Politics and Religion*. Cambridge: Cambridge University Press.

Boon, James A. 1990. *Affinities and Extremes: Crisscrossing the Bittersweet Ethnology of East Indies History, Hindu-Balinese Culture and Indo-European Allure*. Chicago: Chicago University Press.

Bowers, Faubion. 1956. *Theatre in the East: A Survey of Asian Dance and Drama*. New York: Thomas Nelson.

Bruner, Edward M. 1991. 'Transformation of Self in Tourism.' *Annals of Tourism Research* 18(2):238–50.

Bruner, Edward M. 1995. 'The Ethnographer/Tourist in Indonesia.' In *International Tourism: Identity and Change*, edited by Marie-Françoise Lanfant, John B. Allcock, and Edward M. Bruner, 224–41. London: Sage.

Bruner, Edward M. 1996. 'Tourism in the Balinese Borderzone.' In *Displacement, Diaspora, and Geographies of Identity*, edited by Smadar Lavie and Ted Swenedburg, 157–79. Durham, NC: Duke University Press.

Chappell, Frank R. 2011. 'Selling Your Relatives: The Impact of Cultural Tourism on Balinese Ritual Life.' MA diss., Northern Illinois University.

Coast, John. 1953/2004. *Dancing Out of Bali*. Singapore: Periplus Editions.

Connell, John. 1993. 'Bali Revisited: Death, Rejuvenation, and the Tourist Cycle.' *Environment and Planning D: Society and Space* 11(6):641–66.

Connor, Linda H. 1995. 'The Action of the Body on Society: Washing a Corpse in Bali.' *Journal of the Royal Anthropological Institute* 1(3):537–59.

Connor, Linda H. 1996. 'Contestation and Transformation of Balinese Ritual: The Case of Nagaben Ngirit.' In *Being Modern in Bali: Image and Change*, edited by

Adrian Vickers. Southeast Asia Studies Monograph 43, 179–211. New Haven, CT: Yale University Press.

Cooley, Timothy J. 1999. 'Folk Festival as Modern Ritual in the Polish Tatra Mountains.' *World of Music* 41(3):31–55.

Corsaro, William A. 1985. *Friendship and Peer Culture in the Early Years*. Norwood, NJ: Ablex.

Covarrubias. Miguel. 1937/1973. *Island of Bali*. New York: A.A. Knopf.

Cukier, Judie, Joanne Norris, and Geoffrey Wall. 1996. 'The Involvement of Women in the Tourism Industry of Bali, Indonesia.' *Journal of Development Studies* 33(2):248–71.

Cukier, Judie, and Geoffrey Wall. 1994. 'Tourism Employment: Vendors in Bali, Indonesia.' *Tourism Management* 15(6):464–67.

Cukier, Judie, and Geoffrey Wall. 1995. 'Tourism Employment in Bali: A Gender Analysis.' *Tourism Economics* 1(4):389–401.

Cukier, Judith. 1996. 'Tourism Employment in Bali: Trends and Implications.' In *Tourism and Indigenous Peoples*, edited by Richard Butler and Tom Hinch, 49–75. London: International Thomson Business Press.

Cukier-Snow, Judith, and Geoffrey Wall. 1993. 'Tourism Employment: Perspectives for Bali.' *Tourism Management* 14(3):195–201.

Daniel, Yvonne P. 1996. 'Tourism Dance Performances: Authenticity and Creativity.' *Annals of Tourism Research* 23(4):780–97.

Darma Putra, I Nyoman, and Michael Hitchcock. 2006. 'The Bali Bombs and the Tourism Development Cycle.' *Progress in Development Studies* 6(2):157–66.

Darma Putra, I Nyoman, and Michael Hitchcock. 2008. 'Terrorism and Tourism in Bali and Southeast Asia.' In *Tourism in Southeast Asia: Challenges and New Directions*, edited by Michael Hitchcock, Victor T. King, and Michael Parnwell, 83–98. Copenhagen: NIAS Press.

deBoer, Fredrik E. 1996. 'Two Modern Balinese Theatre Genres: Sendratari and Drama Gong.' In *Being Modern in Bali: Image and Change*, edited by Adrian Vickers. Southeast Asia Studies Monograph 43, 158–78. New Haven, CT: Yale University Press.

Desmond, Jane. 1999. *Staging Tourism: Bodies on Display from Waikiki to Seaworld*. Chicago: University of Chicago Press.

Dibia, I Wayan. 1996/2000. *Kecak: The Vocal Chant of Bali*. Denpasar, Bali: Hartanto Art Books Bali.

Dibia, I Wayan, and Rucina Ballinger. 2004. *Balinese Dance, Drama and Music: A Guide to the Performing Arts of Bali*. Singapore: Periplus Editions.

Dunbar-Hall, Peter. 2001. 'Culture, Tourism and Cultural Tourism: Boundaries and Frontiers in Performance of Balinese Music and Dance.' *Journal of Intercultural Studies* 22(2):173–87.

Dunbar-Hall, Peter. 2003. '*Tradisi* and *Turisme*: Music, Dance and Cultural Transformation at the Ubud Palace, Bali, Indonesia.' *Australian Geographical Studies* 41(1):3–16.

Dunbar-Hall, Peter. 2007. '"*Apa Salah Baliku*?" ("What Did My Bali Do Wrong?"): Popular Music and the 2002 Bali Bombings.' *Popular Music and Society* 30(4):533–47.

Eiseman, Fred B. 1990/2004. *Bali: Sekala and Niskala*. Volume 1. *Essays on Religion, Ritual, and Art*. Indonesia: Periplus Editions.

Foley, Kathy, and I Nyoman Sumandhi. 1994. 'The Bali Arts Festival: An Interview with I Nyoman Sumandhi.' *Asian Theatre Journal* 11(2):275–89.

Gibson, Chris, and John Connell. 2005. *Music and Tourism: On the Road Again*. Clevedon: Channel View Publications.

Gold, Lisa. 2005. *Music in Bali: Experiencing Music, Expressing Culture*. New York: Oxford University Press.

Hannah, William. A. 1976/2004. *Bali Chronicles: A Lively Account of the Island's History from Early Times to the 1970s*. Singapore: Periplus Editions.

Harnish, David. 2005. 'Teletubbies in Paradise: Tourism, Indonesianisation and Modernisation in Balinese Music.' *Yearbook for Traditional Music* 37:101–23.

Hatchwell, Emily. 1990. *Travellers Survival Kit to the East: From Istanbul to Indonesia*. Oxford: Vacation Work.

Herbst, Edward. 1981. 'Intrinsic Aesthetics in Balinese Artistic and Spiritual Practice.' *Asian Music* 13(1):43–52.

Herbst, Edward. 1997. *Voices in Bali: Energies and Perceptions in Vocal Music and Dance Theater*. Hanover, NH: Wesleyan University Press.

Herbst, Edward. 1999. *Liner Notes for The Roots of Gamelan: The First Recordings*. Linden Hill Station, NY: World Arbiter 2001. CD Recording.

Herbst, Edward. 2006. *Liner Notes for Dancers of Bali, 1952: Gamelan of Peliatan*. Linden Hill Station, NY: World Arbiter 2007. CD Recording.

Hill, Hal, ed. 1994. *Indonesia's New Order: The Dynamics of Socio-Economic Transformation*. Honolulu: University of Hawaii Press.

Hitchcock, Michael. 2001. 'Tourism and Total Crisis in Indonesia: The Case of Bali.' *Asia Pacific Business Review* 8(2):101–20.

Hitchcock, Michael, and I Nyoman Drama Putra. 2005. 'Bali Bombings: Tourism Crisis Management and Conflict Avoidance.' *Current Issues in Tourism* 8(1):62–76.

Hitchcock, Michael, and I Nyoman Drama Putra. 2007. *Tourism, Development and Terrorism in Bali*. Aldershot: Ashgate.

Hobart, Angela, Urs Ramseyer, and Albert Leemann. 1996. *The People of Bali*. Oxford: Blackwell.

Hobart, Mark. 1978. 'The Path of the Soul. The Legitimacy of Nature in Balinese Conceptions of Space.' In *Natural Symbols in South East Asia*, edited by George Bertram Milner, 5–28. London: School of Oriental and African Studies.

Hobsbawm, Eric. 1983/1991. 'Introduction: Inventing Traditions.' In *The Invention of Tradition*, edited by Eric Hobsbawm and Terence Ranger, 1–14. Cambridge: Cambridge University Press.

Hough, Brett W. 2000. 'The College of Indonesian Arts, Denpasar: Nation, State and the Performing Arts in Bali.' PhD diss., Monash University.

Howe, Leo. 2005. *The Changing World of Bali: Religion, Society and Tourism*. London: Routledge.

James, Jamie. 1999. 'Travel: Ubud, the Heart of Bali.' *Atlantic Monthly* 284(2):26–32.

Johnson, Henry. 2002. 'Balinese Music, Tourism and Globalistation. Inventing Traditions within and across Cultures.' *New Zealand Journal of Asian Studies* 4(2):8–32.

Keeler, Ward. 1975. 'Musical Encounter in Java and Bali.' *Indonesia* 19(April):85–126.

Laerke, Anna. 1998. 'By Means of Re-Membering: Notes on a Fieldwork with English Children.' *Anthropology Today* 14(1):3–7.

Lau, Frederick. 1998. '"Packaging Identity through Sound": Tourist Performances in Contemporary China.' *Journal of Musicological Research* 17(2):113–34.

Long, Veronica H., and Sara L. Kindon. 1997. 'Gender and Tourism Development in Balinese Villages.' In *Gender, Work and Tourism*, edited by M. Thea Sinclair, 89–118. London: Routledge.

Long, Veronica H., Geoffrey Wall, Michael V. Conlin. 1995. 'Small Scale Tourism Development in Bali.' In *Island Tourism: Management Principles and Practice*, edited by Michael V. Conlin and Tom Baum, 237–57. Chichester: Wiley.

MacCannell, Dean. 1973. 'Staged Authenticity: Arrangements of Social Space in Tourist Settings.' *American Journal of Sociology* 79(3):589–603.

MacCannell, Dean. 1976. *The Tourist: A New Theory of the Leisure Class.* London: MacMillan.

MacRae, Graeme. 1999. 'Acting Global, Thinking Local in a Balinese Tourist Town.' In *Staying Local in the Global Village: Bali in the Twentieth Century*, edited by Raechelle Rubinstein and Linda H. Connor, 123–54. Honolulu: University of Hawaii Press.

McCarthy, John. 1994. *Are Sweet Dreams Made of This? Tourism in Bali and Eastern Indonesia.* Northcote, Australia: Indonesia Resources and Information Program.

McGraw, Andrew Clay. 2009. 'The Political Economy of the Performing Arts in Contemporary Bali.' *Indonesian and Malay World* 37(109):299–325.

McIntosh, Jonathan. 2006. 'How Playing, Singing and Dancing Shape the Ethnographer: Research with Children in a Village Dance Studio in Bali, Indonesia.' *Anthropology Matters* 8(2). Accessed 20 March 2012. http://www.anthropologymatters.com/journal/2006-2/index.htm.

McIntosh, Jonathan. 2010. 'Dancing to a Disco Beat? Children, Teenagers and the Localizing of Popular Music in Bali, Indonesia.' *Asian Music* 41(1):1–35.

McIntosh, Jonathan. 2012. 'Preparation, Presentation and Power: Children's Performances in a Balinese Dance Studio.' In *Dancing Cultures: Globalization, Tourism and Identity in the Anthropology of Dance*, edited by Hélène Neveu-Kringelbach and Jonathan Skinner, 194–210. Oxford: Berghahn.

McIntosh, Jonathan. n.d. 'Performing Emotional Connections in a Balinese Landscape: Exploring Children's Roles in a Barong Performance in Keramas, South-Central Bali.' In *Performing Gender, Place and Emotion in Music: Global Perspectives*, edited by Fiona Magowan and Louise Wrazen. Rochester, NY: University of Rochester Press.

McKean, Philip F. 1979. 'From Purity to Pollution?: The Balinese Ketjak (Monkey Dance) as Symbolic Form in Transition.' In *The Imagination of Reality: Essays in Southeast Asian Coherence Systems*, edited by Alton L. Becker and Aram A. Yengoyan, 293–302. Norwood, NJ: Ablex.

McKean, Philip F. 1989. 'Towards a Theoretical Analysis of Tourism: Economic Dualism and Cultural Involution in Bali.' In *Hosts and Guests: The Anthropology of Tourism*, 2nd ed., edited by Valene L. Smith, 119–38. Philadelphia: University of Pennsylvania Press.

McPhee, Colin. 1944/2002. *A House in Bali.* Singapore: Periplus Editions.

McPhee, Colin. 1966. *Music in Bali: A Study in Form and Instrumental Organization in Balinese Orchestral Music.* New Haven, CT: Yale University Press.

Morris, Meaghan. 1995. 'Life as a Tourist Object in Australia.' In *International Tourism: Identity and Change*, edited by Marie-Françoise Lanfant, John B. Allcock, and Edward M. Bruner, 177–91. London: Sage.

Nettl, Bruno. 2005. *The Study of Ethnomusicology: Thirty-One Issues and Concepts.* Urbana: University of Illinois Press.

Noszlopy, Laura. 2002. 'The Bali Arts Festival—Pesta Kesenian Bali: Culture, Politics and the Arts in Contemporary Indonesia.' PhD diss., University of East Anglia.

Oja, Carol J. 1990. *Colin McPhee: Composer in Two Worlds.* Washington, DC: Smithsonian Institute Press.

Picard, Michel. 1990a. '"Cultural Tourism" in Bali: Cultural Performances as Tourist Attraction.' *Indonesia* 49(April):37–74.

Picard, Michel. 1990b. 'Kebalian Orang Bali: Tourism and the Uses of "Balinese Culture" in the New Order Indonesia.' *Review of Indonesian and Malaysian Affairs* 24(2):1–38.

Picard, Michel. 1993. '"Cultural Tourism in Bali": National Integration and Regional Differentiation.' In *Tourism in South-East Asia*, edited by Michael Hitchcock, Victor T. King, and Michael J.G. Parnwell, 71–98. London: Routledge.

Picard, Michel. 1996a. *Bali: Cultural Tourism and Touristic Culture.* Translated by Diana Darling. Singapore: Archipelago Press.

Picard, Michel. 1996b. 'Dance and Drama in Bali: The Making of an Indonesian Art From.' In *Being Modern in Bali: Image and Change*, edited by Adrian Vickers. Southeast Asia Studies Monograph 43, 115–57. New Haven, CT: Yale University Press.

Picard, Michel. 1997. 'Cultural Tourism, Nation-Building, and Regional Culture: The Making of a Balinese Identity.' In *Tourism, Ethnicity, and the State in Asian and Pacific Societies*, edited by Michel Picard and Robert E. Wood, 181–214. Honolulu: University of Hawaii Press.

Picard, Michel. 1999. 'The Discourse of Kebalian: Transcultural Constructions of Balinese Identity.' In *Staying Local in the Global Village: Bali in the Twentieth Century*, edited by Raechelle Rubinstein and Linda H. Connor, 15–50. Honolulu: University of Hawaii Press.

Picard, Michel. 2003. 'Touristification and Balinization in a Time of Reformasi.' *Indonesia and the Malay World* 31(89):108–18.

Picard, Michel. 2008a. 'Balinese Identity as Tourist Attraction: From "Cultural Tourism" (*Pariwisata Budaya*) to "Bali Erect" (*Ajeg Bali*).' *Tourist Studies* 8(2):155–73.

Picard, Michel. 2008b. 'From "Kebalian" to "Ajeg Bali": Tourism and Balinese Identity in the Aftermath of the Kuta Bombing.' In *Tourism in Southeast Asia: Challenges and New Directions*, edited by Michael Hitchcock, Victor T. King, and Michael Parnwell, 99–131. Copenhagen: NIAS Press.

Racki, Christian. 1998. *The Sacred Dances of Bali.* Denpasar, Bali: CV Buratangi.

Ramstedt, Martin. 1991. 'Revitalization of Balinese Classical Dance and Music.' In *Music in the Dialogue of Cultures: Traditional Music and Cultural Policy*, edited by Max Peter Baumann, 108–20. Wiljelmshaven: Florian Noetzel Verlag.

Rees, Helen. 1998. '"Authenticity" and the Foreign Audience for Traditional Music in Southwest China.' *Journal of Musicological Research* 17(2):135–61.

Rosaldo, Renato. 1989. *Culture and Truth: The Remaking of Social Analysis.* Boston, MA: Beacon Press.

Rubin, Leon, and I Nyoman Sedana. 2007. *Performance in Bali.* Abingdon, Oxon: Routledge.

Rubinstein, Raechelle, and Linda H. Connor, eds. 1999. *Staying Local in the Global Village: Bali in the Twentieth Century.* Honolulu: University of Hawaii Press.

Sanger, Annette E. 1986. 'The Role of Music and Dance in the Social and Cultural Life of Two Balinese Villages.' PhD diss., the Queen's University of Belfast.

Sanger, Annette E. 1988. 'Blessing or Blight? The Effect of Touristic Dance-Drama on Village Life in Singapadu, Bali.' In *Come Mek Me Hol' Yu Han': The Impact of Tourism on Traditional Music*, edited by Adrienne L. Kaeppler, and Olive Lewin, 89–104. Kingston: Jamaica Memory Bank.

Sanger, Annette E. 1989. 'Music and Musicians, Dance and Dancers: Socio-Musical Interrelationships in Balinese Performance.' *Yearbook of Traditional Music* 21:57–69.

Sanger, Annette E. 1991. 'Artistic Representation in Social Action: The Case of Bali.' *Dance Research Journal* 23(2):48–9.

Sarkissian, Margaret. 1998. 'Tradition, Tourism, and the Cultural Show: Malaysia's Diversity of Display.' *Journal of Musicological Research* 17(2):87–112.

Sarkissian, Margaret. 2000. *D'Alberquerque's Children: Performing Tradition in Malaysia's Portuguese Settlement.* Chicago: University of Chicago Press.

Seebass, Tilman. 1996. 'Change in Balinese Musical Life: "Kebiar" in the 1920s and 1930s.' In *Being Modern in Bali: Image and Change*, edited by Adrian Vickers, Southeast Asia Studies Monograph 43, 71–91. New Haven, CT: Yale University Press.

Spies, Walter, and Beryl de Zoete. 1938/2002. *Dance and Drama in Bali*. Singapore: Periplus Editions.

Stokes, Martin. 1999. 'Music, Travel and Tourism: An Afterword.' *World of Music* 41(3):141–55.

Stuart-Fox, David J. 2002. *Pura Besakih: Temple, Religion and Society in Bali*. Leiden: Koninklijk Insituut voor Taal-, Land- en Volkenkunde (KITLV) Press [KITLV, Verhandelingen 193].

Sugriwa, I.G.B. Sudhyatmaka. 2000. *Nadi: Trance in the Balinese Arts*. Denpasar: Taksu Foundation.

Talamantes, Maria S. 2004. 'The Cultural Politics of Performance: Women, Dance Ritual, and the Transnational Tourism Industry in Bali.' PhD diss., University of California, Riverside.

Tarplee, Susan. 2008. 'After the Bomb in a Balinese Village.' In *Tourism at the Grassroots: Villagers and Visitors in the Asia-Pacific*, edited by John Connell and Barbara Rugendyke, 148–63. London: Routledge.

Tenzer, Michael. 1991/1998. *Balinese Music*. Singapore: Periplus Editions.

Tenzer, Michael. 2000. *Gamelan Gong Kebyar: The Art of Twentieth-Century Balinese Music*. Chicago: Chicago University Press.

Turner, Victor. 1967. *The Forest of Symbols: Aspects of Ndembu Ritual*. Ithaca, NY: Cornell University Press.

Urry, John. 1990. *The Tourist Gaze: Leisure and Travel in Contemporary Societies*. London: Sage.

Vickers, Adrian. 1989. *Bali: A Paradise Created*. Ringwood, Victoria: Penguin Books.

Vickers, Adrian, ed. 1994. *Travelling to Bali: Four Hundred Years of Journeys*. Oxford: Oxford University Press.

Wall, Geoffrey. 1996. 'Perspectives on Tourism in Selected Balinese Villages.' *Annals of Tourism* 23(1):123–37.

Wall, Geoffrey, and Veronica Long. 1996. 'Balinese Homestays: An Indigenous Response to Tourism Opportunities.' In *Tourism and Indigenous Peoples*, edited by Richard Butler and Tom Hinch, 27–48. London: International Thomson Business Press.

Warren, Carol. 1995. *Adat and Dinas: Balinese Communities in the Indonesian State*. Oxford: Oxford University Press.

Xie, Philip F. 2003. 'The Bamboo-Beating Dance in Hainan, China: Authenticity and Commodification.' *Journal of Sustainable Tourism* 11(1):5–16.

Yamashita, Shinji. 2003. *Bali and Beyond: Explorations in the Anthropology of Tourism*. Translated by Jeremy S. Eades. Oxford: Berghahn.

3 The Staged Desert
Tourist and Nomad Encounters at the Festival au Désert

Marta Amico

Traveling to Mali, Algeria, Libya, Morocco, Niger, and Mauritania in the Sahara desert is often described as a form of 'cultural tourism'. Standing in sharp contrast to 'mass tourism', cultural tourism benefits local economies, enhances cultural sites, is respectful of local inhabitants, and thereby promotes ethical behavior on the part of visitors (Cousin 2006). Its concept suggests 'travelling to discover the culture of indigenous peoples' (Chabloz and Raout 2009, 9).[1] In regard to the Sahara desert, cultural tourism is built around the mythical image of its inhabitants, the Tuaregs, an image that first emerged during 19th-century European explorations.[2] This image was—over the past two decades—maintained by both international institutions, such as UNESCO,[3] and national ones, such as ministries and state founded corporations. The Malian government has invested in cultural tourism since the end of the 1990s when the Minister of Culture and Tourism, Aminata Traoré, launched tourism as a national economic activity (Doquet 2007, 2009). Within the framework of these policies, a festival was organized in the Malian Sahara in 2001, named the Festival au Désert, which is devoted to create a stage for a particular blend of 'desert sounds' and has attracted large numbers of cultural tourists from abroad. This chapter, while drawing on ethnographic research conducted in 2008 and 2009 in Timbuktu and its neighboring desert,[4] focuses on the staging of tourist encounters with the desert through music during the Festival au Désert. Drawing on participant observation and a series of 20 formal and informal interviews completed during the ninth festival (from January 8 to January 10, 2009), I will describe the festival through the categories of 'tourists' and 'nomadic people' and develop some reflective thoughts on my own position as ethnographer as opposed to tourist in the context of the festival. Overall, I seek to illustrate how the Festival au Désert is a means for staging 'the desert' and constructing notions of 'nomadic tradition' disseminated via cultural tourism.

FESTIVAL BACKGROUND AND CONTEXT

The Festival au Désert has been held annually since 2001 in the Malian Sahara desert. According to its organizers, who belong to the Tuareg tribe of the Kel Ansar, its goal is to build a stage for Tuareg music and culture in their homeland and to open their music and culture to the rest of the world. On the festival website, the origins of the festival are associated with the 'longstanding Tuareg tradition of coming together for annual meetings, which are called *Takoubelt* in the Kidal region and *Temakannit* in the Timbuktu region' (Festival au Désert 2009). According to the French manager, Philippe Brix, this 'tradition' was turned into a festival in the late 1990s thanks to the encounter in Bamako, the Malian capital, between some members of the Tuareg band Tinariwen, from the region of Kidal in Northern Mali, and the band Lo'Jo from Angers, in Western France. It was specifically Lo'Jo's manager, Brix, who sought to bring Tinariwen to the global music market and to create an international music festival in the musicians' homeland, which had never existed in Mali or in the Sahara before (Brix 2005). Originally held in the Kidal region some 1,600km from Bamako, the festival was moved in 2003 to the area of Essakane, a village in the Timbuktu region in the territory that the Kel Ansar tribe recognizes as its homeland. For the festival organizers, this cultural project represented an extraordinary means to bring investment into their territory and to create new bridges with the Malian authorities, who in turn have been taking advantage of the growing international reputation of the festival in publicizing an image of the country's beauty alongside the idea of the successful reconciliation with the Tuareg minority. Attended by foreign tourists, local inhabitants, and supported by Malian authorities, the event plays an important role, both for promoting local cultural expressions all over the world and for attracting foreign tourists to Mali. During my fieldwork, for instance, local participants numbered around 10,000 people according to the festival organizers. Those participants had free access to the festival site. Non-African participants numbered around 1,000 people, who included journalists, volunteers, musicians, and festivalgoers. For the latter, the entrance fee was about 150 euros, plus costs related to the trip, lodging, and food.[5] Even so, according to the festival organizers, the number of foreign attendees was starting to drop because of increasing political tension in the Sahara and the Sahel, and the kidnapping of some Westerners in Mali, Mauritania, Niger, and Algeria. A brief historical perspective may help to understand this delicate context: During the 1950s and 1960s, Tuareg territory was freed from French colonial domination and split into five national states, namely, Mali, Niger, Algeria, Burkina Faso, and Libya, all of which instigated different policies concerning the integration of its new inhabitants, some more successful than others. In northern Mali, for instance, Tuareg movements launched four armed rebellions against the state (in 1963, 1990, 2006, and 2012), claiming the loss of land and, with it, their nomadic way of life; the lack of infrastructure and development programs; the lack of representation at a national level; and, more recently, the invasion of drug traffickers, smugglers, Islamic terrorists, and the pressing of corporations who compete for the control of desert resources. In such a complex sociopolitical context, promoting tourism and other economic activities through local cultural heritage transforms the festival into an important national and global symbol to raise recognition and investment in the cultural expressions of the Timbuktu area.

CAMELS AND CAMERAS: THE ENCOUNTER OF/BETWEEN NOMADS AND TOURISTS

'Here is the tourist!' exclaims a young man, whose glancing eyes pierce me through his veil. He immediately invites me to sit on a carpet next to a tent with his sisters and cousins. In the stunning desert sun, they talk and listen to the melodies that sound from farther away, probably an improvised jam session in a tent. They explain to me in good French that they are from the Timbuktu region, and that they joined the festival to meet their friends and family, listen to music, and see the world travelers who come from far away to visit their people. Hama, a child about 9 years old and proudly dressed with a small bow tie, invites me to drink strong, dense tea that is to become the quintessential taste during my fieldwork in Tuareg lands. The tea awakens my senses, weakened by the four-day journey on the river Niger and three-hour drive through the desert in a four-wheel drive car. No sign marked the passage from Niger water to Sahara sand, but it seems I crossed a border and plunged into a new world. On this particular morning, there is strong wind in the Sahara dunes, and the dust grains crunch in my mouth while I drink tea with my new friends. The conversation leaves little time to catch my breath. 'I am not a tourist. I am a researcher,' I resolve any ambiguity. 'Mmmmh, researcher . . . a journalist?' says a man dressed in traditional dress, sunglasses, and baseball hat. 'Well, I also write as a journalist, but research is another job . . . and I play the violin.' 'Ah, then you are a musician!' Another man wearing a turban looks at me with mistrust while he prepares the second cup of tea. He does not care about his relatives' search for answers. He instead wants to sell his 'desert business' to the white girl in front of him. 'And you, what do you do?' I ask him, making out a smile behind meters of cloth. He turns around to me and says: 'My name is Abdallah. I am a camel guide. Look at my document. I wait for the festival and then I take tourists for a ride.' Then he proudly shows me a piece of paper that says in French and English: 'camel guide.' The second cup of tea is less strong than the first one, but I begin to feel nervous. Locals are very friendly with tourists, but I have the impression that they present themselves and behave according to a common canvas, while I need to provoke some more spontaneous kinds of communication in order to gather some good material for my research. For this reason, I feel uncomfortable being seen as a tourist. But how can I explain my presence here, lying on a carpet in the desert sand with a Tuareg family, while participating at a festival that is at the heart of the tourist season? 'That's interesting. And how about when the festival is over? What do you do the rest of the year? Are you a nomad?' I question Abdallah, while listening to the pouring sound of Hama filling a third cup of tea. 'Tuaregs are nomads, so I am a nomad. But now I live in Timbuktu with my family. And there I wait. I wait for the festival, I wait for the world to come, I wait for the tourists,' says Abdallah, already choosing a good camel to take me on a ride.

Abdallah regards himself a nomad, but he actually lives a sedentary life in Timbuktu, where he takes advantage of his traditional craft to take tourists on camel rides. Despite my professional reasons to be in Timbuktu, I have to accept that I am his business target today, a victim of the misunderstanding caused by differing perceptions and expectations of each other. Nevertheless, I use these ambiguities to establish a common ground for communication, which resonates with Sahlins's (1981) notion of 'productive misunderstanding' to describe the paradox that emerges during tourist encounters with local populations (Chabloz 2007). Accordingly, my informants and I are involved in a game of productive misunderstandings that help us better to understand each other's worlds. Our persisting desire for communication is essential here for establishing a common objective and agreement between us. Here, 'cultural tourism' becomes the starting point for my experience as a researcher in a dialectical exploration of different views of identity and Otherness. My fieldwork begins by questioning the role of the ones identified as 'tourists' in the festival encounter, and their relation to the ones identified as 'nomads'. In doing so, I follow Jean-Didier Urbain's (2002, 2012) calls for tourism research that not only focuses on the market side, but also on an 'anthropology of tourists', that takes into account the traveler as a person with his own desires, values, and dreams. This perspective on tourists may help to understand the complex social interplay that manages one of the most exemplar experiences of Otherness of the current time.

Festival publicity makes a clear separation between festival attendees, who are identified as 'nomads' or 'tourists'. On the one hand, nomads participate in the festival because of their 'desire to open the doors to the outside world, while still preserving the cultures and traditions of the desert . . . being listened to and then recognized', while tourists are said to seek 'a way to discover the desert through its inhabitants' values of hospitality and tolerance' (Festival au Désert 2009). This perspective seems to correspond with the way in which people identify each other during the festival. The tension between preservation and discovery—of saving desert cultures and traditions and exploring them—is a powerful means for staging identity, which transforms the festival into a social space where people define themselves in a game of reciprocal gazes. Many tourists, with whom I spoke, said that they are in the desert mainly to encounter the nomads, listen to their music, and experience their way of life. They mainly come from Europe, the US, Canada, and Australia, and they travel in groups to stay for one to two weeks, organized by international tourism agencies with connections to local tourist guides. Either by their own intentions or suggested by the people guiding their trip, Western tourists always hope to meet the local people and discover their environment. The festival represents to many a special journey through 'an authentic country', as is proclaimed in a slogan by the national tourism office Office Malien du Tourisme et de l'Hotellerie (OMATHO).

In her studies on cultural tourism in Mali, the French anthropologist Anne Doquet (2007, 2009) talks about authenticity as it is employed by the tourism industry in Mali, indicating festivals as privileged platforms to create national imageries of local cultures and spread them worldwide. For Doquet, 'the festivals are dialogic enterprises where the current cultural authenticity builds itself at the crossroads between endogenous and exogenous visions of traditions' (2009, 84). The nationally built imagery of the authenticity of Malian cultures is crucial for creating a so-called desert desire that determines touristic travel and displacement to the festival. The global promotion of the desert is especially enabled by a dozen of Tuareg bands who now circulate within the global musical network, labeled as 'Tuareg music'. During the second morning at the festival, I meet Antoine, a French guy around 30 years old visiting Mali with his girlfriend. The two French are enjoying an improvised performance by five Tuareg musicians, who are singing and playing the guitar inside their tent. Antoine tells me that this is not the first time he has listened to Tuareg music, but now he particularly appreciates being at the source of it. Then he explains that he made his first encounter with the desert in Paris, during a concert by the Tuareg group Tinariwen:

> It is the first time that I come to Mali and to the festival. This trip is linked to my encounter with the desert. I made this encounter at a Tinariwen concert two years ago in France and that gave me the wish to travel back to the source. (Antoine, interview, Essakane, January 9, 2009)

The notion of 'encounter' plays a central role here. This spectator becomes a tourist by following his desire to pursue the cross-cultural experiences at home with a journey to the musicians' land. The role of tourism for appropriating Otherness calls for Arjun Appadurai's notion of 'ethnoscape' (1996), indicating a fluid landscape of people in transit, which, in this case, relates to the mobilization of people who cultivate a certain desert imagery. During the festival, this imagery spreads globally through the way the music industry constructs an experience defined by tourists as the total immersion into the desert environment.

The experience of 'authenticity' offered by the festival starts with the journey to the festival location near Timbuktu, which is typically divided into two steps: The first one takes place by car, bus, or boat and usually starts from the capital Bamako some 900km from Timbuktu. The second one requires four-wheel drive cars to travel to the festival location near Essakane village, which is about 70km across the desert. This long journey is often defined by tourists as an adventure or 'expedition' that allows them to gradually leave what they perceive as the 'civilized' world to encounter a world of nomads, sand, and emptiness. Indeed, the journey to the festival does not precede the festival experience, but is an important part of it, a sort of modern 'rite of passage' (van Gennep 1960), where the separation from home is succeeded by a transition between states of being, culminating in the acquisition of a new kind of identity. Once on the festival site, the rite of passage is often completed with the purchase of a turban, seen by tourists as a way to experience a form of 'nomad Otherness'. Called *tagelmust* in Tamasheck, the Tuareg language, the turban is traditionally an exclusively male attire, representing dignity and respect in addition to providing protection from the wind. In the context of the festival, however, the turban becomes a unisex symbol of Otherness. The fact that tourists wear a turban can be seen as an attempt to surpass their simple observer stance toward Tuareg culture, of being passive consumers of Tuareg traditions, by assimilating and incorporating a symbol of 'nomadic culture' into their own (Boulay 2009; Cauvin Verner 2007).

Nevertheless, the festival's 'nomadic culture' is itself the outcome of negotiating and managing the tourist encounter. Dressed in their turbans, tourists are immersed in the festival's role of constructing 'nomadic culture' during the first afternoon when they are invited to a 'camel race', where the nomads cross the dunes on their camels. This celebration is often described in somewhat epic ways, as in a filmed report by Rosie Swash for the Internet site of the *Guardian*, which depicts images of camel herds in the desert sands on their way to the festival scene:

> This is the Tuaregs arriving at the festival which means the open-ing ceremony is going to kick off. Probably about half an hour [into the race], probably I'd say an estimate of about 250 of them arrive *en masse* for the moment. [Roar] That's the sound of a camel. The Festival in the Desert has been running from eight years now and is truly one of the most remote spots to get to. Determined tourists and the nomadic Tuareg people gather here every year to have an amazing showcase of Malian music from desert blues to traditional griot songs. (Swash 2008)

In this quote, journalist Rosie Swash indicates the musicultural experience to be the common objective for tourists. She defines the festival's showcase through the genre of 'Malian music', presented here as a blend of differ-ent sounds, from 'desert blues', a music made by turban-wearing Tuareg guitar players, to 'traditional griot songs', which refer to some regional repertoires now celebrated as cultural heritage. Similarly, the main iden-tity markers describing the desert in the reports of international journalists include white sable dunes, camels, and turbaned nomads with their musical traditions, as in this BBC reportage:

> The Festival of the Desert—held in Mali amongst the dunes of the Sahara—brings to mind images of indigo-clad Tuaregs, camel caravans and the musical tradition of desert nomads. (Jones 2010)

The local authorities use the same images to promote the beauty of their natural and cultural heritage, and to explain the international appeal of the festival. During an interview, Alpha Charfi, the Timbuktu regional director of the OMATHO, a national institution created in 1995 to realize the government policy for tourism, tells me that what makes the festival unique is the relationship with the desert:

> People do not come to the festival for music but for music in the desert; it is this that interests them. It is the relationship with the desert, because the desert, it fascinates us. I think that it is the desert that attracts people from all over the world, with the way of life of people that are called the blue people of the desert. (Alpha Charfi, OMATHO regional director Timbuktu, interview, Timbuktu, January 2009)

The scenery, which is pivotal for the festival attendees, is carefully prepared by the festival organizers, most of whom are Tuaregs from the Timbuktu region who live in Timbuktu or Bamako. 'We lay out everything on the site to make it just like it is in our camps. That is the secret of the festival, to transform tourists into nomads,' explains Mohamed, one of the festival organizers, while accompanying me on a general visit to the festival site. Then he adds:

> If we wanted to continue to do our traditional gatherings for us, we wouldn't need to organize them as we do now. Tuaregs do not need scenes, sound engineers, lights, plastic water bottles, toilettes, Internet sites, fixed dates, publicity panels; we do not need all that to gather and make music. But when we started to open to the others, when we decided to present our culture and to make a festival, we started to think about all that because we wanted to welcome people from abroad and to make them comfortable in our land. This is the reason why we try every year to adapt our desert to their lifestyle. (Mohamed, interview, Timbuktu, January 2009)

Accommodation for foreigners is provided in Tuareg tents across the festival site; there are also tents serving as restaurants, craft and textile markets, and bars. These amenities make the site comfortable to foreigners, while locals can freely set up their tents, make tea, prepare the traditional mutton dish to celebrate their gathering, discuss, sell their products, or look for new social and economic encounters. While nomads 'play' the nomad role by dressing and acting as in their home camps, for three days tourists can experience Otherness in the form of 'desert life'. The success of this experience depends on the creation of a common stage for different cultural worlds that dramatize the tourist desire for Otherness (see Figure 3.1).

Figure 3.1   Attendees of the Festival au Désert in 2009 (photograph by author).

Even if festival organizers take great care in preparing the site for tourists, the conditions are often described by international guests as extreme because of the changes between hot daytime sun and cold nights, the rationing of water and electricity, and the reduction of meal sizes to a rice bowl. But in this scenery, the roughness of the desert environment becomes yet another exciting ingredient that enhances the authenticity of the adventure. BBC journalist Caroline Jones describes this as follows:

> It is very fine sand and it gets everywhere. My digital camera has taken on a worrying new grinding sound and has become reluctant to retract the lens when directed. A mouthful of rice crunches with each chew and it has even appeared in my underwear, but hey! What were you expecting? It's the festival of the *desert*! (Jones 2010)

As an engine of difference in the desert, the bulk of the festival's showcase is reserved to its three afternoons and nights, which is dedicated to a long, rich, and entirely musical program. Here, the encounter between nomads and tourists is mirrored on stage by a blend of bands and musical styles.

NOMAD MUSIC TURNING GLOBAL:
THE STAGING OF MUSICAL DIFFERENCE

While the camel race and the opening ceremony dominate the first festival afternoon, the second and third ones are spent at the so-called traditional stage, also referred to as 'little stage' or 'dune stage' (Figure 3.2). This is a mobile stage, especially dedicated to performances by bands from the Timbuktu region, who are often unknown beyond the desert. It is set out on a sand square and surrounded by carpets and sometimes a big tent, equipped by sound technologies and lit by natural sunlight. When I attended this stage one afternoon during my fieldwork, the desert was still very hot, but some musicians were already playing under the sun. I asked some people for the band name, but they did not share my interest in search for bands' identities. In fact, I found that people tended to wander on and off the stage, some dancing, others joining the band to sing some verses, and finally jumping off the stage. Because of the flexible nature of this performance, my notion of 'band' probably needs a revision here, as this performance seems to be more a gathering and sharing than an imitation of a conventional concert, where the stage clearly separates the musicians from the audience. Here, instead, the audience sits on a sand dune facing the performers, reflecting

Figure 3.2   The 'traditional stage' at the Festival au Désert 2009, here showing a group of Tuareg women (photograph by author).

a colorful mix of different dresses, languages, and reactions to the music. But despite this diversity, the audience seems to be completely captivated, and during the last song everybody rises to dance. The festival achieves one of its climaxes, as the fusion between 'nomads' and 'tourists' is realized thanks to the symbolic power of musical staging for creating new forms of social cohesion and cultural exchange. However, after half an hour of sheer cultural harmony, one of the festival organizers, who seemingly acts as stage manager, announces to the performers that time is over and the schedule has to continue with another band. While this is a reminder of the necessary timekeeping of any ordinary festival, here it takes on a new meaning, revealing the compromise between formal concert and informal gathering that lies behind the scene of this special musical showcase.

Meanwhile, from sunset until late at night, the 'modern stage' or 'big stage' lights up (see Figure 3.3). Its structure is similar to the one that is typical for a contemporary festival stage: It is raised from the ground, faces the audience directly, is equipped by sound and light technologies, and managed by the stage manager and technicians. The majority of bands that play on this stage are known in Mali, and some are certainly known internationally. They come especially from the Sahel and the Sahara (e.g., Tartit, Tinariwen, Terakaft, Etran Finatawa, Bombino, Vieux Farka Toure, and Samba Toure) and from southern Mali (e.g., Bassekou Kouyate, Salif Keita, Cheick Tidiane,

Figure 3.3 The 'modern stage' at the Festival au Désert 2009 (photograph by author).

and Oumou Sangare). Only a few, including some superstars, such as Robert Plant and Manu Chao, come from other parts of the world and spread the festival fame worldwide. Here, the organization is radically different from the traditional stage. The separation between musicians and audience is clearer, the volume is much louder, and the performances seem to be more organized and in line with a concert format. The image of the nomadic camp is replaced by an eclectic showcase that confirms that the Festival au Désert belongs to a global network of cultural events.

The partition between the two stages can be interpreted as a way to model the festival encounter. On the 'traditional stage', local bands show the beauty and richness of regional cultural expressions to an audience that came from abroad to discover them. On the 'modern stage', the sounds are presented as 'different' through the presentation of different types of bands from Mali, Africa, and overseas. When seen together, the staging of local and global music, mixed in the same program, creates an original blend. Seen from this perspective, the staging of music at the festival represents two festival missions embodied by the nomads and tourists, namely, of preserving the self and of discovering the other. For local bands, playing onstage is a way to legitimate their cultural and musical practices, which reinforces their status of keepers of desert traditions and inserts them into new global networks. In turn, for international performers, a concert in the desert is an exceptional experience to connect with 'roots' and refresh the music through their encounter with different sounds. For festival attendees, no matter what role they play, listening to the music creates a space for encounter. This means that the 'play' of nomads and tourists reaches its climax through this particular staging of music, which gives a special feel to the festival experience as a whole. Cultural differences are finally overcome, an 'imagined community' (Anderson 1983), which lasts for the duration of the festival.

Beyond the two stages, the festival also offers spaces for informal encounters and musical exchange between musicians. The exchange between local and international bands is particularly encouraged by the festival organizers, as all musicians are lodged in the same camp and usually end up meeting and jamming outside their tents. It is usually the less well-known artists that promote themselves and their music in this way, while the more famous bands are showcased more formally. Some bands that have turned internationally, such as Etran Finatawa from Niger and Tamikrest from Mali, were equally launched after their initial appearance on the festival stage. In other words, the festival functions as a wider support network for artists and musicians in search for commercial success. For instance, the booklet of the album *BKO* by the Australian-American band Dirtmusic expresses the feeling of Western musicians discovering the 'desert sound':

> The Festival au Desert spreads out across the dunes in a labyrinth of white tents, the distant stage scaffolding silhouetted against a cobalt-blue

saharan sky. Dirtmusic are billeted facing the digs of a young touareg band called Tamikrest. Chris Brokaw grabs the dobro and wanders over to play cross-legged in the sand—kicking off a jam session that will continue for the next three days and gift all concerned with an amazing cross-cultural journey through the common language of sound, rhythm and rock and roll. (Dirtmusic 2010)

In the perspective of this band, the festival experience is cross-cultural because it enabled the encounter with a local Tuareg band. This encounter with the 'local' also turns it 'global' as the band members helped launch Tamikrest in the international market. Indeed, this process of molding global pressures into specific practices becomes an engine for 'producing locality in new, globalized ways' (Appadurai 1996, 22). It is precisely the engagement of the Tuaregs in the production and spreading of their local identity that gives them a new visibility in the global network. On the contrary, to reach local cultures requires the adoption of global practices, such as the one of cultural tourism.

The complex interplay between international and local musicians mirrors the encounter with global tourists. Here, my perceived double role as tourist and researcher in the eyes of my informants is a means to participate in the role play that goes on during the festival. For instance, one afternoon at the 'traditional stage' some tourists join me to tell me their emotions and enthusiasm. They are especially charmed by the sound of the *tehardent*, a lute with three strings played by Tuareg griots, by the slow movement of the dancers, and by the spontaneity of the interplay between the musicians and audience. For them, the performance is without any doubt an expression of the 'pure' nomadic tradition. Their perceptions of 'pureness' seems to be conditioned by comparisons to the big stage, where the music seemed to them 'more common'. Thus, the partition between two spaces of musical encounter shapes tourists' understanding of a 'traditional' performance, and to see it in a different frame than on the big stage. This gives value to a nomad world represented as alternative to the 'modern' one, but stimulates also the harmonization of two worlds into one 'whole' musical and human ensemble.

Once the concert was over, I went behind the stage and interviewed one of the musicians, a young man about 30 years old, elegantly dressed with a white dress and a turban adorned with colored leather and a silver crown. The man tells me that he comes from the desert around Timbuktu, and his band is composed of his family and has existed for a long time, since well before he was born. The band used to play for celebrations like weddings or baptisms, but since the birth of the festival nine years ago, they also learned to stage music for a foreign audience. To him, the festival not only transformed them into a well-known band that presents Tuareg land and culture on stage; it also transformed its musicians into cultural ambassadors. He tells me that he conceived this role as an effort to 'create tradition on stage and open it to a wider audience.' This idea calls to mind Eric Hobsbawm's (1983) concept of 'inventing traditions', where the return to the past is intended as a means to affirm contemporary identities. In this process of 'retro-projection' (Pouillon 1975), the past legitimizes the present and validates a contemporary movement where Tuaregs engage directly in the management of their territory, and in the staging of their local culture.

Here, the use of tourist clichés by locals does not lead to a form of 'folklorization', but rather to a validation and legitimization of particular cultural values. Through the staging of musical tradition and encounter, the Festival au Désert defends the ideal of a nomadic identity harmoniously connected to the outside world and enchased as a source of authenticity and beauty. This gives sense to the tourist experience of the desert, while locals use it to negotiate new nomadic identities that engage them directly with their own cultural heritage. At last, the musician's response to tourist expectations brings me back to my first encounter of the festival, when a camel driver took me as a tourist while I was clearly stating I was a researcher. The misunderstanding is now on the side of the tourists with whom I spoke, who regard the music of a local band as 'nomadic tradition', while the musicians make efforts to 'fit the rules' of formally staging their music and showing a new identity that is turned toward the outside world. But this misunderstanding is also 'productive', as the musicians and the audience can both gain advantages by actively engaging in both the 'preservation' and 'discovery' of local traditions, which are the two major forces evoked by festival publicity, the cornerstones of the 'encounter' with the desert.

CONCLUDING REMARKS

This chapter sought to illustrate the staging of the desert through the lens of the annual Festival au Désert in Mali within the wider context of cultural tourism. In the first place, I described the festival experience as a game of reciprocal gazes between 'tourists' and 'nomads', two categories proposed by the festival official line and interpreted by the festival attendees during three days. In doing so I showed that even the ethnographer takes part in the tourist encounter, managing an ambiguous third role in addition to the dual shaping of the festival's showcase. Here, music and tourism are deeply intertwined in negotiations of nomadic culture and identity. The musical showcase on the traditional and modern stages frames the notion of 'difference' in a dialectical way. The mixing of different music styles and formats gives an exceptional power to the festival encounter, which conveys new ideals of a common world respectful of its diversity and able to use it to create some new forms of dialogue. All in all, the festival allows for new ways to identify with and experience a new brand of 'nomadic culture' that emerges from such issues as preservation and loss, tradition and modernity, difference and encounter, nomads and tourists. It produces a context in which participants—both tourists and nomads—may take advantage of the connections offered by the global movement of cultural tourism. Such an encounter raises hope toward the opening of new routes for showing local meanings being listened to and understood. Ultimately, the festival encounter is a way to support the nomads' claim of visibility by allowing the restoration of new identities connected with a global network.

NOTES

1. All quotations have been translated into English by the author.
2. The first European to describe the Tuareg people was the German Friederich Hornemann, who stayed in Tripoli until 1798, followed by another German Heinrich Barth in 1850 and a French national, Henry Duveyrier, during 1859–61 (Casajus 2000, 8). Lately, the desert has inspired a number of authors, such as Theodore Monod, André Gide, Antoine De Saint Exupery, and Roger Frison-Roche.
3. The UNESCO program 'The Sahara of Cultures and People', initiated in 2001, considers tourism as 'a real tool in sustainable development and struggle against poverty, in particular in the Sahara which is a desertic ecosystem, characterized by a rich cultural, human and natural wealth, and great fragility' (UNESCO 2001).
4. My fieldwork ended before the degradation of Malian political situation that caused the displacement of the festival 2010 edition from Essakane to Timbuktu for security reasons. This chapter will not consider the recent situation in Mali, and its consequences for music and festivals in the north of the country.
5. Apart from the income generated by ticket sales, the festival has been sustained by numerous national and international institutions (e.g., the Malian Government, UNESCO, Norwegian Embassy, European Union) as well as private organizations (e.g., Orange Foundation Mali, TV5 Monde, Africalia Belgium).

REFERENCES

Anderson, Benedict. 1983. *Imagined Communities: Reflections on the Origin and Spread of Nationalism*. London: Verso.

Appadurai, Arjun. 1996. *Modernity at Large: Cultural Dimensions of Globalisation*. Minneapolis: University of Minnesota Press.

Boulay, Sébastien. 2009. 'Culture Nomade versus Culture Savante. Naissance et Vicissitudes d'un Tourisme de Désert en Adrar Mauritanien.' *Cahiers d'Études Africaines* 193–194:95–119.

Brix, Philippe. 2005. *Le Festival au Désert. Journal de Tin Essako*. Angers: Triban Union.

Casajus, Dominique. 2000. *Gens de Parole. Langage, Poésie et Politique en Pays Touareg*. Paris: La Découverte.

Cauvin Verner, Corinne. 2007. *Au Désert. Une Anthropologie du Tourisme dans le Sud Marocain*. Paris: L'Harmattan.

Chabloz, Nadège, and Raout Julien. 2009. 'Corps et âmes. Conversions Touristiques à l'Africanité.' *Cahiers d'Etudes Africaines* 193–194:7–25.

Chabloz, Nadège. 2007. 'Le Malentendu. Les Rencontres Paradoxales du "Tourisme Solidaire."' *Les Actes de la Recherche en Sciences Sociales* 170:32–47.

Cousin, Saskia. 2006. 'De l'UNESCO aux Villages de Touraine: Les Enjeux Politiques, Institutionnels et Identitaires du Tourisme Culturel.' *Autrepart* 40:17–32.

Doquet, Anne. 2007. 'Festivals Touristiques et Expressions Identitaires au Mali.' *Africultures* 73:60–67.

Doquet, Anne. 2009. 'Guides, Guidons et Guitares. Authenticité et Guides Touristiques au Mali.' *Cahiers d'Etudes Africaines* 193–194:73–94.

Dirtmusic. 2010. *BKO*. Beverungen: Glitterhouse Records.

Festival au Désert. 2009. 'L'histoire.' Accessed February 19, 2009. http://www. festival-au-desert.org/index.cfm?m=0&s=2.

Hobsbawm, Eric. 1983. *The Invention of Tradition*. Cambridge: Cambridge University Press.

Jones, Caroline. 2010. 'The Festival of the Desert. A Diary.' *BBC World Service Africa*, January 9. Accessed March 18, 2010. http://www.bbc.co.uk/worldservice/africa/2010/01/100107_desert_festival_diary.shtml.

Pouillon, Jean. 1975. *Fétiches Sans Fétichisme*. Paris: Maspero.

Sahlins, Marshall. 1981. *Historical Metaphors and Mythical Realities: Structure in the Early History of the Sandwich Island Kingdom*. Ann Arbor: University of Michigan Press.

Swash, Rosie. 2008. 'Festival au Désert 2008.' *Guardian*, January 18. Accessed February 18, 2009. http://www.guardian.co.uk/news/video/2008/jan/17/desert2008.

UNESCO. 2001. *The Sahara of Cultures and Men*. Accessed February 19, 2009. http://portal.unesco.org/culture/en/ev.php-URL_ID=10403&URL_DO=DO_TOPIC&URL_SECTION=201.html.

Urbain, Jean-Didier. 2002. *L'Idiot du Voyage. Histoires de Touristes*. Paris: Payot.

Urbain, Jean-Didier. 2012. 'Pourquoi voyageons-nous?' *Sciences Humaines* 240. Accessed December 4, 2012. http://www.scienceshumaines.com/pourquoi-voyageons-nous_fr_29142.html.

van Gennep, Arnold. 1960. *The Rites of Passage*. Chicago: University of Chicago Press.

4 The Golden Fleece

Music and Cruise Ship Tourism

David Cashman and Philip Hayward

For the past 40 years, cruise ship tourism has offered and advertised an integrated leisure experience that provides a mobile 'comfort zone' for passengers as they move between ports of call on prescribed routes. This leisure experience has increasingly focused on the ship as the main destination rather than the actual ports, which have become secondary. Some cruise tourists never leave the ship, not even to make use of ship-sponsored tours. An important component of this integrated leisure product is live musical performance. Depending on the size of the ship, a large pool of musicians may be employed, offering more opportunities to experience live music than land-based tourism (Hertan 2010; Jones 2009; Zhongyan and Xiangxiu 2006). The cruise industry is among the most successful sectors in tourism, having recorded an 8 percent compound annual growth from 1970 projected to 2015 (Dickinson and Vladimir 2008; Wahlstrom 2012). As well as attracting patrons towards ship-based tourism, music actively promotes the generation of revenue aboard ships. While Jason, the hero of the third-century Greek epic poem *Argonautica*,[1] included Orpheus among the crew of adventurers seeking the Golden Fleece in the Mediterranean because he could charm 'unshiftable upland boulders and the flow of rivers with the sound of his music' (Book 1, Lines 23–34), music's role in the modern maritime 'golden fleece' is more about separating guests from their money, thereby ensuring the profitability of the ship.

While destinations and the overall package provide a key element in the design and marketing of cruise ship packages, cruise lines increasingly built expectations of the ship rather than the ports visited, making the ship the destination rather than the ports of call. Whereas ports and their leisure facilities operate independently of cruise ship companies, the ship is a bounded, monopolistic touristic environment. Former CEO of Carnival Cruise Lines Bob Dickinson and cowriter Andy Vladimir surveyed several recent cruise line advertising campaigns and concluded that the ones that were most effective were those that concentrated on the onboard experience (2008, 211–17). Since its early advertising campaigns in the 1970s, Carnival has advertised its fleet as the 'fun ships', while Norwegian Cruise Line advertises its 'Freestyle Cruising' product.

By focusing on the cruise ship as the primary destination, such vessels become a prime example of an 'experience economy' (Pine and Gilmore 1999, 2011), a concept that cites the experience as the most important aspect of a service interaction. The experience must be immersing and take people out of their everyday lives. Examples of the experience economy range from doll-making stores to Disneyland, where people pay for time spent absorbing the experience rather than paying for services provided by a vendor. Cruise ships, though only mentioned briefly by Pine and Gilmore (2011, 4), provide such a quintessential experience. A cruise ship is an experiential cocoon that takes guests to foreign cultures, but it also provides a safe haven to return to, populated and designed with familiar signifiers of Western culture, such as musical performances and predictable cuisine. Even when the guest leaves the safety of the ship, this occurs on ship-sponsored tours, essentially extensions of the cocoon of the ship.

As noted in Figure 4.1, there are three streams of revenue on cruise ships:

1. The 'entrance fee' (or ticket price), which grants access to the essentials of the cruise vacation
2. The onboard 'tipping' system, which allows cruise companies to pay staff while maintaining seemingly low fares[2]
3. The purchase of 'experience enhancements' (that produce onboard revenue)

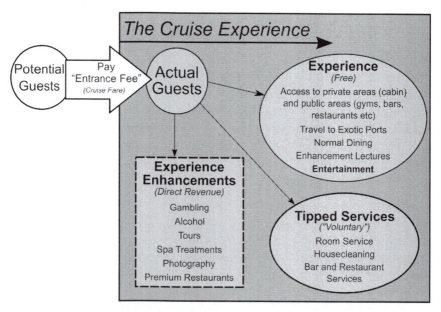

Figure 4.1 A model of a cruise ship 'experience,' by the authors.

When customers buy a cruise ticket, it secures them access to public spaces (dining rooms, gyms, entertainment venues, lido deck, etc.) and the private space of their cabins. Also included in this fee is travel to exotic ports and, significantly, entertainment. A ticket price of $70 per day (common in the 'contemporary' cruise sector) (Cashman 2012) is far cheaper than accommodation on comparable land-based holidays but only suffices to cover the running costs of the ship. The profit of this enormously lucrative business is generated from onboard revenue (Becker 2006, 17; Vogel 2011), a stream of income from 'experience enhancements' that derive from separately charged items such as gambling, drinking, dining in specialty restaurants, shopping, Internet access, and telephone usage.[3]

The consumption of musical performance is a key part of the cruise experience and incurs no additional costs. However, music exists on board cruise ships to encourage consumption rather than to be consumed. For example, music occurs in bars and the disco, as drinks are served there, but rarely in the restaurants of cruise ships. From a cruise line perspective, there is no reason to provide such performances, as they do not directly attract revenue. Dining is also part of the experience of taking a cruise, and a passenger sitting in a restaurant enjoying a performance does not generate additional revenue apart from purchase of wine.[4] Cruise lines would rather guests were out in the bars consuming alcohol or gambling while being entertained by music. Cruise lines design the consumption of experience enhancements into the core of the cruise ship tourism product. It is, for example, technically possible to undertake a cruise and refrain from alcohol consumption, day tours, and gambling, but cruise ships are organized so that, in practice, this rarely occurs. In a bar, while listening to the cocktail pianist, a drinks waiter quickly appears and offers to take an order, and while lying in the sun on sea days, bartenders in colorful outfits tout the 'drink of the day' in souvenir plastic glasses.

This chapter draws on an extended period of participant observation research undertaken by coauthor Cashman, who was employed as a cruise ship musician on contract with eight ships between 2004 and 2007, playing piano in solo and ensemble contexts. Such employment allowed for considerable observation of and socialization and familiarization with fellow performers, other crew members, and passengers. Between 2011 and 2012, a further ethnographic study of cruise ship music was undertaken, which garnered data from 105 participants, including musicians and other staff. In 2012, a further study analyzed 1,601 performances on 91 cruise days aboard 30 ships in order to study performances by genre and by cruise sector. Based on this extensive research, and subsequent analysis by the coauthors, the chapter will discuss the institutional logic, organization, and delivery of music on cruise ships.

MUSICAL PERFORMANCES ON CRUISE SHIPS: IMPORT AND INTERACTIVITY

Musical performances on cruise ships are of various types and include various levels of performer–audience interaction. These vary from the provision of background music to attention-grabbing and/or interactive performance,[5] depending on the purpose of the venue and the time of performance. Musical performances occur all over the cruise ship from late morning until the early morning the next day. When scheduling a cruise ship performance, there are two aspects that must be considered. People attend shipboard musical performances either to watch and be immersed in the musical performance or to relax and talk in a congenial environment. Thus, in some performances, music is of primary importance, such as theatrical performances in the main theater or dance venues. Guests attend specifically to listen to the music and see the performances. In others, music has a secondary role, such as in a cocktail lounge or on the lido deck, where guests attend for different reasons (in these cases, respectively to drink, and to sunbathe and swim), and the music forms a background ambiance. Musicians refer to these performances as 'musical wallpaper'. Bass player Steven Riddle says:

> [In these performances] I'm slightly toning it down. I'm not playing as I would do in the jazz trio because it's not a jazz gig. You can't sort of let rip and do anything like wild or you know. You've got to keep it respectable and polite . . . If you're playing in a jazz venue at home on land, people are coming to hear jazz, whereas when you've booked on a passenger on a cruise ship, you've not booked to go hear jazz unless it's a jazz cruise, you're doing a lot of things, it's incidental. (Riddle, interview, London, October 17, 2011)

A second consideration in cruise ship performances concerns the level of interactivity between audience and musicians. In some performances, guests may desire to immerse themselves in the music (for example, in a highly interactive rock performance in a lounge, or in a sing-along piano bar); in others, musicians perform with physical and psychological barriers to interactivity between them and guests (for example, in the main theater). Considerations of primary/secondary impact and high/low interactivity are integral to every cruise ship performance and, increasingly, cruise lines are insisting on more interactivity. Brian Gilliland, the music specialist for Princess Cruises who books and manages shipboard music, explains:

> Our goal is not just to have a band on a stage; our goal with everything that we're doing right now is to bring in bands that, though they satisfy a pretty common desire amongst the majority of our passengers . . . bring something compelling to the bandstand . . . it's a combination

of the quality of the music they play, their sound, but personality on the stage. Their look is important . . . you know, that's just part and parcel to being on stage in front of an audience, whether it's movies or television or theater or stage, any stage anywhere . . . Whatever we do, we try to vet it as being deliverable and being impactful in some way and that's an intangible, that's kind of hard to put your finger on it, it varies with different groups and with different personalities of bands. (Gilliland, telephone interview, December 1, 2011)

Even within the range of modes described above, cruise ship musical performance is changing as the relationship between audience and performers is increasingly being built into the structure of venues. These changes are occurring in response to developments in consumption of touristic music and the rise of the portable MP3 device as a self-programmed tourist amenity. Tourists are no longer satisfied with merely having an accurate representation of a song they can hear on their MP3 players. As a result, musical performance on cruise ships seeks to emphasize the pleasure of participating in the live experience of music by engaging the audience, and the cruise industry is actively looking to increase the interactivity of performance. In a recent interview, John Smith,[6] a highly experienced cruise director (the shipboard officer in charge of the entertainment department), described a funk band that illustrated the advantage of this approach:

[In their performances, the band] just came out and danced with everyone; they just . . . completely broke the fourth wall. When they played their sax they were walking through the crowds . . . it was like a rock concert. . . . I think they could have been playing classical music and they still would have had that crowd because whatever they give is them, their personalities. (Smith, interview, London, October 17, 2011)

This particular band always played to large crowds. Their performances consequently resulted in very high bar takings. The cruise director contrasted them with the more usual band, which 'played exactly the right music stylistically . . . a little bit of Elvis, a little bit of Beatles. Did they have people waiting in their lounge? No. Were people buying drinks? No.'

Aboard expensive lines, such as Crystal Cruise Line and Regent Seven Seas, music is less interactive than in larger and less expensive fleets, such as Carnival and Royal Caribbean, because of cruise line perceptions of the demographics of their particular market. Often the performance space is designed with these criteria in mind. The main theater, for example, is a large space where patrons sit facing the performers. The stage is often high and sometimes has a pit. Performances here are naturally going to focus on the music, but there are physical and psychological barriers to interactive performance. The sing-along piano bar, by contrast, places the piano in the center of the room. Patrons sit at a specially designed bar encircling the piano. Like the theater, the focus is on the performer, but the audience is physically much closer to the performer, encouraging interaction and the taking of requests. Other bars that feature musical performance may have a stage, but the musical emphasis is on creating an ambiance. The Golden Lion Pub on Cunard's RMS Queen Mary 2, for example, is the location for the jazz piano trio. However, the bar is in a T-shape with the band not visible from the entire venue. People can choose to sit in the middle and watch the band, or go to one of the ends of the crossbeam, chatting and drinking and enjoying the ambience.

MUSICAL PERFORMANCES ON A TYPICAL SEA DAY

While the focus of this chapter (and book) is on music, it is worth emphasizing that one of the important tenets of Pine and Gilmore's experience economy is that *all* senses must be stimulated in an experience. On board a cruise ship, for instance, food may tempt the taste buds and olfactory senses, while a luxurious massage stimulates one's sense of touch, and the luxurious surroundings and beauty of the ocean setting are pleasing to the eyes. Musical performance, however, is the primary method that cruise ships use to create an aurally stimulating environment. Music creates a congenial ambiance that encourages guests to visit and stay in certain places. This is often a location associated with the consumption of experience enhancements. Even more, the sounds of music travel a reasonable distance and can pique guests' interest, drawing them to these locations. Cruise lines use the ability of music to attract and create a congenial ambiance to guide guests to locations of high consumption. The following section provides a descriptive overview of typical performance contexts and practices.

There are many performance locations on a cruise ship delineated by only a grand piano, or a musicians' area where a drum kit, amplifiers, and a keyboard are temporarily set up. Some of these areas, if skillfully implemented, can generate large amounts of revenue, part of which involves appropriate use of musicians. Cade Kupiec, a drummer, contrasts the effect of locations where music is of primary importance with that where music is deemed to be secondary:

> Generally in the show band I was fortunate that most of those gigs were [in] the theater, which was the larger of the two venues to play in . . . Usually after there would be a smaller lounge where they'd have a smaller act play . . . and maybe they'd use a guest entertainer because they knew it wasn't going to get the same draw on the backgrounds . . . Occasionally we do a deck set but this could be demoralizing as guests ignored the band. (Kupiec, interview, New York, October 11, 2011)

Time as well as space affects cruise ship music. There are four types of day on a cruise: the sea day; the port day, when the ship departs the port at around 5:00 p.m.; the embarkation day, the first day of the cruise; and the rare overnight stay in a port. Most musical performances occur on a sea day with around 33 hours of live music per day. It makes sense for cruise ships to invest in the sea day: Guests do not get up early and instead spend the day relaxing around the ship. Because the ship is at sea, all money spent reverts directly to the cruise line, and consequently the company wishes to maximize onboard expenditure on a sea day. As musical performance attracts and retains guests, musicians play extensively and in many locations on sea days, with performances usually starting at 10:00 a.m. and finishing at 1:00 a.m. Sea days usually follow (and precede) port days, as consecutive sea days are rare (although they do occur). On port days, guests have often been sightseeing and go to bed late. For this reason, comparatively later performances are scheduled. Few musical performances are, therefore, scheduled in the morning of a sea day when guests are waking and breakfasting. After breakfast, at around 11:00 a.m., a few pre-lunchtime poolside and solo cocktail performances are scheduled to entice tourists to lie by the pool or sit in a bar before lunch. After lunch, when guests may wish to relax, the lido deck becomes the focus of musical entertainment. Guests are encouraged to relax on a deck chair and buy the drink of the day. These performances peak around 3:00 p.m. and decline in number during the afternoon. From 7:00 p.m. until midnight, performances are few in number. If they are scheduled, they are likely to be prerecorded music and often advertised as 'dancing under the stars'. After 5:00 p.m., solo performances, often cocktail piano sets, come to the foreground while guests are waiting to dine, visiting the bar on the stern or bow of the ship, and watching the sun go down while having a drink. A tinkling cocktail piano in the background makes for a congenial aural environment. Such musical performances are secondary to the main purpose of relaxation and conversation, and the low level of interactivity creates an undemanding ambiance. Such performances dominate the shipboard musicscape (Bitner 1992; Oakes 2000) until 8:00 p.m.

After dinner, many guests attend the evening theatrical show, which may be a guest entertainer cabaret or a production show in the main theater. Both performances usually occur between 8:00 p.m. and 10:00 p.m., which coincides with a slight dip in the number of cocktail performances and the start of the main evening entertainment. Despite the fact that evening performances are finished relatively quickly, usually lasting no more than 45 to 60 minutes, they provide a focus for the evening's entertainment, encouraging guests to stay out rather than returning to their cabins, and to stay in one place, rather than wandering around different events. The evening show is a focal point and is designed to provide high-energy, uplifting experiences that lift guests' mood so they continue their evening while purchasing experience enhancements.

Most modern cruise ships have a large central lobby that extends from the ship's top down through several levels. Access to the main theater is usually via the upper levels of the main atrium, so as guests exit the main evening show in the main theater , the sound of a performance, scheduled on the 'ground' floor, fills the void, encouraging guests to continue on to other musical events. Cruise Director Smith explained:

> [The musical director and I] worked very hard at trying to make sure there was no dead space where people were walking. We didn't want dead space, we also worked really hard at guiding the musicians to play the songs that everyone loves to hear at set times. So, for example, the second show at 8:45 p.m. came out at 9:45 p.m. Did we want [a band in the lobby] at 9:45 p.m., with a thousand people walking past them, playing 'When I Fall in Love'? Or did we want them performing an upbeat, fun song, creating an atmosphere that kept people staying out? We worked really hard at that. We wanted upbeat, fun music so that when people were walking around, they wanted to stop. (Smith, interview, London, 17 October 2011)

Guests who attended the theater can lean over the railing to watch the performance a few decks below, perhaps purchasing a drink or continuing along and watching another performance. It is important at this point in the evening for the ship to be buzzing, as excitement and activity draws guests onward. Those guests who choose to stay out will find a large amount of performers around the ship, especially piano and guitar vocalists, as well as prerecorded dance music in the disco, karaoke, and live jazz performances, all of which provide a number of options for different tastes. These performances peak between 10:00 p.m. and 11:00 p.m. and quickly taper off until 1:00 a.m. As already mentioned, the following day is usually a port day, and guests may wish to get up early, so by finishing musical performances, guests are prompted to retire into their cabins.

MEDIATED ENCOUNTERS WITH THE 'OTHER': COMMODIFIED EXOTICA

Tourism involves the process of the consumption of images (which can include aural images), nurtured and cultivated by the media (Berger 2011; Urry 1990). Imagery is central to increasing the desire to undertake tourism (Williams 2006), and to define and add meaning to the destination itself (Tresidder 2011). The concept 'Tahiti', for example, brings to mind pre-packaged and mediatized images, such as balmy beaches and warm ocean dips, or perhaps a maiden plunking a ukulele under a palm tree.[7] These populist images of Tahiti as a tourism product are manifestations of 'exoticism', a particular mode of representation of a culture different from one's own (Célestin 1996, 2) and 'the borrowing or use of music materials that evoke distant locales or alien frames of reference' (Bellman 1998b, ix). This can occur as musical 'borrowing' of elements of nonfamiliar cultures by artists, or in performance as 'spectacle'.[8] Tourism destinations are defined by such images, using signifiers of a destination that are easily assimilable and nonthreatening, and they are generated by travel programs, advertising campaigns, and popular media. They are specifically designed to generate a desire to consume such images, encouraging consumers to take vacations to exotic locations, thus helping to fuel the tourism industry. Such touristic performances are rarely, if ever, promoted *as anything other than* authentic. Concepts of authenticity are used to sell everything, from objects such as souvenirs, clothing, and fabrics to experiences gained during festivals, rituals, and cruises. Thus, cultural objects or experiences become marketable tourism products (Xie and Wall 2008) negotiated between the tourism provider and the tourist. This authenticity may be considered as *performative*, in that authenticity is suggested by resemblance to popular representations of a culture rather than any essential (indexical) authenticity that may adhere to traditional cultural practices.

One of the most common commodified non-Western cultural and, specifically, musical forms offered on board cruise ships are the 'Caribbean bands' that provide a dependable and palatable version of Caribbean, Latin American, and related Western pop music for guests. These ensembles range from reggae bands using a standard rock lineup to bands featuring steel drums along with amplified instruments and, on occasion, solo steel drum players playing to MIDI accompaniments. This style is so common on cruise boats that it is usually just referred to as 'Caribbean'. The repertoire usually comprises a mixture of calypso classics from various decades, such as 'Yellow Bird' and David Rudder's 'Bacchanal Lady'; Harry Belafonte numbers, such as 'The Banana Boat Song'; soca hits, such as Arrow's 'Hot, Hot, Hot'; Bob Marley compositions, such as 'Jammin' and 'One Love'; and 'tropicalist' Western pop songs, exemplified by Jimmy Buffet's anthemic 'Margaritaville'. This diverse material is integrated into a mellow, mid-tempo, musical flow usually performed on the pool decks as sonic accompaniment to the consumption of afternoon cocktails. It is 'symbolically authentic' as it looks and sounds like expected popular representations of Caribbean bands rather than any actual regional performance style. Any sense of specific place and culture of origin is effaced in favor of a vague Caribbeanistic groove and sense of sun-drenched hedonism.

The experience many travelers have onshore is often just as mediated and 'inauthentic' as their onboard experiences. With regard to tourists' experience of the Caribbean, the 'Island Village' situated next to the cruise terminal in Ocho Rios, on Jamaica's north coast, is virtually an onshore extension of the shipboard environments for those who visit. The 'village', actually a market area, is populated by stalls selling material targeted at brief stopover tourists, such as T-shirts, 'rastacaps' (with dreadlocks attached), and Bob Marley memorabilia along with the quintessentially commodified exoticism of a 'Jimmy Buffet's Margaritaville' café franchise, where consumers can purchase a real 'Cheeseburger in Paradise'. The whole space is sanitized and safe, contained in the guarded and fenced-off area of the cruise terminal, to which locals cannot usually gain access. The reality is past the gate, where beggars sit and assertive young men attempt to persuade unaccompanied passengers and crew to go on unlicensed 'guided tours'. As Garin noted about a visit to this 'village' in 2006, apart from touristic souvenirs, his only brush with Jamaican culture was in:

> the upbeat rhythms of the four-man reggae band giving a free show near the entrance: Dancing in front of them is a young woman dressed up like Aunt Jemima, a fake Carmen Miranda fruit basket on her head and, beneath her dress, great big pads to simulate a plantation 'mammy's' enormous rear end and bosom. As the passengers shuffle appreciatively past the twenty-first century minstrel show, none hears the dreadlocked singer's words. 'Oh God,' he sings as they pass, heads bopping in time to the song. 'Look what they're doing to my soul. . . Oh God! Oh God! Oh God! Look how they take control.' (Garin 2006, 279)

Such performances are represented as 'authentically Jamaican' by virtue of being performed in a tourist location with popular cultural references to local culture, yet they are just as banalized as onboard performances.

Figure 4.2   A Caribbean band playing on the lido deck of a cruise ship. Reproduced with photographer permission.

Even when the cultural/musical commodity on offer is far more specific to a region than the Caribbean commodity circulated internationally on cruise ships, the product is just as diluted. Tahiti in French Polynesia provides a good example. Two types of cruise ships visit Tahiti: those visiting Tahiti among several different ports, and those that are resident there. The visitor ship will visit Tahiti as a part of a longer voyage, with visits to many other ports. These visits may last a few days in the case of a Pacific Island voyage, or several months in the case of a world cruise. For these tourists, Tahiti is one among several places they may visit. Therefore, it is essential that Tahitian culture be presented in an easily and quickly assimilable manner. Three resident ships stay in Tahiti year-round: the small cruise ship M.V. Paul Gauguin, the combined cruise ship/cargo vessel M.V. Aranui 3, and the 22-passenger M.V. Haumana. Princess Cruises often places a smaller ship, such as the 826-passenger M.V. Ocean Princess in Tahiti for the northern winter. These vessels attract guests interested in a longer and more thorough stay specifically in Tahiti and require a closer, though safe, and educational and entertaining introduction to Tahitian culture.

There are three ways in which cruise ships present Tahitian culture to their guests: in dockside performances, local shows, or regular production shows. Different ships use these shows variously to cater to the perceived requirements of their consumers. Dockside performances involve groups of musicians and (at times) dancers performing on the docks of the restricted port areas as passengers embark and disembark. These performances commonly take place near the port entrance, where guests can see them regardless of which ship they are on. Passengers will have a similar experience regardless of the type of cruising undertaken. As the port authority organizes such performances, these are examples of how the government prefers tourists to see Tahiti. Visual and musical signifiers delineate Tahitian culture. Costumes are simple but colorful. Instrumentation usually consists of Tahitian drums, guitars, and the ukulele, the ubiquitous symbol of Polynesian music. Organizers do not design these performances as formal concerts; indeed, many tourists may feel uncomfortable stopping and observing the performance. Rather, they are designed to provide an aural and visual signifier of Tahiti and Tahitian culture, welcoming the visitor to a constructed and packaged Tahiti. While they are carefully organized, dockside performances have many of the trappings of informal performance (e.g., lacking a formal venue such as a theater, stage lighting, seats, etc.). Performances take place in the port area, a multipurpose environment used for both shipping business and, in this case, performance. They usually occur when guests are leaving the ship (the first few hours the ship is in port) and returning (the last few hours before departure), though such performances may consist of several groups performing one after the other with breaks. The port area, a restricted space where locals are not usually permitted to venture, is considered by guests to be a 'safe' place—an extension of the safe cocoon of the ship. Most cruise ship guests also have an opportunity to experience choreo-musical shows performed by local, (shore-based) musicians and dancers on board the cruise ship. Nearly every visiting cruise ship books such a show. If the ship sails in the evening, the local show will occur just before sailing when most guests have returned to the ship. If the ship is overnighting (which is rare, as this practice is expensive for the cruise line),[9] the performance may take the place of the evening cabaret show. These performances are more commodified and controlled than dockside performances. Musicians wear Hawaiian-style shirts and trousers, while dancers are dressed in 'traditional' grass leg skirts, or in skirts and bikini tops, playing to the exotic and sensual expectations of cruise ship guests. Cruise Director Jamie Logan writes of guests, saying that a successful Tahitian performance was 'classy and colorful' (2011). It is significant that classy and colorful, rather than reflective of local culture, is the requisite of the successful local show.

CONCLUSION

As analyzed in this chapter, the intersection of music and tourism takes several forms. Some interactions are primarily event and/or locale based, providing musical experiences in places that appear to be congruent with the cultural context of the form for those able to afford to visit them. These locations may reflect myths and/or actualities of origin (e.g., New Orleans, commonly recognized as the 'birthplace' of jazz), or else institutional traditions (e.g., Wangaratta, in southeastern Australia, which has hosted the premier national jazz festival since 1989). Others may be more concerned with a more diffuse musical and/or countercultural ethos (such as the UK's Glastonbury Festival). Cruise tourism is significantly different in that while the previously mentioned location-based tourism involves the transport of tourists *to* the locations in question, cruise tourism focuses on the transit of tourists between set points in floating 'pleasure palaces'. The cruise travelers' destination is the ship itself. The congruency of musical forms and the place of their performance is complete in that the music performed on board cruise ships is music designed for cruise ship performance. In this regard, it is as 'authentic' as any other form of musical practice. Indeed, as this chapter has demonstrated, cruise ship tourism has distinct repertoires, performance practices, venue and scheduling structures, performer lifestyles, and traditions of audience interaction and consumption that constitute a (living) heritage form. This heritage may be one that has been created within the sphere of commercially crafted popular music and enabled by the financial structures of ship-based tourism operators but it is, nonetheless, distinct and dynamic and as worthy of analyzes as it is patronage. There is also the heritage of consumer exploitation alluded to in the title of this chapter, as cruise ship patrons are smoothly 'fleeced' through their complicity with the profit-generating mechanisms that the lines operate as the core element of their commercial rationale. Commodification is an all-encompassing aspect of the musical experience of cruise ship tourism, making it arguably one of the purest forms of modern commercial musical practice in both tourism and the entertainment sector in general.

NOTES

1. The poem is available open-access online, see, for instance, R.C. Seaton's translation online at http://classics.mit.edu/Apollonius/argon.html.
2. The salaries of onboard service staff are not built into the ticket price and are presented as a 'gratuity' on the final bill. Musicians are not tipped staff, and so this income stream falls outside the current study.
3. This is not a term used by Pine and Gilmore but coined by the authors here, and it applies to the cruise ship as an experience.
4. In the last few years, cruise lines have also begun to develop 'specialty' restaurants that charge an additional fee for an improved dining experience, including supposedly better food and service. In *these* restaurants, music is regularly provided as an encouragement to attend these restaurants and contribute to onboard revenue.
5. A proportion of music on ship is prerecorded, occurring particularly in the disco, in some lido deck performances, and between sets in the ballroom dance venue. While this music is in the minority compared with live performance—a situation at odds with land-based music—this music also functions to guide guests to locations of high consumption and is also considered in this study.
6. At the request of the cruise director, 'John Smith' is a pseudonym.
7. See, e.g., Williamson (1986), who describes how women and island paradise are linked in media images.
8. These approaches are common in Western art music, such as Handel's eastern dramas and Mozart's *Rondo alla Turka* (Locke 2009, 87–100, 123–26), as well as in popular music, such as the influences of Indian music in the music of the British invasion (Bellman 1998a) and modern constructions of 'World Music' (Taylor 1997).
9. Port fees for overnight stays are more expensive than those for day stays as the port authority must employ people for the nighttime as well. For this reason, overnight stays usually occur on long voyages such as a world cruise.

REFERENCES

Apollonius Rhodius. 1912. *Argonautica*. Translated by R.C. Seaton. Cambridge, MA: Harvard University Press.

Becker, Bill. 2006. 'Onboard Revenue Takes Centre Stage.' *International Cruise & Ferry Review* (October):17–18.

Bellman, Jonathan. 1998a. 'Indian Resonances in the British Invasion 1965–1968.' In *The Exotic in Western Music*, edited by Jonathon Bellman, 292–306. Boston: Northeastern University Press.

Bellman, Jonathan. 1998b. 'Introduction.' In *The Exotic in Western Music*, edited by Jonathon Bellman, ix–xiii. Boston: Northeastern University Press.

Berger, Arthur Asa. 2011. 'Tourism as a Postmodern Semiotic Activity.' *Semiotica* 183:105–19.

Bitner, Mary Jo. 1992. 'Servicescapes: The Impact of Physical Surroundings on Customers and Employees.' *Journal of Marketing* 56(2):57–71.

Cashman, David. 2012. 'Musicology and Cruisicology: Music and Cruise Ship Tourism 2003–2011.' PhD diss., Lismore, Australia, Southern Cross University.

Célestin, Roger. 1996. *From Cannibals to Radicals: Figures and Limits of Exoticism*. Minneapolis: University Of Minnesota Press.

Dickinson, Bob, and Andy Vladimir. 2008. *Selling the Sea: An Inside Look at the Cruise Industry*. 2nd ed. New York: Wiley.

Garin, Kristoffer A. 2006. *Devils on the Deep Blue Sea: The Dreams, Schemes, and Showdowns that Built America's Cruise-Ship Empires*. New York: Plume.

Hertan, Richard R. 2010. *An Analysis of the Placement of Music in Miami Beach Hotels. Master of Science in Hotel Administration*. Las Vegas: University of Nevada.

Jones, Peter. 2009. 'A "Sound Strategy" for Intercontinental Hotels.' *Tourism & Hospitality Research* 9(3):271–76.

Locke, Ralph P. 2009. *Musical Exoticism: Images and Reflections*. Cambridge: Cambridge University Press.

Logan, Jamie. 2011. 'Regent Seven Seas Voyager's 2011 World Cruise: Papeete, Tahiti. Same Ship Different Day.' http://www.sameshipdifferentday.com/2011/regent-seven-seas-voyagers-2011–world-cruise-papeete-tahiti/. Accessed 12 May 2011.

Oakes, Steve. 2000. 'The Influence of the Musicscape within Service Environments.' *Journal of Services Marketing* 14(7):539–56.

Pine, B. Joseph, and James H. Gilmore. 1999. *The Experience Economy*. Boston: Harvard Business School Press.

Pine, B. Joseph, and James H. Gilmore. 2011. *The Experience Economy*. 2nd ed. Boston: Harvard Business Review Press.

Taylor, Timothy Dean. 1997. *Global Pop: World Music, World Markets*. New York: Routledge.

Tresidder, Richard. 2011. 'The Semiotics of Tourism.' In *Research Themes for Tourism*, edited by Peter Robinson, Sue Heitmann, and Peter Dieke, 59–68. Wallingford: CABI.

Urry, John. 1990. *The Tourist Gaze*. London: Sage.

Vogel, Michael P. 2011. 'Monopolies at Sea: The Role of Onboard Sales for the Cruise Industry's Growth and Profitability.' In *Tourism Economics: Impact Analysis*, edited by Álvaro Matias, Peter Nijkamp, and Manuela Sarmento, 211–29. Heidelberg: Springer.

Wahlstrom, Ryan. 2012. 'Cruise Market Watch.' *Cruise Market Watch*. http://www.cruisemarketwatch.com/. Accessed 20 March 2012.

Williams, Alistair. 2006. 'Tourism and Hospitality Marketing: Fantasy, Feeling and Fun.' *International Journal of Contemporary Hospitality Management* 18(6):482–95.

Williamson, Judith. 1986. 'Women Is an Island: Femininity and Colonization.' In *Studies in Entertainment: Critical Approaches to Mass Culture*, edited by Tania Modleski, 99–118. Bloomington: Indiana University Press.

Xie, Philip Feifan, and Geoffrey Wall. 2008. 'Authenticating Ethnic Tourism Attractions.' In *Managing Visitor Attractions*, edited by Alan Fyal, Brian Garrod, Anna Leask and Stephen Wanhill, 132–47. Oxford: Butterworth-Heinemann.

Zhongyan, Liu, and Mao Xiangxiu. 2006. 'On the Setting of the Tourist Hotels' Background Music.' *Journal of Huangshan University* 7(2):52–54.

5 Mobilizing Music Festivals for Rural Transformation

Opportunities and Ambiguities

John Connell and Chris Gibson

Economic decline in rural Australia, as in many parts of the world, has become an issue of national importance. Consequently, the infrastructure and community life of many rural and remote towns has slowly disappeared through bank branch closures, the loss of football and cricket teams, and declining populations in some areas, resulting in sometimes desperate efforts to stimulate immigration (Argent and Rolley 2000; Connell and McManus 2011). Restructuring of traditional agricultural industries and a resurgence of mining have also created new patterns of winners and losers—and new flows of people, investment, and infrastructure. Certain regions, such as parts of Queensland and western Australia, where mining has boomed, and Victoria, with better soils, more space, and high-capital-intensive forms of production, have improved their economies of scale, gained export markets, and retained or even boosted their populations. In other regions where farms and exports are smaller and where capital is scarce, local economies have stagnated and young people have left in droves. In some coastal places, stagnation has been avoided by the growth of tourism and in-migration from capital cities (known in Australia as *sea-change* migration because it implies urbanites' downshifting careers and material expectations in order to pursue lifestyle benefits of living in a quiet coastal location; see Burnley and Murphy 2003). In such places, there is a rather different, and dynamic, context of growth and prosperity. Patterns of growth and decline and resultant social problems have not been distributed evenly between, or within, regions: what are now described as patchwork economies. While some centers continue to grow, many smaller towns have become caught in a vicious cycle of decline, losing residents, industries, and confidence about prospects for a sustainable future and fearing neglect from the center.

In this setting, music festivals have emerged and proliferated. This chapter discusses music festivals in the contexts of attempts to stimulate tourism, migration, and regional development, through drawing rural communities together and creating a new element of what has been seen as the 'post-productivist economy,' the switch toward service industries, rural tourism, and the creativity economy (Gibson 2002). Festivals reflect patterns of decline and growth, and the social and economic processes behind them, and generate new mobilities of people, capital, and cultural influence. Music festivals have sometimes been actively incorporated into attempts by places to reinvent themselves (sometimes in surprising ways), have helped turn around economic and population decline, or have played a substantial role in changing the character and distribution of benefits from the local economy. Yet, as we shall show, music festivals have certain limitations—not least the kinds of music and the kinds of patrons—that sometime result in social divisions and antagonism. Festivals are no guaranteed panacea.

The focus of the chapter is on festivals situated in what in Australia are called country towns, usually ranging in size from 5,000 to 30,000 people, though some, like Bermagui, our case study, are considerably smaller. Many small towns have a declining agricultural base and relatively homogenous populations with little in-migration, where indigenous people are a small numerical minority. Others such as Bermagui have received sea-change migrants from big cities and, although ethnically still quite homogenous, feature tensions between longtime residents (often working-class, and once employed in fishing or agriculture) and middle-class, affluent newcomers. Exactly what opportunities and antagonisms result from the new mobilities catalyzed by festivals is our focus here. These mobilities are musical, personal, professional, material—circuits of sounds, performers, stallholders, suppliers, migrants, tourists, and audiences. In a case study we explore in the second section of our chapter, the Four Winds classical music festival in Bermagui, we discover that musical mobilities in particular, far from being peripheral to regional development concerns, are a central concern.

MOBILIZING MUSIC FESTIVALS

Regional festivals are scarcely new. In regional areas of countries as different as China and Australia, the tourism spin-offs deriving from the promotion of festivals are seen as one means of redressing rural decline, reversing flows of out-migration with new, albeit temporary, surges of inward mobility (Walmsley 2003; Xie 2003). In 2003, an annual international music festival was argued to be the only viable means of rescuing the host Shoalhaven River Estate (in New South Wales) from bankruptcy and mounting debts; later that year in the same state, the tiny former gold mining township of Hill End, with just 120 people, launched the inaugural Hill End Jazz Festival, which brought 1,500 visitors, enough to raise sufficient funds to buy a defibrillator for the community (Gibson and Connell 2005). Regional towns, such as Aldeburgh, Glyndebourne, and Glastonbury in the UK, Bayreuth in Germany, and Woodstock in the US, have been so successful that their festivals, across various genres of music, have substantially improved economic and social capital and resulted in those places largely being known, even defined, through their festivals. In such places, festivals have become a long-term place-marketing strategy, rather than simply a short-term, one-off event (Hall 1989). Festivals may bring multiple benefits to rural communities: stimulating short-term employment, improving the skills of residents and their chances of finding future work, enhancing social cohesion, and reinventing places and their images. In short, they can put towns on the map and keep them there. And by and large they are an enjoyable way of doing so. In other places, festivals are small and the real skill is in managing to marshal enough resources, to call on favors, and make ends meet. Festivals also fuel creative frugality.

The contemporary proliferation of music festivals is remarkable—big, small, conservative, radical, alternative; every demographic and niche audience is catered for, from children's music to speed metal, opera to techno. In their proliferation, they fill some of the smallest and most specific niches: as in the Roy Orbison Festival in Wink, Texas, or the Elvis Presley Festival in Parkes, New South Wales, both dedicated to the music of a single (dead) musician. Herräng, in Sweden, an otherwise small and largely anonymous village and described on its own website as 'a sleepy one-horse town in the outskirts of nowhere but still fairly easy to reach by car or public transportation' (quoted in Gibson and Connell 2012, 7), hosts the world's largest annual gathering of jitterbug (swing jazz) dancers. Individual instruments too can be rationales for music festivals, often where regional traditions are strong (or are revived in the face of cultural globalization), where competition for hotel space and visibility is less fierce, or where specialization gives a small-town festival a unique niche. Examples include the Cape Welsh International Harp Festival (in Caernarfon, Gwynedd); Australia's International Guitar Festival (held in Darwin in the country's remote tropical north); and the Yosemite Flute Festival (held on the edge of the national park in California and that specializes in Native American flutes). For violins alone, there is an international network of events, mostly in small towns and rural locations. For bagpipes, there are festivals in Glasgow (Scotland), Malahide (Ireland), Strakonice (Bohemia, Czech Republic), Mihovljan (Croatia), Gela (Bulgaria), Mont Cassel (France), New Jersey (US), and Minsk (Belarus), far beyond where bagpipe festivals might have been expected. Such unusual networks define the geography of music festival mobility.

Festival diversity is no less in Australia, from opera in the Outback (and opera in the Paddock), to heavy metal in Scone, and multiple jazz festivals in wineries and on riverboats. Every state has a major country music festival, and Tamworth (NSW) and Gympie (Queensland) are two towns essentially defined and largely marketed by their country music festivals (Edwards 2011; Gibson and Davidson 2004).

The contemporary proliferation of festivals builds on a legacy of previous generations of rural residents staging agricultural shows and carnivals, but as in the Northern Hemisphere in the late 1960s and early 1970s, it was a particular form of urban-to-rural mobility that really got things going. The hippie rock scene was characterized by festivals staged by urban subcultures in idyllic rural/pastoral locales: examples include the Pilgrimage for Pop festival in Ourimbah, Nimbin's Aquarius Festival, and the Meadows Technicolour Fair in South Australia. Subsequent phases of growth and diversification occurred in the 1980s, with the rise in popularity of commercial country music (both globally and in Australia, where it especially chimed with rural audiences), and in the 1990s, with the increasingly fragmented market for popular music.

That decade saw the emergence of rave culture (in Australia, outdoor techno events in rural locations became known as 'bush doofs,' an onomatopoeic reference to the bass line sounds of the music); the Lollapalooza format of alternative/hard rock festivals (with their Australian equivalents in the Homebake, Meredith, and Falls Festivals); and the creation of a network of blues and roots festivals linked to folk culture, acoustic styles of blues and bluegrass, and World Music. All of them relied on urban audiences traveling to rural and small-town locations to soak up the music and rustic ambience.

By 2007, when we undertook a major audit of music festivals in three Australian states (NSW, Victoria, and Tasmania), there were no fewer than 288 music festivals in rural areas, a remarkable statistic given the numerically tiny contributions made by those areas to the overall residential population. Of those, just under half were country, jazz, or folk festivals, and another third were generic 'music' festivals not pinned to a specific music style (Gibson and Connell 2012). Every town and even most small villages now host a music festival of some sort.

Cairns (Queensland) has a ukulele festival, and Hawkesbury (NSW) hosts the National Fiddle Festival, which 'celebrates the Fiddle from all cultures in all genre of music' (quoted in Gibson and Connell 2012, 8). Bagpipes predominate at the Glen Innes Celtic Festival and the Bundanoon is Brigadoon Scottish Festival (Ruting and Li 2011). Perhaps indicative of just how specialized such music festivals may be is the Australian Gumleaf Playing Championship. Held annually in Maryborough (Victoria), with its coveted Golden Gumleaf Award, it has become a focus for enthusiastic Aboriginal and non-Aboriginal players from around Australia. Gumleaf playing started as an Aboriginal tradition but by the 1920s was highly popular in the wider Australian community, trained in the ancient art of whistling using eucalyptus leaves. The music festival scene has expanded and specialized perhaps more than any other segment of the special event industry.

Festivals also generate income. In the small town of Queenscliff (Victoria), annual tourism income from its music festival totaled over A$2 million at the start of the century. For the festival's manager, Barbara Moss, beyond the direct impact:

> that economic impact is tied to the social fabric of the community. It's directly linked to the social health of the town and confidence is always

a big factor in economic growth. A lot of local people become involved in the festival—up to 400 people volunteer to help out each year—and we've found that to be a big long-term stimulant to the economy. Some of those people might otherwise be lying in bed watching Oprah. Now they're out getting involved. That connectivity, the bringing together of diverse elements, is what social wealth is all about. (Gibson and Connell 2005, 219)

These kinds of interrelated social and economic returns are particularly meaningful in small towns like Queenscliff with limited labor resources and support infrastructure. In small places, festivals can scarcely go unnoticed; large segments of communities are mobilized to invest money, time, and emotion in them. Festivalgoers travel great distances, and performers and marketers may travel even farther.

Despite this involvement, festivals, and particularly small regional festivals—seemingly ephemeral, concerned with fun rather than jobs, often not explicitly commercial, and largely invisible other than when actually being staged—have been overlooked by regional development academics and practitioners, despite obvious examples of successful transformations they have catalyzed (Gibson et al. 2010). Current orthodoxy in regional development research and practice has underplayed the contributions of festivals, an attitude that privileges particular industries and perspectives (often fixated on agriculture, big business, and transport infrastructure) at the expense of smaller-scale, seemingly transient phenomena. Even in the most visible cases, regional development agencies, local council managers, town mayors, and economic planners have taken years to be convinced of the value of festivals because few seem to make much money. But as Australia and other countries move toward a 'post-productivist countryside' (Gibson and Connell 2012), where agriculture is of declining significance relative to other sectors, notably service provision, so the role of festivals becomes even more important, more invaluable, and even critical.

Music festivals have further portrayed and enhanced creative industries outside major cities, namely, in places that are physically and/or metaphorically remote, are small in population terms, or which, because of socioeconomic status or inherited industrial legacies, are assumed by others to be unsophisticated or marginal in an imaginary geography of creativity. Lithgow, a former mining town in rural NSW, might hardly have been expected to host a successful annual Ironfest, described by its website as 'an arts festival with a metal edge, featuring art exhibitions, live music, street performance, historical re-enactments (including the Australasian World Jousting Tournament and a colonial battle re-enactment with three cannons and cavalry)' (Ironfest 2013). The tiny township of Nundle (NSW) has capitalized by combining its 19th-century history of gold mining and Chinese settlement in an annual Go for Gold Chinese Festival (Khoo and Noonan 2011). Heritage, sometimes dubiously, has been invested with new meanings, and festivals and tourism linked to that heritage replace traditional forms of economic development.

In Australia, regional development is particularly challenging, not just because the so-called 'tyranny of distance' (Battersby and Ewing 2005) has historically been considered a national economic problem, but because internally large distances, uneven geographical distribution of wealth, and a polarized urban hierarchy of a few large cities and a large number of scattered, small towns characterize the Australian situation (Gibson et al. 2010). However, remoteness, marginality, and difference can, in certain circumstances, be brokered into a base for a distinctive and successful industry (Gibson, Luckman, and Willoughby-Smith 2010). Provinciality can be a point of distinctiveness and difference.

Some festivals began for no special reason other than for entertainment, and because local authorities wanted to enhance local cultural life. Others started because of desires to promote particular musical genres, because of the efforts of enthusiastic fans and local musical clubs looking for a focal point on their annual calendars of events, or because musicians themselves sought outlets for performance where few previously existed. Frequently in-migrants into rural contexts have been the key movers and shakers behind their establishment. Many music festivals in small towns happened just once, or lasted for a few years depending on the enthusiasm of the local organizing committee or local government-employed festival organizer. Others survived, gained reputations, and developed their own heritages and traditions, rising from small beginnings to national and even international prominence. The more well-known have included the Tamworth Country Music Festival, Woodford Folk Festival, Byron Bay's East Coast Blues and Roots Festival, Meredith Rock Festival, the Wangaratta Jazz Festival, and Goulburn's Blues Festival. All these are now known as leaders nationally in Australia in their respective genres, having grown steadily from modest local beginnings in country towns.

Economic benefits are a function of the particular patterns of mobility and the predilections of those who travel to them. Hotels and restaurants are invariably primary beneficiaries, since festivalgoers must eat and sleep, and direct benefits are also enjoyed by petrol stations, gift and souvenir stores, PA and portable toilet hire companies, local transport companies, and charities (who run raffles, cake stalls, and barbecues). Secondary benefits trickle down to various extents depending on how much visitor spending 'stays local' through subsequent circulation within the location, so that even lawyers, printers, furniture shops, and undertakers receive extra income somewhere down the line. In the case of the Tamworth Country Music Festival and Parkes Elvis Revival Festivals, home-hosting schemes were launched to manage enormous crowds that exceed accommodation capacity. In turn, they directed new flows of money into the wallets of local people, a meaningful spillover benefit for regional development.

Music festivals are not merely local. They rely on supra-local patterns and networks of people, money, and creative talent. In our audit, although most music festivals wished to profile local artists, they also imported musicians from considerable distances, an example of bringing 'culture to the provinces.' Distant businesses also benefit from festivals. A well-established network in regional Australia takes many itinerant stallholders festival to festival, earning a living selling food, clothing, or other items. Much of what is sold, in fact, has nothing much to do with music—clothes, bags, trinkets, garden furnishings; at the Parkes Elvis Revival Festival, itinerant stallholders sell everything from national football club merchandise to Harley Davidson gear, woven rugs, garden gnomes, local goat cheese, and hand cream. Buskers too are part of the same regional circuits.

Much larger companies are involved in similar circuits. The tent providers at Parkes, Tent City Hire, are the same as at Tamworth, from where the idea came. Tent City Hire increasingly dominate the market for tent accommodation at outdoor music festivals in regional Australia, providing tents at the Gympie Muster, Dingo Creek Jazz Festival, the Great Southern Blues Festival, and Splendour in the Grass. Their format of establishing temporary tent communities on festival sites is convenient for patrons and provides helpful order and predictability for organizers, but the monetary benefits return to Queensland. Portable toilets too are very big business, as evocatively portrayed in the hit Australian film *Kenny*. These portaloos tend to be rented through hire companies (such as the evocatively named '1,300 Dunnys') that are organized territorially: For obvious reasons, carting empty (and full) portable toilets around by truck can be both expensive and messy, so the market is broken up into regional providers. Intricate and ever-changing economic circuits link regional music festivals.

The economics might be beneficial, even where income trickles back to the cities, but environmental and social costs may bring conflict and dismay: Festivals can destroy fields, generate waste, ensure traffic jams, and guarantee noise. They can annoy local residents with pollution and congestion and by attracting 'unwanted' types of people (often revealing as much about local residents' imagined picture of themselves as of the behavior of the festivalgoers), and thus conflicting with the image local people might wish for themselves and their towns.

Where crowds have become too much, festivals have even been drummed out of town, as occurred at Byron Bay (Gibson and Connell 2012). One of the most striking and distinctive regional music festivals is the Parkes Elvis Revival Festival in a small town 400km from Sydney. Its genesis was derided as frivolous and inappropriate; it struggled to overcome floods and bushfires in early years but was bolstered by the support of the local rugby club and eventually the council and tourist board. Even still, there was opposition from many local people who hated the noise and congestion and, above all, saw the image of a latter-day Elvis as inappropriate for a town that prided itself as the center of wheat growing in New South

Wales (Gibson and Connell 2012). In Tamworth, huge crowds and perennial pressure to deliver massive tourism and economic development benefits has placed pressure on organizers to broaden its remit from country music to become a more generic music festival. The festival hired teen idol singers and techno-pop bands, alienating the traditionally older crowd. Stalwarts resented 'their' festival losing touch with its country 'roots.'

Festivals do not therefore necessarily bring people together, and communities can be divided over the merits of festivals, both in general (in terms of congestion and noise) and to the specific festival (and who is involved). Change of any kind can be unwelcome, and proponents of change, including festivals, are often derided—however erroneously—and ignored as blow-ins who do not have roots in or understand the local community. Indeed, it is one of the characteristics of most small towns that they are inherently divided—by religion, politics, sport, class, and also race—which divisions may spill over into music festivals, with concerns over who is excluded and who benefits. Conflicts can ensue over local spaces, resources, and the direction and meaning of the event itself. Festivals include and exclude people by drawing boundaries around community, through subcultural affiliation, prerequisite knowledge to appreciate narrow music styles, specialist knowledge required for entry (in the case of, for instance, raves), or meaningful participation.

In the second half of this chapter, we explore some of these tensions and differences by focusing on the Four Winds Festival, a classical music festival in rural New South Wales, at which we have conducted interviews and surveys over a period of some five years (including work by our project colleagues Michelle Duffy, Gordon Waitt, and Andrea Gordon). This case demonstrates that staging a successful festival is rarely easy; requires dedication, commitment, and creativity; and may still be opposed. Yet it also shows that even in the face of occasional antagonism, disinterest, conservatism, and uncertainty, it is possible to thrive, enable some degree of regional growth, and transform the image of a small town. At the heart of that story, notwithstanding antagonisms, has been its steadfast commitment to making quality music mobile, reversing an imagined hierarchy that positions small remote places as distant to creativity. For one weekend, at least, a small coastal town becomes a hub for musical and critical expression.

THE FOUR WINDS FESTIVAL

The Four Winds Festival is held biennially near Bermagui, a small town of around 1,300 people on the Sapphire Coast, 400km south of Sydney. Bermagui, like many country towns, is remote from metropolitan markets, but with two possible advantages for festivals: its coastal setting and some proximity to the national capital, Canberra, from where it is a location for second homes. Once a significant fishing, agricultural, and timber center, as each of these has struggled to survive, it has gradually become a residential, sea-change retirement town, and a small tourist center, slowly going through a process of rural gentrification.

The idea for the Four Winds Festival came from a small group of local people wanting to fill a gap in locally available music. According to Sheila Boughen, chair of the festival's board, 'the community down here seemed to have no or limited access to high quality classic and classical music, so we got together in 1991 to see how we might do something about that. We just don't see why if you live here you shouldn't have access to high quality classical music' (interview, Bermagui, October 2007—all subsequent quotes are from this interview unless otherwise noted). At the same time, classical music represented a new niche: 'Our gig is the classical gig so we don't step on Merimbula Jazz or Cobargo Folk and anything else.' The Four Winds Festival eventually benefited from some complementarities with other quite different festivals and contributed to regional integration by sharing support services such as lighting and food.

While the initial objective was cultural rather than economic, rather later, recognizing socioeconomic changes in the area, the festival committee increasingly felt that, since farming, fishing, and forestry in the region were declining, a new source of economic development was needed. According to Boughen, 'We feel really strongly that culture can be an economic asset for the area and is already an economic asset . . . so we definitely see ourselves as part of a new identity for Bermagui and the area.' Recognition of that role by the wider community was slow to evolve; indeed, 16 years later in 2007, 'the community wouldn't even know that. We think that they just think we're a gig at Easter. But our area is also the start of the Bermagui to Tathra arts trail.' Like many festivals, but especially those with a seemingly elite orientation, and classical music festivals are relatively rare, the festival developed few early links with the wider community. Some locals perceived it as having deliberately chosen an out-of-town site and having made few moves to challenge local notions of elitism. As one commented early on: 'The Four Winds Festival didn't hit my radar over the weekend. I was busy with family and we had plans to go fishing. We hadn't a clue what they were doing. It's crap. They were all still hanging around the park when we went off to the pub with friends.' (quoted in Duffy and Waitt 2011, 54) The festival was set in an outdoor amphitheater at Barragga Bay, close to the ocean some 10km south of Bermagui. Its existence created the site. The amphitheater was a privately owned paddock that was initially temporarily terraced, with marquees at the top of the hill for food, wine, and toilets.

The festival began in 1991 and ran annually until 2000 when it became a biennial event, since the voluntary board 'got a bit exhausted.' The board had ten unpaid members (more than half from the Bermagui area, but some in Canberra and Sydney with local connections) with a paid part-time administrator with high-level financial and accounting skills, a similarly part-time paid artistic director, and a part-time production assistant doing most of the logistics, such as booking artists and stage management. Other workers were hired intermittently, especially at festival times when volunteers were also highly involved.

By the end of the 2000s, the festival board had developed what it called the four pillars:

- The place: inspired by and celebrating nature and its beauty, creating a sense of belonging through the program interpreted around the site and our area.
- People and community: We value relationships by making people feel welcome to our community while increasing our local audience. We are active in developing the role of culture as an asset in our region—local and beyond.
- Music and performing arts: We focus on fine music of all kinds, with a balance between the new and familiar classical, appropriate to the festival site and our core audience. We encourage elements of magic and the unexpected, which both comfort and challenge.
- Outreach through arts and education: Provide a way of taking great quality music to the schools and community in our region, through an interactive creative process leading to students contributing to the development of the arts. We encourage a love of music and the arts (quoted in Gibson and Connell 2012, 146).

The first festival at Easter 1991 was designed as a test run and by invitation only (a policy that may also have unwittingly fueled notions of elitism). Two hundred people came, as did rain, so the festival transferred to Bermagui community hall: 'It ended up being a real event and the whole move showed us that it wasn't just the music, it was the community and the place.' Serendipitously the sense of exclusion and elitism was challenged. The festival was opened by actress Patricia Kennedy reciting poetry, incidentally accompanied by a flight of ducks descending on the lake behind her, a link with nature that the festival has constantly stressed.

Like most festivals, it grew steadily over the years, by 2012 attracting about 1,500 people on each of its two days. By 2008, about a third were local people, from Bateman's Bay to Merimbula and the hinterland. A third came from Canberra, and a further third from elsewhere, mainly Sydney and Melbourne. The goal was to increase the local audience: 'If we increased overall but it was all outside the local area we wouldn't be fulfilling the reason we exist.' By 2010, about 45 percent of audiences were local people. Like most festivals, marketing budgets were small, and marketing was deliberately informal and personal, primarily 'relationship marketing,' as Boughen described it, with a quarterly newsletter and brochures to a database of about 1,500 people. The only overtly commercial marketing was cinema advertisements in Canberra, Narooma, and Merimbula. Such marketing therefore assumes a significant amount of return visiting.

Four Winds attracts a largely middle-aged and middle-class audience, wrapped warmly, with many wearing iconic Australian Akubra hats. Visitors came for several reasons, but ambience played a big role:

> We found there were four reasons why people came; they come because when they come and park their cars we open their car doors and greet them and park their cars and that sort of stuff, so they love the welcoming and it's all low key. They love that it isn't full of corporate banners . . . and they love the connection to the community like going into town . . . everybody wants to be in a little community. Then they love the place and nature; the whole connection to nature is huge because the site is very beautiful. We've done plantings just of native species and it's got a lake behind so you can watch the music and watch the ducks fly in . . . and then it's the music . . . it's only one of four reasons why people come.

The site was 'carefully managed to confirm the idea of Bermagui as "paradise" and little allowed to disrupt the conventional pleasures of this paradise' so that distracting human sounds, like traffic, were banished to the periphery, and the 'power and emotional rewards of the festival were heightened by the combination of sounds of bellbirds, frogs and winds moving through the trees' (Duffy and Waitt 2011, 52). The particularly attractive site and its initial deliberate isolation from urban life created a strong connection between visitors and place. According to Boughen, 'The connection to the place is huge and that's why people tolerate music they don't always like.' Indeed, 'you can lie down and go to sleep at this thing and no one cares, do a crossword or go up and have a coffee' as opposed to a concert 'where you think "oh bugger it, I've paid $50 bucks for this."' Consequently, 'people bring their blankets, picnics and chairs and you'll see someone listening to something else on the radio.' Flexibility and atmosphere were invaluable.

Visitors from the local area offered additional reasons for attendance, providing a more prosaic insight into the role of festivals in rural revitalization. For many, the event was a rare occasion where 'community' was galvanized through simple enjoyment of beautiful music. One festival participant, Belinda, said:

> like in the performance on Friday at the oval and here, getting moved by the music. And then I look around. I think this is my community, you know, I look around and . . . there is the woman from the local corner shop and there is the people I know. And I just think, how luck are we . . . And, also this community has drawn this thing together. (Duffy and Waitt 2011, 52–53)

Nevertheless some locals described the festival as 'snobby' (Gordon 2012, 113) and complained about high ticket prices (e.g., $100), which were actually comparatively inexpensive nationally, but still out of reach of the region's many unemployed young people and low-income retirees.

Cuisine was an integral part of the festival, culminating for some in a Saturday night outdoor feast in adjoining woodland. Food and wine were separately organized. As the 2010 festival website observed:

> As we all know Four Winds is a feast of music and art but equally important we want you to experience some of the culinary pleasures of this special region. We have worked hard with local foodies to provide a range of food and wine options which are fairly simple, use local produce where possible and fit in with the feel of Four Winds and the area . . . [and promised] . . . the opportunity to sample local wines and delicious homemade foods from our marquee. Plunger coffee, fine teas and local patisserie will be available all day. We will be selling oysters grown in pristine Wapengo Lake and baguettes with gourmet fillings. (Four Winds Festival 2010)

By then, a newly arrived Bermagui gelato bar (the Bermagui Gelato Clinic) had deliberately created a 'special Festival gelato:' part of a wider transformation of Bermagui that included the opening of a $5 million retail development including a café, wine bar, and delicatessen at Bermagui's Fishermen's Wharf. As the owner of the gelato bar pointed out, that had stimulated social change: 'Traditionally, Bermagui was not somewhere people went out to eat . . . This summer we've had queues out the door for the first time. We need the region to develop gastro tourism and inspire the locals' (quoted in Baum 2010, 5). Cuisine was a means to buttress impressions of Bermagui as 'cultured,' further improving its appeal to middle-class baby boomers, but also adding to tensions that the town had become more elitist.

Notwithstanding the risks of alienating resistant locals, the festival has continued to emphasize delivering quality music to the whole local community as its central purpose. From the beginning, a diversity of Western classical, Asian, and other non-Western musics were performed—a regional attempt to introduce ideas of World Music—and the Festival sought out some of the best national and international performers, even introducing avant-garde performers to Australia, such as the American Terry Riley, famous as a leading proponent of minimalism. Achieving the right musical balance has been much debated, and is seen as the main constraint to success and sustainability. According to Boughen:

> I think the real risk in people not coming is if we stretch too far into more esoteric music; too much contemporary is definitely a danger . . . so we sort of do a risk assessment of the program. There's no doubt you can't annoy your core audience so they like being stretched a bit.

> But if you turn it into a contemporary music festival it wouldn't work, we'd lose people.

At the same time, part of the festival's goal was to cherish eclecticism and celebrate all forms of musical expression. Eclecticism could both challenge and intrigue audiences, and most festival programs combined new and experimental work with pieces that were likely to be more familiar and accessible. Here, as elsewhere, achieving a balance between musical goals, community goals, and market development was never easy.

By the late 2000s, the festival was bringing in as many as 35 to 40 musicians for each event, which involved an expenditure of about $150,000, half the total budget. According to Boughen, the core of the music

> tends to be familiar, traditional, classical music . . . string quartets and so on and then we added on, after a few years, a Friday night cabaret gig in town because we realize that Barragga Bay is a bit out of sight and a bit cut off. That gets sold out really quickly as lighter music, more fun and a bit jazzy. Now we've added on also in the last festival a lunchtime forum . . . 'Up Close and Personal' . . . you get a chance to meet people, say, living composers and musicians, and they talk about how they do their work and give a little demonstration. Next year we've going to have an opening ceremony on the footy oval in town on the Friday afternoon so it's now a three-day festival.

Among other things, the 2008 Up Close and Personal brought composer Peter Sculthorpe and Aboriginal didgeridoo player William Barton together to discuss musical composition. Meanwhile, staging events on the local football grounds sought to physically bring performances closer to skeptical people in town.

Like most festivals, ticket sales contribute only a small part of the revenue—just a third of the income, with further thirds from grants and donations. The festival has sought corporate support, but according to Boughen, 'we haven't had much luck going to companies and getting money from them, because what's in it for them? It's a little country community.' It also established the 'Friends of Four Winds,' which sponsored events, brought some performers to Bermagui, and gave its members a sense of personal connection. In 2010, $773,000 was raised in a grassroots campaign, and the Australia Council for the Arts approved a $420,000 grant for the festival under the federal government's Creative Communities Partnership Initiative. Exactly how to interpret such funding is a source of contention. For some working-class taxpayers, such grants are viewed as diverting public money away from basic needs toward elitist high culture. In the case of Bermagui, however, this default class politics was cut across by other tensions. The specific grant above was intended to broaden the festival from a focus on professional performances to include greater community participation.

Its purpose was to decenter the elitism assumed to be inherent in classical and art musics. Moreover, the festival, having secured funding from the Australia Council for the Arts, was seen to have 'won' for a tiny rural community funding normally soaked up by established cultural institutions in major metropolitan centers. For local people resistant to the festival, it came as proof that this seemingly exclusionary form of culture could catalyze benefits for the whole town.

Indeed, the need for financial support coincided with the realization of the value of developing and formalizing ties to the local community. The Four Winds Festival was initially criticized for not supporting local people. More than a decade later that perspective had shifted: 'Our big push is to connect more and be more visible in the local community regardless of whether you come or not,' so that 'we want to put roots down in the culture and in the community' (Boughen, interview, 2007). So much so that by 2011: 'We want to reverse the thinking that classical music is made in cities. Our motto is "Born in Bermagui"' (quoted in Frew 2011, 14). Since 2008, the festival developed a community outreach initiative called Barnstorming, which involved initially performing at various local schools and establishing public concerts, so that 'we get some flow on of people, since we've got a big commitment to local education and to the cultural development of the area.' It introduced a free opening-day concert in Bermagui itself, with Aboriginal dancers from the local Yuin tribe (paid at equivalent professional rates), as part of an agenda for greater social inclusion. Later performances in Bermagui were staged in parkland, and performers were brought in on, and often performed from the top of, drays. The subsequent festival two years later was closed by Aboriginal women from The Black Arm Band, who performed a 'celebration of language and cultural survival.' Before the festival, members of the band visited the Wallaga Lake Aboriginal community to share skills through a series of music workshops, while for the first time a young Aboriginal musician performed rap at the festival. Participants were clearly moved by the more substantial indigenous presence. One participant, Sarah, said 'The Didjeridu [Aboriginal wind instrument], and energy down my spine, looking across the sea of faces, more familiar people, more people I know, my community' (quoted in Duffy and Waitt 2011, 52).

One unwitting community connection has been the role played by the festival for nonprofit music groups in the region. Because of the small population and sparse nature of the region's settlements, a commercial music scene is barely viable, if at all (Gordon 2012). Musicians throughout the region are rarely paid for performances anywhere. Audiences are simply too small and incomes too low to support much disposable income being spent on attending musical performances. In a context without much income or wealth, regional residents have found other means to enjoy listening to and performing music, like participating in community music initiatives, organizing nonprofit shows, and finding freely available venues.

Choirs are one such community music phenomenon in the region, with an important link to the Four Winds Festival. In ethnographic work conducted as part of this broader project (see Gordon 2012), it became clear that choral participation was vital to the sense of self, identity, and well-being for a diverse range of local residents, not just incoming middle-class people, but farmers (and their children), old retirees who lived their entire lives in the region, ex-defense force workers, the unemployed, and regular people who during the day work in shops, hairdressing salons, or teach at the local schools (cf. Durrant and Himonides 1998; Hays and Minichiello 2005; Joseph 2007). Singing together delivered simple bodily pleasure and triggered the emotions, but it also generated an unusually inclusive sense of community, capable of overcoming differences in background, gender, and class (although some participation was along gender lines, in men's and women's choirs). Local public schools run choirs and are linked to adult choirs throughout the region. Other than the costs of sheet music, participation is free.

For community choirs, the Four Winds Festival was far from an exclusionary or elitist event. Rather, the attempts by the festival board to integrate with the community have generated important performance opportunities for local choirs. They now perform at the in-town opening ceremony, and during the on-site festival itself. In interviews, choir participants from diverse class, age, and gender backgrounds emphasized the festival as the highlight on their annual performance calendar: a one-off opportunity to perform a paid performance at professional rates, alongside highly acclaimed visiting national and international artists (Gordon 2012). Choir participants rehearse and look forward to this performance, providing energy needed to keep them inspired and engaged. Jessica, a classically trained local musician, said:

> We're lucky to have the Four Winds Festival which is generally a [performance] opportunity for very high standard musicians. So that helps a lot in terms of injecting a bit of lifeblood for the local musicians to connect with . . . that's been fantastic, really fantastic. Without [the festival] it would be a much poorer place I think, musically. (Gordon 2012, 112)

Another chorister, Nick, agreed that for local nonprofit choirs, this was a pivotal occasion:

> Especially since we devised the whole opening ceremony where it's all done with local community members . . . I think it's really good to the point where now there's lots of community involvement before the Four Winds [takes place] . . . and then through the actual festivals there is an element of involving whoever wants to be involved. Even if they are a plumber or something [laughs] they will somehow get them involved. (Gordon 2012, 113)

By 2010, local dancers, school choirs, ballerinas, and musicians were all involved through various community engagement programs. Community involvement also extended to work experience and employment, as Boughen explains: 'In 2006, we invited some local high school students who were doing any sort of arts subjects to come and be . . . production assistants so they understood how a festival gets done. They did everything from going to rehearsals and looking after an artist and one of them is being offered a part-time job at the festival as a result.' By 2011, plans were to turn the festival amphitheater into a permanent 'cultural hub' for new music, master-classes, artist-in-residency programs, and local school music teachers. A federal government grant worth over $1.6 million was won toward this, enabling construction of a sewerage system, broadband infrastructure, and a new road to access the site.

Ultimately, as architect Philip Cox (who designed a new sound shell and permanent hall for the festival) said at the time: 'I think the older farming community is a bit bewildered by the festival but are still supportive because the future lies in culture and tourism' (quoted in Frew 2012). The festival has sought to become a stronger part of a community, though that was never the original intention. Classical music and community ties in a tiny coastal country town sought to invert the typical urban hierarchy of credibility and marginality, and created a new sense of place.

CONCLUSION

The Four Winds Festival is atypical of many regional festivals, by being geographically distant from the local community and primarily performing innovative classical music that might not be to everyone's taste. At the start, it predictably appeared elitist and eccentric to longtime local residents. Yet this case shows how a festival with a long gestation period and lots of sustained attempts at community engagement can eventually transcend its specific status as a classical/art music event, and became more synonymous with the town, and with the wider region. Being a discerning lover of classical music became less important than an engaged member of the community, whether via participation in a local choir or by volunteering support services. As this symbiosis became stronger, the festival grew, drew larger audiences, attracted metropolitan political support and financial grants, and had a social and economic impact on the town and wider region. New linkages and mobilities were forged with metropolitan centers in a deliberate inversion of an imagined geography of creativity that typically marginalizes rural places (Gibson 2012).

This transformation has not been entirely unproblematic. The festival has arguably fueled class tensions and exacerbated the transformation of a once low-income area into a more affluent middle-class destination. Young people growing up in Bermagui may in the future no longer be able to afford to live there, though whether this is the entire fault of the festival is moot. In parallel to experiences in the city, cultural programs such as music and festivals may unwittingly confirm the class politics of gentrification, even when in the case of such events the intention is to transcend class difference toward more inclusive social goals (Gibson and Homan 2004). Festivals are one way in which small rural places gain positive reputations with moneyed urban newcomers, contributing to a cycle of property price rises that can marginalize low-income people from the region.

Yet the story of the Four Winds Festival is not nearly so simply divisive. Efforts to involve the older strand of local community have been persistent and have gradually succeeded, including shifting events within the festival to accessible and free local venues, diversifying programming, and making performance opportunities available for local Aboriginal musicians and choirs (who come from diverse class, age, and gender backgrounds). Unlike large commercial festivals, where tokenistic attempts are often made to smooth over local resistance rather than any genuine local empowerment (see Gibson and Connell 2012 for examples), in this case strong commitment from management as well as gradual incorporation of a diversity of local interests has built a genuine sense of integration. This does not thwart the criticism that such events contribute to upwardly mobile gentrification of the place, but it does provide a more sophisticated view of mobilities of migrants, tourists and musicians, beyond simplistic 'us and them' dichotomies.

In an equally rural setting outside the small town of Inverell (NSW), Opera in the Paddock went through almost exactly the same trajectory, struggling to convince local people that opera was a viable and enjoyable rural pursuit, but nevertheless it became a quirky annual event bringing farmers, shop workers, and the cultural elite together. That inland town has not had the affluent in-migration of Bermagui, and it remains an affordable, pastoral region, but now with access to high-quality opera. Meanwhile, in Parkes, celebration of Elvis was never to everyone's taste, but tolerance steadily grew, especially as economic benefits multiplied and diffused and the town was placed firmly on a metropolitan and national map of cultural renown. In some ways, these festivals are exceptional, based in a particular musical form and initiated by a handful of enthusiasts, and (sometimes consequently) begun in out-of-town settings. Alongside the Tamworth Country Music Festival and a host of others, utterly different in content and genesis, they have experienced similar histories and local tensions. All have negotiated dissent and disagreement to become part of and to build small, otherwise vulnerable places.

Yet festivals invariably reflect the interests of just some local people. They are sites where certain people project visions of place and music that may have limited local relevance, where tastes are those of a minority, and where commerce can dominate decisions about anything resembling local identity. Most festivals have experienced pressures to become more commercially astute, both when they have sought access to arts funding and national support or to acquire larger markets. As that has occurred (and for most, arguably, that has not been the case), festivals have grown and management has become more professional and powerful, but local ownership and identity is challenged. Festivals may also be pressed to retain their creativity and individuality (Quinn 2005). Festivals taking aesthetic risks gain credibility among specialist audiences, but those aimed at engaging a broader spectrum of the community (or where places host a number of festivals catering to different segments of the population) go further in alleviating a sense of exclusion. Festivals may also enable social connections for newcomers to a rural region, people in search of a new sense of identity (Gordon 2012). For such reasons, the incorporation of festivals into regional development policy making requires consideration of questions of cultural expression, vitality, and inclusion. Hence, the Four Winds Festival at Bermagui sought to reconcile concerns for quality programming with strategies to involve the wider community. Evolution, inclusion, innovation, and credibility are the concomitants of successful festivals, and the means of warding off life cycles that end in death.

Small towns are thoroughly capable of producing creativity, despite assumptions that creativity—and the creative industries—are metropolitan phenomena, and that 'best practices' are to be found in the largest cities from where they may trickle down (Gibson 2012). Festivals alone demonstrate that this is no longer tenable, and that many small towns have been able to gain significant economic, social, and cultural benefits. Just as in England, where the media have been astounded at festivals and creativity existing in seemingly improbable places (Voase 2009), so too in Australia have metropolitan commentators slowly begun to acknowledge rural creativity, evident in such festivals as Bermagui's Four Winds. Local people are part of a place that is not merely local, but a place of exchange, and a place that outsiders appreciate and are enthusiastic about (Kozorog 2011). Musical mobility makes that possible.

In Australia, more than in other countries, festivals are antidotes to drought, depression, and part of the regeneration of the countryside. Yet in the end no festival, or even clusters of festivals of different kinds (and most small towns have several), can be a panacea for rural decay. Some festivals fail. Small towns continue to struggle to diversity economies and retain high school leavers. Others, such as Four Winds, contribute tangibly to regional development, but run the risk of fueling the rural gentrification spurred by affluent in-migration, in turn alienating long-term residents. While festivals enable a limited renaissance, there are limits to festival growth because of competition, accommodation constraints, in some cases too frequent repetition, and high prices. Festivals are and are not solely about the music. The Four Winds Festival at Bermagui both takes musical credibility seriously and exists as a social event irrespective of the music. No genre of music can ever be popular with everybody; no town is going to welcome every genre.

But many towns, in Australia and elsewhere, have used music and creativity to stimulate economic and social activity and new directions of mobility in the face of recession.

REFERENCES

Argent, Neil, and Fran Rolley. 2000. 'Financial Exclusion in Rural and Remote New South Wales: A Geography of Bank Branch Rationalisation.' *Australian Geographical Studies* 38:182–203.

Battersby, Bryn and Robert Ewing. 2005. *International Trade Performance: The Gravity of Australia's Remoteness.* Canberra: Federal Government Department of Treasury.

Baum, Caroline. 2010. 'Frozen in Time.' *Sydney Morning Herald*, March 16, 13.

Burnley, Ian, and Peter Murphy. 2003. *Sea Change: Movement from Metropolitan to Arcadian Australia.* Sydney: UNSW Press.

Connell, John, and Phil McManus. 2011. *Rural Revival? Place Marketing, Tree Change and Regional Migration in Australia.* Farnham: Ashgate.

Duffy, Michelle, and Gordon Waitt. 2011. 'Rural Festivals and Processes of Belonging.' In *Festival Places: Revitalising Rural Australia*, edited by Chris Gibson, and John Connell, 44–57. Bristol: Channel View.

Durrant, Colin, and Evangelos Himonides. 1998. 'What Makes People Sing Together? Socio-Psychological and Cross-Cultural Perspectives on the Choral Phenomenon.' *International Journal of Music Education* 32:61–71.

Edwards, Rob. 2011. 'Birthday Parties and Flower Shows, Musters and Multiculturalism: Festivals in Post-war Gympie.' In *Festival Places: Revitalising Rural Australia*, edited by Chris Gibson, and John Connell, 136–54. Bristol: Channel View.

Four Winds Festival 2010. Accessed October 11, 2011. www.fourwinds.com.au.

Frew, Wendy. 2011. 'Grassroots Festival Grows into the Big League.' *Sydney Morning Herald*, December 9, 14.

Frew, Wendy. 2012. 'Change in the Wind for Festival's South Coast Home.' *Sydney Morning Herald*, March 30, 9.

Gibson, Chris. 2002. 'Rural Transformation and Cultural Industries: Popular Music on the New South Wales Far North Coast.' *Australian Geographical Studies* 40:336–56.

Gibson, Chris, ed. 2012. *Creativity in Peripheral Places: Redefining the Creative Industries.* London: Routledge.

Gibson, Chris, and John Connell. 2005. *Music and Tourism.* Clevedon: Channel View.

Gibson, Chris, and John Connell. 2012. *Music Festivals and Regional Development in Australia.* Farnham: Ashgate.

Gibson, Chris, and Deborah Davidson. 2004. 'Tamworth, Australia's "Country Music Capital": Place Marketing, Rural Narratives and Resident Reactions.' *Journal of Rural Studies* 20:387–404.

Gibson, Chris, and Shane Homan. 2004. 'Urban Redevelopment, Live Music and Public Space: Cultural Performance and the Re-Making of Marrickville.' *International Journal of Cultural Policy* 10:69–86.

Gibson, Chris, Susan Luckman, and Julie Willoughby-Smith. 2010. 'Creativity without Borders? Re-Thinking Remoteness and Proximity.' *Australian Geographer* 41:25–38.

Gibson, Chris, Gordon Waitt, Jim Walmsley, and John Connell. 2010. 'Cultural Festivals and Economic Development in Regional Australia.' *Journal of Planning Education and Research* 29:280–93.

Gordon, Andrea. 2012. 'Community Music, Place and Belonging in the Bega Valley, NSW, Australia.' MSc thesis, University of Wollongong.

Hall, C. Michael. 1989. 'The Definition and Analysis of Hallmark Tourist Events.' *GeoJournal* 19:263–68.

Hays, Terrence, and Victor Minichiello. 2005. 'The Meaning of Music in the Lives of Older People.' *Psychology of Music* 33:437–51.

Ironfest. 2013. Accessed December 1, 2012. www.ironfest.net.

Joseph, Dawn. 2007. 'Sharing Music and Culture through Singing in Australia.' *International Journal of Community Music* 2:169–81.

Khoo, Tseen, and Rodney Noonan. 2011. 'Going for Gold: Creating a Chinese Heritage Festival in Nundle, New South Wales.' *Continuum* 25:491–502.

Kozorog, Miha. 2011. 'Festival Tourism and Production of Locality in a Small Slovenian Town.' *Journal of Tourism and Cultural Change* 9:298–319.

Quinn, Bernadette. 2005. 'Changing Festival Places: Insights from Galway.' *Social and Cultural Geography* 6:237–52.

Ruting, Brad, and Jen Li. 2011. 'Tartans, Kilts and Bagpipes: Cultural Identity and Community Creation at the Bundanoon Is Brigadoon Cultural Festival.' In *Festival Places: Revitalising Rural Australia*, edited by Chris Gibson, and John Connell, 265–79. Bristol: Channel View.

Voase, Richard. 2009. 'Why Huddersfield? Media Representations of a Festival of Contemporary Music in the "Unlikeliest" Place.' *Journal of Tourism and Cultural Change* 7:146–56.

Walmsley, Jim. 2003. 'Rural Tourism: A Case of Lifestyle-led Opportunities.' *Australian Geographer* 34:61–72.

Xie, Philip F. 2003. 'The Bamboo-Beating Dance in Hainan, China: Authenticity and Commodification.' *Journal of Sustainable Tourism* 11:5–16.

6 Branding the City

Music Tourism and the European Capital of Culture Event

Simone Krüger

Music is connected with tourism in diverse ways. As an expression of culture, a form of intangible heritage, or a signifier of place, music provides an important and emotive narrative for tourists. Adopting the qualities of a cultural resource, music is actively used to evoke images and associations with specific places. To this end, music tourism constructs nostalgic attachments to musical heritage sites, scenes, sounds, or individuals, while relying on musical events and incidents from the past that can be packaged, visualized, photographed, and 'taken back' home. Nostalgia and memory are thus key motivators for the global music tourist in search for particular kinds of authentic musical experiences. This chapter explores these notions by focusing on the role of music, place branding, and tourism during Liverpool's year as European Capital of Culture (ECOC). To do so, the chapter will illustrate the branding of Liverpool as *The World in One City* to promote tourism and urban regeneration under consideration of migration and settlement, while exploring the staging and commodification of music events and activities during Liverpool's year in 2008 as ECOC.

Music tourism is often built around specific geographical locations—cities, regions, countries—that have acquired special significance through their musical associations. Liverpool provides a well-known and often-studied case in point, with specific focus typically placed on the packaging and marketing of the Beatles and Merseybeat (e.g., Brocken and Davis 2012; Cohen 1994, 2007; Connell and Gibson 2003; Leaver and Schmidt 2009). To many Beatles fans, the city of Liverpool is an emotionally charged place evocative of ideas surrounding pilgrimage, nostalgia, and heritage that center on sites of musical production and performance; the places that shaped their music; the incidents from the past; or the tangible artifacts that can be photographed. A visit to Liverpool is, to many music tourists,[1] a kind of nostalgic and emotional quest in search for an authentic past—a pilgrimage. This prompted local businesses, entrepreneurs, and organizations to package, stage, and market Beatles memorabilia and nostalgia in the 1970s and 1980s, while more recently Beatles and Merseybeat tourism has become officially developed by Liverpool City Council (LCC) in an effort toward the city's regeneration and reversal of its economic decline (see also Cohen 2003, 383). Initiatives to use culture and the creative industries such as TV, cinema, multimedia, music, books, and festivals to contribute to the economy, employment, and cultural diversity of a city for urban renewal and to offset the negative consequences of globalization are also more recently conceptualized under the theme of 'creative cities', which is rapidly attracting the interest of academics and policy makers around the world:

> Based upon the belief that culture is more than just an expensive public good but can play an important role in urban renewal as well, the concept of 'creative cities' has been most thoroughly tested so far in response to the economic decline of industrial cities in Europe, the US and Australia over the last two decades. (UNESCO 2004)[2]

Such initiatives do not only promote economic development, but also seek to contribute to a city's 'charisma', diversity, identity, and image, and thereby to promote cultural tourism (see, e.g., Hughes 2010). According to UNESCO (2004), cultural tourism 'is increasingly important as the tourism industry is moving away from mass marketing toward tailored travel focussed on individuals, and tourists now rate cultural and heritage activities among their top five reasons for travelling', an issue already raised in the introductory chapter. Today it is estimated that a significant proportion of Liverpool's annual 54.5 million tourists visit the city at least partly because of its musical heritage, and it is estimated that more than £400 million per year is now spent in Liverpool as a direct result of Beatles tourism (It's Liverpool 2012), a considerable increase from the estimated £20 million that Beatles tourism generated in Liverpool in 2000 (Cohen 2007, 15). The city's effort to boost its economy through music tourism became most evident in 2008, Liverpool's year as ECOC, during which I conducted an ethnographic study that sought to shed light into the interrelatedness between music, mediation, and place by examining the array of musical events and activities that were mobilized as heritage myths and tourist packages, and the impact of this experience on the city and its people (Figure 6.1; see also Adams 2012 for a useful summary about the nature, scope, applicability, advantages and limitations, and future issues surrounding ethnographic approaches in tourism studies).[3] The data collection was vast, including recorded interviews with city council officials (e.g., Liverpool City Council and the Liverpool Culture Company); researchers of the Impacts 08 team; executive members of local cultural organizations like the Beatles Museum, Liverpool Philharmonic, FACT, Tate, Bluecoat, etc.; and local musicians, composers, and audiences, including local people from all sorts of backgrounds. I also completed observations at a vast number of music concerts, events, performances, festivals, exhibitions, museums, theaters, etc., taking note of the musics, musicians, and audiences in terms of their experiences, perceptions, and attitudes. Collections of print materials in the form of official and promotional material published by LCC and Impacts 08; media coverage in local and national newspapers; websites; and flyers and other noncommericalized publications complemented the ethnographic portion of the research, alongside semiotic analysis, statistical analysis, and virtual observations.

Figure 6.1   On my way to work: A bus depicting Liverpool 08 slogans, architecture, and the Beatles drives along Hope Street (here outside Liverpool Philharmonic Hall). January 2008. Photograph by Simone Krüger.

BRANDING LIVERPOOL: THE WORLD IN ONE CITY

The Liverpool ECOC program, an initiative launched by the European Union in 1985, operates particularly in the context of broad urban regeneration for long-term economic and social change. The ECOC event delivers both a 'major cultural festival', involving multi-annual events with international reputation, and a 'cultural mega-event', usually a one-off event attracting the largest range of participants and media coverage (Langen and Garcia 2009, 7–8). The ECOC event can be seen as an effort to develop, promote, and market a 'place brand' (Hjortegaard 2010; Nobili 2005) in order to enhance a city's image, to attract tourists, and to stimulate regeneration.[4] At the heart of the Liverpool ECOC vision was an aspiration to regenerate and reposition the city nationally and globally. For instance, in the narrative constructed by LCC when bidding for the ECOC title,[5] Liverpool became branded under the theme *The World in One City* in reference to and celebration of its apparent multiculturalism.[6] Liverpool's 'multiethnic' identity, most notably from the African, Arabic, Chinese, and Indian communities, was actively used and promoted in the media campaigns accompanying the ECOC event as a positive signifier of an exoticized and Orientalist form of multiculturalism that sought to stage and museumize Liverpool's diverse cultural heritage. In doing so, the LCC represented Liverpool as a diverse and inclusive festival city based on its multicultural heritage resulting from the movement, migration, and settlement of people (see Belchem 2006 for a comprehensive historical and cultural overview, specifically Belchem and MacRaild 2006, 311–92).[7] More specifically:

> The cultural map of Liverpool is grounded in the experiences of traditionally under-represented groups and individuals. As a port, it acted as a magnet for social migration, as a focus for the slave trade and as a place of settlement for different communities, beginning with the Irish, then the Chinese, West African, seamen from many countries, in particular Somalia and the Yemen, and more recently as a location where refugees and asylum seekers have come for sanctuary. It has a cultural identity which is both local and international—The World in One City. (Liverpool Culture Company 2002, 101)

Indeed, Liverpool's role as a port city, and, resulting from that, its multicultural heritage, is often considered to be one of the key drivers for the city's musical scenes, which also tends to be the starting point in many academic and journalistic writings (e.g., Cohen 1991; Brocken 2010):

> the big factor about Liverpool was it being a port. There were always sailors coming in with records from America, blues records from New Orleans. And you could get so many ethnic sounds: African music, maybe, or Calypso via the Liverpool Caribbean community. (Foreword by Sir Paul McCartney in Du Noyer 2007, xi)[8]

Liverpool was founded by King John on 1207 as a strategic port from which the monarchy could access Ireland, and it remained a small fishing village for good 500 years, when the city rose in prominence as a port for American cargo, sugar refineries, and the slave trade, and later (after the abolishment of the transatlantic slave trade) as a center for the cotton, sugar, and tobacco industry. As industrialization and colonialism in the Americas, Africa, and Far East strengthened during the 19th century, Liverpool—the gateway of Empire (Lane 1987)—became one of the most powerful cities in the world. Liverpool's port shaped the population, as seafarers and migrants from all over the world arrived in the city during the height of British imperialism. Liverpool had strong Celtic influences, specifically from the Irish, but also Welsh and Scottish; Europeans and Scandinavians passed through the city on their way to America; seafarers from Africa and China settled in the city after gaining employment in the docks. Liverpool's financial decline began with the demise of the British Empire (Wilks-Heeg 2003, 44–49), followed by global changes at the end of the 20th century, which left Liverpool in drastic economic decline with 25 percent of its population unemployed.

This, together with the 1980s riots, left an image of Liverpool that was highly negative, connoting a place of deterioration, race riots, decreasing population, crime and unemployment: a symbol of 'urban decline' (Cohen 2007, 1).

As the city came to symbolize the economic and political decline of Britain and its former empire, Liverpool was in desperate need for a new image, urban regeneration, and economic growth. LCC recognized the role of tourism here and in the late 1990s began emphasizing Liverpool's cultural heritage, most notably the Beatles and football, in its marketing campaigns (Cohen 2012). The most dramatic turning point came when bidding for the ECOC title in 2002, while establishing the focus for the Liverpool brand as *The World in One City* (see also Nobili 2005, 316). The constructing of Liverpool as a vibrant multicultural festival city was reinforced subsequently in the promotional materials accompanying the 2008 ECOC event. For instance, images in the official Liverpool 08 program often depicted Orientalist representations of people of Indian, Arabic, or African descent (Figure 6.2), while slogans like 'wondrously diverse' and 'melting pot' used in the backgrounds of most promotional materials further romanticized and celebrated difference and Otherness, all of which reaffirm a certain narrative of collective memory and imaged diversity that became the pinnacle of Liverpool's place brand. The official narrative thereby condensed Liverpool's history into an easily promotable image: a city of movement, initially 'for the slave trade' (Liverpool Culture Company 2002, 101), but today a contemporary global city, marked by diversity and inclusivity. In doing so, the official and promotion material not only constructed the concept 'Liverpool', but also adapted EU rhetoric and agendas to produce and promote 'Europeanness' or European identity (Lähdesmäki 2009), manifested by both the canons of 'high' European art and other forms of European popular culture, and by the cultural diversity of the city.

Yet while representations by migrant groups are clearly evident in the branding of Liverpool as a multicultural city, the particular choices made by LCC also created an 'official culture' that played on and reaffirmed difference and Otherness in the depictions and representations of these groups. This is evident by the fact that local Yemeni culture (rather than international music by, e.g., *raï*-singer Khaled) was featured in representations of Liverpool's migrant Arabic community in official and promotion materials, or that local musicians from African migrant communities like Nigerian Oludele Olaseinde and Senegalese Mamadou Diaw felt the need to 'perform their ethnicity' and thereby tap into preconceived assumptions about 'authentic' African music (Andersson 2011).

In highlighting Liverpool's history as a port city of migration and settlement, the narrative constructed by LCC evoked notions of past and present, local and global as shapers of Liverpool's identity as a 'cocktail of cultures' (Liverpool Culture Company 2002, 1102). Branding Liverpool as

Figures 6.2(a)   Liverpool 08 Program, containing images depicting Indian women in arm bangles and brightly colored skirts, dancing in the (monsoon?) rain (08 Liverpool ECOC 2008, 25 and 94). Published by Liverpool City Council. Reproduced with permission.

Figure 6.2(b)   Liverpool 08 Program, young Arabs in turbans holding large daggers, similar to the characters in 1001 Nights and Aladdin (ibid., 56). Published by Liverpool City Council. Reproduced with permission.

Figure 6.2(c) Liverpool 08 Program, a man of African descent with colorful face paint, wearing a costume accessorized with beads, strings, and feathers (ibid., 74). Published by Liverpool City Council. Reproduced with permission.

The World in One City, which functioned as an umbrella for the multiple strands of cultural experiences that Liverpool had to offer, including heritage, art, football, and music, was sought to be achieved via a vast program of activity, specifically through the main program of events and related activity branded as 'Liverpool 08' that was coordinated by Liverpool Culture Company (Garcia, Melville, and Cox 2010, 12), and included around 300 events themed around music, literature, art, streets, stage, participate, conversation, sport, and exploring.[9]

In considering music, specifically, the Liverpool ECOC event featured an impressive range of musical activities (Figure 6.3), including 'big' names like Paul McCartney and Ringo Starr, and an equally impressive budget (e.g., Garcia, Melville, and Cox 2010, 17; ECOTEC 2009, 60–61). Yet since the staging of an event concentrating on international, rather than local, culture had already caused controversy among some local groups during Glasgow's ECOC event in 1990 (Richards 2000), LCC was keen to involve a nuanced range of international, national, and local artists, with a strong focus on community access and participation:

Of the artists and performers in the programme procured, delivered or large grant funded by the Liverpool Culture Company . . . 32% were from a Black and Minority Ethnic background. . . . Up to 50% of professional artists employed as part of the programme for the Liverpool ECOC were locally based. This was complemented by 30% national and 20% overseas based artists. (Garcia, Melville, and Cox 2010, 14)

Accordingly, around 66 music events of different sizes and musical styles were staged during 2008 (Figure 6.3), which can be grouped according to size of event type on a sliding scale from global—glocal—local: (i) ECOC flagship or highlight events, typically ticketed large-scale (even mega-) events with a

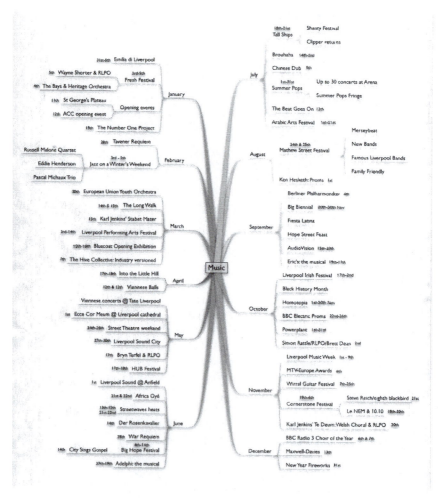

Figure 6.3 Overview of the music program of activity and events during 2008. Provided to the author by Gordon Ross, music coordinator at the Liverpool Culture Company. Reproduced with permission.

one-off nature, which attract the largest range of international participants and media coverage; (ii) mid-range ticketed events like larger concerts, performances, or festivals, which attract a large number of participants from the region and beyond the northwest and national media coverage; and (iii) small-scale events, such as free community events and music competitions, that attract largely local participants with minimal media coverage.

MUSIC, TOURISM, IMPACT: BACK TO THE BEATLES!

The staging and promoting of events of differing scale, varied musical styles, and multicultural nature is reflective of more inclusive, democratic concerns, and shows LCC's attempt to combat the often-voiced criticisms that regard the ECOC event as a capitalist exercise purely aimed at stimulating a city's economic activity and improving the image of a city to attract inward investment, which is, in fact, reflective of a trend toward economic and urban regeneration goals (and away from purely cultural ones) in the shifting policy emphasis of the ECOC event since its inception in the mid-1980s (Richards 2000; see also Hughes 2010, 122–23 for discussions on city marketing more generally). For instance, a local resident raised the following critique early in 2008 titled *Culture of Capitalism?*:

> I AM concerned that the events taking place for the Capital of Culture 2008 are, in most cases events, which would be taking place no matter if Liverpool was the host of Capital of Culture and that these events cost money. All the theatres are open and the Grand National take place each year. I would actually like some one to let me know what I can do with my children that will not cost me a whole day's salary. Also, it would be good to find out what there is for children to do free of charge during the school holidays. Or is the Capital of Culture 2008 taking place for the city council staff and the Liverpool MPs to attend events at the Liverpool resident taxpayer's expense? (Peter R. Anderson-Makinson, reader letter, *Liverpool Echo*, January 8, 2008)

To combat such initial criticisms in the local media surrounding affordability and accessibility, more than 70 percent of cultural activities were free (ECOTEC 2009, 59; see also McLoughlin 2008, which makes special mention of the 'free' nature of The People's Opening). Moreover, LCC actively involved a vibrant scene of local grassroots musical activity inspired by the ECOC title itself—here grouped into the third category of small-scale events—and made efforts to open up cultural participation via, for instance, the Creative Community Programme (Figure 6.4) that encouraged community-based projects by local artists and organizations. In other words, LCC sought to deliver an inclusive program of activity, evident in a vast number of community-based projects. This intensive public engagement program consisted of local events, competitions, or festivals, which attracted predominantly local participants and audiences, and minimal media coverage. Among these activities was the Open Culture initiative that engaged around 6,300 individuals and organizations (ECOTEC 2009, 66). For example, the Liverpool Song project as part of the Open Culture initiative called locals to compose a new 'Song for Liverpool post '08', which was taken up by hundreds of residents and reflects people's enthusiasm to contribute toward and participate in a celebration of 'their' city. One good example of such 'grassroots' engagement is the writing and recording of the song called 'This City' (2008) by former rock band Damascus,[10] which is characteristic of the band's influential New-Wave-Of-British-Heavy-Metal musical style and emotionally expressive of place-based 'Scouse' identity commonly known for working-class pride and good-humored people (Boland 2008), and here includes references to the Catholic influence to the city (Example 6.1).

Chorus:
This city is mine
This city is yours
Stays deep inside my heart
This city is ours
[Repeat]

Verse:
If you wanna know what rocks about this city
It's not the lights or buildings pretty
It's not the statues, church or steeple
What makes it rock, it's gotta be the people
[Repeat]

You think the good things never last
You think the music's in the past
You think the cast have all been cast
Etc.

Example 6.1 'Your City' (2008) by Damascus. Lyrics by David Bridge (guitar) and Billy Downes (vocals); bass guitar by Mike Booth, drums by Bill Campion. Provided to author and reproduced with permission.

However, hundreds of songs (but one) ended up 'in the draw' and were never performed or recorded, while the winning song 'The Pool of Life' by Phil Jones and The Pool Band (the three band members wrote the lyrics) was released as a single recorded at Waterloo-based Mersey Sound Studios (Jones 2008). It is interesting to note here that the winning song was not performed by a local amateur musician, but well-known singer songwriter Phil Jones with an already established profile, which most certainly helped to boost beyond-local recognition, media coverage, and single sales.

World in One City

As in previous years the Creative Communities programme will be supported by a series of seminars and workshops that seek to support community groups in developing or enhancing their skills in planning, organising and delivering their own programmes of work. Learning from previous years the support programme will feature a range of topics people have fed back on and include sessions on working with the media, project management and monitoring, event planning and equalities training.

The community grant programme for 2008 will enable 54 community groups to undertake arts and sports projects. This is the final stage of a 4-year investment in grass roots culture. Since 2004 the Culture Company has awarded nearly £3.37m in funding to a mixture of community groups, arts organisations and individuals enabling them to deliver a massive programme of work which has engaged thousands of participants from all corners of the city. For 2008 there are a variety of events, exhibitions and performances including:

- **Wales and Liverpool 2008**: An exploration by Merseyside Welsh Heritage Society into the distinctive contribution that the Welsh have made to the character and culture of Liverpool.
- **Double Dutch**: A girls' sport project by Pidgin Productions promoting heath, exercise and confidence through team skipping.
- **Lodge Lane Days:** A project involving an artist using the windows of community groups and businesses on Toxteth's Lodge Lane as an open gallery space, while working with the local community to produce new work.
- **Life of Totem Chinese Ethnic Dance Show:** A showcase of Chinese ethnic dance.
- **In the Frame:** An exhibition showcasing the work of disabled artists in Liverpool.

Figure 6.4 A page from the promotional brochure 08 Participate, which promotes the Creative Communities Programme in order to inform the general public about these activities. Published by Liverpool City Council, 2008. Reproduced with permission.

The Liverpool ECOC program of music activity also featured a significant number of midsize concerts, performances, and festivals—here grouped into the second category of events—that attracted a large number of participants locally and from beyond the northwest, alongside regional and (in some cases) international media coverage, while the latter involved predominantly specialized media aimed at niche, rather than global, media audiences. In this category are typically events like the Matthew Street Festival and Liverpool Pops, as well as the 'multicultural' festivals like Milapfest (Indian), Brazilica (Brazilian), the Arabic Arts Festival, and Africa Oyé, although these festival events are already well established and would have taken place in the absence of ECOC designation.

The Liverpool Arabic Arts Festival was first held in 2002, formerly known as the London Yemeni Festival and held under the auspices of the Yemeni Community Association. Since 2002, and growing out of the efforts of Nadey Al-Bluecoat (a partnership between Liverpool Arabic Centre, formerly known as Liverpool Yemeni Arabic Club, and the Bluecoat Arts Centre), the festival attracted sponsorship from the North West Art Board and witnessed rising national and international success (Qassim and Hassan 2009). The 2008 festival (during the ECOC year) was launched at the Family Day in Sefton Park's Palm House and attended by 2,500 people, including the Ambassador of the Republic of Yemen and Councillor Paul Clark, Lord Mayor of Liverpool. While the launch event was broadcast by BBC Radio Merseyside to an estimated audience of 50,000 people (Andrews 2008, 3), the festival was also radio broadcast on national (BBC Radio London) and international (Dubai Eye Radio; BBC Arabic World Service) level, and covered on Sky Channel 166 as part of their 'Best of Summer' 2008 program (ibid.). A total of 27,000 visits to 41 events was recorded (ibid.), while the highlight of the festival was a performance by international *rai*-star Marcel Khalife (known internationally as Khaled) in the Liverpool Philharmonic Hall.

Meanwhile, Africa Oyé resembles the largest African music festival in the UK, which is held annually over two days in Sefton Park and popularized with African food, drinks, arts, crafts, and fashion stalls and workshops (Figure 6.5). Beginning in 1992 as a series of small gigs in the city center, the event grew steadily, moving to its present Sefton Park location in 2002 to cope with rising audience numbers; for instance, the 2007 event attracted an audience of more than 40,000 people, which was expected to be exceeded in 2008. While the festival lineup typically involves international bands and musicians,[11] the festival is attended largely by local and national audiences, and it features in the national and (to a growing extent) international media. For instance, Oyé 2008 was recorded by BBC Radio 3 and The Africa Channel (Sky Channel 281) for future broadcast in the UK, Africa, and the Caribbean, and was thus promoted to niche, rather than global, media audiences. As in previous years, the festival did not feature local African bands or musicians like The River Niger Orchestra (headed by Oludele Olaseinde) or The Super Libidor Band (headed by Mamadou Diaw), which may be so because the festival directors/organizers, Kenny Murray and Paul Duhaney, seek to promote a 'beyond-local', international appeal.

Figure 6.5 Africa Oyé festival, June 21 and 22, 2008. The festival is held in Sefton Park, here also featuring (in the background) the high-rising apartment towers in the L8 area of Liverpool. Photograph by author.

The fact that Liverpool's Arabic or African (or Indian, or Brazilian, or Chinese, for that matter) heritage and (the staging of this heritage during festivals) featured strongly in LCC's bid and subsequent promotional efforts is particularly important, as it taps into the narratives spun around the concept 'Liverpool' as *The World in One City*, which, as already argued, served the strategic performance of multiculturalism. Here, pluralism and difference were turned into a spectacle for consumption through 'museumizing' culture (after Appadurai 1990, 304), creating a staged environment where musicians performed their ethnicity to resemble that of the festival, a common mechanism used in official narratives surrounding multiculturalism.

Meanwhile, LCC supported 14 local artists and organizations (from 150 applicants) for the Liverpool Commissions strand by commissioning 'exciting, innovative art projects of international quality' (ECOTEC 2009, 66) from local artists and organizations. Noteworthy here is The Rightful Owners of the Song project, led by Jonathan Ross, which brought together a small number of Liverpool's pub 'karaoke' singers to perform a one-off concert of pub classics with the Royal Liverpool Philharmonic Orchestra providing the backing music. Jonathan explained the context for this project as follows:

> The Rightful Owners of the Song seeks to acknowledge and celebrate 'working' culture. Working class. . . . To place this economically impoverished musical culture in relation to the incredible richness of resources available to a Symphony orchestra offers the possibility of exposing and bridging such cultural 'rifts'. ('The Rightful Owners of the Song' Project Description, provided to author and reproduced with permission)

While the audience apparently consisted of 'both fans of the orchestra and those of the singers themselves' (McNulty 2008), some selected pub singers clearly already enjoyed a certain musical career: 'William Wenton, 60, who once toured the world with Chris Rea is one of the chosen singers' (Anderson 2008). Even so, the coupling of 'working class' and 'high art' is noteworthy here; indeed, the staging of the event in Liverpool Philharmonic Hall, a resemblant of the art deco period and its idealistic notions of exoticism, exploration, and travel (see Henley and McKernan 2009), and accompanied by the RLPO, is important, not least because 'the award-winning Royal Philharmonic Orchestra is . . . at the height of its powers [with] a global reputation for excellence under the leadership of Chief Conductor Vasily Petrenko' (flyer, Liverpool Philharmonic Hall, 2011). The appointment of Petrenko brought global connections and tourists not only to the Philharmonic Hall, but to the city more widely. The decision to commission this project seems to, at least to me, be made on the basis of its promotional potential to officially celebrate Liverpool's 'working-class' people (local culture) alongside 'high art' (global culture).

Clearly, the Liverpool ECOC event sought to emphasize both, economic and cultural objectives, which it achieved through a combined emphasis on the local and glocal aspects of Liverpool's cultural heritage. It has even been suggested that the commissioning of Liverpool-born high profile international artists and performers (and their visibility) was not a significant priority for Liverpool's ECOC (ECOTEC 2009, 67). Indeed, 'the city's Beatles connections were deliberately downplayed in official Capital of Culture documents (including the original bid and published programme of events) in order to highlight local cultural diversity' (Cohen 2012, 13). Yet despite the official narrative in certain publications that certainly sought to promote the ECOC event in a positive light,[12] a key aim of the Liverpool ECOC was to attract more visitors to the city, and thus:

> to use tourism as a driver for economic development, both directly through visitor spend and the subsequent growth of the visitor economy, and indirectly through changing the image of the city in order to attract inward investment and emphasise the quality of the city's offer for potential residents. (Garcia, Melville, and Cox 2010, 24)[13]

A glimpse at the number of visits to Liverpool motivated by the ECOC title and events program reveals an interesting peak during January/February, May/June, and July/August (Garcia, Melville, and Cox 2010, 25), and, perhaps predictably, this increase in visits to Liverpool coincides with the staging of global music events and international stars, events here grouped into the first category of mega-events. These musical highlight or flagship events, also described as 'world-class' events (ibid., 35), included the Liverpool ECOC Opening Events (January 11 and 12), the MTV Europe Music Awards (November 6), and the Paul McCartney/Liverpool Sound concert (June 1), as well as classical music events (ibid.).[14] These global music events achieved maximum impact economically and culturally, while being themed around 'high art' (e.g., classical music) and Liverpool's popular music heritage (e.g., the Beatles and Merseybeat—the Liverpool Sound, as well as other well-known pop music artists; see also ECOTEC 2009, 59). For instance, the musical billing during the Opening Events drew predominantly on Liverpool's popular music heritage, including Ringo Starr, The Wombats, Echo and the Bunnymen, Pete Wylie, Ian Broudie, Shack, and The Christians (for a useful description of the opening event at St George's Hall, see Cohen 2012, 2–3; 2013).[15] The local newspaper, *Liverpool Echo*, published an article entitled 'Ringo Kicks Off a City Spectacular', announcing the Opening Events and playing on sentiments surrounding the Beatles and Beatles-influenced music:

> This week marks the first big events of 2008, with one of the biggest taking place outside St. George's Hall this Friday. . . . this is a free event which includes former Beatle Ringo Starr on top of the historic hall. . . . The People's Opening promises buckets of spectacle, emotion, humour and surprises with music ranging from Ringo Starr to the Wombats. It's for the people of Liverpool and it's free. (McLoughlin 2008, 5)

It was specifically the city's 'white' popular music heritage (see also Cohen 1994, 123; 2012, 13–14), staged as large-scale mega-events that were used as key drivers for national and international tourism and travel.[16] Music was, once again, actively used to 'sell' place, and place in turn used to market a particular sound, the Liverpool Sound, which began to emerge with the Merseybeat groups of the 1960s like the Beatles, Gerry and the Pacemakers, and The Searchers. Ever since, Liverpool has continued to produce its own particular brand of guitar bands like Echo and the Bunnymen, The La's, The Coral, and, right up to the present day, The Wombats, The Zutons, and The Rascals. The most successful band, the Beatles, became undeniably the biggest global music product and is accredited with lending Liverpool its world-renowned reputation as the Capital of Pop. Both the jingly-jangly guitar sound of early Beatles records and their later experiments with psychedelic pop have become staples of the Liverpool Sound and can be heard in the music of The La's and Echo and the Bunnymen, who in turn have influenced more recent Liverpool bands that specialize in jingly-jangly guitar pop, as well as featuring that popular psychedelic twist.

The Paul McCartney/Liverpool Sound concert that took place on June 1, 2008, in the Anfield Stadium of Liverpool FC resembles another powerful example of a large-scale music event—attended by more than 32,000 fans—that successfully tapped into the pleasures and expectations of the city's global 'customers' by satisfying their nostalgic imaginations and romanticized desires for firsthand experiences with the Beatles and Beatles-influenced music (Figure 6.6). Headlined by Paul McCartney himself, the event also featured Peter Kay as MC and younger bands like Leeds-based Kaiser Chiefs and Liverpool-based The Zutons.[17] Paul McCartney performed the usual Beatles classics,[18] thereby tapping into the city's desire to stage Beatles heritage and nostalgia in order to attract a substantial number of international tourists and, with it, international recognition and revenue. A visitor from Alaska described her 'Beatles pilgrimage' to Liverpool as follows:[19]

> Last winter, Judie and I were offered the opportunity of a lifetime to attend the Liverpool Sound Concert in Liverpool which was being headlined by Sir Paul McCartney on June 1st, 2008. . . . The Magical Macca Tour started on May 29, 2008 at the Premier Inn on Albert Dock, where the tour group was residing for the Liverpool expedition. . . . The next morning, Friday May 30th, we had the customary wonderful English breakfast then went through the Beatle Story Museum & Exhibition. . . . Later that morning Judie and I, along with several other group members, went on the National Trust Tour to see John and Paul's childhood homes. It was a mystical experience to walk in the homes where the two musical geniuses grew up. . . . Sunday, June 1st—Paul McCartney Concert Day!. . . . The Magical Macca Tour group rode to the Anfield Stadium in the Cavern's 'retired' Magical Mystery Tour bus, which was a magically mysterious way to start the evening. . . . It was a surreal occasion to be in Liverpool watching Paul McCartney, from the Beatles, perform in his hometown. . . . When riding

back from the concert, we were in the Magical Mystery Tour bus singing Beatle songs with windows down, while people on the streets waved and took pictures of us. The entire evening was the ultimate magical phenomenon! (Leslie Baker, Nikiski, Alaska. Accessed January 16, 2013. http://www.liverpooltours.com/2008maccatourreport.htm)

Figure 6.6   The Liverpool Sound concert, here promoted in the official Liverpool 08 Program as 'once-in-a-lifetime event'. Published by Liverpool City Council, 2008. Reproduced with permission.

Perhaps because the Liverpool Sound concert, as local rumor had it, was supposed to feature a significantly larger number of bands and musicians, both locally and internationally,[20] but did not manage to do so because of financial problems, the concert reinforced—once again—a particular Liverpool Sound that is closely associated with the Beatles and Beatles-influenced music, a reality that differed significantly to the branding of Liverpool under the theme of *The World in One City*. At least in regard to mega-events, Liverpool was promoted as the city of the Beatles and Capital of Pop, and not necessarily as multicultural festival city, the new city brand, a reality that shows that music tourism tends to build upon, model, and reinforce a certain music canon.

CARNIVALESQUE UTOPIA, OR CAPITAL OF CAPITALISM?

Liverpool ECOC provides a striking example of the ways in which music, place branding, and tourism intersect in a post-globalized world. Under the overall theme of *The World in One City*, the ECOC event sought to promote Liverpool as a world-class cultural city with a positive reputation, to promote international tourism, and to promote urban regeneration through culture. This economic revival of Liverpool due to the ECOC event could be seen as a reason to celebrate globalization, in the local setting of the city at least, where economic ambitions were officially underpinned by more democratic concerns with building community access and participation. The dual nature of LCC's efforts shows how cultural mega-events like the ECOC can contribute toward a 'culture of collaboration', a modern-day cultural phenomenon that helps to explain collective feeling during festivals and construct an artificial atmosphere of inclusivity, eclecticism, and tolerance. In this context, Mikhail Bakhtin's concept/social institution of carnivalesque is highly significant, as the advent of the carnivalesque reflects the transition of city marketing (Hughes 2010, 132). While there exists a historical link between modern-day festivals and the medieval carnival, in carnivalesque audiences are active participants, not simply spectators, which emphasizes the apparent participatory nature of such events and overrides any significance placed on specific, individual performers:

> Carnival is not a spectacle seen by the people; they live in it, and everyone participates because its very idea embraces all the people. . . . Such is the essence of carnival, vividly felt by all its participants [. . .] as an escape from the usual official way of life. (Bakhtin 2008, 7–8)

While carnival is regarded as a spectacle where the serious (as exemplified by 'higher' renaissance culture) and the comic (as reflected in medieval 'folk' consciousness) are simultaneously present and in this process subverting hegemonic assumptions, one pivotal characteristic contained within carnivalesque and relevant here is the suspension of political order and, with it, hierarchical social structure, transforming the carnival into a classless social potpourri of people of different backgrounds. This 'classlessness' is indeed reflected in the official aims of the Liverpool ECOC event. In this regard, the official narrative aimed at dismantling the authoritative voice of the hegemony through the celebration of collaborative culture (and the inclusion of alternative voices) has thus been central to the branding of Liverpool as *The World in One City*. Liverpool ECOC and its representations portray a new urbanity, a postindustrial city that is carnivalesque and festive.

Even so, however, it seems that the staging of different event types and the representations of culture in the promotional materials, as illustrated in this chapter, reflect the workings of the global, capitalist media and music industries, and thereby reinforce certain hegemonic cultural practices. For instance, ECOC official materials emphasized *local* Yemeni culture rather than international Arabic music (e.g., *raï*-singer Khaled). Representations in the official and promotion materials thereby functioned to 'strengthen some forms of culture or culture of some groups in the city or region, and in turn, other forms or other cultures are pushed towards the margins' (Lähdesmäki 2009, 217). Meanwhile, with complete control over what musics or musicians were being heard, 'big names' were staged on the basis of 'international' impact for high costs and were heard by thousands worldwide, globally, while other musicians, particularly from Liverpool's local communities and so-called minorities remained in the periphery and/or were seen by only small audiences, pointing toward the tensions that emerge from initiatives targeted at tourists and international audiences versus those targeted at local residents:

> Yet the Liverpool events also illustrate the emphasis on White, male Anglo-American rock in dominant accounts of Liverpool's popular music past, and how diversity sometimes appeared to be tacked onto such accounts rather than a central component. (Cohen 2012, 13)

Thus while community engagement and participation featured high on the 'official' agenda, local Liverpudlians did not necessarily agree. Many musicians, such as Senegalese-born Mamadou Diaw or Nigerian-born Oludele Olaseinde,[21] with whom I became acquainted over the years while residing in Liverpool, felt that the contribution made by 'black' residents to Liverpool's soundscape, which featured heavily in the bid and subsequent promotional campaigns surrounding the ECOC event, had been overlooked, overshadowed, or marginalized during the actual event (see also Andersson 2011). Meanwhile, Paul Duhaney from Africa Oyé explained that:

> It was a weird one, Capital of Culture, because originally we [Africa Oyé] were . . . would kind of be at the forefront of that. You know we

were featured in the bid video . . . as one of the jewels in the crown of the city, but as time went on . . . we realized that . . . there was more interest in projects that were being brought in from outside of the city, as opposed to existing projects that were going on in the city, which was quite frustrating because . . . most of the arts organizations in the city thought, you know, this is a chance for us to shine and show the world what we are about. But that didn't transpire and they brought in . . . Ringo Starr for £2 million and this mechanical spider thing [for] £2 million pounds. . . . And you know we really didn't benefit in any shape or form from Capital of Culture. (Interview transcript, available in Andersson 2011, 107–12; reprinted with permission from Paul Duhaney)

Liverpool's apparent multiculturalism that resulted from its borderland or gateway city status—a 'melting pot' where different cultures meet and merge as these became constructed in the bid and ECOC event (and, once again, reflects EU rhetoric)—also distracts away from actual injustices, such as racial segregation, and with it, social, economic, and cultural exclusion of certain (notably 'black') ethnic communities in Liverpool (Brown 2005). This shows that the ECOC event tended toward a particular place brand that reflected an 'official culture', rather than to promote to the 'outside' international world an organic culture that already existed within the city (see Wilks-Heeg 2004, 353). These forms of culture did and still do exist, but 'local' culture did not feature for the gazes of the world tourist. Instead, in order to reposition, brand, and market Liverpool internationally as a global, inclusive cultural city, particular emphasis was placed on 'high art' and Liverpool's 'white' popular heritage, reflexive (once again) of EU rhetoric to highlight those works of art and cultural sites valued in Western art and cultural history and seen within the frames of high culture (Lähdesmäki 2009, 219). Important questions may be raised here about what culture is for, as there seem to emerge tensions between more liberal views about using culture to enhance mutual respect and understanding to lead happier and harmonious lives versus views that regard culture as a means to bring about quantifiable economic benefits, and so to promote an official culture aimed at improving a city's image and enhancing economic regeneration. While LCC clearly sought to combine the two, the reality is that globalization and late capitalism have forced cities to use culture as a driver for income generation, a practice usefully termed 'city imagineering' (Hughes 2010). Culture, including music, in the postmodern age is an intangible commodity for potential economic gains, which turns places like Liverpool and its Beatles-themed locations and events into a postmodern tourist site (Urry 1990). Besides a carnivalesque utopia, Liverpool ECOC may thus also be seen as a brand product of a mixture between British neocolonialism and forms of global capitalism and its dominant meanings and experiences.

NOTES

1. Leaver and Schmidt (2009, 225) found during their research that local Liverpudlians categorized Beatles tourists into four categories, namely, fans (who like the music), anoraks (who have a detailed knowledge of the music and recording history), fanoraks (a more extreme fan with greater knowledge), and fundamentalists ('ultra' fans).
2. Two years after the ECOC event, LCC (under the project leadership of Gordon Ross) submitted a bid under UNESCO's Creative Cities programme to become UNESCO City of Music (see also http://www.liverpoolcityofmusic.com/, accessed March 13, 2013).
3. The project was entitled 'Liverpool '08 and Beyond: Music, Mediation and Place' and supported by Liverpool John Moores University.
4. Place-branding is by no means unique to Liverpool and first occurred in the late 1970s in the US as a response to the changes in the global economic system, which left key industrialized enters in decline (Ward 1998, 186).
5. Liverpool City Council (LCC) is the governing and administrative body of the city, which set up Liverpool Culture Company (LCC), the managing and commissioning body for the Liverpool ECOC. Note that Liverpool City Council and Liverpool Culture Company are both abbreviated as LCC and used here interchangeably, as the latter remained a subsidiary to Liverpool City Council when managing the ECOC event.
6. For a useful overview on and critique of multiculturalism, see Werbner (2005, 759–63).
7. The celebration of multiculturalism in the media campaigns that accompanied the ECOC event is overshadowed with controversy. While Liverpool's role as a port city brought people (seafarers, migrants, etc.) from all over the world, Liverpool also played a key role in Britain's empire-building project with its association to the transatlantic slave trade, from which it is said to have benefited (Brown 2005, 3). Furthermore, the infamous (in the British press) 1980s riots were a direct result of the racial tensions bubbling under the city's glossy cover, and even today there are reports about the city's racial and social segregation (Boland 2008).
8. Interestingly, Du Noyer's 2007 edition of the book used the Capital of Culture logo with permission from the Liverpool Culture Company, thereby officially validating the book's relevance to the ECOC event (Cohen 2012, 5).
9. More specifically, 276 highlight events were listed in the official Liverpool 08 Program, while 830 events were listed on the Liverpool 08 website, which included details of cultural activities that were not explicitly branded as 'Liverpool 08' or directly funded through the Liverpool ECOC (Garcia, Melville, and Cox 2010, 14). A total of 7,000 cultural events took place in 2008, highlights of which included La Machine, a giant mechanical spider as part of the Street strands of events; the visit of the Berliner Philharmoniker conducted by Liverpudlian Sir Simon Rattle as part of the music program; and the Gustav Klimt exhibition at the Tate Liverpool, the first comprehensive exhibition of the artist's work ever shown in the UK (ECOTEC 2009, 59).
10. While the band, like so many other bands from Liverpool, never 'made it', given the positive reviews of their EP *Open Your Eyes* (1984), they recently released an album *Cold Horizon* with High Roller Records (Germany 2011), which contains remastered recordings of their 1980s releases (see http://www.hrrecords.de/high_roller/sites/release_detail.php?id=203, accessed March 12, 2013).

11. The lineup during the 2008 festival, as during prior festivals, was largely international: Odemba OK Jazz All Stars (Congo), Body Mind and Soul (Malawi), Bedouin Jerry Can Band (Egypt), Massukos (Mozambique), Bassekou Kouyate & Ngoni Ba (Mali), Candido Fabre Y Su Banda (Cuba), Kenge Kenge (Kenya), and Macka B (Jamaica/UK) (source: http://www.afri-caoye.com/halloffame.html, accessed June 5, 2013). The local River Niger Orchestra (headed by Oludele Olaseinde) featured briefly as a support band.
12. It must be remembered that the Impacts 08 team was commissioned by LCC, thus it is not surprising that in their publications there is an underlying agenda to promote the Liverpool ECOC event as a positive success for the city and its people.
13. In the original bid to win the ECOC title, Liverpool Culture Company identi-fied tourism as a key driver for broader regeneration: 'Tourism is big business for Liverpool. . . . Our vision is to double the annual visitor spend to £1 bil-lion and create 12,000 new jobs in the sector' (Liverpool Culture Company 2002, 1001).
14. For example, the world premiere of Sir John Tavener's Requiem at the Met-ropolitan Cathedral, Jah Wobble's Chinese Dub, and Sir Simon Rattle's *Ber-liner Philharmoniker* at the Philharmonic Hall.
15. The *People's Launch* outside Liverpool's St. George's Hall, attended by 50,000 people, featured performances by former Beatle Ringo Starr and Liv-erpool band The Wombats; while *Liverpool—The Musical* in Liverpool's ECHO Arena, attended by 10,000 people, featured 'a host of musical stars including Ringo Starr, Dave Stewart, Vasily Petrenko, RLPO, No Fakin DJ's, Echo and the Bunnymen, Pete Wylie, Ian Broudie, Shack, and The Chris-tians' (BBC 2007).
16. Specifically, nonresident visitors made up the majority with 63 percent of attendees at the Liverpool Sound concert (ECOTEC 2009, 70).
17. The Zutons formed in 2001 while studying music at the Liverpool Insti-tute for Performing Arts—LIPA, which was cofounded by Lead Patron Paul McCartney and is housed in his former school.
18. When I attended the concert, I was surprised also to see Dave Grohl (lead singer of the Foo Fighters), who accompanied McCartney during three Beat-les songs, as he did not feature in any promotional material for the event. In local circles it is generally assumed that Grohl performed for free, while fulfilling a lifetime dream of performing live with Beatles legend Paul McCa-rtney in Liverpool, which is once again evocative of the nostalgic and roman-ticized perceptions of Liverpool and its Beatles heritage.
19. While discussions of 'pilgrimage' as a modern-day phenomenon in music tourism are outside the purpose of this chapter, rhetoric of this kind illus-trates that people—tourists—'acquire languages of spirituality in which they come to interpret their own acts as acts of devotion and pilgrim-age through complex routes and for complex reasons' (Stokes 1999, 151), while this rhetoric is also exploited by the city's tourism industry and music press.
20. For instance, a local newspaper article by Catherine Jones entitled '£700 Macca Tickets Row' explained that: 'More than 32,000 fans will pack the football ground to see Macca along with other major names from the pop world who have been inspired by Liverpool music. Rumoured acts include U2, Oasis and the Kaiser Chiefs, although culture chiefs have not yet revealed any other names' (*Liverpool Echo*, January 15, 2008).
21. Other local musicians may be named here too, including Oludele's brother Tunji Olaseinde, Liverpool-born Ogo Nzeakor, Congolese-born Felix Ngindu Kasanganayiad, and Pierre Balla from Cameroon.

REFERENCES

08 Liverpool European Capital of Culture. 2008. *Official Liverpool 08 Yearbook*. Liverpool: Liverpool City Council.

Adams, Kathleen M. 2012. 'Ethnographic Methods.' In *Handbook of Research Methods in Tourism: Quantitative and Qualitative Approaches*, edited by Larry Dwyer, Alison Gill, and Neelu Seetaram, 339–51. Cheltenham, UK: Edward Elgar.

Anderson, Vicky. 2008. 'Liverpool's Best Pub Singers at the Philharmonic Hall.' *Liverpool Daily Post*. Accessed February 10, 2013. http://www.liverpooldailypost.co.uk/liverpool-news/regional-news/2008/10/28/liverpool-s-best-pub-singers-at-the-philharmonic-hall-64375-22130416/2/.

Andersson, Emma. 2011. 'African Musics in Liverpool: An Ethnographic Study.' Unpublished MRes thesis, School of Art and Design, Liverpool John Moores University.

Andrews, Nadine. 2008. 'Liverpool Arabic Arts Festival: Evaluation Report 2008.' Culture Probe: Creative Management Research & Consultancy.

Appadurai, Arjun. 1990. 'Disjuncture and Difference in the Global Cultural Economy.' *Theory, Culture, Society* 7:295–310.

Bakhtin, Mikhail. 2008. *Rabelais and His World*. Translated by Hélène Iswolsky. Foreword by Krystyna Pomorska. Introduction by Michael Holquist. Bloomington: Indiana University Press.

BBC. 2007. '08 Opening Ceremony.' Accessed February 10, 2013. http://www.bbc.co.uk/liverpool/content/articles/2007/12/05/08web_opening_ceremony_feature.shtml.

Belchem, John, ed. 2006. *Liverpool 800: Culture, Character and History*. Liverpool: Liverpool University Press.

Belchem, John, and Donald M. MacReid. 2006. 'Cosmopolitan Liverpool.' In *Liverpool 800: Culture, Character and History*, edited by John Belchem, 311–92. Liverpool: Liverpool University Press.

Boland, P. 2008. 'The Construction of Images of People and Place: Labelling Liverpool and Stereotyping Scousers.' *Cities* 25(6):355–69.

Brocken, Michael. 2010. *Other Voices: Hidden Histories of Liverpool's Popular Music Scene, 1930s–1970s*. Aldershot: Ashgate.

Brocken, Michael, and Melissa Davis. 2012. *The Beatles Bibliography: A New Guide to the Literature*. Manitou Springs, CO: Beatle Works.

Brown, Jacqueline Nassy. 2005. *Dropping Anchor, Setting Sail: Geographies of Race in Black Liverpool*. Princeton, NJ: Princeton University Press.

Cohen, Sara. 1991. *Rock Culture in Liverpool: Popular Music in the Making*. Oxford: Oxford University Press.

Cohen, Sara. 1994. 'Identity, Place and the "Liverpool Sound".' In *Ethnicity, Identity and Music: The Musical Construction of Place*, edited by Martin Stokes, 117–34. Oxford: Berg Publishers.

Cohen, Sara. 2003. 'Tourism.' In *Continuum Encyclopedia of Popular Music of the World*. Volume 1. *Media, Industry and Society*, edited by David Horn, Dave Laing, Paul Oliver, and Peter Wicke, 382–85. London: Continuum.

Cohen, Sara. 2007. *Decline, Renewal and the City in Popular Music Culture: Beyond the Beatles*. Aldershot: Ashgate.

Cohen, Sara. 2012. 'Musical Memeory, Heritage and Local Identity: Remembering the Popular Music Past in a European Capital of Culture.' *International Journal of Cultural Policy*. Accessed February 15, 2013. http://dx.doi.org/10.1080/10286632.2012.676641.

Cohen, Sara. 2013. '"From the Big Dig to the Big Gig": Live Music, Urban Regeneration, and Social Change in the European Capital of Culture 2008.' In *Musical Performance and the Changing City: Post-Industrial Contexts in Europe and the United States*, edited by Fabian Holt and Carsten Wergin, 27–51. New York: Routledge.

Connell, John, and Chris Gibson. 2003. *Sound Tracks: Popular Music, Identity and Place*. London: Routledge.

Du Noyer, Paul. 2007. *Liverpool Wondrous Place: From the Cavern to the Capital of Culture*. London: Virgin Books.

ECOTEC. 2009. *Ex-Post Evaluation of 2007 and 2008 European Capitals of Culture: Final Report*. Birmingham: ECOTEC. Accessed January 21, 2013. http://ec.europa.eu/dgs/education_culture/evalreports/culture/2009/capital_en.pdf.

Garcia, Beatrix, Ruth Melville, and Tamsin Cox. 2010. *Creating an Impact: Liverpool's Experience as European Capital of Culture*. Impacts 08. Accessed January 16, 2013. http://www.liv.ac.uk/impacts08/Papers/Creating_an_Impact_-_web.pdf.

Henley, Darren, and Vincent McKernan. 2009. *The Original Liverpool Sound: The Royal Liverpool Philharmonic Society*. Liverpool: Liverpool University Press.

Hjortegaard Hansen, R. 2010. 'The Narrative Nature of Place Branding.' *Place Branding and Public Diplomacy* 6:268–79.

Hughes, George. 2010. 'Urban Revitalization: The Use of Festive Time Strategies.' *Leisure Studies* 18(2):119–35.

It's Liverpool. 2012. 'We Can Work It Out.' Accessed January 19, 2013. http://www.itsliverpool.com/passions/we-cant-buy-their-love-but-can-we-put-a-price-on-the-beatles/.

Jones, Catherine. 2008. ''08 Winning Anthem Is the Pool of Life.' *Liverpool Echo*. Accessed February 10, 2013. http://www.liverpoolecho.co.uk/liverpool-news/local-news/2008/01/11/08-winning-anthem-is-the-pool-of-life-100252-20337758/.

Lähdesmäki, Tuuli. 2009. 'Concepts of Locality, Regionality and Europeanness in European Capitals of Culture.' In *Representation, Expression and Identity: Interdisciplinary Perspectives*, edited by T. Rahimy. Oxford: Inter-Disciplinary Press. Accessed March 17, 2013. htp://www.inter-disciplinary.net/wp-content/uploads/2009/11/rei-v1.3b.pdf.

Lane, Tony. 1987. *Liverpool: Gateway of Empire*. London: Lawrence and Wishart.

Langen, Floris, and Beatriz Garcia. 2009. *Measuring the Impacts of Large Scale Cultural Events: A Literature Review*. Impacts 08. Accessed January 15, 2013. www.liv.ac.uk/impacts08/.

Leaver, David, and Ruth A. Schmidt. 2009. 'Before They Were Famous: Music-Based Tourism and a Musician's Hometown Roots.' *Journal of Place Management and Development* 2(3):220–29.

Liverpool Culture Company. 2002. *Executive Summary*. Accessed January 16, 2013. http://www.liverpool08.com/Images/tcm21-32519_tcm79-56880_tcm146-122188.pdf.

McLoughlin, Jamie. 2008. 'Ringo Kicks off a City Spectacular.' *Liverpool Echo*, January 10.

McNulty, Mark. 2008. 'Rightful Owners of the Song.' Accessed February 10, 2013. http://markmcnulty.typepad.com/mark_mcnulty/2008/12/rightful-owners-of-the-song.html.

Nobili, Valentina. 2005. 'The Role of European Capital of Culture Events within Genoa's and Liverpool's Branding and Positioning Efforts.' *Place Branding* 1(3):316–28.

Qassim, Samira, and Saria Hassan. 2009. *The Liverpool Arabic Centre: A History*. Provided to the author by Taher Qassim.

Richards, Greg. 2000. 'The European Capital of Culture Event: Strategic Weapon in the Cultural Arms Race?' *Journal of Cultural Policy* 6(2):159–81.

Stokes, Martin . 1999. 'Music, Travel and Tourism: An Afterword.' Special issue (Music, Travel, and Tourism) of the *World of Music* 41(3):141–55.

UNESCO. 2004. 'Creative Cities—Promoting Social and Economic Development through Cultural Industries.' Accessed March 13, 2013. http://portal.unesco.org/en/ev.php-URL_ID=34471&URL_DO=DO_TOPIC&URL_SECTION=201.html.

Urry, John. 1990. *The Tourist Gaze: Leisure and Travel in Contemporary Societies.* London, UK: Sage.

Ward, Stephen Victor, 1998. *Selling Places: The Marketing and Promotion of Towns and Cities, 1850–2000.* London: E & FN Spon.

Werbner, Pnina. 2005. 'The Translocation of Culture: "Community Cohesion" and the Force of Multiculturalism in History.' *Sociological Review* 53(4):745–68.

Wilks-Heeg, Stuart. 2003. 'From World City to Pariah City? Liverpool and the Global Economy, 1850—2000.' In *Reinventing the City? Liverpool in Comparative Perspective*, edited by Ronaldo Munck, 36–52. Liverpool: Liverpool University Press.

7   Goatrance Travelers
Psychedelic Trance and Its Seasoned Progeny

Graham St John

This chapter examines how a heterogeneous post-1960s haven for cultural exiles evolved into a globalized traveler dance music phenomenon. In the late 1960s and into the 1970s, Goa, the former Portuguese colony of India, was a destination for traveler 'freaks' making departure from the worlds of their upbringing. In Goa, these travelers procreated a live dance music scene that developed in the 1980s as a seasonal paradise for 'trance dance' parties led by pioneer DJs, who mixed diverse electronic music for travelers from locations around the world. These parties were the product of flows of travelers carrying the latest sounds out of scenes from Paris to London, Rimini to Ibiza, Berlin to Amsterdam; from a *psychedelic tribalism* nurtured in the seasonal DJ-led scene that escalated by the turn of the 1990s, reaching a peak by the mid-1990s, around which time several factors conspired in its demise. Among these was the emergence of Goa Trance,[1] a psychedelic trance music that intended to capture the 'essence' of the idyllic parties in Goa through a *psychedelic orientalism*, a marketed theme compelling the growth of trance tourism. While the genuine Goa scene declined as a result, Goatrance, and subsequently psytrance, flourished around the world as evidenced by its paramount expressions, *psychedelic festivals*. Once traveler festivals, and thus homes for Goatrance travelers, these events grew to become recreational destinations for the *psychedelic traveler*, who is now less likely to have visited Goa, nor perhaps traveled far from home. Today, in regional party and festival organizations, the romance of the traveler sensibility infuses a global event-culture.

I explore the globalization of Goatrance with attention to these four *psychedelic* developments—tribalism, orientalism, festivals, and travelers. I thus investigate key elements of a psychedelic diaspora, a responsive and yet diverse artistic counterculture in which Goatrance and its global progeny has been a chief development. The 'trance dance' culture evolving in Goa over many consecutive seasons from the 1960s to the 1990s formed in response to repressive and untenable conditions in the home countries of travelers, chief among which was the prohibition of cannabis, LSD, and other psychoactive plants and compounds. In Goa, an amorphous mix of cultural fugitives and holidaymakers, exiles and outlaws, visionaries and vagrants, sought a multitude of freedoms from the domestic criminalization of lifestyles. They were also escaping from what many believed was an impending nuclear conflict. This exodus gave shape to the post-Goa event culture that is discussed in this chapter by way of detailed analyses of diverse global scenes and events composed through participant observation at events (notably Portugal's Boom Festival), interviews with DJs, event organizers, and partygoers, and analysis of movement niche and micromedia. Attention is directed throughout to key figures, acts, and music releases, along with principal moments, national translations, and festival productions within the transnational psychedelic trance movement. Drawing upon this multimodal research conducted on psychedelic trance history, culture, and music—psyculture—I then trace the development of this neonomadic cultural expatriation from Goa outland to global events.

GOATRANCE AND PSYCHEDELIC TRIBALISM

Psytrance music and culture was born from winter (November–April) experiments on Anjuna and proximate beaches in Goa. Goatrance/psytrance derived from the repeated seasonal influx (1960s–1990s) of aesthetics, performance techniques, and drugs imported by transnational travelers experienced in bohemian enclaves, world cosmopolitan centers, and clubbing capitals, and who sought newer, exotic, and protected plateaus of experimentation. During the 1980s, expatriate DJs transported and mixed techniques and music styles from these locales to cultivate a unique, experimental, open-air trance dance culture relatively isolated from elements suppressing and regulating cultures of conviviality elsewhere. As relatively affluent and resourceful travelers holding passports from countries across Europe, Israel, Japan, North America, Australia, South Africa, and with growing numbers from Central and South America in more recent years, trance travelers have consistently differentiated themselves from 'amateurs' and non-'freaks', including those cohorts arriving in Goa in later seasons. While domestic tourists (Indians) have been among those excluded from parties demonstrably elitist (Saldanha 2007b), as D'Andrea (2009) points out, phenotype is not the principal measure of exclusion in the Goa scene, but one's characterization as a 'tourist', the fleeting and coddled visitor removed from risk and contact with the locals, a loathed specter against whom freaks have traditionally identified themselves. Scorning the packaged commodification of experience associated with conventional tourism, as independent budget travelers, 'neonomads . . . present a pragmatic engagement with native cultures, and more closely emulate the skeptical, romantic and elitist gaze of the "post-tourist"' (D'Andrea 2007, 177).

While Goa Trance emerged as a marketable genre between 1994 and 1997, its principal gestation period was during the late 1980s/early 1990s, a period of international optimism, which saw the collapse of the Soviet

Union and the end of the Cold War, the dismantling of apartheid in South Africa, the popularization of Ecstasy (or MDMA), and the birth of the World Wide Web. At this premillennial juncture, which also saw the emergence of acid house rave culture in the UK and elsewhere, a transnational electronic dance movement was born, whose chief expression was ecstatic open-air dance parties, the inspiration for labels, communities, and party organizations dedicated to reproducing the Goa 'state of mind'. Goa has been consistently euphemized as a 'state of mind' (see Elliott 2010), a sentiment extolled, for instance, by seminal scene figure Goa Gil, and reproduced, for example, on the cover of documentary *Last Hippie Standing* (Robbin 2002). The euphemism evokes a quintessentially liminal condition, a state of being-in-transit nurtured and optimized by countless practitioners over more than 25 seasons. The Goa traveler and heirs are committed to a world of transit, an exodus with physical and mental parameters. Their transition has been achieved as participants have traveled physically from 'home' locations and mentally from normative mind states, freedoms of movement enabled by relative disposable wealth and assisted by transpersonalizing digital, chemical, and virtual media. In D'Andrea's (2007) study of 'nomadic spirituality', alternative travelers are mobile across exotic sites and transcendent states, a psychogeography of experience, which positions freak travelers at the crossroads of 'horizontal' (geo-spatial) and 'vertical' (metaphysical, psychedelic) 'trips'.

Freaks figure within a 'global countercultural diaspora', which includes Osho sannyasins, New Age DJs, raving nomads, and other figures in an 'expressive expatriation' that can be traced back to the 1930s when intrepid travelers first fled to Ibiza, 'a node in an international circuit of Romantic travelling', which would include Goa (D'Andrea 2007, 171). These hypermobile expatriates are implicated in what D'Andrea identifies as a 'negative diaspora'. That is, they see themselves as

> part of a trans-ethnic dispersion of peoples that despise home-centered identities. Their identity as a diasporic formation is not based on ethnic or national nostalgias, but rather on a fellowship of counter-hegemonic practice and lifestyle. Other than making one's soul the Promised Land, expressive individualism opposes diaspora as a basis of personal identity (ibid., 13–14).

Furthermore, subjectivity formation in what may effectively be an anti-diaspora diaspora possesses differentiated and yet complementary trends: 'New Agers cultivate the self as an inner substance to be shaped within holistic ideals, whereas Techno freaks implode the ego during pounding rituals of Gothic digitalism' (D'Andrea 2007, 225). Unlike other dance music and cultural expatriate movements, such as African-Caribbean sound systems in the UK (Partridge 2010), ethnicity, faith, and racial oppression are not defining characteristics of a 'freak diaspora' (D'Andrea 2007, 127), consisting, at least in its formative occasions, of those from privileged (and often European) backgrounds. D'Andrea's study is also important since it begins clarifying the internal diversity of this movement composed of a complexity of experimental behaviors, holistic to self-destructive, utopian to leisured, bohemian to capitalist, evident in communities of expatriates worldwide. In my own research (St John 2012a), I have explored further the heterogeneous character of the Goa experience, where those seeking freedom from repressive laws and oppressive structures in the lifeworld gave shape to the seasoned trance dance experience evolving at 'the end of the world'. This context subsequently shaped a diverse transnational Goa/psytrance music culture (St John 2010), now concentrated in the heterotopian mosaic of the psychedelic festival (see St John 2012b, Forthcoming).

While Goatrance has been identified amid the strands of complex globalization—hypermobility, digitalization, and neoliberalism (D'Andrea 2007)—and possesses a socioeconomic aesthetic that, not unlike other electronic dance music (EDM) cultures, is decidedly cosmopolitan (Rietveld 2010), the globalization of psychedelic trance music post Goa has received relatively little scholarly attention. One key research dilemma is the ambiguous status of psytrance as a popular music (although, for Israel, see Schmidt 2012). With a globalization that differs markedly from that of other styles thought to exemplify music globalization, commodification, and exploitation, notably World Music (see White 2012), psytrance operates independent from major music industry labels (Gebesmair and Smudits 2001); is an electronic dance music (EDM) culture possessing modes of production, performance, and distribution that are decentralized and DiY (see St John 2009); and is cultivated within an increasingly diversified event culture that envisions an alternative transnationalism.

The emergence of this transnational EDM culture is characterized by a sociality that is intrinsically psychedelic. That is, psytrance is a social dance movement purposing technologies of the senses to magnify perception, expand the mind, dissolve the ego—processes of redefining the self that are cultivated in parties. The current analysis would be best situated within the study of the globalization of psychedelia, a field that has received scant attention partly due to a 40-year moratorium on research investigating psychedelic drugs and culture. The resulting lacuna has left a gaping hole in scholarship. Take, for instance, the post-military backpacking sojourns of Israelis, who have had a considerable presence in Goa since the late 1980s, importing the psychedelic trance aesthetic back to Israel (see St John 2012b, chap. 7). Other than Maoz's (2005) classification of disparate traveler sensibilities in India (i.e., 'conquerors', 'Manalis', and 'settlers'), research on Israeli psychedelic travelers is nonexistent, including the critical 1988–93 period. Given the popularity of psytrance in Israel and the prevalence of Israelis in psytribes worldwide, this research paucity is disappointing, although perhaps unsurprising given state-sponsored funding imperatives and prejudices.

Insufficient research attention aside, since the early period of the Goa exodus, a self-identified 'tribal' sensibility has evolved in the context of ecstatic dance gatherings worldwide. The individual patron's inviolable status is challenged in ways not dissimilar to pilgrimage and other cultic events identified as exemplary contexts for 'communitas', the Latin term referring to 'a relatively undifferentiated community, or even communion of equal individuals' (Turner 1969, 96), the social liminality potentiating 'a flash of mutual understanding on the existential level, and a "gut" under-standing of synchronicity' (Turner 1982, 48). As Goa went viral, regional psytribes emerged to replicate the experience and the 'psychedelic com-munitas' (see Tramacchi 2000) proliferated around the world. Not unlike other EDM technotribes, in these initiatives, electronic sound media, psychoactive compounds (e.g., LSD, MDMA, cannabis, and *psilocybin*-containing mushrooms), and Internet communications media have been assembled and purposed to maintain independence, with control over the means of production, distribution, and perception established in ways only imagined by forebears. Post-Goa psytribes typically absorb diverse musics, which are subject to metagenre 'psychedelicization' (see Lindop 2010), a process that sees multiple styles mixed and refined to form new subgenres around which microcommunities identify (e.g., Dark, Progressive Psyche-delic, Dub, Full-On, Ambient). The profusion of electronic music styles impacting and influencing populations who themselves continuously cut 'n' mix from this profusion speaks of the 'compositional sensibilities' of the last few decades (Bennett 1999, 610), and of the 'cosmopolitan emo-tion' (Rietveld 2010) felt by citizens of global cities, who seek attachments outside ethnonationalism, circumstances oiled by post-1960s psychedelia, amplified by post-1980s electronic and digital arts scenes, and virtualized by post-1990s–2000s net culture.

These developments have assisted the formulation of a translocal imagi-nation (Appadurai 1996) where individual creativity, vernacular trans-lations, and regional innovations feed back into a global milieu where experimentalism, syncretism, and the arts of the remix ensure the repro-duction of psychedelic trance culture. Global cities and cosmopolitanism have been instrumental, overseeing these translocal flows but also contex-tualizing distinct modes of being together, or more accurately, being altered together, in the radically reflexive contexts of late modernity. As a trope commonly adopted within this movement, 'tribe' designates both a distinct form of identification and the obliteration of difference, a dynamic native to neotribalism (Maffesoli 1988/1996). In late modernity, the disenchanted seek sensation, difference, and expatriation in the radical immanence of the dance party, a circumstance potentiating the dissolution of difference (ethnonational, class, gender, sexuality, age). Within these contexts, assem-bled technologies of the senses dubbed 'psychedelic'—psychoactive com-pounds, music and audio systems, lighting and visual projections, decor, etc.—facilitate the expression of difference (e.g., alternative consumption options, transgressive artifice) via the liquidation of differences (enabled by optimized and prolonged alteration of normative spatiotemporal conditions). This is a circumstance replicated across global EDM, though hyper-activated in psychedelic trance, where 'tribal gatherings' are the product of complex global influences and peoples from multiple countries, who, for a brief period, shed their differences and unite around commonalities.

THE SEASONED CULTURE AND MUSIC OF GOA

From 1966 to 1967, freaks like the noted Eight Finger Eddie began descending on Goa, which after 450 years of Portuguese rule, held a reputation as one of the most hospitable locations on the subcontinent, and in the East. In Elliott's (2010, 28) estimation, 'whether it was intrinsic affability or economic hardship that motivated the amicable relations, most accounts of the 1970s in Goa cast the villagers of Calangute, Baga, Anjuna, Vagator as friends and business partners.' Goa was among the most permissive and tolerant locations in India, where *charas* (hashish) was legal until the mid to late 1970s and was (and remains) cheap. While various Goa beaches had been host to ecstatic dance gatherings from the late 1960s, Anjuna became the location for the famed full-moon gatherings. These foundation events were sumptuous and extravagant occasions encouraging the most spectacular individual style among participants. As Swedish Anders (Anders Tillman) recalls, 'in the seventies, we were the deco . . . and we spent the whole month creating our dressup.'[2] By the mid-1970s, those parties were an experimental showcase for what Steve 'Madras' Devas called the 'Cosmo Rock movement.'[3] By the mid-1980s, electronic music had completely dominated what by then had become a DJ-led scene in Anjuna. There were numerous pioneers in the development of this scene, among them the renowned Goa Gil (see St John 2011), but also Anders, German Paoli (Paoli Münchenbach), Frenchmen Fred Disko and Laurent, and Ray Castle from New Zealand. While Paoli, for instance, was a keen selector of Krautrock, Afrobeat, Latin Funk, and Dub Reggae, Fred Disko played German punk New Wave from the 1979–80 season, and producers Goa Gil (Darkpsy) and Ray Castle (experimental Goa) became confident spokesmen for the trance dance ritual, albeit championing divergent music aesthetics. Genuine remixers of sound and traditions, and typically estranged from the cultural popstream, each of these cultural brokers maintained vast collections of fresh material enabled by networks of exchange, which, by the late 1990s, was in no small way facilitated by the Goa DJ's instrument of choice—the Sony Walkman DAT (especially the Digital Audio Tape-Corder TCD-D3). In contrast to vinyl—which was not played in Goa since records warped in the heat and proved difficult to transport—DAT devices and their tapes were small and highly transportable, enabling DJs to 'dub' or edit existing material and to exchange (i.e., duplicate tape to tape) new releases efficiently and rapidly in the field.

DJ Laurent is commonly understood to have had a prodigious impact on the Goa sound, with one experienced commentator, Dave Mothersole (2010), identifying Laurent as 'the real father of Trance. A true legend ... just as Chicago had Ron Hardy and Detroit had The Electrifying Mojo, Goa had a DJ called Laurent.' Laurent arrived in Vagator (from Paris) in early March 1984, and did not leave India for ten years. Maintaining harvest of a steady supply of fresh audio-cargo from Europe and the US, he used tape cutup techniques—using the same Sony devices he mixed with—to remove vocals and extend the rhythmic sections of New Wave, Italo Disco, EBM, New Beat, Goth, Electro, Hi-NRG, Synth-Pop, House, and Acid House material, which were mixed to create mesmerizing sets through the 1980s. Right through the decade, the re-edited work of Blancmange, Cabaret Voltaire, A Split Second, DAF, Konzept, Microchip League, Revolting Cocks, Shriekback, Signal Aout 42, Trilithon, and other outfits favored by Laurent were stitched together sans the vocals to animate the proto trance massive for up to ten hours at a time. Laurent's style simply resisted categorization.[4]

The diversity of sounds propagating across the beaches and thumping within the jungle hinterlands of Goa were resounding echoes of the scene's roots in a global network of cosmopolitan centers and dance scenes, and a profusion of 1980s electronica: Industrial, EBM, Acid House, Techno, and Trance sounds. The circulation of MDMA had become a crucial factor by the end of the 1980s, fueling formative domestic dance scenes like the Acid House scenes in London and Spain. By the turn of the 1990s, the Goa sound was carrying what Hillegonda Rietveld (2010, 79) calls a 'psychedelic *motorik*' amplified in the Trance or Hard Trance produced in Germany at that time, notably the 'Frankfurt sound',[5] though a veritable noise of influences—e.g., New Wave, Synth Pop, Eurodisco, New Beat, EBM, Industrial, and House—shaped the sound to come. As artists attempted to refine and define the seasonal mixes in tracks released on EPs and albums, by 1995–96, Goa Trance had emerged as a recognized genre.[6] Although this sound received great variation according to stylistic influences, fusional developments, and regional aesthetics, there emerged a 'classic style' led by a strong four quarter-note kick drum pattern in 4/4, with a more or less constant accentuation of the 16th-note layer at bpm's between 130 and 150. Prominent early artists experimented with analogue sound sources, digital and hybrid synthesizers, samplers, and digital drum machines to build evolving patterns with layered synth sounds and sub-bass frequencies in hypnotic arrangements. Artists used Multiple Instrument Digital Interface (MIDI), computers, and software. Among the most familiar sounds were the fast arpeggio-patterns and strong sawtooth-wave leads running through a resonant band-pass or high-pass filter, such as found in the work of Astral Projection and Etnica. Early works employed additive rhythmic characteristics in the bass line, like the Latin-American tresillo (the duple-pulse rhythmic cell) or variations of 'oriental patterns'. While syncopation receded in later developments, intricate triple-meter accenting embedded in a 'straight' duple-framework persisted in the higher frequency layers, arpeggios, percussive elements, and leads. These embedded alternative signatures combined with the frequent use of the Phrygian Major scale to give Goa Trance an 'Eastern' feel. The tracks were programmed into eight- to ten-minute pieces.

This emergence in sound was indebted to the interventions of a few key figures, chief among them Martin 'Youth' Glover, who played bass guitar in The Killing Joke, wrote, produced for, and performed bass with The Orb, and worked with Ben Watkins (Juno Reactor) and Alex and Jimmy Cauty (of The KLF). Having made ten seasons in Goa, Glover founded the first Goa Trance label, Dragonfly Records (sub-label to Butterfly Records), in 1993. Dragonfly rapidly became the engine-house of the London (and global) psychedelic trance scene. 'As it became more and more popular and the sound followed this evolutionary curve into high-octane trance,' Glover confirmed that 'the bandwidth of expression' suddenly became narrow. 'But in some ways,' he added, 'that was good. It did cut out a lot of chaff from the wheat. It had to be really good to fit into that bandwidth and some artists really redefined it because of that and took it even further' (in Photon 2005). Leading the psychedelic trance aesthetic was Simon Posford, studio engineer at Butterfly. As Hallucinogen (and member of many other acts and collaborations), Posford pushed the boundaries of the possible, with his 'LSD'—released on the Hallucinogen 12-inch *Alpha Centauri/ LSD* in 1994, and rereleased almost 50 times—probably defining Psychedelic Trance more than any other single track. Posford was cofounder of Shpongle, the chief act in the psychedelic diaspora, formed with expat Australian Ron Rothfield (aka Raja Ram), who is a principal Goa Trance architect. With backgrounds in diverse styles and scenes, these producers —along with others like Germany's X-Dream, Israel's Astral Projection, Frenchmen Total Eclipse, the UK's Doof and James Monro (cofounder of Flying Rhino Records), Japan's Tsuyoshi Suzuki (founder of Matsuri Records), and Finland's Kalle Pakkala (member of GAD and owner of Exogenic Records)—and with the momentous work of labels like Blue Room Released and Spirit Zone, became members of an emergent global psychedelic trance network.

PSYCHEDELIC ORIENTALISM

India has long been regarded as a topos for Westerners to become unburdened of the rational Occident and luxuriate in the mystique of the Orient. For the most serious trailblazers—not least among them Helena Blavatsky and the theosophists—India has been a spiritual reservoir potentiating an evolution in consciousness. The 'hippie trail' from Turkey, through Iran, Afghanistan, and Pakistan to India and Nepal, might have been trekked by those Rory Maclean, in *Magic Bus* (2006), calls the 'Intrepids' of the 1960s and 1970s, but as Saldanha (2007a, para. 48) conveys, 'India, the idea and the place, has itself shaped the self-images of others' for centuries, with trailblazers long returning with epiphanous insights. Inspired by the writings of Hermann Hesse, including *The Journey to the East* and *The Glass Bead Game*, Timothy Leary, the ex-Harvard psychologist had traveled to India in 1965, in the wake of his coauthored manual for psychedelic induced ego-death and rebirth modeled on the *Bardo Thodol* (the *Tibetan Book of the Dead*) (Leary, Metzner, and Alpert 1964). Experienced as an exotic and disorienting 'trip', the ultimate 'set' for the journey, Leary wagered that 'the impact of a visit to India is psychedelic' (Leary 1965/1981, 115). Romanticists, artists, and mystics touring the semiotic wealth, metaphysical heights, and abject depths of the East, and motivated by the opportunity to become liberated from what they recognized as 'structures of oppression', were returning to states of innocence and amnesia, smoking *charas*, and living naked next to the beach. India was the context for a *rite de passage* with deep transcendentalist roots and more than a thin slice of romantic Orientalism (Said 1978/1995) that inheres in present representations and desires. For transnational rave-trance tourists, according to Victoria Bizzell's (2008, 288) frank assessment, Goa became a 'place of "pilgrimage" that is far removed from the lived reality of Goa's indigenous inhabitants, local culture, and actual religious practices,' with India, and Indian people, 'rendered static and immobile, bereft of progress and development.' Among the most elite of 'freaks', romantic and essentialized depictions of India and Indians are adopted as media of subcultural capital, while Indians who do not match the ideal—i.e., domestic tourists—are excluded from parties since they contaminate the purity of the vibe (see Saldanha 2007b).

As the production houses of this estranged Orientalist aesthetic, labels sought to replicate the spiritual journey to, and from, the East, on cassette, vinyl, and CD, with covers and sleeves typically imprinted with Hindu imagery. The Orientation of the self is a project evident on the first Goa Trance compilation, *Project II Trance*, released in August 1993 on Dragonfly Records, but was more clearly apparent in early DJ compilation releases—essentially hour-long DJ sets released on CD and distributed globally as Goa Trance. Featuring recurring golden Buddha statues on its cover, in 1995, Psychic Deli (sub-label to UK's Phantasm Records) released one of the first mix albums, Mark Allen's *Deck Wizards—Psychedelic Trance Mix*. Early classics, such as Elysium's 'Monzoon' (*Monzoon*, 1996), Shakta's *Silicon Trip* (1997), and Chi-A.D.'s 'Pathfinder' (*Anno Domini*, 1999) were all stamped with Eastern timbres. To implement the *Orientation*, Goa Trance labels, albums, and events emerging in the mid-1990s would promote and package the trance experience as a transcendent journey adopting Oriental imagery and iconography to assist the telos.

With the Goa aesthetic so transposable, enthusiasts on the dance floor could consume Goa, be exposed to the mystique, and access the metaphysical lore without ever having set foot in India. By the turn of the century, it would grow increasingly unlikely that 'Goa' producers and DJs had themselves visited India. In efforts to induce Visions of Shiva, the name Paul van Dyke chose for his outfit formed in 1992 with Harald Blüchel (aka Cosmic Baby), or to project *The Colours of Shiva*, the compilation series produced by Tua Records (1997–99), or to reduce the *Distance to Goa*, the successful compilation series released by French label Distance (founded in 1995), promoters, producers, and designers were concocting label aesthetics, album cover art, track titles, music structures, and festival concepts saturated with Orientalism. All through this period, trance was infused with OMs and mandalas, an iconic pandemic reminiscent of the essentializing motifs of the earlier counterculture. While Orientalism had been an identifiable theme, it should be recognized that many key Goa Trance artists have drawn inspiration from a medley of symbols, sources, and traditions, not exclusively Eastern (or Indian). Thus while psyculture and its festivals, to which I now turn, became influenced by Eastern essentialisms, these are sometimes difficult to distinguish from a cornucopia of spiritual and popular cultural influences on the psychedelic aesthetic.

PSYCHEDELIC FESTIVALS

That Goa was exported back to the world in a transnational network of events is a process illustrated by the recent anthology *Goa: 20 Years of Psychedelic Trance* (Rom and Querner 2011). The book uncovers the progression from Goa freak exodus (as recounted by Goa Gil, who wrote the first of 42 chapters) to the emergence of global psychedelic festivals, the subject of the book's final part, featuring chapters on various festivals, including Voov (Germany), Boom (Portugal), Universo Parallelo (Brazil), Ozora (Hungary), and Burning Man (US). The anthology also features a part entitled 'Global Culture,' where readers are guided through chapters on various key national cosmopolitan scene developments, most often written by figures integral to the psychedelic diaspora. As *Goa* illustrates, many countries were host to foundation clubs and parties importing and translating the Goa sensibility. These included those in Germany from 1989—i.e., from the time of Unification—such as Hamburg's Atisha and parties south of Hamburg at the Waldeim Inn at Sprötze and DJ Antaro's parties in Lüneburger Heide, Lower Saxony, which became the foundation for the Voov Experience (now VuuV Festival), regarded as 'the mother of all parties'. In London, Ahimsa and Pangaea crews, the TIP, Flying Rhino, and Dragonfly label parties, and Brixton's Fridge (home to Return to the Source parties) sprung up in the early 1990s, when full-moon gatherings were also being held in Thailand (on Koh Panghan), on the Nizanim beaches of

Israel, in the Mojave Desert in California (Moontribe), and at bush 'doofs' around Melbourne (e.g., Green Ant). Elsewhere, regional cosmopolitan and bohemian scene hubs for the psytrance movement included The Geoid in Roppongi Japan, the Aeorodance Rave Centre in the old Moscow air terminal, the Epicentre in Australia's Byron Bay (home to the Beyond the Brain parties), an old shipbuilding yard in Stockholm called Docklands, Vienna's Shambala Club, Zurich's Toggi and the Scarabäus parties, and San Francisco's Consortium of Collective Consciousness parties. In South Africa, Cape Town's Alien Safari and Vortex Productions were among the chief promoters, and in Brazil, beach parties at Vegetal, Trancoso, and later Universo Parallelo in Bahia were important traveler venues. Many of these event organizations and initiatives were run by or catered to travelers, whose networks included the very artists who were releasing work defining the psychedelic trance aesthetic.

These and many other venues became homes for the development of identifiable aesthetic trends within psytrance music and culture. As the psychedelic trance music industry evolved, psytrance festivals emerged as expressly commercial operations, often conceived as free parties and evolving into multistage dance music venues host to diverse music and practices. Where the Goa seasonal parties were typically 'free' (or by donation) events, and where DJs were most often not paid for their performances, the contemporary psychedelic trance festival, like other EDM festivals, are branded corporations possessing admission fees, employees, contracted artists, hired security personnel, market stalls, and fences. While these developments have been the subject of considerable debate within a culture with countercultural roots, these events typically afford event-goers with multiple freedoms. Extraordinary recreational topographies, they combine leisure activities common to popular music festivals with the experience of the sacred associated with pilgrimage destinations, and the labors of festival workers, many of whom are volunteers—swapping their labor for admission—with most mixing business with pleasure in close quarters. As interstices of undisciplined embodiment, cognitive liberty, and ethical consumption, these events are sites for the variable expression of free culture (see St John 2012a). Freedoms are expressed in the ways events cater to transgressive and disciplinary pursuits that, combined in the contemporary event, are downstream from the mosaic of exile sensibilities performed at sites of origin. These events exist among extreme and experimental leisure industries facilitating the performance of psychosomatic risk taking in the tradition of voluntary 'edgework', which, according to Stephen Lyng (2005, 9), includes recreational pursuits like skydiving and motorcycle riding as a 'means of freeing oneself from social conditions that deaden or deform the human spirit through overwhelming social regulation and control.' Here 'edgework' resonates with 'raving' as an extreme and concentrated exercise in transgression, where, in the early 1990s UK and later in the teknival movement (see St John 2009, chap. 2), 'rave' came to designate a cultural practice combining travel to locations remote from domestic sites with the journey out of one's mind. The physical 'trip' to remote and exotic regions at the risk to one's health and person, and the psychological 'trip' resulting from the use of psychoactive compounds risking one's rational consciousness, and possibly one's mental health, combined in the psytrance festival to potentiate liberation and fulfillment in ways paralleling risk taking within 'extreme sports' and other forms of wild recreation in which one abandons 'home', sobriety, and certainty. It is no coincidence that publications like *Psychedelic Traveller* magazine promote psytrance scenes in nations like New Zealand alongside other adventurous and risk-laden leisure pursuits, such as white-water kayaking and bungee jumping. At the same time, however, discipline is also compelled in situ through redressive ecological principles implemented in event design, an ethos that encourages participants to comport themselves in accordance with an awareness of human symbiosis with nonhuman nature. As apparent 'incubators of novelty', such events have been identified as 'petri dish of possibility where the future forms of community and consciousness are explored' (Davis 2008, 54).

This last statement was made with regard to Portugal's Boom Festival. Initiated in 1997 by Diogo Ruivo and Pedro Carvalho (who met as children in Goa) and held on lake Idanha-a-Nova near the village by that name in the mountainous Beira Baixa Province, the biennial Boom Festival is akin to a pilgrimage center for the global psytrance and visionary arts community. Boom was specifically founded in efforts to reproduce the sensibility of Goa beyond its physical and seasonal borders. I attended four consecutive Boom Festivals (in August 2006, 2008, 2010, and 2012, with official attendances ranging between 20,000 and 30,000, including participants from more than 100 countries). On my initial field trip in 2006, I converged upon Idanha-a-Nova with dozens of fellow travelers from Australia and elsewhere, many of whom had, like me, never been to Goa. I was immediately impressed by what seemed like an epic compression of what I imagined to be an entire Goa season in one week. The event is timed in August so as to include the full moon, which is celebrated on one of the main nights. There were several dance floors featuring various styles of EDM (Progressive Psychedelic, Full-On, Darkpsy, and Ambient, along with other prominent styles like Techno and Minimal Techno), as well as live acoustic and World Music. Across this range, music offers variable means for facilitating transcendence in 'trance', from the decidedly optimistic and evolutionary atmosphere of Progressive to the gothic sensibilities of Darkpsy intended to orchestrate the obliteration of the self. While Psytrance would continue to be showcased on the event's main arena—the Dance Temple—music aesthetics diversified over subsequent years (including Dubstep, Glitch-Hop, and various other sounds), a diversification apparently mirroring that of the seasonal mix of the 1980s that was influential to the Goa Trance sound. But Boom is not simply a music festival. Promoted by its organizing body of the time, Good Mood Productions, as a weeklong 'harmonic convergence of people, energy, information and philosophies from around the planet earth and beyond,'[7] Boom accommodates diverse countercultural strands drawn toward ecstatic trance and visionary culture across its various areas, from the dance floors (including the Dance Temple) to the Liminal Village. Hosting a weeklong program of workshops, films, and lectures, the Liminal Village is subject to a variety of concerns—such as sustainability, cognitive liberty, transpersonal consciousness, and integral health—preoccupying festival attendees. As the premiere event in the gulfstream of Goa, Boom is an exemplar of radical immanence, autonomy, and the progressive discourses that psychedelic spirituality shares with other alternative, ecological, and New Age dispositions evolving in the 20th century.

Boom exemplifies the merger of ecstatic and reflexive dispositions within the environment of the festival, not least because, as a psychedelic festival in the Goa tradition, the 'mind-manifesting' dissolution of boundaries that separate different participants enables the experience of difference. Here, 'psychedelic' refers to a range of techniques and practices—including, albeit not exclusively, psychoactive compounds—that facilitate 'mind manifesting'. Since the dissolution of boundaries is affected by an assemblage of techniques and practices, the narrow-band understanding of 'psychedelic' as synonymous with LSD (or other psychoactive compounds) requires revision. As the psychedelic festival illustrates, psychoactives are among an assemblage of options available for participants to become expansive, creative, and interactive. In an event tradition to which the UK Free Festivals (see McKay 1996) and Burning Man (Doherty 2006) belong—that is, visionary arts events where each participant is reckoned to be an 'artist' and not simply as a consumer or an audience to a spectacle—a cornucopia of experiential freedoms are worked at and played with. Outlands accommodating psychonauts, neomystics, and other fissiparous seekers of spirituality identified by Sutcliffe (1997, 105) who 'select, synthesize and exchange among an increasing diversity of religious and secular options and perspectives,' psychedelic festivals permit the condition of *being in-transit*, a desirable mobile sensibility for cultural exiles and architects of the possible, who launch venues like spacecraft or 'UFOs', and model themselves as 'aliens', the ultimate signature of difference to the popstream from which they seek expatriation. These scenes are connected historically to spaces of experimentation long inhabited by artists and utopians, queers, and bohemians, expats and esotericists, whose cosmopolitan aesthetic is fueled by the artifacts and artifice of consciousness alteration concentrated under the roofs of cafés and chai tents, and promulgated in head shops and chill-out spaces, danced into being on remote beaches, in forest parties, and at desert doofs. The world over, these islands of radical immanence maximize the potential for self-exiles to accumulate experience and build repertoires of knowledge and practice expressive of their transitional lifestyles. Augmenting conditions in which knowledge, truth, and wisdom are acquired through direct experience, where artistic expressions afford the highest credibility, and where being loose, open, and liminal are desirable objectives, these festivals enable habitués to become their own shamans, mystics, and healers. Riffing ideas from his book *Prometheus Rising*, as Robert Anton Wilson conveyed, 'we're all evolving into something different . . . . In the higher and higher circuits everybody becomes their own psychic, and their own magician and life gets more interesting', thoughts conjured by psybient artist Androcell sampling the 'agnostic mystic' on 'Higher Circuit Experience' (*Entheomythic* 2010).

PSYCHEDELIC TRAVELER AND VISIONARY DANCE CULTURE

By the end of the 1990s, in the initiatives of nascent labels and event crews, this *traveler* dance music culture became translated by national scenes—often through the lead work of sannyassins initiated at Osho's (Bhagwan Shree Rajneesh) ashram in Pune, Maharashtra (the state to the north of Goa), which opened in 1974. At the beginning of the new millennium, the Goa sensibility was transposed to locations worldwide amid waves of new state optimism, post-revolutionary hope, and nascent countercultural formations. From Goa to London, Hamburg to Tel Aviv, Paris to Tokyo, Amsterdam to San Francisco, Melbourne to Cape Town, Koh Phangan to Bahia, Lithuania to Lisbon, in the events cultivated by charismatic DJs and visionary promoters, in the European circuit of festivals, and in countless other seasonal events in regions worldwide, psychedelic traveler culture proliferated. Throughout this development, travel became an initiatory experience for backpackers from Israel, Europe, Australia, Japan, South America, and elsewhere, with annual circuits of events enabling entrants to remain in a state of mobility. An alternative travel industry evolved over the first decade of the 21st century, whose spruikers purveyed the view that the experience once encountered at the end of a dirt track in Goa could be rediscovered at trail's end all around the planet. Kicking off in 1999, Slovakia's Hill-Top Festival, for instance, was promoted inviting 'travellers of the world', 'The road ends in Lipovec and it feels like the end of the world, with huge forests stretched on the mountain tops' ('Spirit of Goa' 2005, 22). Scene publications *Mushroom Magazine*, *Psychedelic Traveller*, and Chaishop.com reported on the proliferation of brief seasonal enclaves of the Goa 'state of mind' around the planet, from Baltic region states such as Lithuania and Estonia to South American countries such as Chile and Argentina, with stories of 'isolated', 'pure', and 'lively' places as yet untouched by jaded sensibilities and commercial interests. *Psychedelic Traveller* functions like a trance-travel brochure, with imagery of dance floor scenes across the world—complete with scene hotspots, reports of popular and favored festivals, artists, and labels within any of the dozen national scenes featured. Rather than simply ports of call for the seasoned traveler, seasonal parties became homes for *the traveler experience*, enabling worldly countenance and cultural accreditation for those who may not have traveled far from home at all. The romantic liminality of the traveler is programmed into psychedelic trance music and culture. On their *Uncharted* compilation (2007), Wouter Thomassen and Sander Visser (aka Citizen), for instance, offer a traveler aesthetic rooted in the Goa experience. In an interview for *Progressive Tunes* magazine (Citizen 2007, 6), these artists stated how they wanted to engineer

> a kind of traveller vibe, going out into exotic countries, away from the trendy tourist places and take the unpaved roads into the jungle in search of some obscure hidden outdoor party. Also that feeling we had when we started out DJing in the 90s and electronic music was just more fresh, obscure and edgy. In search of those hidden treasures at the local record store.

Their comments indicate the intention of musicians to create music that echoes the desire for 'global' discovery, making rendezvous with the exotic, being intimate with the 'authentic' experience, an occurrence approximated as one becomes less like tourists and more like travelers. Psytrance cultivates the mystical adventure, carried in the sampling, the chanting, the space journeying, in the Eastern and native imagery reproduced on album covers, event posters, and fliers. 'That's the real use of music. It's not for listening to, it's for travelling,' reads the sample aboard Laughing Buddha's 'Astral Traveller' (1998). Space travel tropes have enjoyed considerable popularity in Goa Trance acts like The Infinity Project, Evolution, Astral Projection, Pleiadians, Cosmosis, and Space Tribe, with samples from science fiction cinema (e.g., *2001: A Space Odyssey*) and TV series (e.g., *Star Trek*) deployed to allegorize the journey outside the Self to encounter one's alien Other (see St John 2013). Such samples worked in conjunction with, among other elements, the arpeggio technique, which, as Ray Castle indicates, was successful in affecting 'ascending cosmic melodies' in techno-trance productions by way of MIDI sequencers and quantization.[8] Listening to and dancing to such music, one becomes transported just as one participates in the sensibility of the traveler grafted from sites where exiles once relocated, but is now made available to domestic audiences, who may enter liminal states without traveling far and perhaps without using psychedelics. Thus the spatio-geographic experience becomes thoroughly replicated in the mind-escapades endemic to psychedelic trance culture, with the 'state of mind' sold to young seekers from world cities still thirsty for the 'real thing'. Thus, in 2010, a *sadhu* with his face and forehead pasted with *vibhuti*, sacred white ash, pulls from a chillum on the cover of TIP Records' *Goa Classics 1*.

Effected via an assemblage of technics (chemical, digital), the Goa-trance dance event evolved as an epic journey in an exotic location removed from routine domestic life, a liminal experience (i.e., of being-in-transit) transposed to optimized traveler festal heterotopias. This experience was replete with risks to the stability of conventional values and commitments, potentiating reevaluations of one's life and relationships. Existing art forms were modified and repurposed, innovations tested, and music curated to the goals of transformation, with the traveler enclave ultimately becoming the model for psychedelic arts dance festivals like Boom and Germany's Antaris Project, which is, as stated in the 2009 *Antaris Project DVD*, 'a once in the year opportunity to revive the Goa scene.' Documenting how wizened travelers and neophytes converge 'to experience the power of Antaris and understand the origin of its vibration,' the film employs footage from Goa parties of the late 1980s, thus connecting the event with its cultural roots. Festivals such as the weeklong Ozora and Boom festivals hire many artists associated with the Goa emergence, like Shpongle, Man With No Name, James Monro, and Dick Trevor to orchestrate continuity, with the effect that event-goers complete events like satisfied travelers returning from their adventures abroad, and who, like the Goa traveler, return to the party next season. They may otherwise maintain a more enduring presence in the culture by participating in an annual circuit of festivals as participants, market vendors, performance artists, décor designers, and DJs. Many participants in this event culture have direct involvement in the various industries that have mushroomed on the verge of the dance floor. These artists and service providers, along with organizers, staff, and volunteers of events themselves, dwell in the event-culture throughout the year, with the effect that their lifestyles are liminalized.

True to their fragmentary, pluralistic, and subversive origins, psychedelic festivals enable entrants to perform a defiance of limits corresponding with 'edgework', as well as integralist and well-being practices like yoga and meditation, and sustainable consumer and waste management practice. These arts of the senses and consciousness are integral to what has evolved as a 'visionary arts' event-culture, which possesses a variety of esoteric and occultic influences (and not simply the seasoned Goa party culture), as well as offering a reflexive response to conditions of contemporary crises. The work of artists like Martina Hoffmann, Luke Brown, and Alex Grey are showcased in arenas like The Sensorium Project, a community-based mobile arts project with a multidisciplinary collaborative gallery, featuring interactive media and sculpture that first appeared at various dance music festivals in Australia, including Rainbow Serpent and Earth Frequency over the summer of 2011–12. The Sensorium Project represents a condensation of multimedia interactive artistry, involving music, lighting, and installations flourishing within these events-spaces and concentrated on dance floors, where art constellations are described as

> a game of forms and colours, lights and fantasy. Like in the *Glasperlenspiel (The Glass Bead Game)* of Hermann Hesse the different aspects of art, fantasy, mythology and science are being consolidated. Pictures,

sculptures, objects, lasers, visuals and animations, projections, string art, performances, fire and light show interblend into a sensual firework—in the best tradition of Pink Floyd. (Antano and Werner 2011, 114)

The artist's ability to orchestrate transportation of the mind is championed in such events, as are the artistic sensibilities of each participant encouraged. Here, *visionary* art is not simply visual art, but notably includes music, with much output in the psychedelic spectrum inspired by transpersonal states of consciousness or mystical experiences, which, when performed in the context of a highly optimized event, facilitates the potential for dancers to travel outside their routine states of awareness. The entire sensory-scape of the visionary arts dance festival is impregnated with sonic and optical art, with the dance floor itself offering a condensation of how various art forms work in symbiosis: the DJ/producer mixing tracks or playing live; VJs synchronizing acoustics with optics using 3-D imagery; the lighting technicians and installation artists providing organic backdrops; and the dancers themselves, who are provided the opportunity to be visionary artists, interpreting the bass frequencies and melody patterns with head, feet, and hand movements, becoming moving canvases to an array of lights, including black lights illuminating geometric and fractal designs on UV-reactive clothing. The latter are produced by designers in a clothing fashion industry, including those from many countries who are dedicated to innovation and accessories conducive to inner and outer travel, transpersonal, and terrestrial mobility. Multi-pocketed Aladdin pants, utility belts, four-part jackets, and other garments designed for psychogeographical mobility are sold at market stalls. Event-goers are familiar with equipment enabling utility, comfort, and style in exposure to elements, like hoodies, face-hugging sunshades, hammocks, and parasols. Other readily available equipment facilitate improved techniques of transpersonal journeys, such as glass-blown pipes, chillum, and jet flame lighters for smoking *charas*, cannabis, and DMT, all of which have their origins of use in exotic contexts. Finally, there is no question that these events, not unlike other alternative cultural events, accommodate ludic practice, rhythmic arts, and exotic techniques imported by travelers who set up stalls selling items like poi (traditionally used by Maori), fire staff (with origins in India and the Pacific rim), juggling clubs (India), and rhythm sticks (China).

CONCLUSION

Over the last 20 years, the exile mosaic of Goa has proliferated in traveler-derived dance music venues—clubs, parties, and festivals—emerging around the globe and promoted in publications like *Psychedelic Traveller*. This chapter has explored this development, from the psychedelic tribalism fomenting in the seasonal paradise of Goa, an expatriate DJ-led trance dance culture shaped by the countless inputs, technics, and aesthetics of travelers from around the world, to a global psychedelic/visionary event-culture. These event islands of psychedelic trance owe part of their success to the appeal of the psychedelic Orientalism inhering in the Goa Trance genre emergent in the mid-1990s. This appeal signifies that Goa travelers and their successors are imbricated in transition as a globalized lifestyle practice, an exodus with physical and mental parameters, a transformative experience catered to by contemporary event organizations. The event proliferation signifies a complex cultural liminalization with transgressive and progressive dimensions. International festivals, such as Boom and Ozora, are optimized sites for being-in-transit, a circumstance facilitated by the assemblage of music, lighting, decor, installations, fashion, and psychoactive drugs in conjunction with the physical travel required to arrive at event venues. While these essentially liminal domains are heir to the seasonal tradition of party-making in Goa, and to its fusional aesthetic heritage, basic differences are apparent. While Goa was a destination for well-resourced and networked expatriates, the festal culture born in its wake would become attractive to a great many entrants whose profile does not match the privileged status of forebears, a circumstance certainly deserving further ethnographic investigations of emergent scenes and events. While, as a veritable 'state of mind', Goa evolved as a kind of placeless space for the anesthetic abandonment of concerns and worries at home, its visionary progeny saw regional event venues emerge as a means to evoke and celebrate local heritage and cultural causes. Furthermore, rather than simply venues for 'getting off' from the world, intentionally visionary arts events are occasions through which a variety of ecological, holistic, and planetary ideas and concerns shape transformative experience. As seen in design and management, events like Boom are mirrors to their times, which can be determined in the scheduling of music representing the currency of 'trance' across EDM genres and world acoustic music, but also in the response to planetary crises. As visionary artist Martina Hoffmann writes, 'as we are becoming more and more challenged as a species, an internationally-connected, alternative family has been creating large festivals and events that have become a forum for all visionaries' (Hoffman and Venosa 2011, 119). With artifice mixed and purposed to the goals of transforming social and environmental practice as demonstrated in situ, Boom in particular provides a destination intended to be other than that which simply resembles Castalia, the province in Hesse's *Glass Bead Game* whose elite occupants are learned in the most abstract game of forms and are oblivious of crises mounting in the world beyond its boundaries. As a world summit of visionary arts and trance, Boom self-identifies as a 'united tribe of the world', with many participants recognizing themselves as conscious participants in a 'global tribe'. The growing understanding cultivated by the Boom festival is not simply one's membership in a global fraternity, but a recognition that the planet upon which transnational travelers dwell and across which they move is wracked by crises—the threat of ecological apocalypse, economic collapse, humanitarian disaster, and psychological turmoil. As such, more than any other known to the author, it is this plateau-event in the traveler circuit that demonstrates how travel, music, and transformation, embodied movement and social movement, rhythm and change, are intricately calibrated. Seeking to understand the role of Boom and other events emerging in the gulfstream of Goa/psychedelic trance, this chapter is part of a broader project charting the development of visionary arts dance music culture.

NOTES

1. Note on terminology: In this chapter I use 'Goa Trance' specifically for the marketed music genre and 'Goatrance' for the associated cultural movement and its various scenes. I use 'Psytrance' and 'psytrance' in comparable fashion. I also interchange 'Goatrance' and 'psytrance' with the broader 'psyculture'.
2. Anders Tillman, e-mail to the author, December 21, 2011.
3. Devas was instrumental to the conception of the live band music scene in November 1974, when he returned from the Tsang Fook Music Store in Hong Kong (and successfully negotiating customs at Bombay Airport) with 'two Stratocasters, Fender bass guitar, two Fender amps, bass amp, mics and bits and pieces' (Steve 'Madras' Devas, e-mail to the author, March 10, 2011).
4. Most of these artists turned up on track lists that Laurent himself provided on a Discogs discussion thread, as further detailed in St John (2012a).
5. The 'Frankfurt sound' was 'trance' emerging with considerable input from DJ Talla 2XLC whose Technoclub parties kicked off in 1984. Trance pioneer Sven Väth was one of many who performed at Technoclub before opening the club The Omen, a subsequent trance laboratory where Väth played legendary 12-hour sets without a break. Väth's Eye Q Records and Harthouse were seminal trance labels with considerable influence on Goa DJs (Wolfgang Sterneck, e-mail to the author, December 5, 2007).
6. For a detailed ethnomusicological analysis of Goa Trance with a focus on Finnish contributions to and development of the sound, see Aittoniemi (2012). Deep thanks to Toni Aittoniemi, whose feedback has been crucial to the formulation of this paragraph.
7. See http://www.boomfestival.org (accessed June 9, 2008).
8. Ray Castle, communication with the author on Facebook, September 18, 2011.

REFERENCES

Aittoniemi, Toni. 2012. 'Cultural and Musical Dimensions of Goa Trance and Early Psychedelic Trance in Finland: The History, Translation and Localization of an Internationally Mobile Electronic Dance-Music Scene.' MA thesis, University of Helsinki, Faculty of Arts, Department of Philosophy, History, Culture and Art Studies.

Antano (aka Infin-E.T) and Julia Werner. 2011. 'Decoration and Design.' In *Goa: 20 Years of Psychedelic Trance*, edited by Tom Rom and Pascal Querner, 108–15. Verlag, Solothurn/Switzerland: Nachtschatten.

Antaris Project and Psynema. 2009. *Antaris Project* [DVD]

Appadurai, Arjun. 1996. *Modernity at Large: Cultural Dimensions of Globalization*. Minneapolis, MN: University of Minnesota Press.

Bennett, Andy. 1999. 'Subcultures or Neo-Tribes? Rethinking the Relationship between Youth, Style and Musical Taste.' *Sociology* 33(3):599–617.

Bizzell, Victoria. 2008. '"Ancient + Future = Now": Goa Gil and Transnational Neo-Tribalism in Global Rave Culture.' *Comparative American Studies* 6(3):281–94.

Boom Festival. 2006. Accessed June 9, 2008. http://www.boomfestival.org.

Citizen. 2007. Interview in *Progressive Tunes* 1(May):6.

D'Andrea, Anthony. 2007. *Global Nomads: Techno and New Age as Transnational Countercultures in Ibiza and Goa*. New York: Routledge.

D'Andrea, Anthony. 2009. 'Chromatic Variation in Ethnographic Analysis. Review of Arun Saldanha's *Psychedelic White: Goa Trance and the Viscosity of Race*.' *Dancecult: Journal of Electronic Dance Music Culture* 1(1):147–50. Accessed January 16, 2013. http://dj.dancecult.net/index.php/journal/article/view/30/26.

Davis, Erik. 2008. 'The Festival is a Seed.' *Pathways: Liminal Zine* 02:50–54.

Doherty, Brian. 2006. *This Is Burning Man: The Rise of a New American Underground*. Dallas: BenBella Books.

Elliott, Luther C. 2010. 'Goa Is a State of Mind: On the Ephemerality of Psychedelic Social Emplacements.' In *The Local Scenes and Global Culture of Psytrance*, edited by Graham St John, 21–39. New York: Routledge.

Gebesmair, Andreas, and Alfred Smudits. 2001. *Global Repertoires: Popular Music within and beyond the Transnational Music Industry*. Aldershot: Ashgate.

Hoffmann, Martina, and Robert Venosa. 2011. 'Visions and Psychedelic Art.' In *Goa: 20 Years of Psychedelic Trance*, edited by Tom Rom and Pascal Querner, 116–25. Verlag, Solothurn/Switzerland: Nachtschatten.

Leary, Timothy. 1965/1981. *The Politics of Ecstasy*. Berkeley: Ronin.

Leary, Timothy, Ralph Metzner, and Richard Alpert. 1964. *The Psychedelic Experience: A Manual Based on the Tibetan Book of the Dead*. New Hyde Park: University Books.

Lindop, Robin. 2010. 'Re-Evaluating Musical Genre in UK Psytrance.' In *The Local Scenes and Global Culture of Psytrance*, edited by Graham St John, 114–30. New York: Routledge.

Lyng, Stephen. 2005. 'Edgework and the Risk-Taking Experience.' In *Edgework: The Sociology of Risk-Taking*, edited by Stephen Lyng, 3–16. London: Routledge.

Maclean, Rory. 2006. *Magic Bus: On the Hippie Trail from Istanbul to India*. London: Penguin.

Maffesoli, Michel. 1988/1996. *The Time of the Tribes: The Decline of Individualism in Mass Society*. London: Sage.

Maoz, Darya. 2005. 'Young Adult Israeli Backpackers in India.' In *Israeli Backpackers: From Tourism to Rite of Passage*, edited by Chaim Noy, and Erik Cohen 159–88. Albany: State University of New York.

McKay, George. 1996. *Senseless Acts of Beauty: Cultures of Resistance since the Sixties*. London: Verso.

Mothersole, Dave. 2010. 'Unveiling the Secret—the Roots of Trance.' April 14. Accessed January 21, 2011. http://www.bleep43.com/bleep43/2010/4/14/unveiling-the-secret-the-roots-of-trance.html.

Partridge, Christopher. 2010. *Dub in Babylon: The Emergence and Influence of Dub Reggae in Jamaica and Britain from King Tubby to Post-Punk*. London: Equinox.

Photon, Nigel. 2005. 'Youth—A Potted History.' *Revolve*. Accessed January 14, 2013. http://www.revolvemagazine.co.uk/Interviews/youthtemp.htm.

Rietveld, Hillegonda. 2010. 'Infinite Noise Spirals: Psytrance as Cosmopolitan Emotion.' In *The Local Scenes and Global Culture of Psytrance*, edited by Graham St John, 69–88. New York: Routledge.

Robbin, Marcus. 2002. *Last Hippie Standing* [DVD]. Tangiji Film.

Rom, Tom, and Pascal Querner. 2011. *Goa: 20 Years of Psychedelic Trance.* Solothurn/Switzerland: Nachtschatten Verlag.

Said, Edward. 1978/1995. *Orientalism: Western Conceptions of the Orient.* London: Penguin.

Saldanha, Arun. 2007a. 'The LSD-Event: Badiou Not on Acid.' *Theory and Event* 10(4). Accessed September 21, 2011. http://muse.jhu.edu/login?uri=/journals/theory_and_event/v010/10.4saldanha.html.

Saldanha, Arun. 2007b. *Psychedelic White: Goa Trance and the Viscosity of Race.* Minneapolis: University of Minnesota Press.

Schmidt, Joshua. 2012. 'Full Penetration: The Integration of Psychedelic Electronic Dance Music and Culture into the Israeli Mainstream.' In *Dancecult: Journal of Electronic Dance Music Culture* 4(1):38–64.

'Spirit of Goa.' 2005. *Mushroom Magazine* 120(June):22–23.

St John, Graham. 2009. *Technomad: Global Raving Countercultures.* London: Equinox.

St John, Graham, ed. 2010. *The Local Scenes and Global Culture of Psytrance.* New York: Routledge.

St John, Graham. 2011. 'DJ Goa Gil: Kalifornian Exile, Dark Yogi and Dreaded Anomaly.' *Dancecult: Journal of Electronic Dance Music Culture* 3(1):97–128. Accessed January 16, 2013. http://dj.dancecult.net/index.php/journal/article/view/94.

St John, Graham. 2012a. *Global Tribe: Technology, Spirituality and Psytrance.* Sheffield: Equinox Publishing.

St John, Graham. 2012b. 'Seasoned Exodus: The Exile Mosaic of Goa Trance.' *Dancecult: Journal of Electronic Dance Music Culture* 4(1):4–37. Accessed January 16, 2013. http://dj.dancecult.net/index.php/journal/article/view/111.

St John, Graham. 2013. 'Aliens Are Us: Cosmic Liminality, Remixticism and Alienation in Psytrance.' Journal of Religion and Popular Culture 25(2): 186–204.

St John, Graham. Forthcoming. 'The Logics of Sacrifice at Visionary Arts Festivals.' In *The Festivalisation of Culture: Place, Identity and Politics*, edited by Andy Bennett, Jodie Taylor, and Ian Woodward. Aldershot. Ashgate. Forthcoming.

Sutcliffe, Steven. 1997. 'Seekers, Networks, and "New Age."' *Scottish Journal of Religious Studies* 18(2):97–114.

Tramacchi, Des. 2000. 'Field Tripping: Psychedelic Communitas and Ritual in the Australian Bush.' *Journal of Contemporary Religion* 15(2):201–13.

Turner, Victor. 1969. *The Ritual Process: Structure and Anti-Structure.* Chicago: Aldine.

Turner, Victor. 1982. *From Ritual to Theatre: The Human Seriousness of Play.* New York: Performing Arts Journal Publications.

White, Bob W. 2012. *Music and Globalization: Critical Encounters.* Bloomington: Indiana University Press.

DISCOGRAPHY

Androcell. 2010. *Entheomythic.* CD. Celestial Dragon Records: CDREC22.

Chi-A.D. 1999. *Anno Domini.* CD. Velvet Inc.: NTD 92511–22

Citizen. 2007. *Uncharted.* CD Comp. Flow Records: FLR0720CD.

DJ Goa Gil. 1995. *Techno Spiritual Trance from Goa*. CD, Mixed. Javelin Ltd: 3005392.

Elysium. 1996. *Monzoon*. CD. YoYo Records: YOYO10.

Hallucinogen. 1994. *Alpha Centauri/LSD*. 12-inch. Dragonfly Records: BFLT 14.

Laughing Buddha. 1998. *Astral Traveller/Acid Rain*. Vinyl. Transient Records: TRA043.

Mark Allen. 1995. *Deck Wizards—Psychedelic Trance Mix*. CD Comp, Mixed. Psychic Deli: PDCD001.

Shakta. 1997. *Silicon Trip*. CD. Dragonfly Records: BFLCD23.

Various. 1993. *Project II Trance*. CD, Comp. Dragonfly Records: bflcd4.

Various. 2010. *Goa Classics 1*. File, Comp. TIP Records: TIPR02.

Part II
Music and Migration

8 Global Balkan Gypsy Music

Issues of Migration, Appropriation, and Representation

Carol Silverman

When Lady Gaga recently declared, 'I'm a gypsy . . . I can't plan my life out like that so much,'[1] she called attention to the freedom and spontaneity linked to the label 'Gypsy' in popular culture. Gypsies, both real and imagined, are appearing everywhere now—in spring 2011 fashion houses, on reality television shows in England, the US, and Hungary, and in music venues on several continents. As both the romantic stereotype and the criminal stereotype come into play in these stagings, I suggest we examine how non-Romani producers and performers market Gypsy culture as the 'new exotica'.

Gypsy music, once the purview of esoteric collectors, has now become globalized—it is performed in European and American festivals and concerts, found in film scores such as *Borat* and *Sherlock Holmes*, played by youth bands, posted on YouTube and Facebook, and remixed by DJs in dance clubs in New York, San Francisco, Tokyo, Melbourne, Istanbul, and Mexico City, and in every city and some small towns in Western Europe. In addition, Gogol Bordello, circulating their Gypsy Punk fusion of East European folk music and rock, and Balkan Beat Box, with their Nu-Med hybrid of Middle Eastern, dub and Gypsy, have successfully infiltrated the rock scene. Madonna's 2008–9 Sticky and Sweet tour included a 'Gypsy' section featuring the Russian Romani Kolpakov Trio; and Shakira (*Gypsy*) and Jennifer Lopez (*Ain't It Funny*) have recently recorded Gypsy themed songs.

What does all this mean for Romani musicians? Before we celebrate too glibly we need to investigate not only the transmission of musical styles, but also the flow of capital and media attention. Ironically, as Balkan Roma migrate westward to seek better lives, they are faced with growing hostility, evictions, and deportations precisely at the same time that their music is generating growing acclaim. This chapter interrogates the changing sonic landscape, as well as the political economy of music making as more non-Roma appropriate and consume Balkan Gypsy music. I argue that the current configuration of global consumer capitalism promotes the consumption of Gypsy music that is marketed as both hybrid and authentic (Taylor 2007). Noting that Roma are rarely in charge of their own representations,

I illustrate how the image and sound of the fantasy Gypsy is created, and ask who benefits from the popularization of Romani arts.

Migration forms the framework of my argument; Roma are a diasporic people originally from India. Not only has Romani music recently traveled from Eastern European communities to Western markets, but also Roma themselves have migrated from east to west, and they are now being deported back to the east from France and other West European nations. Xenophobes accuse Roma of not belonging in Europe, not having 'their own' music or culture, and not having 'civilized European' values. Having no written history, Roma are often rendered invisible, slippery, or hard to define. They are routinely excluded from national cultural and musical projects both in Western and Eastern Europe. Furthermore, the nomadism characteristic of some groups has been translated into slurs such as rootlessness and shiftiness.

At the same time that Roma are rejected as 'Others', Romani music is celebrated by Western journalists, marketers, and scholars as 'hybrid, fusion, borderless, bricolage'. This discourse often gives non-Romani performers license to appropriate from Roma; in effect they have been pushed out of some of their traditional musical spheres. I argue that Roma are twice erased: first by being relegated out of the core of European values and nation-state frameworks, and then being stereotyped as ultimate hybrids with no music of their own.

Heeding Timothy Taylor's call to provide ethnographic details of the processes of globalization. i.e., 'what happens in specific places and historical moments' (Taylor 2007, 115), I provide three cases studies of the migration of Romani music from communities to World Music festivals to popular music stages via the interventions of non-Romani arrangers, producers, mangers, and DJs. These case studies are united by the genre of brass bands. Brass bands have become a symbol of Balkan Roma, a brand to negotiate on the world stage. Through representational analysis of texts, imagery, repertoire, and live and digital performances, I examine the interplay of hybridity and authenticity in the marketing and consumption of Gypsy music via the arranger Goran Bregović, the *Balkan Brass Battle* tour/album, and the Balkan Beats DJ scene.

ROMA

Linguistic evidence shows that Roma are a diasporic ethnic group that migrated from northwest India to the Balkans by the 14th century and Western Europe a century later. Roma have been indispensable suppliers of diverse services to non-Roma, such as music, entertainment, fortune-telling, metalworking, horse dealing, woodworking, and agricultural work. Many of these trades required nomadism or seasonal travel. Initial curiosity about Roma by Europeans quickly gave way to discrimination, a legacy that has continued until today (Hancock 1987, 2002). Petrova (2003, 128) suggests that negative stereotypes of Roma blossomed in 15th-century Western Europe and spread eastward. Roma were viewed as intruders probably because of their dark skin, their non-European physical features, their foreign customs, and their association with magic and invading Turks.

In the southern Romanian principalities, Roma were slaves from the 14th to the 19th centuries. Despite their small numbers, Roma inspired fear and mistrust and were expelled from virtually every Western European territory. Bounties were paid for their capture and repressive measures included confiscation of property and children, forced labor, prison sentences, whipping, and branding. Assimilation was attempted in the 18th century in the Austro-Hungarian Empire by forcibly removing children from their parents and outlawing nomadism, traditional occupations, and Romani language, music, and dress; similar legislation was enacted in Spain after 1499 (Petrova 2003). In the Balkans, the policy of the Ottoman Empire towards Roma was, in general, more lenient than state policy in Western Europe, at least from the 16th to the 18th centuries. Perhaps the most tragic period of Romani history was World War II, when more than 500,000 Roma were murdered (Hancock 2002).

The communist regimes in Eastern Europe defined Roma as a social problem. They were targeted for integration into the planned economy, forced to give up their traditional occupations, and assigned to the lowest-skilled and lowest-paid state jobs (e.g., street cleaners). Specific policies varied by country and by decade, e.g., forced sterilization (Czechoslovakia) and tracking of children into schools for the disabled (Bulgarian, Hungary, Czechoslovakia). Nomadic Roma were forcibly settled, settled Roma were forcibly moved, and aspects of their culture, such as music and language, were prohibited in some regions.

In the post-socialist period, harassment and violence towards the Roma of Eastern Europe have increased, along with marginalization and poverty. They are the largest minority in Europe (10–12 million), and despite a huge human rights campaign, they still have the lowest standard of living in every country, with unemployment reaching 80 percent in some regions. Balkan Roma face inferior and segregated housing and education, including tracking of children into special schools for the disabled. Poor health conditions, specifically higher infant mortality and morbidity, shorter life expectancy, and higher frequency of chronic diseases all plague Roma. Discrimination is widespread in employment and the legal system, and even educated people routinely express disdain for Gypsies. Hate speech and racial profiling are common in the media. Perhaps most troubling are the hundreds of incidences of physical violence against Roma perpetrated by ordinary citizens and also by the police.[2]

Considering the above situation, Romani refugees from the crisis of post-socialism can now be found in every Western European nation and in the US and Canada. Because of dire living conditions, many Balkan

Roma would like to emigrate to the West, but immigration has become extremely difficult. Western European nations are deporting Roma, nationalist parties are on the rise, and xenophobia is growing. With their racial taint, their low class stigma, and their baggage of historic stereotypes, East European Roma are among the least desirable immigrants; Muslim Roma are even more suspect because they are assumed to be Islamic terrorists.[3]

According to the *Economist*, Roma remain at the 'Bottom of the Heap' (2008, 35). Rather than being the purview of extremists, anti-immigrant and anti-Romani sentiment is becoming more mainstream. For example, in 2008, the Italian government started to fingerprint all Gypsies living in camps in an effort to crack down on crime; from 2010 the French government began deporting Romani European Union citizens back to Bulgarian and Romania; in 2010 right-wing militias patrolled Hungarian villages against Gypsies; and in 2011 Bulgarian anti-Gypsy demonstrations erupted into violence.

In April 2012, Kooijman wrote:

> In spite of the efforts made by NGOs and the distribution of EU funds, Europe's main minority is no better off than it was 10 years ago. A lack of appropriate supervision in Brussels, the corruption of local leaders and the indifference of national governments are at the root of the problem. On International Roma Day, which falls on 8 April, the significant proportion of Europe's 12 million Roma who live in deplorable conditions will not have much to celebrate. And poverty is not the only worry for the community. Ethnic tensions are on the rise. In 2008, Roma camps came under attack in Italy, intimidation by racist parliamentarians is the norm in Hungary, and in September of last year thousands of Bulgarians took to the streets to chant such slogans as 'Turn the gypsies into soap'. Speaking in 1993, Vaclav Havel prophetically remarked that 'the treatment of the Roma is a litmus test for democracy': and democracy has been found wanting. The consequences of the transition to capitalism have been disastrous for the Roma. Under communism they had jobs, free housing and schooling. Now many are unemployed, many are losing their homes and racism is increasingly rewarded with impunity.

The positive yet dangerous coding of Romani Otherness hinges on their historical romanticization by non-Roma as free souls (outside the rules and boundaries of European society), their rootlessness/nomadism, their association with the arts, especially music and the occult, and their proximity to nature and sexuality. Using Said's (1978) concept, we can claim that Roma are 'Orientalized' and exoticized. Todorova (1997), discussing whether the Balkans are Orientalized in reference to the rest of Europe, points out that we are not dealing with a colonial situation; nevertheless, the Balkans are posed as 'Other' to Europe, and Roma are posed as 'Other' to the Balkans. Ken Lee specifically extends Said's argument to Gypsies: 'Whilst Orientalism is the discursive construction of the exotic Other *outside* Europe, Gypsylorism is the construction of the exotic Other *within* Europe—Romanies are the Orientals within' (2000, 132).

Trumpener emphasizes the association of Roma with an ahistoric, timeless nostalgia: 'Nomadic and illiterate, they wander down an endless road, without a social contract or country to bind them, carrying their home with them, crossing borders at will' (1992, 853). Simultaneously they are reviled as unreformable, untrustworthy, liars, and rejected from civilization. This contrast expresses the 'ideology of Gypsy alterity—feared as deviance, idealized as autonomy' (ibid., 854). Roma, then, serve as Europe's quintessential Others.

Music is one of oldest Romani occupations, but it is not a profession in some Romani groups; in the current period of post-socialist transnational mobility, music remains one of the only viable professions for Balkan Roma. Historically, writers claimed either that Roma are 'sponges', i.e., they merely borrow and rework, and have no music of their own, or that they are the staunchest preservers of tradition. As early as 1910 Serbian music scholar Djordjević disparaged Gypsies because they failed to preserve their own music, and, when adopting Serbian music, 'they decharacterize and gypsify it' (1910/1984, 38). In 1977 Gojković wrote that Gypsies 'corrupt not only national music of various countries but also new music, for instance, jazz' (48). Thus, the typical older Balkan scholarly attitude toward Romani musical innovation was one of contempt; in these accounts, 'Gypsy style' (most notably innovation) threatened the preservation of 'authentic folk music'.

Because of their professional niche, Roma creatively molded the popular repertoire and interacted dynamically with local musics. For centuries, Roma have performed for non-Romani peasants and city dwellers of many classes for remuneration in cafés and taverns and at events such as weddings, baptisms, circumcisions, fairs, and village dances. This professional niche, primarily male and instrumental, requires Roma to know expertly the coterritorial repertoire and interact with it in a creative manner. A nomadic way of life, often forced upon Roma due to harassment and prejudice, gave them opportunity to enlarge their repertoires and become multi-musical as well as multilingual. In addition, large groups of sedentary Roma in major European cities became professionals who performed urban folk, classical, and/or popular music. There is, thus, neither one worldwide nor one pan-European Romani music. Roma constitute a rich mosaic of groups that distinguish among themselves musically.[4]

Recently, Roma hailing from many regions of the diaspora have been performing side by side in festivals. Although their styles may be quite disparate, journalists and marketers often assume that a pan-Romani culture unites all Roma. This becomes part of the marketing scheme that advertises the supposed musical brotherhood of Gypsies. In reality, Romani music exhibits many distinct styles and genres depending on location and history; disparate Romani musics often share little (Silverman 2007, 2012).

HYBRIDITY AND AUTHENTICITY

The role of the exotic in the representation of many world music styles has been noted by numerous scholars (Taylor 1997). Roma are a prime example of this phenomenon, iconically pictured as sexual, Eastern, passionate, genetically musical, and defiant of rules and regulations (Szeman 2009). It is precisely their outsiderness, their Otherness, that makes them a valuable 'authentic' marketing commodity; many performers know this very well and capitalize on it. But performers are always negotiating the fine line between authenticity/exoticism and rejection, between being a Gypsy onstage and passing as a non-Roma offstage to avoid discrimination. Furthermore, this 'authentic' label is ironic, considering that Roma have been historically excluded from state-mandated categories of 'authentic folk music'.

Europeans may be attracted to 'authentic' Gypsy music because they mourn their own loss of authenticity. Perhaps authenticity emanates magically from marginal artists: folks who look like they come from real communities with real rituals, songs, and dances, the very things most Europeans and Americans have lost, or think they have lost. Although the label 'authentic' may valorize Romani music, it can also serve as a straitjacket, limiting choices of performers. For example, Roma have complained to me that Western audiences prefer acoustic instruments; perhaps consumers can then be sure they are getting 'the real thing'. Roma, on the other hand, often prefer electric and synthesized instruments; they were among the first to introduce them into Balkan folk music. As Hutnyk states: 'The ghettoization of purity and authenticity serves only to corral the "ethnically" marked performer yet again' (2000, 31).

In the 1990s, new concepts of globalization emerged that produced a heightened consumption of difference. Taylor observes: 'Everything is for sale, everything is appropriable in the name of making one's identity—or music' (2007, 118). Several scholars have analyzed how 1980s multiculturalism went hand in hand with the consumption of difference (Dirlik 1997, 2000, 2002; Gilroy 2004; Taylor 1997, 2007). Globalization 'fosters a new way of taming difference in order to commodify it' and distribute it via new technologies (Taylor 2007, 126).

In its newest incarnation, globalization embraces hybridity as its major trope, 'sometimes displacing lenses of authenticity' (Taylor 2007, 141). In an ironic twist, the hybrid often becomes a mark of authenticity (even purity), and the two terms can even be found side by side in music marketing. For example, Tomić (2006) asserts in the liner notes for the CD *Rromano Suno 2*, 'they found themselves in a strange place where their repertoire is described both as the deepest repository of tradition and a generator of irresponsible innovation.' Similarly, in the liner notes for the album *Balkan Brass Battle* discussed below, Cartwright (2011) writes that Fanfare Ciocarlia 'existed in isolation, part of no larger brass band tradition' in 'rural obscurity' surrounded by mud and sheep; yet they developed an 'eastern funk . . . more akin to hardcore punk or techno than any recognized Western brass tradition.' According to Taylor, there has been a shift from 'authenticity-as-pure to authenticity-as-hybrid'; now, world musicians are expected to be hybrid, and this characteristic 'allows them to constructed as authentic' (2007, 143–44).

The fluidity of Romani musical creativity grows from the multiple rediasporizations of Roma (from India to Europe and within and from Europe), their openness to adopt non-Romani and multiple Romani styles, and their outsider status. For centuries Roma have not had a singular state or a national language, territory, religion, or culture. Historically, the professional marginal musician was a hybrid to survive; multiple patrons required multiple musical repertoires. So what is different about the current situation? The post-socialist context has amplified factors such as marketing, migration, celebrity patronage, and digital sampling (which I will explore via DJs below).

Taking a step back, I note that hybridity can be a problematic concept because of both its vagueness and its theoretical positioning. Hybridity is now so fashionable and applied to so many situations that it has begun to lose its specificity and its political mooring. Furthermore, the power of hybridity can be harnessed by reactionary as well as progressive causes. 'Hybridity in and of itself is not a marker of any kind of politics but a deconstructive strategy that may be used for different political ends' (Dirlik 2000, 187). Rey Chow elaborates the position that hybridity, while valorizing difference and disjuncture, may acquiesce to and support the status quo of global consumer capitalism: 'The enormous seductiveness of the postmodern hybridite's discourse lies . . . in its invitation to join the power of global capitalism by flattening out past injustices' (1998, 156). Hutnyk similarly writes that there is no problem with the creative trading of cultures, but rather we must investigate the terms of the trade: 'To think that a celebration of the trade is sufficient is the problem. Celebration of multicultural diversity and fragmentation is exactly the logic of the mass market' (2000, 135). Along these lines, below I investigate the appropriation of Romani music by non-Roma.

Dirlik (2002) points out that hybridity means different things to different class constituencies: To business investors it means internationalizing consumption markets, as I mentioned above, but to postcolonial scholars like Bhabha and Soja it means a new kind of radical politics. Concepts of multiculturalism, transnationalism, and globalism have been successfully used by corporations to recruit wider markets (Dirlik 1997, 94–95). Gilroy (2004, xix) similarly points out that hybridity has been annexed by corporate culture, and Žižek (1997) underlines that multiculturalism is manipulated by commerce.

Hutnyk (2000) reminds us that hybridity is above all a marketing label used by World Music promoters. What does the embrace of heterogeneity by global capitalism really mean? Bringing the musics of marginal peoples into the mainstream may provide visibility and even hard cash for formerly impoverished performers but only if they have fair contracts. However, the valorization of hybridity rarely changes the structures of inequality. For Roma it is true that some performers have become rich (even supporting whole villages in the Balkans), and Gypsy styles have been appropriated by mainstream non-Romani artists. But the overall structural inequality has not changed.

Hutnyk shows how certain cultural forms become 'the flavour of the month [. . .] the seasoning for transnational commerce [. . . .] Hybridity sells difference as the logic of multiplicity' (2000, 3–4). Hybridity in its meekest form is not too far from the Disney version of multiculturalism: watered-down, safe, distant. Liberals can feel good when buying a hybrid product like a World Music CD because of the imputed connection to the dispossessed. In fact, marginality can become a kind of asset, a type of political cache, because of the assumption that marginal folks make good music, and we owe it to them to buy their products. It is certainly no accident that African Americans and Roma occupy similar positions vis-à-vis race and music. Hutnyk writes that 'other love (anti-racism, esotericism, anthropology) can turn out to be its opposite' (2000, 6). This is reminiscent of Renato Rosaldo's concept of 'imperialist nostalgia', whereby the powerful destroy a form of life and then yearn for it aesthetically. 'Imperialist nostalgia uses the pose of "innocent yearning" both to capture people's imaginations and to conceal its complicity with often brutal domination' (Rosaldo 1989, 69–70). Thus Roma (or African Americans or Native Americans), suffer discrimination for years and then white folks idolize and appropriate their music (or spirituality) as a means to erase this history and feel good.

Although marginality may be an attraction in music, it also may be erased by the illusion of success onstage. Part of the deceptive seductiveness of hybridity for audiences is its aura of equality. The logic goes something like this: If Africans or Gypsies use Western harmony and electric instruments and appear in large festivals, they must be already integrated into the West and successful. We assume they are compensated fairly and accepted fully by the mainstream as musicians and people. Of course, these are all false presumptions. Hutnyk writes: 'Difference within the system is a condition and stimulus of the market—and this necessarily comes with an illusion of equality' (2000, 33). Few audience members bother to find what performers are paid, what Western styles and instruments mean to performers, or how performers are treated once the show is over. Romani musicians relate many stories of being idolized onstage but being suspect walking down the street (Silverman 2012). Furthermore, successful performers are unrepresentative of the vast majority of poverty-stricken Roma. Neither can we presume that rich Romani musicians care about poor Roma—most do not.

The celebration of hybridity is occurring precisely at a time when identities are becoming more political and battles are being waged for representation and turf. Hutnyk asks: 'Why is it that cultural celebration rarely translates into political transformation? [. . .] At a time when explicit class politics in the West seems blocked, does the shift to identity, hybridity and the postcolonial express a decline in aspirations (to transform the entire system)?' (2000, 119). I respond to Hutnyk's and Taylor's calls for an engaged cultural studies where hybridity is not merely celebrated aesthetically and discursively but enmeshed in political struggles. The challenge I accept from Dirlik and Gilroy is to keep a focus on representation, performance, and aesthetics while still maintaining a solid connection to material conditions and history.

Thus I turn to the relationship of music to politics and representation via Balkan brass bands, a genre that has become so ubiquitous that a Balkan or Gypsy festival without one would be an oxymoron; the terms 'Balkan', 'brass', and 'Gypsy' are now used interchangeably in marketing. I argue that brass solves the 1990s question of authenticity and also suggests the hybrid dimension. Many Europeans wonder if, with all the digital fusions available, there is any 'authentic' Gypsy music. Most Europeans shun the electrified wedding music played on synthesizers that is characteristic of Romani community events, even though this is perhaps the most vital genre in the Balkans. Brass bands, on the other hand, are acoustic and seem older and more authentic; Western audiences can relate to Balkan brass because Western Europe and the US have their own brass musical traditions; audience members also regularly note their energy, loudness, and visceral power. Furthermore, brass bands are depicted as hybrid because of their innovative repertoires and collaborative projects. Finally, brass is ubiquitously employed in the digital sampling of Balkan Beats DJs. In tracing how brass come to dominate the DJ repertoire in Western Europe, I turn to the significant role of Goran Bregović.

GORAN BREGOVIĆ

Goran Bregović is a good example of a non-Romani appropriator who has become more famous and wealthy than most Roma; he is perhaps the most widely known performer/arranger of Gypsy music in the world, earning top billing and fees of $30,000 at Gypsy, Balkan, and World Music festivals. Figure 8.1 shows him in a publicity photograph.

Figure 8.1   Goran Bregović in a publicity photograph taken by Sergey Kozlov. Reproduced with permission.

On the other hand, he is routinely an object of wrath by Roma and is even described as a thief and robber. Why do Roma speak of him in condemning terms? Born in Bosnia of mixed heritage, Bregović was a guitarist who pioneered in performing rock/folk fusions of all the ethnic groups in Yugoslavia. He became internationally famous for his musical scores for Bosnian director Emir Kusturica, whose films (*Time of the Gypsies*, 1988; *Underground*, 1995) dealt with Romani themes and employed Romani actors (Marković 2008, 2009). Precisely Bregović's arrangements of Romani brass music have become the iconic Gypsy sound in festivals and DJ club culture. At the same time, Roma hate Bregović because he copyrighted his arrangements under his own name and has not given credit to his Romani sources.

The case of Bregović's dubious ethics can be compared with other cases of World Music collaboration such as *Graceland* (Feld 1988; Meintjes 1990) and *Deep Forest* (Feld 2000b).[5] Taylor points out that in the 1980s collaboration was the dominant trope of world music projects. Feld asks: 'Is world music a form of artistic humiliation, the price primitives pay for attracting the attention of moderns?' (2000b, 166). Similarly, do Roma need appropriators like Bregović to achieve popularity in the modern world? Feld points out that collaborations with famous artists are often presented as part of 'a politically progressive and artistically avant-garde movement. . . . This process has the positive effect of validating musicians and musics that have been historically marginalized, but it simultaneously reproduces the institutions of patronage' (2000a, 270).

The issue is how music migrates between multiple contexts of commercial power. For many non-Roma, Bregović has come to stand for all Balkan Romani music; for example, the program notes for a 2006 concert state that he has developed 'a reputation as an eloquent spokesperson for Gypsy culture in Eastern Europe' (Lincoln Center, 2006). He is actually taken to be Romani by many fans; indeed a Serbian Romani activist cynically called him part of the 'Gypsy music industry'.

We may clearly place Bregović in the 'celebratory camp' of fusion artists. Feld has noted the divide between 'anxious' and 'celebratory' narratives of World Music appropriation. Celebratory narratives valorize hybridity, feature hopeful scenarios about economic fairness, and 'even have romantic equations of hybridity with overt resistance' (Feld 2000b,152).[6] Anxious narratives fret over purity and underline the economics of exploitation. I believe that we need to interrogate both narratives. Celebratory scholars eschew ownership and valorize the fertile artistic exchange of musical styles. George Lipsitz (1994), for example, shows that appropriations create cultural zones of contact where intercultural dialog between ethnic groups can happen; he says hybridity produces an immanent critique of contemporary social relations. He thus equates hybridity with resistance.

On the other hand, Lipsitz may 'overstate the relative cultural power of these musics' (Born and Hesmondhalgh 2000, 27) to effect change.[7] Celebratory tales tend to naturalize globalization, emphasizing its inevitability (Feld 2000b, 152). They espouse a 'democratic vision for world music,' which then becomes part of the marketing scheme. When audiences observe the incredible diversity of music available, they see it 'as some kind of sign that democracy prevails that every voice can be heard, every style can be purchased, everything will be available to everybody' (Feld 2000b, 167). But, in celebrating diversity, we shouldn't confuse the flow of musical contents with the flow of power relations (Feld 1994b, 263). Often too much attention is paid to the sound aspect of hybrid musics and not enough to the social, political, and economic relationships that produce them. Anxious narratives often narrowly focus on the pitfalls of more commercial forms, less pure forms. 'This fuels a kind of policing of . . . authenticity' (Feld 2000b, 152). Regarding Roma, I am not concerned about authenticity; the music that is produced by Roma is becoming neither more homogeneous nor less authentic. Rather, a narrow aesthetic analysis ignores 'who is doing the hybridity, from which position and with what intention and result' (Born and Hesmondhalgh 2000, 19). Thus we need to focus more on questions of transmission, agency, profits, and representations. Along these lines, I turn to the Balkan Brass Battle.

BALKAN BRASS BATTLE

Balkan Brass Battle is a collaboration between two brass bands, Boban and Marko Marković Orkestar from Serbia and Fanfare Ciocarlia from Romania, that began in 2011 (see Figure 8.2 for a photograph of the two bands).

Figure 8.2   Balkan Brass Battle, © Arne Reinhardt. Reproduced with permission.

Collaboration is one of the hallmarks of the marketing of world and popular music; novel combinations of artists provide fresh ideas and supposedly fuel creativity. However, many collaborations are motivated not merely by artistry, but by profit; moreover, not all collaborators have equal roles, and some collaborations are more top down than other. Balkan Brass Battle is a tour, an album, and a branding concept developed in Berlin by the production and management company Asphalt Tango. Asphalt Tango has been a key player in the Gypsy music industry, producing a steady stream of albums of Balkan Romani music, winning awards for production, and orchestrating several collaborations such as the *Gypsy Queens and Kings* tours and albums (Silverman 2012, 270).

I have already mentioned how Goran Bregović's arrangements and Emir Kusturica's films helped solidify brass as the iconic Gypsy sound. The frenzy over brass can be seen in Serbia, where thousands of Western tourists visit the Guča brass band festival, and also in the West where festivals like Guča na Krasu in Trieste, Balkan Trafik in Brussels, and Balkan Fever in Vienna regularly invite Balkan Romani brass bands. In 2011 Balkan Trafik invited three brass bands from the Balkans: Boban and Marko Marković; Ekrem Mamutović also from Serbia; and Brakja Kadrievi, who are from Macedonia, although half of their members live in Belgium. These brass bands, along with Goran Bregović, who also performed with a brass band, received top billing and played at the most prestigious times. Ekrem Mamutović and Brakja Kadrievi's performances were staged as a battle of brass bands; battles have now become a common performance trope.

Asphalt Tango manager and producer Henry Ernst conceived the idea of a brass battle and spent years arranging the daunting logistics of combining two 12-piece brass bands from two countries and from different management agencies into one show. Asphalt Tango's marketing narrative emphasizes how the two groups became curious about each other and wanted to compete; however, the idea was hatched from above. Asphalt Tango describes the 'showdown' in its marketing:

> Prepare yourself: here comes the heavy, heavy monster sound! From the wild, wild East—Romania & Serbia—the two foremost Gypsy brass bands are taking the stage to see who blows hottest and hardest. There's gonna be a showdown! . . . Neither act is willing to play support. . . . A sound clash? More like a battle royal! The Gypsies are ready to get in the ring! (Asphalt Tango 2013)

The narrative continues by painting a portrait of a typical Gypsy musician:

> A successful Gypsy musician lives like a 17th-Century aristocrat. He will drape his body in gold, drive late-model jeeps, surround himself with the most beautiful women, eat the finest cuts of meat and drink

only vintage wine. But unless he can be acknowledged as No. 1 he can never truly be at peace. Respect, this is what he craves more than anything else. The respect that comes with knowing the world says he is The Greatest Living Trumpet Player. With such respect then, why, even if you live in a shanty you are still King! . . . Victory will not be decided by a knockout blow but by the enthusiasm of the audience. Who are the real Gypsy Kings of Balkan brass? Dancing feet and cheering voices will tell! (Asphalt Tango 2013)

The battle trope accomplishes important ideological and symbolic work that resonates with historical stereotypes: Gypsies are portrayed as naturally flamboyant, competitive, wild, belligerent, seeking status and showing off; they can be menacing and potentially violent, but, the battle is only with music, so we are 'safe'. In fact, not only will we will be privy to an age-old rite, but we will also determine the winner by dancing and cheering. Simultaneously, this is a portrait of Roma who are talented but scary; however, they are rendered amiable by the cozy setting.

Asphalt Tango's video clips marketing the battle depict miniature staged dramas of competition between Fanfare Ciocarlia, pictured as peasants from a village (they are from Zece Prajini, Moldavia, Romania), and the Marković Ork., pictured as cowboys.[8] The rural wildness of Fanfare Ciocarlia's village is deployed by multiple shots of animals (the musicians dance with and hug sheep), mud, carts with wood, old houses, old cars, and a chicken inside a drum. The musicians sing 'Born to Be Wild', a rock song they reworked for the movie *Borat* (see Silverman 2012) and boast of their skills. Members of Marković's band, in cowboy hats and bandannas, also deal with geese, as they display their prowess and stomp on Fanfare's posters. Alcohol is common to the two groups, as well as depreciating hand gestures, shouting, facial expressions, and boasts about how they can play faster, louder, and better.[9] This staging of the rural peasant boisterous exotic is reminiscent of Kusturica's films that depict Roma as mired in mud, larger than life, and outside the bounds of normal society. All dialogue is in the English language even though the musicians in reality speak little English. This personalizes the musicians for Western audiences.

Garth Cartwright, who wrote the liner notes to the album *Balkan Brass Battle*, explained to me that he thought that the dramatic battle element was necessary for a good show; he recommended that the two lead trumpet players enact a duel on stage, standing back to back, walking three paces, and turning around to face each other and play their trumpets. On the other hand, backstage stories that I heard and backstage videos of the making of the album all point to camaraderie and respect among the musicians. They talked, played, smoked, ate, and drank together and became good friends. Unlike some Romani music projects in which the Roma cannot communicate with each other because they do not share a language, musical style, or repertoire (see Silverman 2007, 2012), here the musicians all spoke Romani and shared some repertoire. The choice of repertoire on the album/tour, however, was coordinated more by the label than the musicians. The album begins with a 'Battle Call'. The representative regional genres appear: *čoček*, (Romani dance in syncopations of 4/4); *kolo* (Serbian dance in 2/4), and *hora* (Romanian dance in 2/4); however, there are also popular Western hits such as 'I Am Your Gummy Bear', released in 40 countries since 2006. In addition, jazz standards like Duke Ellington's 'Caravan' are featured, as well as the 'James Bond Theme'. The typical formula for Balkan brass albums and shows now includes jazz, Latin, and popular music.

In sum, the Brass Band Battle reworks a familiar performance trope 'the battle of the bands', known in New Orleans and in 1960s pop music, and inserts familiar stereotypes about Roma. It hints at danger and belligerence but creates a safe context for enjoyment and for vicarious participation in determining the outcome of the battle.

DJ REMIXES

Recent digital sampling techniques have made all recorded music available to anyone at any time, to replay, manipulate, loop, and then repackage. The word 'producer' now means a DJ as well as a coordinator of events. As Taylor writes: 'This sampling and collecting of "world music" is caught up in the complexly intertwined phenomena of travel, tourism, globalization, and new consumption pattern, covered and justified with the veneer of collaboration' (2007, 134).

Most non-Roma performing or remixing Gypsy music subscribe to the belief that hybridity and fusions are inherently celebratory. Roma, on the other hand, are aware of the slippery slope from collaboration to appropriation to exploitation. By appropriation I mean taking music from one group and using it in other musical projects, usually for profit.[10] I am aware of the underlying essentialism in the concept of appropriation: music cannot be ultimately assigned to unitary 'sources'. Postmodernists would argue that neither music nor any other part of culture is owned by individuals or groups, and I would agree that music cannot be ultimately owned—intermingling has always occurred. Notwithstanding this observation, certain musics are associated with certain groups and do get used in new contexts.

I prefer to avoid the terms 'source' and 'origin' and instead focus on the process of transmission, that is, giving and taking. As mentioned above, historically Roma have been characterized as the ultimate music appropriators. While it remains true that Roma have taken numerous musical elements from coterritorial peoples (as well as from Western classical and pop music), it must also be remembered that they do not take indiscriminately, but rather borrow selectively and creatively rework what they take. Conversely, Roma have also contributed to many musical genres in the Balkans (Silverman 2012).

When Roma appropriate, however, their class relationship is rarely altered; no matter how powerful their music, they have not become powerful politically. They may provide a desirable commodity, but they have not lost their stigma. Furthermore, Roma still need patrons; even the most famous performers are managed by non-Romani producers. Appropriations by the powerful are different from appropriations by the marginal; when the powerful appropriate, the marginal often lose in the process because they can't fight back in terms of ownership and copyright. Musical appropriations by non-Roma from Roma, thus, need to be investigated in terms of motivation, profit, and artistry. Along these lines I turn to DJs.

As mentioned earlier, clubs on four continents draw large crowds of young non-Roma to dance to remixed Balkan Gypsy music. Approximately 90 percent of DJs' core repertoire is brass music, including many songs popularized by Bregović. The remaining 10 percent of the repertoire is composed of string bands such as Taraf de Haidouks from Romania, Hungarian Romani string bands that feature vocables, and Klezmer bands (frequently the Amsterdam Klezmer Band). These bands share an acoustic style; most DJs, like Western audiences discussed above, shun amplified music that feature electric instruments, even though this is the most widespread music in Balkan Romani communities.

There are hundreds of DJs, some young and naive about the Balkans and Roma and a few from the Balkans; none, however, are Roma. On the one hand, some DJs remix for the love of it and make little money; on the other hand, Shantel, the highest paid, receives as much as 2,000 euros for one night. The most popular pan-European DJ enterprise is trademarked under the name 'Balkan Beats'. It was coined in the 1990s by legendary Bosnian DJ Robert Šoko, who initially attracted Balkan immigrants to his Berlin parties as part of the boom of Yugo-nostalgia; later Šoko expanded his purview to Germans and other West Europeans (Dimova 2007). Today Balkan Beats is an international trademark that brings Šoko to numerous international cities.

A cursory glance at the discourse and the visuals advertising Balkan Beats and other DJ events reveals the trafficking in iconic Gypsy motifs. DJs adopt names like Gypsy Jungle, Gypsy Box, Gypsy Sound System, Tipsy Gipsy, and the Tsiganization Project; advertising imagery draws on the circus, carnivals, travel, animals, Yugo-nostalgia, and brass instruments (see Figure 8.3 of a 2011 Balkan Beats party in Antwerp, Belgium).

One group of DJs trademarked the name Balkan Circus; clearly the romantic fantasy of the carefree musical Gypsy is invoked. For example, a poster advertising a 2009 London event promises 'another night of lush and gypsy mayham, balkan luxuries and exilarant dances [sic].'

Figure 8.3   Balkan Beats poster, Antwerp, 2011. Reproduced with permission.

All DJs are in the 'celebratory camp': They disavow ownership theories of music and believe that all music is available to everyone to use. They celebrate creativity and reject any hint that artistic or economic exploitation could exist. They valorize their own artistry and truly admire Romani musicians; furthermore, they claim they are helping Roma by popularizing their music by increasing the number of audience members who listen to it. This is true. However, young audience members rarely buy CDs, and even if they did, Romani artists rarely receive royalties because recording contracts are usually exploitative. Moreover, only a handful of Romani bands have recorded on Western CDs. Most Balkan Romani bands, even brass bands, are suffering because of decreased demand at home in the Balkans.

Are DJs putting Romani musicians out of work? Are they being hired instead of Romani musicians? It is certainly cheaper to hire one DJ than to bring a band from the Balkans. But DJs have underlined to me that because of their club shows, audiences are growing. A few DJs invite guest Romani musicians. In some clubs, at about 1:00 a.m., a live act performs for an hour for a modest fee. But live acts are increasingly composed of non-Roma; there are dozens of non-Romani brass bands that charge less than Romani bands and play similar repertoires (albeit poorly in some cases). In general, if non-Roma perform Gypsy music well, share gigs, and do not exploit, Roma are supportive. If non-Roma profit at the expense of Roma, they are angry; however, they will rarely object in public because they do not want to lose the chance of future collaborations.

How do Roma feel about remixes? Most Roma are extremely practical and do not want to alienate possible 'collaborators' from whom they may derive future revenues. In private most dislike the music and disregard the club scene, preferring to focus on markets they can influence, like weddings and festivals. Feld similarly observes that third world musicians want more exposure, sales, and 'a greater cut of the action. If their perception is that the same process that is screwing them over is the process that is eventually going to give them a larger cut, then how to you tell them to take a smaller cut?' (Keil and Feld 1994, 315–16).

With the globalization of Balkan Gypsy music, we can observe a process that resonates with the historical example of the appropriation of African American blues and jazz by white musicians. A musical genre of a marginalized, racialized minority captures the pulse of fashion, but the group itself may be edged out of profit, fame, and credit, because of appropriation and hierarchical market forces. Most remixes are played in clubs and shared on digital platforms without securing legal permission (laws in Western Europe vary regarding remixes). If DJs produce CDs, their label needs to obtain permission, but music is produced and copyrighted by a label, which decides whether to issue permission for remixing. The revenues go to the label, which may or may not have a revenue-sharing agreement with their artists. The music business is supported by three pillars: record companies, major contract artists (like Madonna) who have control over their art, and 'musicians [who] are laborers who sell their services for a direct fee and take the risk (with little expectation) that royalty percentages, spin off jobs, tours, and recording contracts might follow from the exposure and success of records with enormous sales' (Feld 1994a, 245).

GYPSY MUSIC AND MULTICULTURALISM

One strand in the celebratory discourse of appropriators is the feel-good, peacemaking 'multicultural' aspect of the music. Bregović, for example, sees himself as transcending the conflicts of the Balkans through Gypsy music. Shantel similarly views the DJ club experience as bringing people together: 'It's only music, you know. It's to make people happy, not to fight against each other' (Lynskey 2006). I wonder how some producers can claim that racism has declined in Western Europe due to dance clubs. There are virtually no Romani patrons in remix clubs—some Roma cannot afford to attend, and most cannot relate to the scene. Many Roma in Western Europe have a precarious legal, political, economic, and social status as refugees or as illegal immigrant workers. The popularity of Gypsy remixes hardly mitigates racism and discrimination. However, a multicultural fantasy of harmony overlays the club scene. For example, when I asked DJs if they knew anything about the plight of Romani refugees in the same neighborhoods of the clubs (e.g., evictions), most were ignorant, but some said their music could help dispel stereotypes. Most put their work in the realm of art as opposed to politics. Many were surprised to learn that the labels Gypsy and *Tsigan* could be insulting to some Roma.

Several European Balkan festivals, such as Balkan Trafik, receive liberal city, national, and European Union funding for multiculturalism despite having little educational programming. Sometimes a festival or concert that merely features Gypsy music is assumed to promote multiculturalism. In reality, festivals often replicate or promote stereotypes. And Romani musicians, who are not in charge of creating their own images (Hancock 1997), sometimes participate in their own self-stereotypification (Silverman 2012).

Paradoxically, many Europeans love Gypsy music at the same time that they revile Roma. For example, Federico F. posted this comment objecting to an article (Kooijman 2012) detailing discrimination against Roma:

> . . . a western liberal democracy is NOT compatible with nomadic people, put simply!!! . . . Romas create constant problems because they do not accept the rules of the game. . . . Mind you there's no racism at play here. For one I love Tzigan music and I'm aware of the contribution folk Roma culture has brought to our European heritage. And I strongly condemn 'Far West' style actions by private citizens or worse paramilitary militias. However every honest person will admit that Romas way of living is incompatible with the contemporary European society. (Federico F. 2012)

It is clear that loving Gypsy music does not necessarily entail accepting Roma as equal members of European society. In fact, the superficial multiculturalism of Balkan music festivals and Gypsy music marketing can mask underlying racism.

In sum, Balkan Romani musicians face multiple exclusions. Very few are represented by Western managers and labels; rather, most rely on live wedding work, which tends to be poorly paid and erratic, except for a few bands. Those that have Western contracts tour more often and make more money, but even they are rarely in charge of designing their own images and charting their own collaborations. My case studies of Balkan brass music in the West, Goran Bregović, Balkan Brass Battle, and DJs remixes all raise questions about the effects of globalization on marginalized peoples. Global corporate capitalism has initiated 'new communication technologies, new regimes of consumerism, and new approaches in advertising and marketing' (Taylor 2007, 11). As Balkan Romani music has migrated to the West and encountered fame and larger audiences, it has been framed by dual discourses of authenticity and hybridity, often masking inequalities. Simultaneously, Roma have migrated West, encountering hostility and panic. At the intersection between these musical and population flows stand non-Romani managers and producers who design the salable Gypsy. This imagined Gypsy, created by non-Romani cultural brokers, resonates with historical stereotypes but also invokes new tropes of authenticity and hybridity, and it claims a legitimating place in multicultural discourse.

ACKNOWLEDGMENTS

The research was funded by the Oregon Humanities Center and by the Guggenheim Foundation. Fieldwork took place in New York, San Francisco, London, Brussels, Frankfurt, Berlin, Cologne, Dusseldorf, Vienna, and Lisbon, 2009–2011, in addition to 25 years of fieldwork in the Balkans with Romani musicians in their communities (see Silverman 2012). Portions of this chapter were reworked from Silverman (2011) and Silverman (2012) by permission of Oxford University Press, US.

NOTES

1. See http://www.actressarchives.com/news/lady-gaga-im-a-gypsy (accessed November 15, 2012).
2. For detailed information on these topics, see European Roma Rights Centre (www.errc.org).
3. Landler (2004, 4) reported the hysteria of Germans in reference to the 'human tidal wave' of incoming Roma. In January 2007 the *Los Angeles Times* published an article titled 'EU's Ugly Little Challenge', which claimed that for many Western Europeans, the inclusion of Romania and Bulgaria in the EU 'spells the inclusion of 3 million potential problems: yet more Gypsies . . . . Yet European newspaper editors are stumped by how they should

address the largest minority on the continent. Town mayors all over Eastern Europe often avoid the term altogether and talk instead of "whitening out" their inner cities' (McCann 2007).

4. In the quest for the universal and unique in Romani music, some scholars have claimed to find musical links with India (Hancock 2002, 71). This work has been highly speculative and remains unproven.

5. *Graceland* (1986), a collaboration between Paul Simon, Ladysmith Black Mambazo, and others, won awards, sold millions of copies, and even figured in the anti-Apartheid movement. Simon's lyrics contributed to the project, and he clearly respected his collaborators, paid them well, toured with them, and donated to political causes. But in terms of ownership, Simon's name appeared above the title and he copyrighted the music (Feld 1994a). In the end, perhaps, 'Musicians fill the role of wage laborers' (Feld 1994a, 242). Also see Taylor (2007, 127–29) for a discussion of other collaborations between Western stars and non-Western musicians.

6. For example, 'Hybridity can rebound from its discursive origins in colonial fantasies and oppressions and can become instead a practical and creative means of cultural rearticulation and resurgence from the margins' (Born and Hesmondhalgh 2000, 19). Postmodernists tend to see a 'resolution of issues of appropriation into unproblematic notions of crossover and pluralism.' Aesthetic pluralism is then divorced from extant socioeconomic differences and 'held to be an autonomous and effective force for transforming those differences. The aesthetic is held to portend social change; it can stand for wider social change' (Born and Hesmondhalgh 2000, 21). Hutnyk (2000) critiques this stance of postmodernists.

7. African Americans provide a useful comparison as a marginal group with musical power. Ingrid Monson's statement that 'African-Americans invert the expected relationship between hegemonic superculture and subculture' (1994, 286) could apply equally to Roma. But is this another form of exploitation? Has the socioeconomic position of blacks improved as a result of their music becoming popular throughout the world? Celebratory scholar Simon Jones (1988) asserts that when white British youth adopt black musical styles they are implicitly rejecting racism. Others, however, focus on how black music never lost its imputed exoticism and primitiveness even when taken into white commercial forms (Born and Hesmondhalgh 2000, 22–23). In jazz, white musicians have tended to receive greater rewards; similarly, in rock, 'its white stars have generally been paid much more attention than black innovators' (Born and Hesmondhalgh 2000, 23).

8. See www.youtube.com/watch?v=BNJUArES7yw&feature=fvwp&NR=1 (accessed November 15, 2012).

9. See www.youtube.com/watch?v=S8ca4WggBs&feature=player_embedded#! (accessed November 15, 2012).

10. Ziff and Rao define cultural appropriation as 'the taking—from a culture that is not one's own—of intellectual property, cultural expressions or artifacts, history and ways of knowledge, and profiting at the expense of the people of that culture' (1997, 1).

REFERENCES

Asphalt Tango. 'Balkan Brass Battle: Fanfare Ciocarlia vs. Boban i Marko Marković Orchestra.' Accessed January 16, 2013. www.asphalt-tango.de/ciocarlia-markovic/artist.

Born, Georgina, and David Hesmondhalgh, eds. 2000. 'Introduction: On Difference, Representation, and Appropriation in Music.' In *Western Music and Its Others: Difference, Representation, and Appropriation in Music*, edited by Georgina Born and David Hesmondhalgh, 1–58. Berkeley: University of California Press.

Cartwright, Garth. 2011. Liner notes for Balkan Brass Battle: Fanfare Ciocarlia vs. Boban i Marko Marković Orchestra. Asphalt Tango, Berlin, ATR 2911.

Chow, Rey. 1998. *Ethics after Idealism: Theory, Culture, Ethnicity, Reading*. Bloomington: Indiana University Press

Dirlik, Arif. 1997. *The Postcolonial Aura: Third World Criticism in the Age of Global Capitalism*. Boulder, CO: Westview Press.

Dirlik, Arif. 2000. *Postmodernity's Histories: The Past as Legacy and Project*. Lanham MD: Rowman and Littlefield.

Dirlik, Arif. 2002. 'Bringing History Back In: Of Diasporas, Hybridities, Places, and Histories.' In *Beyond Dichotomies: Histories, Identities, Cultures, and the Challenge of Globalization*, edited by Elisabeth Mudimbe-Boyi, 93–127. Albany: State University of New York Press.

Dimova, Rozita. 2007. 'BalkanBeats Berlin: Producing Cosmopolitanism, Consuming Primitivism.' *Ethnologia Balkanica* 11:221–35.

Djordjević, Tihomir. 1910/1984. 'Cigani I Muzika u Srbiji.' *Naš Narodni Život* 7:32–40.

Economist. 2008. 'Briefing: Europe's Roma: Bottom of the Heap.' June 21, 35–38.

Federico F. 2012 Internet comment, April 9, on Kooijman, Hellen, Roma: Bleak Horizon. Presseurop. Accessed June 10, 2013. http://www.presseurop.eu/en/content/article/1757331–bleak-horizon.

Feld, Steven. 1994a. 'Notes on World Beat.' In *Music Grooves*, edited by Charles Keil and Steven Feld, 238–46. Chicago: University of Chicago Press.

Feld, Steven. 1994b. 'From Schizophonia to Schismogenesis: On the Discourses and Commodification Practices of "World Music" and "World Beat."' In *Music Grooves*, edited by Charles Keil and Steven Feld, 257–89. Chicago: University of Chicago Press.

Feld, Steven. 2000a. 'The Poetics and Politics of Pygmy Pop.' In *Western Music and Its Others: Difference, Representation, and Appropriation in Music*, edited by Georgina Born and David Hesmondhalgh, 254–79. Berkeley: University of California Press.

Feld, Steven. 2000b. 'A Sweet Lullaby for World Music.' *Public Culture* 12(1):145–71.

Gilroy, Paul. 2004. 'Migrancy, Culture, and a New Map of Europe.' In *Blackening Europe: The African American Presence*, edited by Heike Raphael Hernandez, xi–xxii. New York: Routledge.

Gojković, Adrijana. 1977. 'Romi u Muzičkom Životu Naših Naroda (Roma in the Musical Life of Our People).' *Zvuk* 3:45–50.

Hancock, Ian. 1987. *The Pariah Syndrome*. Ann Arbor, MI: Karoma.

Hancock, Ian. 1997. 'The Struggle for the Control of Identity.' *Transitions* 4(4):36–44.

Hancock, Ian. 2002. *We Are the Romani People: Ame Sam e Rromane Džene*. Hatfield: University of Herfortshire Press.

Hutnyk, John. 2000. *Critique of Exotica: Music, Politics, and the Culture Industry*. London: Pluto Press.

Jones, Simon. 1988. *Black Youth, White Culture: The Reggae Tradition from JA to UK*. Basingstoke: MacMillan.

Keil, Charles, and Steven Feld. 1994. *Music Grooves*. Chicago: University of Chicago Press.

Kooijman, Hellen. 2012. Roma: Bleak Horizon. April 6. Presseurop. Accessed June 10, 2013. http://www.presseurop.eu/en/content/article/1757331–bleak-horizon.

Landler, Mark. 2004. 'A Human Tidal Wave, or a Ripple of Hypsteria?' *New York Times*, May 5, A4.

Lee, Ken. 2000. 'Orientalism and Gypsylorism.' *Social Analysis* 44(2):129–56.

Lincoln Center. 2006. Program for Goran Bregović Wedding and Funeral Orchestra. July 13.

Lipsitz, George. 1994. *Dangerous Crossroads: Popular Music, Postmodernism and the Poetics of Place*. London: Verso.

Lynskey, Dorian. 2006. 'Dorian Lynskey on Bands Looking to the Balkans for Inspiration.' *Guardian*, November 24. Accessed January 16, 2013. http://www.guardian.co.uk/music/2006/nov/24/worldmusic?INTCMP= SRCH.

Marković, Alexandra. 2008. 'Goran Bregović, the Balkan Music Composer.' *Ethnologia Balkanica* 12:9–23.

Marković, Alexandra. 2009. 'Sampling Artists: Gypsy Images in Goran Bregović's Music.' In *Voices of the Weak: Music and Minorities*, edited by Zuzana Jurkova and Lee Bidgood, 108–21. Prague: Slovo 21.

McCann, Colum 2007. 'EU's Ugly Little Challenge.' *Los Angeles Times*, January 6. Accessed June 10, 2013. http://www.latimes.com/news/la-oe-mccann6jan06,0,476912.story.

Meintjes, Louise. 1990. 'Paul Simon's Graceland, South Africa, and the Mediation of Musical Meaning.' *Ethnomusicology* 34(1):37–73.

Monson, Ingrid. 1994. 'Doubleness and Jazz Improvisation: Irony, Parody and Ethnomusicology.' *Critical Inquiry* 20(2):283–313.

Petrova, Dimitrina. 2003. 'The Roma: Between a Myth and a Future.' *Social Research* 70(1):111–61.

Rosaldo, Renato. 1989. *Culture and Truth: The Remaking of Social Analysis*. Boston: Beacon Press.

Said, Edward. 1978. *Orientalism*. New York: Vintage.

Silverman, Carol. 2007. 'Trafficking in the Exotic with "Gypsy" Music: Balkan Roma, Cosmopolitanism, and "World Music" Festivals.' In *Balkan Popular Culture and the Ottoman Ecumene: Music, Image, and Regional Political Discourse*, edited by Donna Buchanan, 335–61. Lanham, MD: Scarecrow Press.

Silverman, Carol. 2011. 'Gypsy Music, Hybridity and Appropriation: Balkan Dilemmas of Postmodernity.' *Ethnologica Balkanica* 15:15–32.

Silverman, Carol. 2012. *Romani Routes: Cultural Politics and Balkan Music in Diaspora*. New York: Oxford University Press.

Szeman, Ioana. 2009. '"Gypsy Music" and DeeJays: Orientalism, Balkanism and Romani Music.' *TDR: The Drama Review* 53(3):98–116.

Taylor, Timothy. 1997. *Global Pop: World Music, World Markets*. London: Routledge.

Taylor, Timothy. 2007. *Beyond Exoticism: Western Music and the World*. Durham, NC: Duke University Press.

Todorova, Maria. 1997. *Imagining the Balkans*. New York: Oxford University Press.

Tomić, Djordje. 2006. 'Balkan Hot Step.' Liner notes for CD *Rromano Suno 2: Gypsy Music from the Balkans*. B92CD215, Serbia.

Trumpener, Katie. 1992. 'The Time of the Gypsies: A "People without History" in the Narratives of the West.' *Critical Inquiry* 18:843–84.

Ziff, Bruce, and Pratima Rao. 1997. 'Introduction to Cultural Appropriation: A Framework for Analysis.' In *Borrowed Power: Essays on Cultural*

Appropriation, edited by Bruce Ziff and Pratima Rao, 1–27. New Brunswick, NJ: Rutgers University Press.

Žižek, Slavoj. 1997. 'Multiculturalism, or, the Cultural Logic of Multinational Capitalism.' *New Left Review* 225(September–October):28–51.

DISCOGRAPHY

Balkan Brass Battle: Fanfare Ciocarlia vs. Boban i Marko Marković Orchestra. 2011. Liner notes by Garth Cartwright. Asphalt Tango, Berlin, CD ATR 2911.

Fanfare Ciocarlia: Gypsy Queens and Kings. 2007. Liner notes by Garth Cartwright. Asphalt Tango, Berlin, CD ATR 1207.

Rromano Suno 2: Gypsy Music from the Balkans. 2006. Liner notes by Djordje Tomić. B92CD215, Serbia.

9 From the *Shtetl* to the Gardens and Beyond
Identity and Symbolic Geography in Cape Town's Synagogue Choirs

Stephen P.K. Muir

In the popular South African tourist destination of Cape Town, Western Cape, a vibrant Jewish community, supporting at least ten synagogues of varying sizes and affiliations,[1] plays out a complex musical narrative that both represents and projects an equally complex range of identities. In this chapter, much of which is based on fieldwork conducted in Cape Town in early 2012, I address only a small aspect of that musical narrative, the Ashkenazi Orthodox community's liturgical choral tradition,[2] but in doing so I hope to shed light for the first time on some of the ways in which, through the agency of musical practice, members of this community negotiate a variety of identities as Jews, and (re)construct diverging symbolic geographies from apparently similar historical and cultural backgrounds.

Symbolic geographies represent perceived, perhaps yearned-for, spheres of experience and existence, rather than actual and material spaces. Separate from 'physical or political reality', they become expressions of 'unfulfilled dreams, frustrations and aspirations' (Trandafoiu 2003, 6). Mark Slobin has argued along similar lines that music plays a vital role in our understanding of the character and dynamic of a community 'because it embodies any number of imagined worlds' (1992, 57). Music, it seems, can provide a means of comprehending these different worlds, charting the sometimes conflicting ontological realms that feature in diasporic communities. In this chapter, through an exploration of the geographies—symbolic, imagined, and otherwise—inhabited by the synagogue choirs of Cape Town, I seek to offer an insight into the multifaceted identity dynamics of a Jewish community whose musical modes of expression have hitherto received almost no scholarly attention.

'A COLONY OF LITHUANIA?'
SYMBOLIC GEOGRAPHY IN THE MAKING

During my interviews with a broad spectrum of Cape Town Jews (see 'Methodology' below), the belief was unanimously expressed that the South African Jewish community's heritage is almost exclusively

Lithuanian. Although, as Gideon Shimoni (1980, 12) has observed, the common description 'a colony of Lithuania' is a somewhat oversimplified version of the country's Jewish history, it nevertheless represents the community's actual perception. How this feeling of kinship with Lithuania helps to create, and sometimes collides with, the different symbolic geographies inhabited by Cape Town's synagogue choirs is a fundamental aspect of my investigation.

South Africa's Jewish history has been well documented by scholars.[3] Jews were almost certainly present in Cape Town when the very first European settlers, the Dutch East India Company, arrived at the Cape in 1652 (Cohen 1984, 1), but the first organized communal body was not established until 1841, when the Society of the Jewish Community of Cape Town, Cape of Good Hope was formed (ibid., 2). By this time, the British had taken control of the area, and Jews were permitted to reside in the colony and practice their religion openly. Although it contained a good number of German Jews, the community was essentially 'a colony of Anglo-Jewry' (Shimoni 1980, 18) in character, and certainly not at all Lithuanian at this stage.

By 1880, the Jewish population of South Africa was approximately 4,000, now spread throughout the country (Cohen 1984, 3), but this grew rapidly in the last decades of the 19th century with the arrival of large numbers of Jews from Eastern Europe, mostly from the northwestern part of the Russian Pale of Settlement,[4] and even more specifically from the Kovno (Kaunas) Province that largely equates to modern-day Lithuania (Shimoni 2003, 2–3). These so-called *Litvaks* (the name given to Jews from the area) swelled the South African Jewish population to some 38,000 by 1904 and nearly 50,000 by 1911 (Cohen 1984, 3). Today, according to the South African Jewish Board of Deputies, the country's Jewish community is thought to number 70,000–80,000 out of a total of nearly 50 million South Africans. Approximately 16,000 of these Jews live among some 3.5 million Cape Town inhabitants, constituting less than half of 1 percent of the city's total population.[5]

Running alongside the social and political history of South Africa's Jews is a rich and colorful musical narrative that has featured some of the most prominent figures in world Jewish culture, *chazzanim* of the caliber of Berele Chagy, Israel Alter, and Simcha Kusevitsky.[6] Accompanying such world-class *chazzanim* has been a strong choral tradition. Among my interviewees were a number of older choristers who had been members of Cape Town synagogue choirs since childhood. They spoke nostalgically of a bygone age when every synagogue in the city had a choir. Together, these reminiscences comprise a powerful collective memory of a recent but now disappearing 'Golden Age' of synagogue choral music in Cape Town. Bryan (pseudonyms are used unless otherwise stated) was born in the city and had sung in a number of different choirs before settling, in his 60s, into the Cape Town Hebrew Congregation choir around 1990; he reminisced:

We used to have, years ago we used to have a choral competition—not a competition, a choral sort of festival. So we had, going back to those days, we had Rondebosch *shul*,[7] we had Gardens *shul*, Sea Point *shul*, Milnerton *shul*, Claremont *shul*, Camps Bay *shul*. . . . There's only the two *shul*s with choirs now. We used to have a, as I say, a concert with all the choirs singing separately. And it went down well. We liked it, everybody loved it. (Bryan, interview, Cape Town, February 23, 2012)

Philip, another born-and-bred Capetonian, had received musical instruction as a child before pursuing a nonmusical career, and he had joined the Cape Town Hebrew Congregation choir in the late 1990s because his former synagogue choir, in which he had sung since his youth, disbanded:

It was one evening, and all the choirs, there used to be about six or seven choirs that came, and each did two or three pieces to entertain the community. It was very good, and it was very keenly, you know, we practiced very hard for it, but now there's only, I think there's us and Sea Point that has a serious choir. The rest I don't think—Milnerton tries, and I think Claremont does on the High Holy Days, and that's it. (Philip, interview, Cape Town, February 24, 2012)

A number of reasons were suggested by my informants for the dramatic decline in choral participation. Most thought that modern society offers too many other distractions and popular musical outlets for young people, and that because liturgical music is not generally taught in Jewish seminaries (*yeshivot*), most new rabbis, being *Chabad*-trained, are more interested in communal congregational singing than in maintaining any sort of choral tradition.[8] Thus, institutional changes common to many Jewish communities around the world have combined with symptoms of globalization—particularly the infiltration of American popular musics, as described more fully below—to reduce choral participation in Cape Town to much lower levels. The result is that, as my informant Philip attested, only two full-time permanent choirs remain in the city's Orthodox community—at the Cape Town Hebrew Congregation (known locally as the Gardens *shul*), and at the Green and Sea Point Hebrew Congregation (usually called the Marais Road or Sea Point *shul*). These choirs are the focus of the two case studies that follow after a brief discussion of my methodological models.

METHODOLOGIES, MODELS

It was into the context outlined above that I arrived in Cape Town in February 2012 for an intensive fieldwork visit among the city's Jewish community. My lifelong involvement with choirs as a singer and conductor, coupled with my Zambian birthplace and an intense fascination with Judaism and its music, guided my choice of subject. Like Abigail Wood (2010), whose excellent account of the 'Singing Diplomat' choir in Jerusalem was published while I planned my visit, my investigation emphasizes the local circumstances of the singers involved, as have others specific to South African music (see, for example, Erlmann 1996; Meintjes 2003).

My choice of choirs as a focus was personally motivated, of course, but also guided by recent musicological advances. As Karen Ahlquist's important collection *Chorus and Community* aims to establish, choirs as a global phenomenon are important for a number of reasons. Ahlquist observes that 'choral performance can assert artistic and educational achievement, aesthetic merit, and social, national, religious, or ethnic identity' (2006, 2). In South Africa, choirs appear even more important than in many other places; indeed, a frequent expression that I heard during my conversations with Cape Town musicians (both Jewish and non-Jewish) ran along the lines that 'of course, South Africa is a choral-based society.' The precise meaning of this often-repeated phrase is not completely clear and goes beyond the scope of this chapter. However, a number of studies have charted the history and ethnomusicology of choirs in South Africa, most typically focusing on various 'black' churches (see, among others, Blacking 1987; Erlmann 1999; Gilbert 2008; Olwage 2002, 2005, 2008). As Carol Muller puts it, these studies help dispel the myth that 'African music is only about drumming and complex rhythms when it is about so much more' (2008, xv).

I therefore hoped to gain a better perspective of the broader community's range of Jewish identities by attending choral synagogue services and choir rehearsals, speaking to rabbis, *chazzanim* and choral directors, and arranging private interviews with the members of the two choirs involved. I also explored the community's varied uses of modern communication media, including websites and social networking sites like Facebook and YouTube, in order to understand how identities were projected in a more global context, sometimes with striking and surprising results, as seen below.

As Jeffrey Summit (2000, 8–11) has observed with great sensitivity, there are a number of methodological challenges associated with researching Jewish musical phenomena, particularly (though not exclusively) in Orthodox communities. While all those involved in my study consented generously to our conversations being recorded and used in my research, the use of electronic devices, and even the act of writing, is prohibited on the Sabbath. Out of respect for these communities, I wrote up field notes from memory if they concerned events on the Sabbath, and a degree of interpretative distancing is therefore inevitable. Furthermore, as quickly became evident, the choristers often knew each other extremely well, and usually had for most of their lives. While they took evident pride in the fact that a visiting scholar was researching their activities, the frankness of some of their stories risked causing friction if set down in writing. I have therefore used pseudonyms when quoting from interviews, believing, like Summit, that I serve no real purpose in 'revealing anything that should not be revealed' (2000, 11). Where revealing an identity might be unavoidable, I limit any information conveyed to the factual and uncontroversial.

However, there would be little point in attempting to disguise the identity of the two synagogues involved, as my chapter celebrates their achievements in sustaining a choral tradition in the face of considerable difficulties. Both have reacted to the threat of dwindling congregations in innovative ways, but with very different musical consequences. My two case studies explore the manner in which musical choice in a worship context (as outlined in Kartomi and McCredie 2004) has been exercised and incorporated into strategies to attract new members to the synagogues, demonstrating how choral music and participation has been adapted and molded in both localized and globalized contexts.

'TOP HAT AND TAILS . . .': A LITTLE PIECE OF ENGLAND IN THE COMPANY GARDENS

My first case study involves the choir of the Cape Town Hebrew Congregation (the Gardens Synagogue), and illustrates how the community's collective self-identity as predominantly Lithuanian can sometimes be challenged and displaced by other historical and contemporary factors, revealing symbolic geographies coexisting side by side, or even nested within each other, in apparent contradiction.

It's 6.15pm, Friday February 3, 2012. Against the breathtaking backdrop of Cape Town's Table Mountain, and with the Friday evening sun warming my back, I cross the landscaped piazza of the Cape Town Hebrew Congregation, the oldest synagogue in South Africa.[9] I enter the synagogue, and am immediately greeted by the rabbi. When he learns that I've travelled all the way from the UK to study the music of Cape Town synagogues, he declares, 'You must have come to hear our choir!' Clearly he is proud of the *shul*'s musical tradition. As I take a seat, a man asks me where I'm from and what brings me there. Upon hearing my story, he too exclaims, 'You've come to the right place! You'll get to hear our choir sing tonight. We're very proud of them; next month is their centenary concert. They're the longest continually-running synagogue choir in the world.' Other congregants join in, agreeing with the first speaker. There is clear, palpable pride in the choir. Shortly after this, the choir enters, a group of twelve men aged between approximately twenty and eighty years dressed in dark suits, smiling and exchanging friendly glances as they ascend the large *bimah*.[10] An expectant hush descends as the *chazzan* begins to intone the opening notes of the Friday night *Kabbalat Shabbat* service. Suddenly the atmosphere changes; it's theatre as well as liturgy now. The choir gathers round the *chazzan*, who doubles as the choirmaster and conductor; all present are visibly impressed with him. [...] After the service the *chazzan* and choir assemble on the steps in the piazza outside the *shul* to sing the blessings for the *brocha*.[11] The rest of the congregants gather round and listen in respectful silence. Singing in the choir clearly puts people in a special place in this community. (Field notes, Gardens Synagogue, February 3, 2012)

The beautiful Gardens Synagogue shares a campus today with the South African Jewish Museum and Cape Town Holocaust Centre. Consecrated in 1905, the current building sits alongside an earlier 1863 synagogue that now forms the opening exhibition of the Jewish Museum. The Gardens Synagogue is important in the South African context. Analyzing the collection of institutions that occupy the campus, which he terms 'South Africa's Jewish Complex', Oren Stier observes that 'it is important to see the Gardens Synagogue both as a physical structure and as a complex symbol and reference point for South African Jewry' (2004, 128). Being the country's oldest, it is often referred to as the Mother Synagogue of South Africa, and it occupies a special place for the nation's Jews. Derek, a stalwart of the Gardens Synagogue community and a member of its choir since the age of eight, related that 'it's an icon in the Jewish Community of South Africa' (interview, Cape Town, February 13, 2012). The choir plays a key role in the synagogue's image and sense of prestige; indeed, it is hard to read about the synagogue without, sooner or later, finding reference to its excellent *chazzan* and choir. Stier's 'Jewish Complex' article, although nothing to do with music, reports the synagogue as 'boasting a men's choir' (2004, 128); on the synagogue's website, the choir features prominently as one of only six rolling images (see Gardens *Shul* 2012a); and even its very brief Wikipedia entry states that 'the congregation is particularly noted for its choir' (Gardens *Shul* 2008).

The Friday night *Shabbat* (Sabbath) service that I recall above was part of an ongoing strategy to attract more members to services: On the first Friday of each month the synagogue holds a special event, 'Friday Night Live'. As the initiative's web page explains, 'the concept of Friday Night Live was created as a means to encourage people of all ages, particularly those who were not *shul* regulars, to increase their *shul* attendance if only once a month' (Gardens *Shul* 2012b). Separate services for children and teens complement the main service in the Gardens Synagogue, all followed by a themed 'Brocha in the Piazza'. Figure 9.1 shows the flyer for the 'Carvo and Croissants' event that I attended; other themes have included 'Pizza and Peroni'. 'Sushi and Blue Label', and 'Bokke, Beer and Biltong'.

Figure 9.1   Flyer for the 'Friday Night Live' service at Gardens Synagogue, February 3, 2012.

Source: Gardens *Shul* (2012c). Reprinted by permission of the Cape Town Hebrew Congregation.

While the various themes and glossy advertising might seem to suggest a degree of 'dumbing down', in fact the prominent role of the choir in 'Friday Night Live' mitigates against this. The website for the initiative proclaims:

> The *Chazzan* and choir singing *Shalom Aleichem* and making *Kiddush* on the front steps has brought tears to many an eye and the evenings are regarded as being from the most memorable *Shabbat* experiences in Cape Town's history. (Gardens *Shul*. 2012b)

Even more interesting in this respect is the YouTube video promoting the initiative's fourth anniversary in November 2011 (see Gardens *Shul* 2011). Toward the climax of the video (1'32"), the *chazzan* and choir restate the 'Wassup?!' motif that runs through the video—itself a spoof of a famous 1999 Budweiser beer advertisement (see Budweiser Wassup Advert 1999)—but now sung to a cadential figure redolent of the mostly 19th-century choral pieces performed at regular services. The message is quite clear: Internet technology is embraced 'with particular social effects in mind' (Lysloff and Gay 2003, 8), here embedding closely guarded tradition (the *chazzan* and choir) at the heart of an innovative strategy to attract new members. At the same time, it also offers the opportunity to market the Cape Town 'Friday Night Live' brand to a more global audience. Such services began in Cape Town in 2007, but the concept is rather older, existing in some American communities for at least 14 years (see Torok 2011). Whether the Gardens Synagogue version was started independently or in emulation of other such events is unclear; however, with its professionally produced video and elegant flyers, it demonstrates an eagerness to engage with global media phenomena, if only to draw in its own community.

Despite this modern, globalizing tendency, the choral music of 'Friday Night Live' is perhaps paradoxically almost indistinguishable from other *Shabbat* services at the Gardens Synagogue. The choir's repertoire (performed with considerable expertise) consists mostly of works from the 'classical' Jewish tradition in common with most Orthodox synagogues that sustain a choir—primarily music by Louis Lewandowski (1821–94).[12] In many respects, use of this music binds the Gardens Synagogue together with a large number of others around the world with a musical equivalent to Robin Cohen's 'diasporic rope' (2008, 16).

Notwithstanding the predominantly 19th-century German Reform origins of this choral music, and its similarity with Lutheran musical models, one word consistently recurs in the characterization of the Gardens Synagogue, its choir, and its music: English. Stier's description of the Gardens Synagogue speaks of 'a distinctly English style of worship that is maintained up to the present day' (2004, 128), and this image is reflected in the comments of my informants, regardless of synagogue affiliation. When speaking of the Gardens Synagogue specifically, they consistently played down the community's Lithuanian heritage in favor of England, at the same time often referring to the early history of the community, when Lithuanian immigrants were not particularly welcome at the Gardens. Andrew, for example, had been a member of the Marais Road choir since childhood and now helps run the choir. His grandparents were all from Lithuania and had shared their experiences with him earlier in life:

> You know, historically the Garden's *shul* was called the 'English'. [. . .] and what happened was that when the Lithuanians, or the *Litvaks*, as they were known, when they arrived they were kind of, excluded. Almost like a Jewish Apartheid! And they had to form their own communities outside of the Gardens *shul*, because the Garden's *shul* was, you know, top hat and tails. So that's different . . . It's actually, it's fine because now we're all one community, but then it was very different. [. . .] The tradition is still there. The history is still there.[13] (Interview, Cape Town, February 22, 2012)

Derek (quoted earlier) reflected broadly on the place of the choir within the wider Jewish community:

> My theory here is that people come to the Gardens *shul* to listen. They go to the other *shuls* to participate. You take *Ohr Somayach*,[14] or you take some of the other *shuls* where there're no choirs. Everybody participates, and people will tell you that they prefer to be in a *shul* where they can sing, and they can participate. [. . .] Whereas at the Gardens *shul* we have very little participation—we try to encourage it, but people have said, 'we've come to listen, coz we enjoy the music so much that it's better to listen than to participate.' So if you're asking if there's a reflection, a reflection of *shtetls* in Lithuania: it was never predominant in the Gardens *shul*, because the Gardens *shul*, if you know the history of the Cape Town community. This was, of course, the first *shul*. When your Lithuanians started arriving here with the pogroms after, in the 1880s and thereon, they weren't very welcome here. [. . .] Because this *shul* consisted of, of English and German families. (Interview, Cape Town, February 13, 2012)

Particularly interesting here is an unspoken conflation of nonparticipation at the Gardens Synagogue with a downplaying of the importance of Lithuanian heritage. Conversely, institutions like *Ohr Somayach*, whose worship is participatory and influenced by popular notions of Hasidism, are, in the minds of my informants, more connected to their East European past. As Mark Slobin has noted, 'congregants find weekly services much more enjoyable when they can sing catchy, rhythmic Hasidic tunes [. . .] rather than sit back and listen to the authority figures—rabbi and cantor—run the show' (1992, 71). Rabbi Smith, formerly a member of the Gardens choir but now involved in the leadership of a different synagogue, made strong allusions to these concepts, rejecting any notion that Hasidic styles of worship had any influence on the Gardens Synagogue:

> And in that service you see, there again, the Gardens Synagogue, because of the ambience, because of the aura, of the beauty of that building, it does influence the performance level of the choir. So to say that the Hasidic way of doing things has infiltrated—no, I don't think so. (Interview, Cape Town, February 9, 2012)

I return later to the question of Hasidism and its connection to the Cape Town community's self-expressed Lithuanian identity, as it is somewhat contradictory. However, the distancing of the Gardens Synagogue choir from the community's Eastern European roots was striking and consistent. Stier's interpretation of the Gardens Synagogue–Holocaust Centre–Jewish Museum campus is perceptive in this respect; he observes that the structure and narrative of the Jewish Museum diminishes the importance of the community's East European past, 'conveying the sense that the world of religion and the *shtetl* is no longer relevant to present-day South African Jews' (2004, 135). For the Gardens Synagogue and its choir, the 'imagined world' (Slobin 1992, 57) of the synagogue and its music creates much more of an English than a Lithuanian symbolic geography.

'*SHABBAT* UNPLUGGED': SUMMER NIGHTS IN SEA POINT

My second case study involves the choir of the Green and Sea Point Hebrew Congregation (the Marais Road Synagogue). Superficially, the choir and its community share many features with the Gardens Synagogue, particularly their involvement in strategies to increase service attendance. However, the musical expressions of this community's identity are shaped to a much greater extent by engagement with globalizing phenomena, resulting in a much more surprising nexus of overlapping symbolic geographies.

> It's 6.00pm, Friday February 17, 2012. The location is the street outside the Green and Sea Point Hebrew Congregation, the Marais Road *shul* in Sea Point, a suburb of Cape Town nestled at the foot of the imposing Lion's Head mountain that forms part of the spectacular Table Bay skyline. As I arrive, the rabbi draws up in a hired red open-top sports car as the sounds of 1950s-style American rock 'n' roll drift up the street. I'm given a coke and some popcorn; a few minutes later I'm ushered into the synagogue. As I take a seat, the sound of men's voices filters through the background hubbub of conversation; I can make out the bass-line introduction to 'Summer nights' from the musical *Grease*, to a vocalized 'bom bom,' accompanied by off-beat finger clicks. An

Figure 9.2 Flyer posted on Facebook for the '*Shabbat* Unplugged' service at Marais Road Synagogue, February 17, 2012.

Source: Marais Road Shul (2012b). Reprinted by permission of the Green and Sea Point Hebrew Congregation.

dressed as a kind of John Travolta figure and seated at the wheel of the red convertible, he is clearly comfortable with the new '*Shabbat* Unplugged' concept. Tradition and innovation sit side by side, at least at the surface level. 'Come watch our world class choir sing *Shabbas* [*Shabbat*] melodies to the sounds of Grease Lightening [*sic*]', exclaims a comment next to the flyer on Facebook (see Marais Road *Shul* 2012b, comment posted February 5, 2012). While the juxtaposition of the choir and the advertised musical style might strike some almost as heretical, the potential incongruity does not appear significant to the anonymous commenter.

Marais Road also created a YouTube video to promote their new initiative (see Marais Road *Shul* 2012a), but it contrasts markedly with the produced professional movie of the Gardens Synagogue. Here the rabbi and *chazzan*, Ivor Joffe, informally discuss the ideas behind '*Shabbat* Unplugged'. Seated at an electric keyboard, Joffe plays the rabbi a new tune he has heard (1'01"), which the rabbi suggests is by Shlomo Carlebach (1925–94). Carlebach was an enthusiastic proponent of Hasidic styles of worship, and continues to be hugely influential, 'greatly influenc[ing] communities in America and around the world' (Tarsi 2002, 201) as 'the most popular—and prolific—composer' of 'neo-Hasidic' worship music (Wood 2007, 230). Speaking of this new Hasidic-flavored tune and how it might be incorporated into '*Shabbat* Unplugged', Joffe declares in the video that 'everybody's going to join in and sing along' (1'37"). Toward the end of the video the rabbi echoes this sentiment, exhorting the viewer to 'be part of the choir, be part of the service! Inspirational songs, uplifting tunes' (3'11"). The message could not be more different to the Gardens: Participation is expected, and the classical tradition espoused by the Gardens' choir is apparently eschewed in favor of the Carlebach-Hasidic style so popular in many other synagogues.

Use of Carlebach in the service indicates an engagement with global Jewish liturgical trends prevalent since the 1960s. The interesting thing about this music is that it has quickly become accepted by many as 'traditionally' Jewish. According to Mark Kligman, 'so quickly and completely did [Carlebach's] music penetrate the Jewish world that many who hear or sing the tunes assume that they are traditional melodies' (2001, 102). Similarly, in her study of Hasidic influences on contemporary Yiddish music making, Abigail Wood refers to an 'imagined Hasidism' (2007, 231) that draws on the sound-world of the hit musical and film *Fiddler on the Roof* as a way of connecting Jews to East European roots that no longer exist.

It is therefore no surprise that, alongside Carlebach, *Fiddler* was one of the early choices for the music of '*Shabbat* Unplugged' in August 2011. Jacob, who earlier outlined the centrality of the choir within the Marais Road community, explained:

> We started off with *Fiddler on the Roof.* So that was—but there, you see, you have more of that, the tunes, you know [sings the opening of 'If I Were a Rich Man']—that sort of music, so it's more acceptable than—but everybody enjoyed it. (Interview, Cape Town, February 23, 2012)

Significant here is that apparently *Fiddler* was considered 'kosher' by this singer as it signaled continuation with the past, with the familiar. Given that the use of Broadway show tunes has persisted since the use of *Fiddler*, it seems that the 'tradition' of a lost age has first been reconstructed and then based on a new one invented 'by repetition,' implying 'continuity with the past' (Hobsbawm and Ranger 1983, 1). Put differently, once *Fiddler* had been used, future selected shows, while losing the immediate association with Jewish culture, were nevertheless deemed acceptable because they perpetuated this new tradition. The use of Carlebach and the encouragement of a more participatory style in the YouTube video supports this attempt to draw on tradition, however detached from the reality of the music of the past that tradition actually is.

As we might expect from the above descriptions, when I discussed Marais Road with the members of the two choirs, the community's Lithuanian heritage and a Lithuanian influence on its music came to the fore. Comments such as the following were very typical from this synagogue's choir. After describing his grandparents' early experience of feeling unwelcome at the Gardens Synagogue, Andrew gave his views on his synagogue's musical approach:

It's both sets of grandparents. Yah. Lithuanian background. [. . .] Yes, absolutely [that has an influence on the music that we do]. Because the type of music that our *shul* actually has always been involved in, and the one that I was at previously, has definitely got a Lithuanian flavor. So we, for example, would not be doing a lot of Lewandowski. [. . .] one of the terms used to describe what that music is, is *freygish*. [. . .] When I think of the music of Lewandowski, I think of more, I don't wanna say the word 'classy', because then there, then it means that Lithuanian music isn't classy! [*laughs*] But, you know, the Lewandowski stuff is more, is just more, I don't even wanna use the word sophisticated. It's more . . . Germanic. (Interview, Cape Town, February 22, 2012)

As Wood explains, *freygish* is the 'Yiddish term for the Phrygian dominant mode' (2007, 225), used extensively in Yiddish and neo-Hasidic music. It is also in essence one of the three principle musical modes of Jewish prayer, known as the '*Avaha rabba*' ('with abundant love') mode, after the eponymous prayer with which it is primarily associated. Its characteristic augmented second interval between the second and third degrees of the scale is what gives much music labeled as 'Jewish' its characteristic sound. The use of the word by my informant Andrew—a musically literate person often involved in the running of his choir—is revealing, and links the style of music increasingly used in the Marais Road synagogue with the neo-Hasidic music that he and his fellow singers associate with the community's Lithuanian past. His downplaying of Lewandowski and similar composers is also striking, since his choir does actually sing a good amount of that very same 'classical' music that predominates at the Gardens. But the importance attributed to it is very different in the context of a choir that apparently looks much more to its East European past for its sense of identity.

Rabbi Smith, who had earlier rejected any genuine Hasidic influence on South Africa's choral music, nevertheless reflected on the influence of *Fiddler* and neo-Hasidism during our lengthy conversation:

I believe that *Fiddler on the Roof* brought a wrong message; [I believe] that being Jewish in the *shtetl* was not all 'yupee-yupee-yupee' singing and dancing, but as portrayed to some extent by Tevye. [. . .] I mean, life in the *shtetl* was not joyous. It was miserable. It was mud up to your knees, and disease and pestilence, and poverty and hunger and cold. It was miserable! But *Fiddler on the Roof* had a different take to it. And I believe it was because of the awareness, or the growing awareness, the developing awareness of the Jews of this city and of this country that they saw [*Fiddler*] as authentic Judaism, an authentic Jewish music. (Interview, Cape Town, February 9, 2012)

The search for some kind of 'authenticity' is a recurring theme in studies of Jewish musical phenomena—see, for example, Summit's (1993) survey of the relationship between music and identity in the greater Boston area. While the Gardens choir seem content with the 'authenticity' and security provided by their symbolically English geography, the Marais Road choir exhibit a far more complicated nexus of identities that seeks to identify at once with an East European symbolic geography that is only partially based on reality, but at the same time with more global phenomena in the shape of American popular musicals.

But there is a final twist in the story to consider. Rabbi Smith also pointed to a situation that I have already briefly alluded to as 'somewhat contradictory', but which deserves a little further consideration in the context of the above discussion:

> Being Lithuanian, of course, we were all the *Misnagdim* ['opponents'], the opponents to the Hasidic movement, so much so that Hasidism was physically kept out of this country 'til about 40–50 years ago. There was one remnant of a Hasidic congregation here in Cape Town, but they were always kept down by the Lithuanian *Misnagdim*. [. . .] There's a whole history. So, because of that the music of the synagogues originally in this country was not of Hasidic content. (Interview, Cape Town, February 9, 2012)

Scholars concur regarding Lithuanian Jewry; Shmuel Feiner speaks of the 'fierce campaign that was being waged against Hasidism in Lithuania from 1772' (2004, 105). Ironically, then, the neo-Hasidic music espoused by the Marais Road community in the form of Carlebach and *Fiddler*, and the 'new tradition' of '*Shabbat* Unplugged', runs in almost diametrical opposition to the actual, historical position of Lithuanian Jewry as *Misnagdim*, the historical opponents of *Hasidism*.

Thus, at Marais Road several apparently contradictory symbolic geographies collide through musical expression, located in yearned-for spheres of experience and existence rather than reality: The neo-Hasidic, the reinvented Lithuanian, and the global exist side by side, yet the contradictions are accepted without difficulty by the members of the choir concerned, and by implication, their supporting community.

CONCLUSIONS: IDENTITY, SYMBOLIC GEOGRAPHY, GLOBALIZATION

As my two case studies have shown, via the agency of choral participation a multifaceted range of overlapping identities emerges in Cape Town's Ashkenazi Orthodox Jewish community. All my informants felt passionately and distinctively Jewish, but this identity means different things in different contexts. For some, an English musical identity sometimes pushes aside an otherwise powerful collective Lithuanian identity when viewed through the lens of the Gardens Synagogue and its music; for others, the Hasidic and the Lithuanian—historically polar opposites on the scale of Jewish Orthodoxy—have merged into a reimagined symbolic Lithuanian geography resituated in a broader, more generically East European musical locus.

The role of globalization complicates things further. Infrastructural changes common to many Jewish communities around the world, particularly the rise of *Chabad* and similar movements, have been compounded by other factors such as the predominance of popular musics, leading to a decline in synagogue choir participation, particularly among the young. It is therefore highly ironic that a very similar global musical phenomenon, the musical, has subsequently been used in an attempt to reverse the overall decline in synagogue attendance. The initial engagement by the Marais Road choir with the music of *Fiddler on the Roof* has legitimated the appropriation of popular secular music without overtly Jewish connotations as a vehicle for modernization and intracommunal outreach, creating a bridge of (actually quite tenuous) connectedness to the community's past (imagined and actual) but also with contemporary global musical hegemonies represented by the Broadway musical. Symbolic geographies thus emerge on even more levels, including now a more global Jewish one. As Philip Bohlman concludes, music is 'not only an object of exchange across social and religious boundaries, but fundamentally reconfigure[s] those boundaries' (2008, xix). In this way, Cape Town's Jewish choral communities construct and negotiate an interweaving and apparently conflicting range of identities that reference 'a sense of multiple "homes"' (Garbin 2010, 159), whose symbolic location and boundaries are indeed continually shifting, ranging from the *shtetl*s of Eastern Europe, to the Englishness of the Gardens, and beyond, to a modern, globally connected South Africa.

ACKNOWLEDGMENTS

My thanks are extended above all to the many choristers, choirmasters, *chazzanim*, rabbis (independent and affiliated), and community members who willingly sacrificed their time to participate in this project, allowed me to attend their rehearsals, tolerated my questions, and in many cases welcomed me into their homes, offering hospitality and meals. I am particularly grateful to *chazzanim* Ian Camissar (Gardens Synagogue) and Ivor Joffe (Marais Road Synagogue), without whose support and enthusiasm I could not have conducted my research, and to the rabbis of the two synagogues, who graciously welcomed me into their congregations.

I wish also to acknowledge the following for their generous support: The Worldwide Universities Network Research Mobility Programme and the School of Music, University of Leeds, whose financial backing made possible my fieldwork visit to Cape Town; Milton Shain and Janine Blumberg at the Isaac and Jessie Kaplan Centre for Jewish Studies and Research at the

University of Cape Town, without whose logistical, scholarly, and professional advice I would not even have made it to Cape Town; Milton Shain also particularly for his encouragement and valuable comments on my later drafts; the staff of the South African college of Music, University of Cape Town, particularly Morné Bezuidenhout, Sylvia Bruinders, and Rebekka Sandmeier; my colleagues Kevin Dawe and Derek Scott for their helpful comments on early drafts; my wife, Claire, and friends Nicki and Ian Sapiro for reading drafts and for their assistance rescuing corrupt computer files; and David Garbin for providing prepublication copies of his work. Notwithstanding these generous contributions, all errors and omissions in the text are of course my own.

NOTES

1. Lists of synagogues in the Western Cape area of South Africa, of which Cape Town is the major city, can be found via http://www.uos.co.za/uos (Orthodox communities; accessed January 12, 2013) and http://saupj.org.za (Progressive communities; accessed January 12, 2013). The lists are not necessarily comprehensive or accurate, since a number of the listed synagogues have either closed or amalgamated in recent years. Nevertheless, they serve as useful starting points for orientation.
2. Cape Town also plays host to a small but active Sephardic congregation with a choir, and three Reform synagogues, constituents of a single congregation named Temple Israel, which also features choirs. Regrettably, space does not permit the consideration of these parts of the community, which consequently will have to await a future opportunity for exploration.
3. Notable accounts of South Africa's Jewish history can be found in, among others, Abrahams (1955); Cohen (1984); Saron and Hotz (1955); Mendelsohn and Shain (2008); Shain (1983, 1994); Shain and Mendelsohn (2002); Shimoni (1980, 2003).
4. Created in 1791 by Empress Catherine the Great, the Pale of Settlement was the area outside which Jewish settlement was largely prohibited in Imperial Russia. It encompassed much of modern-day Lithuania, Latvia, Poland, Belarus, Ukraine, and Moldova, along with some areas of western Russia (see Pipes 1975 for a general historical outline).
5. Statistics derived from 'SA Jewish History—A Brief Overview' from the website of the South African Jewish Board of Deputies at http://www.jewishsa.co.za, applying the search term 'Jewish population' (accessed January 12, 2013).
6. *Chazzanim*: plural of *chazzan*, meaning cantor. For more on the extremely significant role of the *chazzan*, see Slobin (1989).
7. *Shul*: the Yiddish term used by most Ashkenazi Jews to mean synagogue.
8. *Chabad* is the common abbreviation for the ultra-Orthodox *Chabad-Lubavitch* movement, a branch of Hasidism known today for its powerful international Jewish outreach program (see http://www.chabad.org; accessed January 12, 2013). Notable exceptions to the general *Chabad* avoidance of classical Jewish choralism are the rabbis of the two synagogues at the focus of this study, both of whom are *Chabad* trained but both of whom wholeheartedly support their choirs.
9 The synagogue is situated in a small campus adjacent to the Cape Town Company Gardens, from which it (and the surrounding vicinity) derives its name.

10. *Bimah*: a raised platform located—in most Orthodox synagogues—in the center of the prayer hall, from which the prayer leader, often but not necessarily the *chazzan*, conducts the service. Choirs do not normally perform from the *bimah*, but the Gardens Synagogue boasts a particularly wide one, permitting *chazzan* and choir to remain together.
11. *Brocha*: literally 'blessing', but used by South African Jews to denote the refreshments provided after certain services. The term normally used in the UK is '*kiddush*'.
12. Goldberg (1992) provides a succinct summary of the nature and development of this so-called 'classical' Jewish choral tradition.
13. More detail on the tensions between different Jewish groups in Cape Town can be found in Shimoni (1980, 13).
14. *Ohr Somayach*, Cape Town, is affiliated to the *yeshiva* in Jerusalem of the same name. Rather like *Chabad* (the two were often spoken of in the same breath by my informants, regardless of their actual differences), both institutions focus on bringing non-observant Jews back to a stricter lifestyle (see http://www.ohrsom.co.za; accessed January 12, 2013). The style of worship is heavily influenced by Hasidism, with an emphasis on participation.
15. Photographs are not taken during the actual hours of *Shabbat*, but usually during the preservice street entertainment. The Gardens *shul* also has a Facebook page, but it had yet to feature any activity at the time of revising this chapter (January 2013).

REFERENCES

Abrahams, Israel. 1995. *The Birth of a Community: A History of Western Province Jewry from Earliest Times to the end of the South African War, 1902.* Cape Town: Cape Town Hebrew Congregation.

Ahlquist, Karen. 2006. 'Introduction.' In *Chorus and Community*, edited by Karen Ahlquist, 1–15. Urbana: University of Illinois Press.

Blacking, John. 1987. 'Intention and Change in the Performance of European Hymns by some Black South African Churches.' In *Transplanted European Music Cultures: Miscellanea Musicologica*, edited by G. Moon, 193–200. Adelaide: University of Adelaide Press.

Bohlman, Philip. 2008. *Jewish Music and Modernity.* Oxford: Oxford University Press.

Cohen, Robin. 2008. *Global Diasporas: An Introduction.* London: Routledge.

Cohen, Stephen. 1984. 'The Historical Background.' In *South African Jewry: A Contemporary Survey*, edited by Marcus Arkin, 1–22. Cape Town: Oxford University Press.

Erlmann, Veit. 1996. *Nightsong: Performance, Power and Practice in South Africa.* Chicago: Chicago University Press.

Erlmann, Veit. 1999. *Music, Modernity, and the Global Imagination.* New York: Oxford University Press.

Feiner, Shmuel. 2004. *The Jewish Enlightenment.* Translated by Chaya Naor. Philadelphia: University of Pennsylvania Press.

Garbin, David. 2010. 'Symbolic Geographies of the Sacred: Diasporic Territorialisation and Charismatic Power in a Transnational Congolese Prophetic Church.' In *Traveling Spirits: Migrants, Markets and Mobilities*, edited by G. Hüwelmeier and K. Krause, 145–64. London: Routledge.

Gilbert, Shirli. 2008. 'Singing against Apartheid: ANC Cultural Groups and the International Anti-Apartheid Struggle.' In *Composing Apartheid: Music for and against Apartheid*, edited by Grant Olwage, 155–84. Johannesburg: Wits University Press.

Goldberg, Geoffrey. 1992. 'Jewish Liturgical Music in the Wake of Nineteenth-Century Reform.' In *Sacred Sound and Social Change: Liturgical Music in Jewish and Christian Experience*, edited by Lawrence Hoffman and Janet Walton, 59–83. Notre Dame, IN: University of Notre Dame Press.

Hobsbawm, Eric, and Terence Ranger. 1983. *The Invention of Tradition*. Cambridge: Cambridge University Press.

Kartomi, Margaret, and Andrew D. McCredie. 2004. 'Introduction: Musical Outcomes of Jewish Migration into Asia via the Northern and Southern Routes c. 1780–c.1950.' *Ethnomusicology Forum* 13(1):3–20.

Kligman, Mark. 2001. 'Contemporary Jewish Music in America.' *American Jewish Yearbook* 101:88–141.

Lysloff, René, and Leslie C. Gay Jr. 2003. 'Introduction: Ethnomusicology in the Twenty-First Century.' In *Music and Technoculture*, edited by René Lysloff and Leslie C. Gay Jr., 1–22. Middletown, CT: Wesleyan University Press.

Meintjes, Louise. 2003. *Sound of Africa! Making Music Zulu in a South African Studio*. Durham, NC: Duke University Press.

Mendelsohn, Richard, and Milton Shain. 2008. *The Jews in South Africa: An Illustrated History*. Jeppestown: Jonathan Ball.

Muller, Carol. 2008. *Focus: Music of South Africa*. 2nd ed. New York: Routledge.

Olwage, Grant. 2002. 'Scriptions of the Choral: The Historiography of Black South African Choralism.' *South African Journal of Musicology* 22:29–46.

Olwage, Grant. 2005. 'Discipline and Choralism: The Birth of Musical Colonialism.' In *Music, Power, and Politics*, edited by Annie Randall, 25–46. New York: Routledge.

Olwage, Grant. 2008. 'Apartheid's Musical Sings: Reflections on Black Choralism, Modernity and Race-Ethnicity in the Segregation Era.' In *Composing Apartheid: Music for and against Apartheid*, edited by Grant Olwage, 35–54. Johannesburg: Wits University Press.

Pipes, Richard. 1975. 'Catherine II and the Jews: The Origins of the Pale of Settlement.' *Soviet Jewish Affairs* 5:3–20.

Saron, Gustav, and Louis Hotz, eds. 1955. *The Jews in South Africa: A History*. Cape Town: Oxford University Press.

Shain, Milton. 1983. *Jewry and Cape Society: The Origins and Activities of the Jewish Board of Deputies for the Cape Colony*. Cape Town: Historical Publication Society.

Shain, Milton. 1994. *The Roots of Antisemitism in South Africa*. Charlottesville: University Press of Virginia.

Shain, Milton, and Richard Mendelsohn, eds. 2002. *Memories, Realities and Dreams: Aspects of the South African Jewish Experience*. Johannesburg: Jonathan Ball.

Shimoni, Gideon. 1980. *Jews and Zionism: The South African Experience (1910–1967)*. Cape Town: Oxford University Press.

Shimoni, Gideon. 2003. *Community and Conscience: the Jews in Apartheid South Africa*. Hanover, NH: Brandeis University Press.

Slobin, Mark. 1989. *Chosen Voices: The Story of the American Cantorate*. Urbana: University of Illinois Press.

Slobin, Mark. 1992. 'Micromusics of the West: A Comparative Approach.' *Ethnomusicology* 36(1):1–87.

Stier, Oren Baruch. 2004. 'South Africa's Jewish Complex.' *Jewish Social Studies* 10(3):123–42.

Summit, Jeffrey. 1993. '"I'm a Yankee Doodle Dandy?": Identity and Melody at an American Simchat Torah Celebration.' *Ethnomusicology* 37(1):41–62.

Summit, Jeffrey. 2000. *The Lord's Song in a Strange Land: Music and Identity in Contemporary Jewish Worship*. Oxford: Oxford University Press.

Tarsi, Boaz. 2002. 'Observations on Practices of "Nusach" in America.' *Asian Music* 33(2):175–219.

Trandafoiu, Ruxandra. 2003. 'Racism and Symbolic Geography in Romania: The Ghettoisation of the Gypsies.' *Global Built Environment Review* 3(2):6–12.

Wood, Abigail. 2007. 'Stepping across the Divide: Hasidic Music in Today's Yiddish Canon.' *Ethnomusicology* 51(2):205–37.

Wood, Abigail. 2010. '*Singing Diplomats*: The Hidden Life of a Russian-Speaking Choir in Jerusalem.' *Ethnomusicology Forum* 19(2):165–90.

INTERNET SOURCES

Budweiser Wassup Advert. 1999. Accessed January 12, 2013. http://www.youtube.com/watch?v=eLh_01ynKRo.

Gardens *Shul*. 2008. 'Gardens *Shul*.' Accessed January 12, 2013. http://en.wikipedia.org/wiki/Gardens_Shul.

Gardens *Shul*. 2011. 'Whats Up—Friday Night Live—4th Anniversary.' Accessed January 12, 2013. http://youtu.be/h0G9tZhHe7g.

Gardens *Shul*. 2012a. 'About the Gardens *Shul*.' Accessed January 12, 2013. http://www.gardensshul.org.

Gardens *Shul*. 2012b. 'Friday Night Live.' Accessed January 12, 2013. http://www.gardensshul.org/index.php/events/special-events/friday-night-live.

Gardens *Shul*. 2012c. 'Garden *Shul* Presents Friday Night Live #39.' Accessed January 12, 2013. http://www.gardensshul.org/index.php/blog/90–friday-night-live-39–carvo-a-croissants.

Marais Road *Shul*. 2011. 'Marais Road Shul.' Accessed January 12, 2013. http://www.maraisroadshul.com.

Marais Road *Shul*. 2012a. 'The Birth of *Shabbat* Unplugged.' Accessed January 12, 2013. http://www.youtube.com/watch?v=IMqahby6b9U.

Marais Road *Shul*. 2012b. 'Let's Get Together, 17 Feb.' Accessed January 12, 2013. http://www.facebook.com/photo.php?fbid=358023450875492&set=pb.159950867349419.-2207520000.1353596329&type=3&permPage=1.

Torok, Ryan. 2011. 'Friday Night Live's Road to the Ford.' *JewishJournal.com*. Accessed January 12, 2013. http://www.jewishjournal.com/los_angeles/article/friday_night_lives_road_to_the_ford_20110628.

10 Reimagining the Caucasus
Music and Community in the Azerbaijani *Aşıq* Tradition

Anna Oldfield

I recall one afternoon in the summer of 2006 in the far north of Azerbaijan. Around me a garden of mulberry trees, in front of me the Caucasus mountain range rising white-capped into the horizon to blend imperceptibly with Georgia and Dagestan. Enjoying the legendary hospitality of my hosts while listening to the stirring rhythms of Caucasian music, it was easy to imagine a time when peoples moved freely through these lands, before administrative, political, and national boarders had sliced them into discreet units. As John Colarusso illustrates in *Nart Sagas* (2002), a collection of heroic narratives that have been shared across ethnicities of the Caucasus for centuries, when traveling I saw more not what divided the peoples of the region, but rather how much they shared: pride in their unique cultures, respect for their long-held traditions, and love for their mountainous lands. In my fieldwork, I found all these qualities embedded in musical cultures that were specific to every locale, even every village, yet with elements that were shared throughout the region. It was this dynamic interplay between local and regional movements of musical traditions that inspired me to frame my research in the borderlands and to explore the musical migrations that I found there.

Specifically, this chapter will illustrate two examples of *aşıq* [ash-UGH] bards from northern Azerbaijan, examining the relationship of the traveling bard to 'imagined communities' that cross national, linguistic, geographical, political, and religious boundaries. The ultimate aim of this study is to explore the role of bardic music in creating flexible communities that privilege local, hybrid, and vernacular identities in contrast to monolingual/national communities based on the authority of texts and the imposition of standardized written languages.

THE AZERBAIJANI *AŞIQ* TRADITION

The *aşıq* tradition is Azerbaijan's oldest living bardic art. This 500-year-old genre is the primary venue for the transmission and creation of oral literature, including epic narratives called *dastan*, lyric poetry, and riddle contests. The practitioners of the art are professional bards called by the title *Aşıq*, meaning 'one who is in love'. *Aşıq* minstrels perform their works in song, accompanying themselves on a long-necked lute called the *saz*. Considered a calling rather than a performance genre, the *aşıq* role has its origins in the Central Asian shaman, who used music to communicate between human and spiritual worlds (Qasımlı 2003). Since the 18th century, there have been both male and female *aşıq* bards. The genre has been woven into the public life of Azerbaijan for centuries, and is traditionally performed at weddings, life cycle ceremonies, holidays, and national festivals. Passed down orally from master to apprentice for generations, *aşıq* arts have persisted into the present, evolving with the historical and social changes that have engaged Azerbaijan over the centuries.

The Republic of Azerbaijan begins as the Caucasian mountain chain completes its southeastern stretch and melds into the plains that reach the Caspian Sea. Small but geographically diverse, Azerbaijan grows everything from Lenkoran lemons to Quba apples to Absheron figs. Azerbaijan's biodiversity is matched by a cultural and ethnic diversity typical of the Caucasus. The population of Azerbaijan is approximately 80 percent Azeri with more than 30 minorities, the largest of which include Lezghi, Talysh, and Avar (Arzumanli 2002). The majority of Azeris are Shi'i Muslims, while minority populations include Sunni Muslims, Christians, and Jews. The official language of the country is Azerbaijani, a Western Turkic language closely related to Turkish and Turkmen. Minority languages are used in local communities and Russian is widely spoken as a second language, especially in the capital city of Baku.

Azerbaijan is bordered by Iran to the south, Russia and Georgia to the north, and Armenia to the west. Azeri people live in a region that stretches from the Caucasus into northern Iran. In 1828, those living north of the Araxes River were incorporated into the Russian Empire, then later into the Soviet Union, and since 1991 into the sovereign Republic of Azerbaijan. The southern Azeris remained in Iran and are that country's largest minority. The Republic of Azerbaijan, with a population of approximately 9.4 million, shares the language and cultural heritage of its relatives to the south, including the *aşıq* tradition, which flourishes on both sides of the border. The *aşık* tradition performed in Turkey is also closely related to the *aşıq* of Azerbaijan.

In a region as complex as Central and Western Asia, the similarities and differences of musical traditions across regions can reveal much of the subtle ways in which cultures dialogue while preserving a sense of distinctiveness. Working on comparative traditions in Afghanistan, Mark Slobin writes that 'music may be one of those features of social interrelationship that reflect underlying patterns of ethnic boundary maintenance' (1976, 1), underscoring that while music is one of the spheres in which cultures interact the most, it is also a sphere that is used to distinctly define one ethnicity from another. This phenomenon has been noted consistently in the former Soviet Union, where threads of the complex relationships between music, state hegemony, and national culture are still in a process of being unraveled as peoples recover from the Soviet experiment (Frolova-Walker 1998; Levin 1996; Naroditskaya 2003; Olsen 2004; Sultanova 2005; and others). In many such cases, folk genres are reshaped in the waves of past histories and mythologies as the process of national identity is renegotiated in the present.

It is no less so in Azerbaijan, where *aşıq* arts are often seen as a unique and defining aspect of national culture, as 'high as the mountains, deep as the ocean, eternal as the sky, and as great as our history' (Bunyadov 1975, 5). In both official and local cultures, *aşıq* arts and classical *muğam* art music are strongly associated with national pride, identity, and, as Slobin indicates, 'ethnic boundary maintenance'. This is especially understandable in the Caucasus, a small region with more than 150 ethnicities that has been, since before the Soviet era, impacted by the influence of romantic nationalism and the identification of identity with ethnicity—perhaps even more so in Azerbaijan, which has recently suffered a devastating territorial war with Armenia, a country with which it had several shared many musical traditions, including *aşıq* arts (Pahlevanian 2001). Breakaway Republics in Georgia, violence in Dagestan and Ingushetia, and the Russian war in Chechnya have cast a pall over the region that can be difficult to see beyond. Seen through the lens of the political, the Caucasus bristles with disputed boundaries; it is a region tragically destabilized after the fall of the Soviet Union that still has not recovered. Some even *define* the Caucasus in terms of conflict; as Bruce Grant (2009, xiv) points out, since Greek antiquity the region has been romanticized by outsiders as a primitive 'zone of violence', an image embodied in centuries of Russian literature and prevalent until this day.

On the ground, however, the Caucasus is home to communities that have lived together for many hundreds of years. Local narratives may give a window into the older and more fundamental patterns of multiculturalism that have allowed this complex region to function peacefully for much of its history. Seen at the grassroots level, the *aşıq* emerges less as a figure to champion the nation and more of a community builder, linking regions and peoples with the power of shared music and narrative.

Historically, the *aşıq* genre is thought to have arisen in 16th-century Tabriz, fusing Turkic epic poetics with Islamic mysticism in the atmosphere of early Safavid Iran (Qasımlı 117). During the 17th and 18th centuries, *aşıq* bards fanned out into the Caucasus and distinct schools developed around masters who had settled in various regions. Regional schools merged the original tradition with local music and folklore, creating new cannons based on their own legends and heroes. Once the companions of powerful leaders such as Shah Ismail I (İsmailzadə 2004, 33), glowing with the prestige of the urban court, by the late 18th century the *aşıq* was associated with rural, unlettered peasants, versifying in vernacular Azeri at a time when Farsi was the literary language of the elites. In the 19th century, intellectuals under the influence of romantic nationalism became interested in the *aşıq* tradition, which they saw as carrying the pure Azerbaijani spirit, and *aşıq* verses began to be collected and appear in print (Eldarova 1984).

The 20th century brought significant changes to Azerbaijan. When the Russian Empire dissolved after the 1917 Bolshevik Revolution, the Azeri intelligentsia seized the chance to declare an independent state, the Azerbaijan Democratic Republic (ADR) (Altstadt 1992). The ADR was formed as a progressive democracy with an impressive constitution and universal suffrage; however, the fledgling state was not able to withstand the Soviet Army, and the country was incorporated into the USSR in 1920. As part of the Soviet Union, Azerbaijani society was subjected to the same upheavals in the 1920s to the 1940s that affected other Soviet territories, including the persecution and killing of intellectuals and an intense campaign against religious institutions. In rural regions, forced collectivization of agriculture led to resistance and oppression in the countryside (Altstadt 1992). After World War II and the death of Stalin both the social and economic condition of the USSR improved, and by the 1960s Azerbaijan had become modernized and industrialized. Literacy was now universal, but the education was Soviet, which for Azerbaijan meant a rewriting of history in a way that cut off their ties with Iranian and Turkish cultures, described their pre-Soviet society as 'feudal' and backward. The alphabet was changed from Arabic script to Latin, then Cyrillic, and most books in the Arabic alphabet were burned (Jafarzade 2006). Russian was taught in schools and became a prestige language needed for success in higher education and government, although Azeri was spoken in homes. In a generation, no Soviet Azerbaijanis could read the Arabic alphabet, cutting them off from the Azeris of northern Iran and from the literature of their own past (Shaffer 2002, 65).

The role of the *aşıq* during the Soviet period was complex. The genre was quickly championed by Soviet policies as the people's authentic musical culture, while 'elite' *muğam* art music was discouraged (Huseynova 2006). An Aşıq Union was created and state sponsored 'Qurultay' registered all the performers in the country, regaling them with speeches such as 'The Role of *Aşıq* Arts in the Communist Workers Revolution' and instructing them to replace their outworn lyrics with songs praising Lenin and the struggle of the masses (Eldarova 1984, 23). By using the *aşıq* to give a stirring Azeri voice to the Russian Revolution, the state harnessed the genre to the official program 'National in Form, Socialist in Content,' which tried to localize Soviet ideals through national languages and cultures (Frolova-Walker 1998). *Saz hava* were taught in local cultural centers, *aşıq* bards were given enhanced performance opportunities on stage and later on television, and the genre thrived under official sanction.

Back home in the village, however, the same bards who sang Lenin's praises were still telling *dastan* about the 17th-century mystic Qurbani and the 18th-century bandit Koroğlu, saving the very narratives that the Soviet powers had tried to burn. By the second half of the century a few *aşıq* bards, most notably Mikayil Azafli (1924–90) were openly critical to the Soviet government. Singing about problems such as censorship and cultural repression, Azafli was arrested several times for his courage (Kafkasyalı 1996). Azafli, who still commands tremendous respect in Azerbaijan, was part of a growing wave of unrest that included artists and intellectuals who became increasingly vocal in the 1980s. His momentum, taken up by his family and apprentices, gave the *aşıq* genre a new wave of energy and integrity with which to meet the challenges of independence after 1991.

The Republic of Azerbaijan has faced serious challenges since it became a sovereign state. Infrastructure in vital areas such as energy and water distribution, health care, public safety, education, and agriculture were seriously disrupted after the fall of the Soviet Union, with disastrous results for the lives of ordinary people. Besides the legacies of bureaucratic mismanagement and environmental irresponsibility that challenge the entire former Soviet Union, Azerbaijan has been plagued with tragedy over the Autonomous Region of Nagorno-Karabakh, a crisis that shattered the Southern Caucasus and created monoethnic territories in a region where Azerbaijanis, Armenians, and other ethnicities had lived together for centuries.

Figure 10.1   Aşiq Mikayil Azafli with his *saz*. Photographed in the 1980s.

Source: From the collection of Gulare Azafli. Photographer unknown. Reproduced with permission.

Many years in the making, the conflict erupted catastrophically in 1992, causing more than 25,000 casualties and nearly a million displaced people (Human Rights Watch/Helsinki 1994, vii). Since a 1994 cease-fire, a series of reconciliation efforts by the OSCE Minsk Group have failed to ease the conflict, which has had enormously painful human and economic repercussions for all sides (de Waal 2003, King 2008).

The onset of the post-Soviet world after 1991 was also difficult for Azerbaijani *aşıq* bards, as the country began the painful transition to a market economy with drastic effects on musical culture. *Aşıq* bards faced a sudden cutoff of state sponsorship and a market where they needed to compete with a newly available world of international pop music. While the popularity of Azeri *muğam* art music soared, *aşıq* bards found themselves needing to overcome an association with being communist, conservative, rural, and old-fashioned: 'When *aşıq*s come on TV, we turn them off', a young urban professional told me (personal communication, Baku, 2005). Because the western mountain regions affected by the Karabakh war were also some of the strongest *aşıq* regions, many *aşıq*s and their core audiences became refugees. Consequently, despite having passionate supporters, many have become displaced and disadvantaged. In addition, the bard's main opportunity to earn a living, the wedding, has changed from a multiday event

Figure 10.2　Map of Azerbaijan and bordering countries.

Source: 'Physical Map of Azerbaijan' at http://www.freeworldmaps.net/asia/azerbaijan/map. html (accessed November 20, 2012; this map has been modified from the original).

performed outside in a tent to a ceremony of a few hours at a rented 'Palace of Happiness'. Weddings now present no opportunities for the telling of lengthy *dastan*, and it can be hard to even hear the *aşıq* over the electric ensemble. Today, it may seem that the winners of the 2011 Eurovision contest more accurately represent the new, modern Republic of Azerbaijan than the traditional *aşıq*.

Nonetheless, after leaving the urban center of Baku, the traveler through Azerbaijan will soon hear the sound of the *saz* from houses and cars. In western and northern mountains the *aşıq* bard still remains central to the local community, and it is there that we will now turn our gaze.

SƏNƏM OF GULUZAN—THE TAMBUR *AŞIQ*

In 2004, I was fortunate enough to meet with the family of Aziza Jafarzade (1921–2003), one of the most prominent literary historians of 20th-century Azerbaijan. Jafarzade had been tireless in collecting and publishing women's writing and folklore, and her articles and books showcased more than 100 women poets, writers, and *aşıq*s from the 12th to the 21st century.

In 1975, Jafarzade published an article about a mystery. In 1970 she had encountered a brief article about an Aşıq Sənəm from the Zagatala-Balakan region of northern Azerbaijan. The article included a photograph of Aşıq Sənəm playing a musical instrument that Jafarzade had never seen before: a two-stringed instrument 'shaped like a plank' but held like a lute (Jafarzade 1975, 14). Then in 1974, Jafarzade spotted a letter to the editor of *Azerbaijani Woman* magazine that mentioned Aşıq Sənəm and gave this verse:

> To my dear town of Guluzan,
> The day has dawned on Guluzan
> If you want to meet with Sənəm
> You have to come to Guluzan.[1] (Jafarzade 1975, 14)

'It was as if she were calling to me,' Jafarzade wrote, and headed off to Balakan to search for Aşıq Sənəm. When she got to Balakan, her inquiries revealed that there indeed was a village called Guluzan, and that *Aşıq* Sənəm still lived there. After arriving at the family residence, Jafarzade quickly spotted the instrument she had seen in the first picture, hanging on the wall—it was a *tambur*. 'In Guluzan, Balakan, Qax, and Zagatala, you won't find any house without a *tambur*,' they told her (Jafarzade 1975, 14).

When I visited Zagatala in 2006, I found the same thing—it was not *saz* but *tambur* that was played among the people there. The Zagatala-Balakan region is the home of Azerbaijan's Avar minority, who consider the *tambur* their national instrument. There are approximately 600,000 Avars living in a mountainous region divided between Azerbaijan, Georgia and Dagestan (Clifton 2003, 1). Although small in number, the Avar have been important players in the history of the Caucasus, including the famous Imam Shamil and Haji Murat. The Avar speak a North Caucasian language and are generally Sunni Muslims.

Variants of the *tambur* are played widely in the Northern Caucasus and by peoples in Central Asia. Avar Esabali Makhmudov, who makes and plays *tambur*, told me that he believes the instrument came with the Mongolic Kalmuks from Central Asia (interview, Zagatala, July 2006). Made of a solid piece of wood, the two-stringed *tambur* is played by strumming vigorously downwards with the fingers. *Tambur* music features fast, driving rhythms that, as Charlotte Albright (2002) noticed of *aşıq* music, bring to mind images of a galloping horse.

The Avar tambur tradition is quite different from the Azeri *aşıq* tradition. 'We love equality and freedom,' Esabali told me, explaining that among the Avars *tambur* playing is not the province of specially trained professionals but is enjoyed by all (interview, Zagatala, July 2006). Most Avars male and female can pick up a *tambur* and play. This is distinct from the Azeri tradition, where an *aşıq* undergoes years of apprenticeship and learns a repertoire that can be traced to a lineage of past masters, earning a special status in the community. The Avar tradition reflects the self-consciously democratic culture of Caucasian highlanders, and their musical culture highlights their differences with the more structured Azeri society, which especially appreciates the excellence of highly trained artists.

Avar and Azeri peoples have lived together in this region with several other ethnic groups for centuries. As a region of cultural heteroglossia, it is no surprise that the Azerbaijani *aşıq*s in that region play *tambur*. The first researcher to notice *tambur aşıq*s was Sadnik Pirsultanlı (2002), who wrote an article based on his own 1969 fieldwork in Tala, a village of Azeris living in an Avar region. What he found was that *tambur* playing *aşıq* bards had developed a unique style of singing the traditional seven syllable *bayati* to *tambur* music, adopting Azeri versification to the local instrument.

Jafarzade's 1975 article, however, was the first to closely examine the creativity of a *tambur aşıq*. Aşıq Sənəm proved to be a remarkable woman, artist, and community leader. In her interview with Jafarzade, Sənəm estimated her own age to be 120, and she was still playing and singing professionally. Though she remarks that her voice wasn't 'what it used to be,' her undaunted liveliness is apparent in Jafarzade's article. A strong figure in the local community, Sənəm says that 'among these peoples not one wedding, not one *iməçilik* (voluntary workday) goes on without me' (Jafarzade 1975, 15), and when Jafarzade asks Sənəm why she didn't ever get married she replies:

Sənəm: Well you know, child, when I was young a husband bossed you around like a master. I didn't want a master. Aren't I my own master?

Jafarzade: But if you didn't fall in love and get married, where do you get all of your poems about love?

The elderly *aşıq* replied with a youthful sparkle in her eye:

Sənəm: Love is one thing, getting married is something else. In our time, those who loved each other didn't get married. Maybe just like Leyla and Majnun were connected, I was bound to someone too. . . .

And once again, the strings of the tambur sounded [She sings]:

Hey boy with the black pants
Boy with the mole on your face
My father will not give you his girl
Come and beg him, boy.[2] (Jafarzade 1975, 15)

This exchange is a rare window into the life of a village-based woman *aşıq* of the 20th century. Here her sense of personal and social authority and confidence are apparent. Jafarzade (1975) writes that after Sənəm's death in 1977, the people of the town named a mountain spring after her, testifying to her high status in the community. At the same time, she seems to have embraced the spontaneity and freedom of the surrounding Avar culture, bursting mischievously into song and remaining independent of social conventions. Sənəm's example also indicates that becoming an *aşıq* could be an alternative for a young woman, especially one who did not want to get married. Scholars who have written close studies of urban Azerbaijani women, such as Tohidi (1996) and Hayat (2000, 2005), reveal that marriage is important to the status of even highly educated professional women. Tohidi writes that 'single women who have never been married, suffer from a negative stigma,' from cultural customs that expect 'self-sacrificing motherhood; docility and subservience' (1996, 114).

Aşıq Sənəm's example, which I saw repeated in many of the women *aşıq*s whom I interviewed, shows an alternative model, deeply embedded in traditional culture yet free from the 'stigma' of spinsterhood. Distinct from Soviet/Russian models of the new, empowered woman, often seen as antithetical to Azeri values, the *aşıq* role is one in which women can gain respect as individuals, explore their artistic talents, and express a powerful public voice in the most traditional communities. Sənəm's example combines the high status of the Azeri *aşıq* with the Avar spirit of independence, perhaps contributing to her role as a powerful local figure in her multicultural community. Traveling from village to village, a carrier of news, current events, narratives, and music, Aşıq Sənəm gives a remarkable example of small scale, rural community building in a complex borderland region. In her life spanning a century she created a community bound both horizontally, across the Zagatala-Balakan region, and vertically, binding generations through 100 years of history and change.

Figure 10.3 Aşıq Sona of Borchali, contemporary of Aşıq Sənəm and a representative of the Azeri minority living in Georgia, circa 1984.

Source: From the collection of Gulare Azafli. Photographer unknown. Reproduced with permission.

THE *AŞIQ* COUPLE OF QUBA: SOLTAN AND QƏNDƏB

Quba, as the northeastern spur of Azerbaijan is called, is part of a larger region with a primarily Lezghi population that stretches up beyond the political border into Dagestan. The Lezghi, who speak a North Caucasian language and are primarily Sunni Muslim, are the largest minority in Azerbaijan (Clifton 2002, 21). Like Zagatala, Quba is an area where many ethnicities have lived together for centuries, and is also a region where the Iran-influenced Shi'a legacy of Azerbaijan meets the Arab-influenced Sunni legacy of Dagestan. The city of Derbend in Dagestan was historically a center of Sufi activity centering on a pilgrimage site called the *Qirxlar pir* ('Shrine of the Forty Saints'), which inspired a strong *aşıq* tradition among both Azeris and Lezghis (Qasımlı 2003, 210).

Recently, folklorist Azad Nəbiyəv published a body of work that he recorded and collected from Soltan and Qəndəb Katruxlu, a 20th-century husband and wife *aşıq* duo originally from Derbend. They composed and performed their *dastan* together, alternately singing and narrating the male and female parts. Soltan hailed from the village of Katrux, an Azeri village near Derbend. Soltan himself had learned *aşıq* arts from his parents, Hani and Züleyxa. Hacı had learned the art from his own father, Aşıq Seyyid (1773–1863) whose master had been the famous Aşıq Lezghi Ahmed. Soltan's mother Züleyxa was born in 1876 in Katrux village in Dagestan, to a 'poor village family' and:

> From a very young age she showed a propensity for poetry and art. She knew the Arabic alphabet well. She took lessons and learned to recite the Quran like a skillful master. Her youthful passions led her to become and *aşıq*. In 1902 Züleyxa married Aşıq Hacı from the same village, and they started a family and performed together as *aşıq* bards. (Katruxlu 1996, 391)

Züleyxa became well known in her region, and along with Aşıq Sənəm was one of two women who took part in the first official *aşıq* Qurultay in 1928. The story of Hacı and Züleyxa's courtship was transformed into a *dastan*, which they themselves sang and then passed on to their children. The *Hacı and Züleyxa Dastan*, recorded as it was told by Soltan and Qəndəb, is typical of an *aşıq* narrative, merging historical and fictional events and people to turn a prosaic life into a poetic legend. The *dastan* begins when young Hacı falls asleep at the *Qirxlar Pir* in Derbend and is given 'Arab nectar' in a dream by the Forty Saints, who give him and Züleyxa to each other as their beloved (Nəbiyəv 2005, 125). But before they can become engaged, the rich Ağalar Khan claims Züleyxa as a bride for his own son. Hacı objects and is banished from Derbend. As the *dastan* narrates, he first goes to Mecca to perform the Hajj. Next he goes to Turkey, where he visits the 13th-century poet Rumi's grave, then goes to Ankara to see Atatürk speak, then to Şivas to meet with the famous Aşık Veysel. He and Veysel have a verbal dueling contest where it is proved they are equals, then they go to Istanbul together. Upon returning to Derbend, Hacı finds Züleyxa and convinces her to marry him by besting her in a riddle contest. They have a gala 40-day wedding, attended by famous bards from across the Caucasus. Finally, in a dream Hacı sees his (as yet unborn) son Soltan playing *saz* and singing the *dastan* of his father's life (Katruxlu 1996).

With such parents, it is no wonder that their son Soltan (1925–99) married an *aşıq* himself. We know of Soltan and Qəndəb's courtship from the 'Soltan and Qəndəb' *dastan*, which the two of them also sang together. As the narrative goes, 'at age seven, Soltan started school and also began learning *aşıq* arts. As he had a agile tongue for telling tales, within a few years he learned to sing, play *saz*, and how to perform' (Nəbiyəv 2005, 249). In school, he met a girl named Qəndəb, who became one of his apprentices:

> After a time they fell in love, but they didn't say a word about it to anyone. Together they played at weddings and gatherings, time passed. Qəndəb was a real 'Qəndəb' [sweet as sugar]: tall, black eyebrows, black eyes, a chin of crystal, apple cheeks. (Nəbiyəv 2005, 249)

In the *dastan*, Soltan is sent to Moscow to perform at an important state function, then comes back to find his apprentice Qəndəb leading weddings by herself. He declares his love and they go to tell her father that they want to marry. Her father objects and hides her by taking her from village to village all over the Quba region. Soltan follows them, hearing in each village how Qəndəb has just been there playing at a wedding. As he travels, he celebrates every town in song. Finally, he is invited to a huge festival of 'workers and shepherds' in Baku (which he calls a 'paradise'), where he finds Qəndəb leading the gathering. He declares his love, and her father drops his objections. The *dastan* ends with a gala wedding attended by famous *aşıq* from all over Azerbaijan as well as Iran and Turkey.

In real life, Qəndəb was Soltan's wife and mother of their seven children. Both were originally from Katrux in Derbend. She began to perform as an *aşıq* in 1948, when she was 13 years old, and Soltan was indeed her *saz* teacher. Soltan and Qəndəb married and moved to the Quba region of northern Azerbaijan, where they became very well known in the local regions and also nationally. Both were sent to perform in Moscow in 1961. Soltan and Qəndəb were known as accomplished performers and could sing in Lezghi and other languages as well as Azerbaijani (Nəbiyəv 2005, 279), which must have contributed to their success in their multicultural region. Qəndəb was active in her community, worked at the Quba House of Culture, and was elected several times as a local representative (Nəbiyəv 2005). The couple performed frequently at official gatherings, where *aşıq* arts were directed towards championing Soviet identity and accomplishments.

The above *dastan* told by Soltan and Qəndəb is a particularly interesting example of *aşıq* arts performed during the Soviet Union at the nonofficial level—that is, outside government-sponsored festivities, which banned any mentions of the Islamic religion, the Arabic language, or references to Turkey or the Middle East. Reported to have been told to workers at '*kholkhozes* and *sovkhozes* (collective farms and state farms) all over Azerbaijan' (Nəbiyəv 2005, 4), one can imagine the appeal of these *dastan*, part romance, part travelogue, and part affirmation of suppressed religious and cultural heritage. Soltan and Qəndəb were very much a couple of the Soviet era; one of their published verbal duels is between the 'cotton' and the 'worker' who will meet the production plan (Katruxlu 1996). At the same time, however, they were deeply embedded not only in the *aşıq*, but in local religious traditions. The easy combination of being Soviet, Muslim, Quban, and Azeri expressed in their *dastan* reveals a remarkable fluidity in the identities of Azerbaijanis living in multicultural areas during the Soviet regime.

The geography of these *dastan* express an *aşıq* geography that is much wider and more inclusive then the reigning political geography, including Azerbaijan, Dagestan, Turkey, Mecca, and a nod toward Moscow. The community-building aspects of their art are evident in binding the Quba region (with its primarily non-Azeri population) with the rest of Azerbaijan in a cultural whole created by the traveling and meeting of *aşıq*s with local

Figure 10.4 Aşık Gulare Azafli performing at a cotton festival in rural Azerbaijan, circa 1985.

Source: From the collection of Gulare Azafli. Photographer unknown. Reproduced with permission.

communities, giving the country not only a shared present, but a shared past. Soltan and Qəndəb's *dastan* expresses a gracefully melded identity that integrates Azeri, Lezghi, Soviet, Muslim, Shi'a, and Sunni into a whole that is Azerbaijani, reflecting the real complexity of the country far more effectively than statistics or histories could manage. In his *Imagined Communities*, Benedict Anderson (1983) theorized the growth of 'imagined communities' related by the reading of texts. By carrying living, flexible texts, and by physically traveling from place to place, *aşıq* minstrels create real communities with real people bound into imagined relationships made real by narrative. It is hard to believe that there could be any written text that could fulfill this function as effectively, unless one could imagine a novel that adjusted to the language, culture, interests, history, and current events of each audience.

AŞIQ BARDS AS ALTERNATIVE COMMUNITY BUILDERS

The examples of Aşıq Sənəm and Soltan and Qəndəb are of course only two out of many in what is still a little studied area. However, they do give us a rare window into identity construction in Azerbaijan among the nonelite, non-Russified classes who lived in the rural regions. During my own fieldwork in Azerbaijan (2004–6), I found that many *aşıq* bards and their rural audiences shared a similar attitude toward the Soviet Union. Although the terror and repression of the 1930s was abhorred, the World War II era was a time of increased patriotism and Soviet community building, as Azerbaijani regiments fought alongside soldiers from all republics. In the ensuing decades the Soviet Union was seen as a positive force that brought economic stability and education to rural regions. Over time Soviet identity was absorbed as just another facet of identity along with many others stemming from Azerbaijan's unique history as a cultural crossroads between Turkic, Iranian, and Caucasian cultures. The positive attitude shown towards the Soviet Union found in much 20th-century *aşıq* poetry should not be seen as simply pandering to the demands of the government; *aşıq* arts from the 20th century demonstrate how the Soviet era was partially synthesized into the existing cultural system—accepting what was positive, such as universal suffrage, women's emancipation, education, electricity, rural development, roads, running water, and employment, while rejecting that which was not wanted—assumed Russian superiority, atheism, hostility to Islamic culture, and loss of ethnic, linguistic, historical, literary, and geographic identity.

Thus, while being part of Soviet discourses, *aşıq* poetry simultaneously carried a strong subtext of resistance to certain aspects, particularly the dominance of Russian language and the encouragement of foreign literary forms such as the novel, short story, and free verse. By keeping the classic repertoire of poetry and *dastan* alive in the oral tradition, Soviet-era *aşıq* minstrels saved many of these works. It is remarkable that decades after the Arabic alphabet had been outlawed and books in that script burned, musicologist Emina Eldarova (1984) found *aşıq* bards in the 1970s still singing and composing the *alefbey-aleflem* form, in which the first letter of each line starts with a letter of the Arabic alphabet, thus preserving knowledge of the entire alphabet in oral form. In addition, poetry sung by bards became a major source of communication between ethnic Azeris living in Iran and Azerbaijan, who could not read each other's alphabets (Sultan-Qurraie 1998, 13).

A striking feature of the works of most *aşıq* bards of the 20th century is that they are not intended to rebel against Soviet hegemony—they are, instead, written from within as a way of changing the very meaning and structure of the hegemony from the inside. As mentioned before, many aspects of the Soviet Union worked well for Azerbaijan. What the *aşıq* worked to subvert and replace was Russian cultural chauvinism; alienation from related cultures, such as Turkey and Iran; the lack of respect paid to their literary, religious, and cultural heritage; and the treatment of Azerbaijani as a second-class language. This narrative subversion, reconsolidated every single time that an *aşıq* began a performance with the traditional appeal to 'the beloved, Ali', was embedded in the content of every *dastan*, and every *aşıq* song, embodying a constant, unwavering resistance to the colonization of the language and culture. The fact that *aşıq* bards still knew and sang 18th-century *dastan* such as *Abbas and Gulgez*, set in the court of Safavid Shah Abbas (1587–1629) and including riddle contests on Quranic philosophy, shows the extent of the alternative education offered by oral literature. In a constant play between acceptance and resistance—being very careful about what they accepted and what they resisted—Azerbaijani *aşıq* bards and the people who loved and memorized their songs kept important alternative conversations alive at both local and national levels.

The creation of community by the *aşıq* was enacted through a combination of oral text, legendizing of real places and people, and actual physical travel by the bard him- or herself. Because *aşıq* minstrels traveled to perform and meet with each other, they were also able to form webs of associations that connected their local communities and their concerns with other communities across the country. It is instructive to compare this process with the creation of national 'imagined communities' as conceptualized by Benedict Anderson. In his exploration of the growth of national consciousness across cultures and continents, Anderson describes how national communities form across large groups of people who had never met each other, yet can imagine each other to be real. As Anderson describes it, national consciousness grew along with the capitalist/industrial developments that led to print culture, which created communities of 'fellow readers, to whom they were connected through print' (1983, 47). Print served the function of a bridge, providing 'unified fields of exchange and communications' in which individuals could imagine themselves as part of a larger whole (ibid.). An important component of this process is the standardization of languages and cultures demanded in order to bridge large-scale national populations. As Ernest Gellner points out, 'a modern industrial state can only function with a mobile, literate, culturally standardized, interchangeable population' (1983, 46).

These processes, including the transformation of Azerbaijani from a vernacular to a standardized print language, the introduction of and universal education, and the shift of populations from rural regions to the capital of Baku, have all contributed to the development of the modern Azerbaijani state.

Rural and local identities, however, present alternatives to models that require 'interchangeable' people and standardized cultures. Comparing the work of *aşıq* bards as community builders through oral narrative culture, a number of points stand out. *Aşıq* narratives also create 'fields of exchange and communications' during their performances, but not by the method of creating a standardized print language to whom every subgroup must submit in order to share in the community, a process that privileges a centrally produced uniform standard over the local, different, and unique. This is an important aspect, because as Anderson points out, 'print capitalism created languages of power. . . . Certain dialects inevitably were "closer" to each print-language and dominated their final forms' (1983, 48), giving the dominant dialect an advantage and better access to education and government.

Aşıq arts, spread by oral tradition, use a different method of community building: although there are many shared stories, rituals, and musical forms, the *aşıq* adjusts them to each village, privileging the local culture of his or her audience rather than forcing them to bow to a standard. Since the 16th century, *aşıq* bards have worked in multiple languages as an inherent feature of the genre wherever it exists. Yilderay Erdener (1995) points out that Turkish *aşıq* singers performing in Kars adjust to the language, dialect, and local culture of the audience. *Aşıq* narratives privilege the local, singing the praises of real villages, real people, and real geographies, countering standardization and interchangeability with the small and unique. This orientation is found in the lyric songs of *aşıq* bards from every region of Azerbaijan—for example, this lyric song by Aşıq Bəsti, who lived in the Kelbajar region of Western Azerbaijan from 1836 to 1936:

Shepherd Mountain

The Water of Life flows from you,
Your water is honey, Shepherd Mountain.
You are dressed up like a bride,
How magnificent you are, Shepherd Mountain!

Cackling and cackling,
The partridges land on a branch.
Everywhere you look there is a lovely show,
It is a dream, Shepherd Mountain.

Every kind of flower blooms in your breast,
In your meadows are flowers that can be found nowhere else.
Bəsti is with you in the season of spring
She has stayed as your guest, Shepherd Mountain.[3] (Pirsultanlı 2001, 43)

Here Bəsti relates the uniqueness of this mountain, with 'flowers that can be found nowhere else,' emphasizing her own belonging in this generative environment that provides the 'Water of Life'. Poems such as this keep love for the local strong and diminish the pull of powerful centers, such as Baku or Moscow.

Print cultures, tied to the existence of a printing industry, distribution systems, and schools that train large numbers of people to read in standard dialect, require a government structure. In turn, government structures are able to control what is printed and distributed. In the Soviet Union, writers were expert at subverting censorship, either by using Aesopian language or *samizdat* publishing (typing out literature and passing it hand to hand). *Aşıq* narratives also evaded censorship by avoiding the fixity of print completely. Despite the attempt to control the genre through the state gatherings and official concerts, *aşıq* narratives were ultimately uncontrollable because their production was independent of government sponsorship—any *aşıq* in a village could sing from his or her store of oral narrative and teach it to others. Thus *aşıq* bards could promote illegal languages, such as Arabic, banned books, such as the Quran, and alternative geographies. Their narratives could travel to Turkey, Iran, or Mecca, subverting the Soviet attempt to identify community inside the borders of the USSR and cut Azerbaijanis off from their cultural and religious identity.

Thus, the *aşıq* genre, spread by oral narrative performed by local bards, presents an alternative model for 'imagined community' building, one which celebrates the local (for it has no 'center'—every region is central to the people that live there) and includes minority languages and cultures. Performance of the art connects a large number of individuals, who, like Anderson's readers, have never met each other; but in this case the model is a living literature that can adjust to the languages and cultures of its readers. Sənəm, Soltan, and Qəndəb were only three of hundreds of bards crisscrossing and connecting different parts of the country, sharing legends, rituals, and music. Their art contributed to the creation of a community that was alternative to both the identities of the Soviet Union and of separate ethnicities, and *aşıq* bards were able to sustain this community through time over a number of drastic and violent changes in the governments and social orders over the last 100 years.

One can imagine the factors that have led to the contemporary persistence of alternative modes of community building in the Caucasus. Russian rule in the Caucasus brought the imposition of administrative borders based on ethnic divisions over what were naturally multiethnic regions, already long connected not just by culture but physically by travelers such as *aşıq* minstrels. The division of the region also created religious tensions between Muslim and Christian populations who had both participated in the *aşıq* arts in earlier centuries, as in the example of Armenian minstrel Sayat Nova (1712–95), who sang Armenian, Persian, Azeri, and Georgian lyrics at the court of the Georgian king (Eldarova 1984). A more contemporary cross-cultural example is the 1988 film *Ashik Kerib*. Based on an Azeri *aşıq dastan*, the film was codirected by Armenian Sergei Paradjanov and Georgian Dodo Abashidze with music by Azeri composer Djavanshir Quliyev, and dedicated to the Russian filmmaker Andrei Tarkovsky. Like the *Nart Sagas* and other narratives generated in the Caucasus themselves, the *aşıq* tradition can give insight into to the methods by which the many ethnic groups of the Caucasus shared geographic and cultural space before they were disrupted by the administrative and conceptual divisions that came with colonization.

As a model of community building, one that is rooted in the local while connecting a large number of people in a larger community, the *aşıq* model presents an alternative to the nation based on the hegemony of a dominant language and ethnic group. This is especially relevant to discussions of the relationship of the national vernacular (both rooted and limiting) with the international cosmopolitan; for example, Sheldon Pollock, in an article that discusses the relationship of texts in international print languages such as Sanskrit and Latin mourns:

> what seems to be the single, desperate choice we are offered: between on the one hand, a national vernacularism dressed in the frayed period costume of violent reaches and bent on preserving difference at all costs, and, on the other, a clear-cutting, strip mining multinational cosmopolitanism that is bent, at all costs, on eliminating it. (2002, 17)

In this article Pollock discusses literary texts, excluding the oral. However, it is perhaps in oral narrative that cultures can negotiate this relationship between themselves as local and rooted, with their belonging to larger multicultural communities. Many of the *dastan* narratives that Azerbaijani bards tell are told in localized variants over a huge region, spreading farther than many print languages because of the built-in ability of an oral narrative to change without losing integrity in a way that a text never can; in oral arts, a narrative is not translated, it is recreated anew. It is no surprise that this model developed among the heterogeneous communities of the Caucasus.

I can recall many afternoons in backyard gardens across Azerbaijan and Georgia, every one them hospitable, compelling, and unique. While the Caucasus as a harmonious, intercultural mountain garden may seem hopelessly out of reach, this concept has long been viable in the narrative imaginations of the people who live there. As Charles King (2008, 250) reminds us, we might think about how Europe has reimagined itself to master its destructive legacy of conflict, to see that there can be peace in the Caucasus. Although now so embroiled in what seem like truly 'desperate choices' of nationalism and identity in today's desperate times, it is encouraging to know that there are deeper layers of multinational community building embedded in the oral narrative culture, and one cannot but hope that these traditional models could have a role in bringing peace back to the region.

ACKNOWLEDGMENTS

I am extremely grateful to the many bards, scholars, and community members in Azerbaijan who not only assisted my research, but also extended their hospitality to me and my family. Special thanks is due to the Azafli family for their help and kindness. I am also very thankful to the editors of this volume and the reviewers of the manuscript; their excellent suggestions drove me to look deeper and greatly improved this chapter. My thanks also to Sarah Moment Atis, who reviewed earlier drafts of this project. Poems from the archives of journalist Aziza Jafarzade reproduced with permission by her son.

I would also like to acknowledge Fulbright IIE and Fulbright-Hays for financial and logistical support of my research in Azerbaijan, 2004–6. This research was also assisted by an award from the Eurasia Program of the Social Science Research Council.

NOTES

1. Translations are my own unless otherwise indicated. The original reads:
   Əzizim Guluzana,
   Gün düşüb Guluzana
   Sənəmi görmək istəsən
   Gəlkinən Guluzana
2. Ay qara şalvar oğlan
   Üzundə xal var oğlan
   Atam sənə qız verməz
   Gəl ona yalvar, oğlan
3. Çobandagi
   Səndən axır abı-kövsər,
   Suyun baldır, Çobandagi.
   Bəzənmisən gələn kimi,
   Nə cəlaldı, Çobandagi!

   Qaqqıldaşa-qaqqıldaşa,
   Kəkliklərin qonu daşa.
   Hər görən eylər tamaşa,
   Bir xəyaldır, Çobandagi.

   Hər dürlü çiçək sinəndə,
   Tapılmaz qeyri çəməndə.
   Bahar fəsli Bəstə səndə,
   Qonaq qaldı, Çobandagi.

REFERENCES

Albright, Charlotte. 2002. 'The Aşıq and His Music in Northwest Iran (Azerbaijan).' In *The Garland Encyclopedia of World Music*, vol. 6, *The Middle East*, edited by Virginia Danielson, Scott Marcus, and Dwight Reynolds, 843–52. New York: Routledge.

Altstadt, Audrey. 1992. *The Azerbaijani Turks: Power and Identity under Russian Rule*. Stanford, CA: Hoover Institution Press.

Anderson, Benedict. 1983. *Imagined Communities: Reflections on the Origin and Spread of Nationalism*. London: Verso.

Arzumanli, Vagif. 2002. 'National Policy and Ethnic Minorities in the Republic of Azerbaijan.' In *Studies in Languages of Azerbaijan*, vol. I,, edited by John Clifton, 1–12. Baku: SIL International.

Bunyadov, Teymur. 1975. *Əsrlərdən gələn səslər*. Baku: Genclik.

Clifton, John. 2002. *Studies in Languages of Azerbaijan*, vol. I. Baku: SIL International.

Clifton, John. 2003. *Studies in Languages of Azerbaijan*, vol. II. Baku: SIL International.

Colarusso, John. 2002. *Nart Sagas from the Caucasus: Myths and Legends from the Circassians, Abazas, Abkhaz and Ubykhs*. Princeton, NJ: Princeton University Press.

de Waal, Thomas. 2003. *Black Garden: Armenia and Azerbaijan through Peace and War*. New York: New York University Press.

Eldarova, Emine. 1984. *Iskusstvo ashugov Azerbaidjana*. Baku: Ishiq.

Erdener, Yildiray. 1995. *The Song Contests of Turkish Minstrels*. New York: Garland.

Frolova-Walker, Marina. 1998. "National in Form, Socialist in Content': Musical Nation Building in the Soviet Republics.' *Journal of the American Musicological Society* 51(2):331–71.

Grant, Bruce. 2009. *The Captive and the Gift: Cultural Sovereignty in Russia and the Caucasus*. Ithaca, NY: Cornell University Press.

Gellner, Ernest. 1983. *Nations and Nationalism*. Ithaca, NY: Cornell University Press.

Heyat, Farideh. 2000. 'Azeri Professional Women's Life Strategies in The Soviet Context.' In *Gender and Identity Construction: Women of Central Asia, the Caucasus and Turkey*, edited by Feride Acar and Ayşe Güneş-Ayata, 177–201. Leiden: Brill.

Heyat, Farideh. 2005. *Azeri Women in Transition*. Baku: Chashioglu.

Human Rights Watch/Helsinki. 1994. *Azerbaijan: Seven Years of Conflict in Nagorno-Karabagh*. New York: Human Rights Watch

Huseynova, Aida. 2006. 'Stalin's Era and the Struggle of Azerbaijani Composers.' *Azerbaijan International* 14(2):56–64.

İsmailzadə, Mirzə, 2004. *Şah İsmail Səfəvi (Xətai)*. Baku: Alhoda.

Jafarzade, Aziza. 1975. 'Aşıq Sənəmlə goruş.' *Azərbaycan Qadını* 11:14–15.

Jafarzade, Aziza. 2006. 'Burning our Books: The Arabic Script Goes up in Flames.' *Azerbaijan International* 14(1):24.

Kafkasyalı, Ali. 1996. *Mikayıl Azaflı: Hayatı, sanatı, eserleri*. Erzurum: Erzurum.

Katruxlu, Soltan. 1996. *Telli Sazim*. Edited by Vurğun Soltan and Azad Nəbiyəv Derbend: 3 Nomreli Matbaa Naşriyyati.

King, Charles. 2008. *The Ghost of Freedom: A History of the Caucasus*. Oxford: Oxford University Press.

Levin, Theodore. 1996. *The Hundred Thousand Fools of God: Musical Travels in Central Asia*. Bloomington: Indiana University Press.

Naroditskaya, Inna. 2003. *Song from the Land of Fire: Continuity and Change in Azerbaijanian Mugham*. New York: Routledge.

Nəbiyəv, Azad, Compiled and Edited. 2005. *Qafqaz xalqların məhəbbət dastanları*. Baku: Şırvannəşr.

Olsen, Laura. 2004. *Performing Russia: Folk Revival and Russian Identity*. New York: Routledge.

Pahlevanian, Alina. 2001. 'Aşıqner.' In *The New Grove Dictionary of Music*, vol. 2, edited by Stanley Sadie and John Tyrrell, 16–17. New York: Grove.

Pirsultanlı, Sadnik Paşa. 2001. *Aşıq Bəsti : Bənovşələr*. Baku: AGAH.

Pollock, Sheldon. 2002. 'Cosmopolitan and Vernacular in History.' In *Cosmopolitanism*, edited by H. Bhabha, C. Breckenridge, D. Chakrabarty, and S. Pollock, 15–53. Durham, NC: Duke University Press.

Qasımlı, Məhərrəm. 2003. *Ozan aşıq sənəti*. Baku: Uğur.

Qasımlı, Məhərrəm, ed. and intro. 2005. *Azərbaycan dastanları, vols. 1–5*. Coll. M. Təhməsib and Ə. Axundov. Baku: Lider Nəşriyyat.

Shaffer, Brenda. 2002. *Borders and Brethren: Iran and the Challenge of Azerbaijani Identity*. Cambridge, MA: Harvard University Press.

Slobin, Mark. 1976. *Music in the Culture of Northern Afghanistan*. Tucson: University of Arizona Press.

Sultanova, Razia. 2005. 'Music and Identity in Central Asia: Introduction.' *Ethnomusicology Forum* 14(2):131–42.

Sultan-Qurraie, Hadi. 1998. *Selected Works of Bakhtiyar Vahabzada*. Bloomington: Indiana University Turkish Studies Publications.

Tohidi, Nayereh. 1996. 'Soviet in Public, Azeri in Private: Gender, Islam, and Nationalism in Soviet and Post-Soviet Azerbaijan.' *Women's Studies International Forum* 19 (1/2): 111–124.

11 From Burger Highlife to Gospel Highlife
Music, Migration, and the Ghanaian Diaspora

Florian Carl

This chapter deals with music in the context of Ghanaian migration, with a particular focus on the Ghanaian diaspora in Germany that emerged over the course of the past three to four decades. Germany constitutes one of the preferred destinations of Ghanaian migrants in Western Europe and it assumed a prominent role in the production of Ghanaian popular music in the 1980s and 1990s. In the following discussion, two different, though interrelated, fields of musical activity will be highlighted, namely, burger highlife and gospel highlife, and the role of these in the negotiation of social status and identity in the context of migration discussed. While the early and formative years of Ghanaian highlife music have received relatively much scholarly attention (Asante-Darko and van der Gerst 1983; Collins 1986, 1989, 1996; Coplan 1978), developments in Ghanaian popular music from the 1980s onwards have often been neglected, if not openly dismissed for their alleged 'inauthenticity', because of the heavy reliance on computerized sounds and the lack of live performed musical instruments (Collins 1996, 289–95). It is only recently that researchers have begun to direct their attention to more current trends (Carl 2012; Collins 2012; Shipley 2009, 2012). As far as musical production and performance in the context of Ghanaian migration over the past decades is concerned, the sociocultural significance of this transnational field has thus far not been explored.

Burger highlife and gospel highlife both emerged in the early 1980s (Collins 2012), a development that can, as we will see, be understood as an effect of the massive emigration that characterized the so-called Rawlings era in Ghana (Akyeampong 2000, 204–8). While burger highlife enjoyed great popularity among Ghanaians at home and abroad throughout the 1980s and 1990s, gospel highlife has in a way 'outlived' burger highlife, which is now, in a positive sense, considered 'classic', or, particularly among the younger generation, seen in a more negative sense as old-fashioned and anachronistic. Today, gospel highlife is arguably the most successful genre of popular music both in Ghana and its diaspora (Atiemo 2006; Carl 2012; Collins 2004). I will argue in the following that the shift towards gospel music, which is a shift in popularity, but also in social relevance, can be understood as a response to a particularly difficult paradox in Ghanaian diasporic experience.

The increased mobility of music, musicians, and audiences that characterized the second half of the 20th century has been addressed in the literature on musical globalization and 'World Music' (Erlmann 1998, 1999; Connell and Gibson 2003; Guilbault 1997; Meintjes 1990; Slobin 1993; Stokes 2004; Taylor 1997). For the purpose of my discussion of highlife music since the 1980s, which has actually never really crossed over into the Euro-American world music market (see Collins 2002), the growing body of literature that deals with music in the context of transnational migration and in various diasporic communities is of particular relevance (Kiwan and Meinhof 2011a, 2011b; Ramnarine 2007; Slobin 1994, 2003; Toynbee and Dueck 2011; Zheng 2010). Focusing on the ways in which relationships between diasporas and their—real or imagined—homelands are established and maintained, music has been a lens through which the negotiation of diasporic identities (Knudsen 2001; Manuel 1997; Um 2000; Ramnarine 1996; Solís 2005), the generation and transformation of gender relations in diaspora communities (Niranjana 2006; Sugarman 1997), or the relationship between migration and historical memory in the diaspora (Muller 2006; Shelemay 1998) have been examined. Reconfigured by Paul Gilroy's (1993) discussion of the Black Atlantic, the role of music in African diasporic experience has received particular attention (Feldman 2005; Monson 2000; Oliver 1990). Ingrid Monson even holds that the African diaspora has 'become the paradigmatic case for the closing years of the twentieth century' (2000, 1; see also Akyeampong 2000).

The concept of diaspora has mostly been employed 'in an effort to characterize the contact zones of nations, cultures, and regions' (Clifford 1994, 303). As such, it is, as James Clifford (1994) noted, linked to a number of other terms such as 'border', 'creolization', or 'hybridity' that emerged in the wake of the critical reconceptualization of anthropology since the 1980s (Appadurai 1996; Fox 1991; Gupta and Ferguson 1992; Hannerz 1996; Marcus and Fischer 1986). By now, 'diaspora' has undergone a similar process of critical scrutiny as the culture concept itself a decade earlier (see Brubaker 2005; Clifford 1994; Safran 1991). As Rogers Brubaker (2005, 12) remarks, while 'diaspora can be seen as an *alternative* to the essentialization of belonging, [. . .] it can also represent a non-territorial *form* of essentialized belonging' (emphasis in the original). Brubaker therefore suggests to treat diaspora 'as a category of practice, project, claim and stance, rather than as a bounded group' (2005, 13; see also Slobin 2003). A similar critique has been raised in recent work on migrating African musicians (Kiwan and Meinhof 2011a, 2011b), where a one-dimensional relationship between diaspora and homeland has proved problematic (see also Hutchinson 2006). To escape this simple dualism, Kiwan and Meinhof (2011a), for instance, argue for a subject-centered multisited approach that examines the complexity and fluidity of the individual networks of African musicians that transcend not only national but also ethnic boundaries.

If the idea of diaspora as bounded community is problematic, as work on music and transnational migration has demonstrated, it is a sense of diaspora as 'state of mind' (Slobin 2003, 292) or as what Anderson (1991) called 'imagined community' that is more relevant for our discussion. From this angle, the Ghanaian diaspora can be understood as a public or social imaginary (Dueck 2011). As Byron Dueck writes, 'social imaginaries have particularly important implications for migrants, who through acts of attention, performance and publication play a role in extending homelands across borders' (2011, 23). It is here that music and dance are crucial, since:

> the 'border-crossing nation' [is not] the end of the matter: social imaginaries often come into being around forms of affiliation quite distinct from nationhood or ethnicity. Of particular interest are those publics that emerge through the circulation of embodied and expressive practices, such as music and dance, and religious activities, such as worship and exhortation. (Dueck 2011, 23)

In the following discussion, which is based on research in Berlin and Accra (see also Carl 2009, 2011, 2012),[1] I argue then for an understanding of both burger highlife and gospel highlife as expressive practices through which the negotiation of social status and diasporic identity is mediated (Stokes 1994; Turino 1999, 2008), as well as embodied practices that help to maintain social relations across geographical space and also to create new forms of social intimacy (Dueck 2011). George Marcus (1995) has suggested a number of 'tracking' strategies for multisited ethnographic projects, namely to follow people, things, metaphors, and biographies, among other things. In multisited musical ethnography, subject-centered approaches focusing on individual musical experience (Rice 2003) or on the social networks of individual traveling musicians (Kiwan and Meinhof 2011a) have been proposed. While I have discussed some of the methodological implications of my own research at greater length elsewhere (Carl 2012), my rhetorical strategy in the following analysis is basically discourse centered; that is, I chiefly follow musical objects, metaphors and narratives, rather than individual people's life stories and musical experience.[2] To contextualize my argument, the following section will outline the demographic implications of Ghanaian migration and introduce some of the public spaces in which musical performance and consumption in the Ghanaian diaspora in Germany takes place. The latter half of the chapter will then discuss the social imaginaries associated with, first, burger highlife and, then, gospel highlife and elucidate the ways in which musical style is involved in the production and negotiation of social status and diasporic identity.

MUSIC AND THE GHANAIAN DIASPORA IN GERMANY

While from the late 19th well into the first half of the 20th century the former Gold Coast attracted substantial numbers of labor migrants from other parts of West Africa, the net migration rate gradually reversed after Ghana attained political independence from British colonial rule in 1957. From the 1960s onwards, due to political and economic instability, increasing numbers of Ghanaians turned their back on their homeland in search of 'greener pastures'. Whereas Ghanaian migrants up until the 1960s were mostly young men of higher social status in search of education, from the late 1970s Ghanaian migration 'encompassed the professional and non-professional classes, elites and commoners, male and female, on a scale that was stupendous' (Akyeampong 2000, 206). The outward migration reached a peak in the 1980s, when the country was at the brink of collapse, and by the mid-1990s Ghana had the highest emigration rate of all West African countries. It is estimated that currently about 10 percent of Ghana's total population lives abroad (Bump 2006; Peil 1995; Tonah 2007).

Emigration receded slightly in the wake of the introduction of multiparty democracy in 1992 and the gradual improvement of socioeconomic conditions in Ghana, but it still constitutes a major demographic as well as sociocultural factor. Today, the Ghanaian expatriate communities that emerged in the post-independence era form a wide-ranging transnational network that spans over virtually all continents, with larger clusters in Western Europe and North America, interconnecting Ghana and its diaspora in various and often complex ways (Akyeampong 2000, 204–13; Bump 2006; Nieswand 2005). One area that was directly affected by the political and economic turmoil of the late 1970s and early 1980s, resulting in the mass exodus of Ghanaians over subsequent decades, was musical production. Many prominent highlife musicians left Ghana in this period. Additionally, almost two and a half years of night curfew from 1982 to 1984, under the military PNDC government, drastically affected urban nightlife and the entertainment industry in Ghana. Many of those musicians who stayed in the country during this time moved into the Pentecostal-Charismatic churches that started mushrooming in the late 1970s and that provided a space for live performed popular music (Gifford 2004; Meyer 2004). Eventually, these developments resulted in a shift of highlife music from the secular realm towards gospel music (Collins 2002, 2004).

At the same time, secular highlife music was transformed by Ghanaian musicians who migrated to Western Europe. It was particularly musicians who settled in Germany who created a new blend of older forms of guitar-band highlife, funk music, and contemporary styles such as disco and synthesizer-based pop that came to be known as burger highlife (Collins 2012). This genre has thus become particularly associated with travel traffic between Ghana and Germany. One reason why Germany became a preferred destination for Ghanaian migrants, including musicians, were the relatively relaxed immigration laws in the 1980s (Carl 2009, 11). Today, Germany hosts the second-largest Ghanaian community in Europe, after the UK and before the Netherlands, with regional concentrations in the larger urban centers, particularly Hamburg, Berlin, Bremen, Frankfurt, Cologne, and the Ruhr region. The exact size of the Ghanaian population in Germany is statistically difficult to determine, but different authors estimate that there are currently between 40,000 and 50,000 Ghanaian nationals residing in the country (Nieswand 2008; Schmelz 2009; Tonah 2007).

Over the past decades a Ghanaian infrastructure emerged in Germany that comprises Ghanaian-owned shops, enterprises, associations, as well as numerous religious bodies, among which Pentecostal-Charismatic churches are the most important ones (Nieswand 2010; Tonah 2007). There are ethnic and hometown associations, branches of Ghanaian political parties, and also numerous Ghanaian national associations in German cities (Tonah 2007, 10). Media networks cater for the Ghanaian diaspora in the form of printed newspapers and periodicals. Increasingly, the internet assumes a central role with portals such as ghanaweb.com or modernghana.com that include specific diaspora news sections. In Berlin, Ghanaians make use of a weekly one-hour time slot on the private radio station Afro FM to announce events and discuss issues of concern to Ghanaians in the city, and in Hamburg the FM station TopAfric Radio serves the needs of the African diaspora. While these stations also play Ghanaian music, the Internet now provides better opportunities for people in the diaspora to keep up with developments in Ghana. Most major Ghanaian FM stations today provide streaming services and on websites such as ghanamusic.com or YouTube the latest video clips of Ghanaian artists can be watched.

Important places for informal networking in the diaspora are Ghanaian-owned stores, so-called Afro Shops, which sell groceries, cosmetics, hair products, and sometimes clothes, music, and movies, but that also, and more importantly, serve as communication centers. In these shops, social events such as naming ceremonies, weddings, and funerals are announced, people might drop a letter for someone without legal resident status, sometimes international money transfer services that circumvent the official banking sector are offered, and often people simply come to chat and exchange the latest gossip. In Berlin, a fluctuating number of about a dozen of such shops that are owned by Ghanaians are found. In Hamburg there are about 20 (Erika Eichholzer, personal communication, January 26, 2006). To some extent, collective music consumption also takes place in Afro Shops, as people spend time together and might discuss and listen to new releases by Ghanaian artists. More important contexts for the collective consumption of both secular and gospel highlife music in the diaspora, as well as opportunities for social dancing, are provided at naming ceremonies, funeral celebrations, and other social events to which customarily 'all sympathizers and well-wishers' are publicly invited. While big sound systems are rented to entertain guests at such events, family ties and other social relations both within the diaspora and between diaspora and homeland are reaffirmed at these occasions. In this context, the circulation of video recordings of the events, for which specialists are usually hired, or, sometimes even their real-time transmission through video calls, are of crucial importance.

Both burger highlife as well as gospel highlife artists also perform live concerts in the diaspora, though such shows are rather scarce and, if they take place in Germany, are mostly restricted to Hamburg, where the potentially largest Ghanaian audience can be found. For gospel artists, performances in diasporic churches are much more common and it is here where the transnational networks of Ghanaian Christianity come into play. More generally, diasporic churches, and particularly those of Pentecostal-Charismatic orientation, provide a public space in which gospel highlife is collectively performed alongside other expressive practices such as prayer, prophecy, healing, or speaking in tongues (Carl 2012). In Hamburg alone, there are more than 30 Ghanaian-initiated churches; in Berlin more than a dozen have been established. The fellowship of these ranges anywhere between a dozen to some 300 people. Several authors have pointed out that Ghanaian-initiated churches, some representing branches of existing ones in the homeland, some newly founded abroad, form an important link between Ghana and its diaspora (Ter Haar 1998; Tonah 2007; van Dijk 1997). Particularly Pentecostal-Charismatic churches have therefore taken on a mediating role, both in the transnational movement of people, as they also assist with the formalities and paperwork involved in international travel (Nieswand 2010), as well as in the circulation of expressive and embodied practices.

THE STYLE AND AESTHETICS OF BURGER HIGHLIFE

The significance of Germany as a site for the production of burger high-life is evident in the genre's name. According to popular etymology the word 'burger' is derived from the name of the city of Hamburg, where the largest Ghanaian community in Germany is located (see Collins 2004, 419; for an alternative etymology, see also Martin 2005, 11–13). As a social type, the 'burger' symbolizes in many ways the process of redefinition of social identity that took place in the wake of the massive emigration waves of the post-independence era and it became a metaphor for the accumulation of economic and symbolic capital through migration (Bourdieu 1989). More generally, we might think of the 'burger' and the way it configures social interaction in terms of what Pierre Bourdieu called 'habitus,' which describes 'a subjective but not individual system of internalized structures, schemes of perception, conception, and action common to all members of the same group or class and constituting the precondition for all objectifications and apperception' (1977, 86; see also Turino 2008, 120–21).

Featuring prominent in Ghanaian social discourse and popular culture, as for instance in video film productions, 'burger' refers to a Ghanaian who lives or has lived abroad and who adopted a specific habitus and style, a way of walking and dressing, as well as speaking (Martin 2005). The term is also used to refer to somebody who has never traveled abroad but who imitates the lifestyle and habitus of a 'burger', popularly referred to as 'home burger' (John Dankwa, personal communication, Cape Coast, April 25, 2011). As a social type, the *burger* is associated with economic capital accumulated through travel and its public display, for example, in the form of expensive cars, clothing, and other assets. It implies at the same time a generous attitude, denoting somebody who shares his wealth by inviting and helping others. Much of the symbolic capital linked to the 'burger' is derived from the prestige attached to transnational travel itself. As a young dancer and musician in Ghana, who himself aspired to travel to Western Europe, told me, a 'burger' is somebody who has the means 'to move freely' (personal communication, Accra, January 16, 2005). Burger highlife musicians have come to embody these connotations, at the same time that they helped shaping the image of the 'burger'.[3] The performance and consumption of burger highlife music allows people to participate in the ongoing negotiation of identity and social status that takes place in the transnational field spanning between Ghana and its diaspora.

The 'invention' of burger highlife is often credited to the guitarist and singer George Darko, who moved to Germany in the early 1980s and in 1983 released the hit song 'Ako te brɔfo' (The Parrot Understands English) with his band Bus Stop (Collins 2012; loc 4919). Darko and his band were, at that time, based in Berlin, where they also produced the other songs for their album *Friends*, as a former member of his band related (Bob Fiscian, personal communication, Berlin, June 30, 2005). When analyzing the song we can identify a number of stylistic features that came to define a new era in highlife music.[4] First of all, the song's instrumentation—including drum set, bass and rhythm guitar, a lead guitar, electric piano, two synthesizers, and a tenor saxophone that features as solo instrument—sets a new standard for subsequent highlife productions. The horn section of classic highlife songs has been replaced here completely by synthesizers. While in later productions of burger highlife even the drum set is substituted by an electronic drum computer, in the 1983 version of 'Ako te brɔfo' it is more the sturdy and dry sound that was assigned to the drums that distinguishes this recording from earlier productions and that is reminiscent of disco music in the 1980s. The song starts with a futuristic keyboard sound. An upbeat on a syncopated dominant seventh chord then gives way to the laid-back groove based on the funky bass line, the rather straightforward four-four drum beat, as well as the rhythmic accompaniment provided by guitar, electric piano, and synthesizer. The tonal structure of the song, on the other hand, is rather typical for highlife and consists of four measures that are repeated throughout (B—F#^{7}—B—B, F#^{7}/C#—C#^{7}—F#^{7}—F#^{7}).

Overall, both the harmonic as well as the rhythmic *ostinato* with its prominent offbeat that is characteristic for the highlife topos (Agawu 2003, 129), create the strong forward-moving feel of the song, constantly inviting further repetitions.

Other Ghanaian musicians who in the 1980s and 1990s emigrated or frequently traveled to Germany and produced their music there include Pat Thomas, Charles Amoah, the Lumba brothers (Charles Kojo Fusu aka Daddy Lumba, Nana Acheampong, and Sarkodie), Ofori Amponsah, and Amakye Dede, to mention just a few of the more prominent examples. Most of them settled in the Rhineland, in the western part of Germany, where many successful burger highlife albums have been produced. There are two recording studios in particular that stand out in this connection which are Skyline Studios in Düsseldorf, owned and run by sound engineer Peter Krick, who worked with Rex Gyamfi and Charles Amoah, among others, and Bodo Staiger's Rheinklang Studio in Cologne, where a number of Ghanaian musicians have produced, among them Daddy Lumba, Amakye Dede, and Ofori Amponsah. The importance of Staiger in the creation of the sound of burger highlife was stressed in a meeting of several Ghanaian musicians, among them George Darko and Charles Amoah, that took place in Accra in March 2006.

In an interview conducted by Martin Ziegler on August 19, 2004, in Cologne, Staiger confirmed that Ghanaian musicians approach him to produce their music and he related that many of them ask him to emulate a particular sound. Rather than requesting acoustic instruments that would be favored in German productions and that nowadays can conveniently be emulated with the help of digital samplers, Ghanaian musicians would prefer synthesized sounds that immediately reveal the impact of technology rather than conceal it (Martin Ziegler, personal communication, April 22, 2011). Take, for instance, the song 'Sika ne barima' (Money Makes a Man) by Amakye Dede, produced at Rheinklang Studio and released in 1997, which apart from an electric guitar exclusively employs synthesized instruments. Another prominent example for the impact of technology is the so-called 'Cher effect', a digital manipulation of the voice created with the pitch-correcting plug-in device Auto-Tune by Antares, which was widely popularized through Cher's 1998 world hit 'Believe'. Many Ghanaian musicians subsequently utilized the Auto-Tune plug-in, featuring prominently, for instance, on Ofori Amponsah's 2005 *Otoolege* album, parts of which were also produced with Staiger in Cologne.

From its beginnings in the 1980s and throughout the following two decades, the sound of burger highlife increasingly came to be defined through the use of modern technology, incorporating more and more purely electronic instruments such as synthesizers and drum machines. By the late 1990s burger highlife productions had moved to an entirely electronic environment with often no other acoustic sounds than the voice, as evident, for example, on Daddy Lumba's 1998 album *Highlife*

2000 that featured the hit song 'Aben wɔ ha' (It Is Cooked Here). Auto-Tune eventually enabled musicians and producers to even work on the voice parts in such a way that the impact of technology on them becomes deliberately audible. While in its musical structures burger highlife is, as we have seen, a continuation rather than a radical break with earlier forms of highlife, its actual sound came to index the modern, cosmopolitan and prosperous way of life for which the 'burger' stands. This imagery also features prominently in music videos that since the 1990s became an important medium in marketing burger highlife. If we look at the video for 'Aben wɔ ha', for instance, we get a glimpse of the 'burger' style in terms of dressing, hairstyle and other accessories signifying luxury and wealth.[5] In the clip, we see Daddy Lumba riding a white stretch limousine, dressed in a stylish suit, drinking champagne, and dancing with beautiful women (see Figure 11.1).

Burger highlife illustrates the significance of sound technology and, more generally, of timbre, in the mediation of everyday-life experience and the production of social difference that different authors have pointed out (Lysloff 1997; Meintjes 2003; Taylor 2001). It is not so much its musical structures but the electronic sound of burger highlife itself that plays a crucial role in this mediation, understood as 'a process that connects and translates disparate worlds, people, imaginations, values, and ideas,

Figure 11.1   Screenshot from the music video *Aben wɔ ha* by Daddy Lumba.

Source: Aben wɔ ha, Lumba Productions (1998). Reproduced with permission.

whether in its symbolic, social, or technological form' (Meintjes 2003, 8). It is important to note that technology is also constitutive of the social imaginary of the Ghanaian diaspora both in its symbolic and material dimension, technology thus being at the very heart of Ghanaian diasporic experience itself. As far as the symbolic dimension of burger highlife is concerned, paradoxically the use of technology that indexes 'modernity' and expresses aspirations to participate in a global cosmopolitan public, by and large prevented Ghanaian highlife musicians to access the more lucrative world music market and restricted them to audiences in Ghana and its diaspora (Collins 2002). After all, the kind of 'audio hyper-realism' (Lysloff 1997, 211) that characterizes the aesthetics of burger highlife seems diametrically opposed to the trope of authenticity and an aesthetics of 'liveness' that has been central, for instance, in the marketing of world music (Lysloff 1997, 209–11; Meintjes 2003, 129–30).

THE PARADOX OF MIGRATION

While the use of sound technology that indexes global modernity in the social imaginary of burger highlife paradoxically also marks the genre's locality, the fundamental tension arising for African musicians who 'desire to participate in the world as cosmopolitans who can move with ease across geopolitical divides, unfettered from nation or locality as a primary source for identity' results more generally from 'a pressure to metaculturally mark their global participation as ethnically specific and emplaced' (Meintjes 2003, 220). This becomes obvious in the fact that those Ghanaian musicians in Germany who, to at least some degree, established their presence in the transcultural World Music scene were able to do so not with the performance of burger highlife, but with ethnically marked forms of African music such as 'traditional' dance-drumming and hybrid forms of popular music that blend in various 'ethnic' elements (Carl 2011).

It must be stressed, that the form of symbolic capital embodied by the 'burger' is not a form of 'transcultural capital' as Kiwan and Meinhof (2011b) use the term, but represents a culturally bounded form of symbolic capital that comes into play within diasporic networks and in interaction with the homeland. In contrast to this, the notion of 'transcultural capital', while building on the work of Bourdieu and others, was developed in an effort to 'foreground the capacity for strategic interventions of migrant and minority groups' vis-à-vis 'the symbolic and social networking power of hegemonic groups in majority society' (2011b, 8). As such, 'transcultural capital' describes the capacity of migrant musicians to assume power positions in the status systems of both their homeland and the host society at the same time. The 'burger's' symbolic capital, however, is restricted to homeland and diaspora.

The marginalization of migrants in their host society is sometimes addressed in burger highlife songs. Here, we are confronted with the flip side to the image of a prosperous life abroad without worries and problems. Though the darker aspects of transnational migration are often not openly discussed, there are some burger highlife songs that capture the hopes and anxieties of migrants and deal with the more problematic realities of migration in their lyrics. In these texts it becomes clear that diasporic subjects are often trapped in what Homi Bhabha referred to as 'inbetween space' (1994, 56), alienated from both homeland and host country. Under the broader theme of love, which undoubtedly represents the most common topic of burger highlife, we find songs that address issues related to transnational migration. A prominent recent example is Kwabena Kwabena's (George Kwabena Adu) 'Aso', released in 2005 on the same-titled album, which deals with the experience of a disappointed husband who travels abroad, leaving his wife back home in the hands of a trusted friend, just to find out upon his return that she and his best friend have started an affair behind his back.[6]

Another theme related to migration addressed in burger highlife are the social expectations towards the migrant. In an extended family system as we find it in Ghana, migration is not an individual decision alone, but often a family affair. Whether family members contribute financially or not, they will expect the person who travels to share some of the associated 'benefits,' generally assuming that migration leads to prosperity. One of the greatest fears, consequently, of migrants is to fail economically and to return home 'empty-handed' (see Martin 2005). In a highly metaphorical way the song 'Ako te brɔfo', for instance, deals with the expectations and social pressure that weigh on migrants, concluding that no matter how travels turn out, migration cannot change the basic identity of a person. Darko evokes the ancestors and tradition—the parrot (Twi, *ako*) is the totem of the Asona clan to which Darko belongs and it generally symbolizes eloquence—and makes reference to an Akan proverb saying that everybody should focus on his or her own burden: *Woso wo twe, menso meso me twe* ('you carry your antelope [i.e., burden], I carry mine'). The song suggests that even if one is not successful in the endeavor to become prosperous through travel, at least not instantly, one can always return home, just as when a trap is sprung, it returns to its original position: *Metu bata na annyɛ yie a, Yaw George, e mɛsan makɔ m'akyi* ('when I travel and it doesn't end well, Yaw George, I will go back where I came from'). However, looking at the realities of migration, there are migrants in the diaspora who are barred from traveling back home, because they have actually not 'made it'. The psychological pressure this puts on individuals can be immense.

In a similar vein, Amakye Dede's song 'Sika ne barima' deals with the hardships involved in the struggle to make money abroad. While at the beginning of the song the protagonist notes that one cannot progress by staying at one place, he realizes at the same time that migrants' struggle for money abroad sometimes borders on enslavement: *Ɛno nti na baabi adehyeɛ, yɛadane nkoa baabi akuro so yi* ('even though we're royals in our place, we've turned into slaves in somebody else's town'). In stark contrast to the pleasures of a luxurious and successful life as depicted in the clip to Lumba's song 'Aben wɔ ha', life abroad in Dede's account is nothing but struggle. In this struggle, the song makes clear, one can only rely on oneself and it might take long before one can see success. As Amakye Dede puts it quite drastically, the only thing that counts is money, without which a man remains a nobody: *Sika ne barima. Na wiase wo sika sua a, w'asɛm sua* ('Money is what makes a man. If you have little money in this world, your word counts little.').

There is then a paradox attached to the accumulation of economic and consequently symbolic capital through migration, for in order to raise one's status in the homeland, one has to make oneself first a 'slave' (Twi, *akoa*, pl. *nkoa*) in somebody else's country. This resonates with Akyeampong's remark that class distinctions among African immigrants in the diaspora are often erased as the 'educated and the semiliterate, the highborn and the lowborn, rub shoulders as they vie for the same menial jobs' (2000, 186). Nieswand (2008) makes a similar point with regard to the Ghanaian diaspora in Germany. He concludes that we are basically dealing with two different status systems into which migrants are incorporated at the same time and which results in what he calls the 'status paradox' of migration. While experiencing marginalization and stigmatization in their host societies, Ghanaian migrants are considered successful 'burgers' back home—if only, that is, they are able to regularly send remittances to family members and possibly also to build a house (see also Martin 2005).

GOSPEL HIGHLIFE AND PENTECOSTAL-CHARISMATIC CHRISTIANITY

In contrast to burger highlife, gospel highlife can be understood as part of the social imaginary of Pentecostal-Charismatic Christianity, which has been tremendously successful over the past decades both in Ghana and its diaspora (Gifford 2004; Nieswand 2010; Ter Haar 1998; van Dijk 1997). Participation in the Pentecostal-Charismatic public offers Ghanaian migrants alternative modes of identification, a process in which gospel highlife as embodied expressive practice plays a central role. Structurally similar to its secular variants, gospel highlife's distinguishing feature is, first and foremost, the symbolic content, generally drawing on Christian themes and particularly the imagery associated with Pentecostalism. Other than burger highlife, there is no direct association of commercial gospel highlife with the Ghanaian diaspora as production site, though quite a few musicians and producers do actually operate within this transnational field nowadays. Since the 1990s it is increasingly churches themselves that have also played a role in the production of gospel music, putting up their own recording studios and distribution networks that encompass Ghana and its diaspora (see Awuah 2012; Collins 2012, loc 5211).

The transnational networks of Ghanaian churches that have emerged over the past decades do not only play their part in the production and distribution of commercial gospel highlife, but, as briefly mentioned earlier, more importantly provide a network for the transnational movement of people as well as embodied expressive practices both between homeland and diaspora and within the diaspora. Thus, in Ghana the rise of 'urban Pentecostalism has very much become a window to the world' (van Dijk 1997, 139), creating a 'moral and physical geography whose domain is one of transnational cultural inter-penetration and flow' (van Dijk 1997, 142). In the diaspora, on the other hand, African churches provide, as Akyeampong writes, 'some security in racially hostile cities [and] are thus an important substitute for kinship and family networks, while extending the emotive religious experience initiated by Pentecostal churches in the homeland' (2000, 209).

The central figure around which Pentecostal-Charismatic identity revolves is the born-again Christian, which is principally somebody who accepts Jesus Christ as personal Lord and Savior. The implications of being born again have, we might note, parallels to the imagery associated with the 'burger', as notions of prosperity and financial success are also central to Pentecostalism. In the evangelistic logic, however, prosperity and personal success are reinterpreted as signs of divine grace (Twi, *adom*), as expressed in the so-called 'gospel of prosperity' (Coleman 2000, 27–40). Mediated by images of prosperity and Western modernity, imagining abroad (Twi, *aburokyire*) is also part of the social imaginary of Ghanaian Pentecostal-Charismatic Christianity, though here, again, the imagery is framed by the moral geography of Pentecostalism. As Gerrie Ter Haar in his study of Ghanaian diasporic churches in the Netherlands noted, 'although many Africans who have come to Europe are appalled by its spiritual poverty, at the same time its material abundance seems to them hardly less than what a Christian may expect to find in heaven' (1998, vi). In Ghana, to be able to travel abroad is therefore an important aspect of the 'gospel of prosperity' and equally seen as a sign of divine grace, a fact that many churches capitalize on by offering 'prayer support' not only for financial success and health, but also for success in traveling and particularly the acquisition of an entry visa for Western countries. As much as burger highlife musicians, as we noted, embody the attributes of the 'burger' as part of their habitus, gospel highlife musicians embody the attributes of the born-again Christian, and stressing success abroad—which, in this context, means in the diaspora—constitutes an important part of an artist's self-representations.[7]

In the symbolism of gospel highlife we are therefore also confronted with images of a luxurious, cosmopolitan lifestyle, but these images are framed by the moral discourse of Pentecostal-Charismatic Christianity which adds to them a dimension that Timothy Rommen (2007, 27–46) conceptualized as the 'ethics of style'. An example that illustrates this is the song 'Moving Forward' by Christiana Love, which was released in 2008 and became one of the most popular Ghanaian gospel songs in 2008 and 2009.[8] The song sets out with a simple descending melodic line played by a synthesizer that is then answered by the backing vocalists, singing 'I am moving forward, I am going forward.' The descending line is taken up by the lead singer, adding the words 'through Jesus Christ.' In the video to the song, we see the singer-protagonist at the same time getting into a bright yellow Mercedes-Benz convertible. Scenes of Christiana Love driving around in this (obviously expensive) car are then alternated with groups of dancers and scenes where she is seen singing and dancing in the interior of a big, luxurious mansion. Other visual elements we can discern are, for instance, the image of a blond, long-haired, white Jesus ascending to heaven. When Christiana Love sings the line 'Jesus died for you, he died for all your problems,' more realistic, Hollywood-mediated images of Jesus on the cross, covered in blood, as they featured prominently in Mel Gibson's *Passion of Christ*, are additionally edited into the video (see Figure 11.2).

Apart from the message of the 'gospel of prosperity' that is conveyed in songs like 'Moving Forward', but also Ohemaa Mercy's 'Wobɛyɛ kɛseɛ' (You Will Be Great), or Philips Baafi's 'Go High', to mention just a few examples, gospel highlife assumes its perhaps most crucial significance as participatory performance in the context of Pentecostal-Charismatic worship. It has been noted that music is at the heart of Pentecostal worship (Gifford 2004, 35; Hackett 1998, 263), and the fact that church bands are constantly integrating new songs into their repertoires that circulate in various audiovisual formats in the mediascape between homeland and diaspora

Figure 11.2 Screenshot from the music video *Moving Forward* by Christiana Love. *Source: Moving Forward*, Big Ben Productions (2008). Reproduced with permission.

has actually contributed to the blurring of boundaries between religion and popular culture (Collins 2004; Meyer 2008). Though Pentecostal-Charismatic churches generally stress spontaneous inspiration by the Holy Spirit and their liturgy can therefore vary greatly, a common feature of Pentecostal worship are so-called 'praise' and 'worship' sections in which musical performance is central. A service in a Ghanaian-initiated church in Berlin—the Gospel Believers Center International—that I witnessed in March 2004, was typical in that regard. The first part was a 'worship' section, the music being overall slow and unmetered, where people sang, prayed with their hands lifted up into the air, some bowing down in devotion, others breaking out in tears or speaking in tongues. This was followed by an upbeat 'praise' section, where the music was faster and people danced and sang, shouting 'Praise the Lord!' and uttering other expressions of joy. Over the years, I have witnessed services in which collective performances like this could last for close to two hours.

Gospel artists in their commercial productions have adapted the praise/worship format and often release the same song in two different versions, enabling consumers, as it were, to carry the worship experience from the public spaces of Pentecostal churches to the private spaces of their homes. VCD releases like Evangelist Diana Asamoah's *Gospel Old Tunes*, which is a collection of popular Pentecostal worship songs, explicitly emulate the worship experience in churches and feature long video extracts of actual church services. It is also noticeable that live performed instruments, and particularly the trumpet, feature prominently not only in the sound, but also the visual imagery of gospel highlife. The video clips to songs like Ohemaa Mercy's 'Wobɛyɛ kɛseɛ' or Baafi's 'Go High' attest to this, just as Cecilia Marfo's 2010 hit 'Afunmu Ba' (Donkey's Foal).[9] Mediated by the worship experience in Pentecostal-Charismatic churches, we can observe that an aesthetics of liveness has reentered highlife music through the idiom of gospel. The notions of authenticity that go along with this aesthetics are, however, quite distinct from geographical or ethnic constructions of place as evident, for instance, in world music (see Connell and Gibson 2003, 19–44; Stokes 1994, 6–7). Transcending the confines of ethnicity and nationhood, the liveness celebrated in gospel highlife links its participants with the religious experience of Pentecostal worship and provides a means, at the same time, to participate in the social imaginary of Pentecostalism.

While diasporic churches provide networks of emotional and financial support for migrants and, thus, partly compensate for the attenuation of traditional social networks like the extended family in the migrational setting, gospel highlife constitutes the central musical as well as religious experience for many Ghanaians in the diaspora. Overall, the significance of gospel highlife in the context of Ghanaian migration resonates with Martin Stokes's observation that 'in migrant communities in Western Europe and North America, religious institutions and their media networks increasingly provide social and cultural infrastructure, and a sense of home' and that in this context 'music is [. . .] a particularly important means of making a home, and imagining a future' (2011, 31).

CONCLUSION

In this chapter, I have argued for the crucial role of music in the ongoing negotiation of social status and identity that takes place within the social space spanning between Ghana and its diaspora. I have traced the emergence of this transnational field and described how from the 1980s onwards it became an important arena in the production, dissemination, and consumption of burger highlife as well as gospel highlife music. Both genres in their particular ways construct and comment on the popular notion of abroad (Twi, *aburokyire*) as a place of prosperity, success and material abundance, an image that in turn plays a crucial role in the constitution of the Ghanaian diaspora as a social imaginary. Yet we have also seen that the realities of migration create a paradox, since the elevation in social status through migration is often paralleled by marginalization in the host country.

While addressing this paradox in different ways, neither burger highlife nor gospel highlife resolve the basic problematic of status production in the Ghanaian diaspora. However, gospel can nonetheless be understood as a powerful response to the paradox of migration, as it provides, particularly in its highly participatory forms as part of Pentecostalist worship, 'a means of attaining a sense of well-being and empowerment' (Dueck 2011, 25) by establishing new forms of social intimacy in the context of diasporic churches. By evoking a social imaginary that clearly transcends nationhood and ethnicity (see also Glick-Schiller, Çağlar, and Guldbrandsen 2006), the empowerment that can be experienced through the performance of and participation in gospel highlife might then represent truly a form of 'transcultural capital,' understood as a 'strategic intervention of migrant and minority groups' (Kiwan and Meinhof 2011b, 8) in the context of the social power structure of majority society. It is then the combination of popular and religious expressive modes and embodied practices characteristic for gospel highlife and their transnational circulation that seems particularly powerful with regard to what Dueck describes as 'the complex dialectical dance between intimacy and public culture' (2011, 26) in the context of migration.

ACKNOWLEDGMENTS

I am grateful to the Volkswagen Foundation that funded parts of the research on which this chapter is based. For the help with translations, fruitful discussions, and helpful comments on earlier drafts of this chapter,

I particularly thank John W. Dankwa. The attendants of the Arts Faculty Lecture at the University of Cape Coast, Ghana, where I first presented this chapter, also provided constructive critique. I am equally indebted to Martin Ziegler, Byron Dueck, and two anonymous reviewers for the critical scrutiny with which they read earlier versions of this text. Their critique and suggestions greatly helped to improve the chapter, though I alone am, of course, responsible for the final result.

NOTES

1. Field research was done over several time periods since March 2004. In the time between March 2004 and February 2006 my research was mainly based in Berlin, interspersed with a 12-week stay in Ghana from November 2004 to February 2005. In this time I became acquainted with professional Ghanaian musicians and dancers who operated within the transcultural African music scene. Apart from performing 'traditional' African music at multicultural events and festivals for German audiences, my Ghanaian friends in Berlin also played and danced to highlife music in diasporic churches and at social events such as naming ceremonies, weddings, and funerals. As they invited me to church services and 'Ghanaian parties' in the city, I became familiar with those aspects of life in the diaspora where Ghanaians remain mostly among themselves. In Berlin, I also interviewed several highlife musicians who migrated to Germany in the 1980s and 1990s. My research in Accra, where I lived from 2006 to 2009, concentrated particularly on a smaller Pentecostal-Charismatic church in Nungua, Christ Victory Ministries International. In these three years I attended many Sunday services and other church programs, in the course of which I had the chance to interview the head pastor and other church officials as well as church musicians, choristers, and congregation members. Since 2006 I also witnessed services in numerous other churches in Ghana and danced to gospel as well as burger highlife at public concerts, as well as private events with friends.
2. While many people in Berlin and Accra shared their views with me along the way, I am particularly indebted to Seth Darko, Gordon Odametey, Kay Boni, and Ofei Ankrah for introducing me to the Ghanaian musical scene in Berlin and, in the case of Ofei, also the 'culture' scene in Accra. Likewise Samuel Kwaku Yeboah, Margaret Dzikpor, as well as Mark Kofi Asamoah and his wife, Elizabeth Abena Asamoah, gave me important insights into Ghanaian musical life in the diaspora and also shared their religious views with me. Their hospitality and openness is much appreciated. In Accra, I am particularly grateful to Bishop Joseph G. Bart-Plange and his wife, Christiana, Apostle Joseph Kwei, and Eunice Kwei of Christ Victory Ministries International, who gave me a deeper understanding of Charismatic believes and worship practices. I very much enjoyed the musical ministry of Sarah Adaku Armah and Fifi Folson, as well as the insightful conversations we had about gospel music. To all other members of Christ Victory Ministries International at Nungua, I am thankful for letting me worship with them.
3. A popular movie that draws on the image of the 'burger' is, for instance, the film *Italian Burger* with Agya Koo. In parts of the Brong Ahafo and Ashanti Regions in Ghana, so-called Burgers' Wives Associations can be found. In their meetings the public display of wealth and conspicuous consumption feature prominently (Kwadwo Adum-Attah, personal communication, Cape Coast,

April 26, 2011). Similarities between Ghanaian *burgers* and Congolese *sappeurs* might also come to mind—an observation I owe to Byron Dueck.
4. A sound file of the 1983 version can be found on YouTube under the link http://www.youtube.com/watch?v=yk_TOtzFJ7w (accessed November 16, 2012).
5. The full clip is on YouTube under the link http://www.youtube.com/watch?v=25gWNvrRDPU (accessed November 17, 2012).
6. The song is on YouTube under the link http://www.youtube.com/watch?v=Q7mHO-6rWlA (accessed November 18, 2012).
7. The profiles of gospel artists like Ohemaa Mercy or Esther Opiesie on Facebook are interesting in this connection. See https://www.facebook.com/ohemaa.mercy and https://www.facebook.com/opiesie.esther (both accessed November 18, 2012).
8. See the video clip on YouTube under the link http://www.youtube.com/watch?v=z-ajdMe6yP0 (accessed November 18, 2012).
9. The clip to Ohemaa Mercy's song can be found on YouTube under the link http://www.youtube.com/watch?v=EzsIjtyBdXY, Marfo's song under the link http://www.youtube.com/watch?v=-xv9GGVp9RQ (accessed November 18, 2012).

REFERENCES

Agawu, Kofi. 2003. *Representing African Music: Postcolonial Notes, Queries, Positions*. New York: Routledge.
Akyeampong, Emmanuel. 2000. 'Africans in the Diaspora: The Diaspora and Africa.' *African Affairs* 99:183–215.
Anderson, Benedict. 1991. *Imagined Communities: Reflections on the Origin and Spread of Nationalism*. Rev. ed. London: Verso.
Appadurai, Arjun. 1996. *Modernity at Large: Cultural Dimensions of Globalization*. Minneapolis: University of Minnesota Press.
Asante-Darko, Nimrod, and Sjaak van der Gerst. 1983. 'Male Chauvinism: Men and Women in Ghanaian Highlife Songs.' In *Female and Male in West Africa*, edited by Christine Oppong, 242–55. London: Allen and Unwin.
Atiemo, Abamfo Ofori. 2006. "Singing with Understanding': The Story of Gospel Music in Ghana.' *Studies in World Christianity* 12(2):142–63.
Awuah, Joe. 2012. 'Gina Antwi Shines in London.' *Daily Guide*, August 14.
Bhabha, Homi K. 1994. *The Location of Culture*. London: Routledge.
Bourdieu, Pierre. 1977. *Outline of a Theory of Practice*. Translated by Richard Nice. Cambridge: Cambridge University Press.
Bourdieu, Pierre. 1989. 'Social Space and Symbolic Power.' *Sociological Theory* 7(1):14–25.
Brubaker, Rogers. 2005. 'The 'Diaspora' Diaspora.' *Ethnic and Racial Studies* 28(1):1–19.
Bump, Micah. 2006. *Ghana: Searching for Opportunities at Home and Abroad*. Washington, DC: Migration Policy Institute. Accessed January 9, 2013. http://www.migrationinformation.org/USFocus/print.cfm?ID=381.
Carl, Florian. 2009. *Berlin/Accra. Music, Travel, and the Production of Space*. Münster: LIT.
Carl, Florian. 2011. 'The Representation and Performance of African Music in German Popular Culture.' *Yearbook for Traditional Music* 43:198–223.
Carl, Florian. 2012. '"Never Go Back": Ghanaian Gospel Music, Born-Again Christianity, and the Nonconformity of the Ethnographer.' *Norient Academic*

Online Journal 1. Accessed January 9, 2013. http://norient.com/en/academic/ghanaian-gospel/.

Clifford, James. 1994. 'Diasporas.' *Cultural Anthropology* 9(3):302–38.

Coleman, Simon. 2000. *The Globalisation of Charismatic Christianity: Spreading the Gospel of Prosperity*. Cambridge: Cambridge University Press.

Collins, John. 1986. *E.T. Mensah: King of Highlife*. London: Off the Record Press.

Collins, John. 1989. 'The Early History of West African Highlife Music.' *Popular Music* 8(3):221–30.

Collins, John. 1996. *Highlife Time*. 2nd ed. Accra: Anansesem Publications.

Collins, John. 2002. 'The Ghanaian Music Industry: A Quarter Century of Problems.' *West Africa* (19–25):8–13.

Collins, John. 2004. 'Ghanaian Christianity and Popular Entertainment: Full Circle.' *History in Africa* 31:407–23.

Collins, John. 2012. 'Contemporary Ghanaian Popular Music since the 1980s.' In *Hip Hop Africa: New African Music in a Globalizing World*, Kindle ed., edited by Eric Charry, chap. 11. Bloomington: Indiana University Press.

Connell, John, and Chris Gibson. 2003. *Sound Tracks: Popular Music, Identity and Place*. London: Routledge.

Coplan, David. 1978. 'Go to My Town, Cape Coast! The Social History of Ghanaian Highlife.' In *Eight Urban Musical Cultures: Tradition and Change*, edited by Bruno Nettl, 96–113. Urbana: University of Illinois Press.

Dueck, Byron. 2011. 'Part 1: Migrants—Introduction.' In *Migrating Music*, edited by Jason Toynbee and Byron Dueck, 21–27. London: Routledge.

Erlmann, Veit. 1998. 'How Beautiful Is Small? Music, Globalization and the Aesthetics of the Local.' *Yearbook for Traditional Music* 30:12–21.

Erlmann, Veit. 1999. *Music, Modernity, and the Global Imagination: South Africa and the West*. New York: Oxford University Press.

Feldman, Heidi Carolyn. 2005. 'The Black Pacific: Cuban and Brazilian Echoes in the Afro-Peruvian Revival.' *Ethnomusicology* 49(2):206–31.

Fox, Richard G., ed. 1991. *Recapturing Anthropology: Working in the Present*. Santa Fe, NM: School of American Research Press.

Gifford, Paul. 2004. *Ghana's New Christianity: Pentecostalism in a Globalising African Economy*. London: Hurst.

Gilroy, Paul. 1993. *The Black Atlantic: Modernity and Double Consciousness*. Cambridge, MA: Harvard University Press.

Glick Schiller, Nina, Ayşe Çağlar, and Thaddeus C. Guldbrandsen. 2006. 'Beyond the Ethnic Lens: Locality, Globality, and Born-Again Incorporation.' *American Ethnologist* 33(4):612–33.

Guilbault, Jocelyne. 1997. 'Interpreting World Music: A Challenge in Theory and Practice.' *Popular Music* 16(1):31–44.

Gupta, Akhil, and James Ferguson. 1992. 'Beyond "Culture": Space, Identity, and the Politics of Difference.' *Cultural Anthropology* 7(1):6–23.

Hackett, Rosalind I. J. 1998. 'Charismatic/Pentecostal Appropriation of Media Technologies in Nigeria and Ghana.' *Journal of Religion in Africa* 28(3):258–77.

Hannerz, Ulf. 1996. *Transnational Connections: Culture, People, Places*. London: Routledge.

Hutchinson, Sydney. 2006. 'Merengue Típico in Santiago and New York: Transnational Regionalism in a Neo-Traditional Dominican Music.' *Ethnomusicology* 50(1):37–72.

Kiwan, Nadia, and Ulrike Hanna Meinhof. 2011a. *Cultural Globalization and Music: African Artists in Transnational Networks*. New York: Palgrave Macmillan.

Kiwan, Nadia, and Ulrike Hanna Meinhof. 2011b. 'Music and Migration: A Transnational Approach.' *Music and Arts in Action* 3 (3): 3–20.

Knudsen, Jan Sverre. 2001. 'Dancing Cueca "With Your Coast On": The Role of Traditional Chilean Dance in an Immigrant Community.' *British Journal of Ethnomusicology* 10(2):61–83.

Lysloff, René T. A. 1997. 'Mozart in Mirrorshades: Ethnomusicology, Technology, and the Politics of Representation.' *Ethnomusicology* 41(2):206–19.

Manuel, Peter. 1997. 'Music, Identity, and Images of India in the Indo-Caribbean Diaspora.' *Asian Music* 29(1):17–35.

Marcus, George E. 1995. 'Ethnography in/of the World System: The Emergence of Multi-Sited Ethnography.' *Annual Review of Anthropology* 24:95–117.

Marcus, George E., and Michael M.J. Fischer. 1986. *Anthropology as Cultural Critique: An Experimental Moment in the Human Sciences.* Chicago: University of Chicago Press.

Martin, Jeannett. 2005. *'Been-To', 'Burger', 'Transmigranten'? Zur Bildungsmigration Von Ghanaern Und Ihrer Rückkehr Aus Der Bundesrepublik Deutschland.* Berlinr: LIT.

Meintjes, Louise. 1990. 'Paul Simon's Graceland, South Africa, and the Mediation of Musical Meaning.' *Ethnomusicology* 34(1):37–73.

Meintjes, Louise. 2003. *Sound of Africa! Making Music Zulu in a South African Studio.* Durham, NC: Duke University Press.

Meyer, Birgit. 2004. 'Christianity in Africa: From African Independent to Pentecostal-Charismatic Churches.' *Annual Review of Anthropology* 33:447–74.

Meyer, Birgit. 2008. 'Powerful Pictures: Popular Christian Aesthetics in Southern Ghana.' *Journal of the American Academy of Religion* 76(1):82–110.

Monson, Ingrid, ed. 2000. *The African Diaspora: A Musical Perspective.* New York: Garland.

Muller, Carol A. 2006. 'The New African Diaspora, the Built Environment and the Past in Jazz.' *Ethnomusicology Forum* 15(1):63–86.

Nieswand, Boris. 2005. 'Die Stabilisierung Transnationaler Felder: Grenzüberschreitende Beziehungen Ghanaischer Migranten in Deutschland.' *Nord-Süd Aktuell* 19(1):45–56.

Nieswand, Boris. 2008. 'Ghanaian Migrants in Germany and the Social Construction of Diaspora.' *African Diaspora* 1:28–52.

Nieswand, Boris. 2010. 'Enacted Destiny: West African Charismatic Christians in Berlin and the Immanence of God.' *Journal of Religion in Africa* 40:33–59.

Niranjana, Tejaswini. 2006. *Mobilizing India: Women, Music, and Migration between India and Trinidad.* Durham, NC: Duke University Press.

Oliver, Paul, ed. 1990. *Black Music in Britain: Essays on the Afro-Asian Contribution to Popular Music.* Milton Keynes: Open University Press.

Peil, Margaret. 1995. 'Ghanaians Abroad.' *African Affairs* 94:345–67.

Ramnarine, Tina Karina. 1996. '"Indian" Music in the Diaspora: Case Studies of "Chutney" in Trinidad and in London.' *British Journal of Ethnomusicology* 5:133–53.

Ramnarine, Tina Karina. 2007. '"Musical Performance in the Diaspora: Introduction." *Ethnomusicology Forum* 16(1):1–17.

Rice, Timothy. 2003. 'Time, Place, and Metaphor in Musical Experience and Ethnography.' *Ethnomusicology* 47(2):151–79.

Rommen, Timothy. 2007. *'Mek Some Noise': Gospel Music and the Ethics of Style in Trinidad.* Berkeley: University of California Press.

Safran, William. 1991. 'Diasporas in Modern Societies: Myths of Homeland and Return.' *Diaspora* 1(1):83–99.

Schmelz, Andrea. 2009. *Die Ghanaische Diaspora in Deutschland: Ihr Beitrag Zur Entwicklung Ghanas.* Eschborn: Deutsche Gesellschaft für Technische Zusammenarbeit (GTZ).

Shelemay, Kay Kaufman. 1998. *Let Jasmine Rain Down. Song and Remembrance among Syrian Jews*. Chicago: University of Chicago Press.

Shipley, Jesse Weaver. 2009. 'Aesthetic of the Entrepreneur: Afro-Cosmopolitan Rap and Moral Circulation in Accra, Ghana.' *Anthropological Quarterly* 82(3):631–68.

Shipley, Jesse Weaver. 2012. 'The Birth of Ghanaian Hiplife: Urban Style, Black Thought, Proverbial Speech.' In *Hip Hop Africa: New African Music in a Globalizing World*, Kindle ed., edited by Eric Charry, chap. 1. Bloomington: Indiana University Press.

Slobin, Mark. 1993. *Subcultural Sounds: Micromusics of the West*. Hanover, NH: Wesleyan University Press.

Slobin, Mark. 1994. 'Music in Diaspora: The View from Euro-America.' *Diaspora* 3(3):243–52.

Slobin, Mark. 2003. 'The Destiny of "Diaspora" in Ethnomusicology.' In *The Cultural Study of Music: A Critical Introduction*, edited by Martin Clayton, Trevor Herbert, and Richard Middleton, 284–96. New York: Routledge.

Solís, Ted. 2005. '"You Shake Your Hips Too Much": Diasporic Values and Hawai'i Puerto Rican Dance Culture.' *Ethnomusicology* 49(1):75–119.

Stokes, Martin, ed. 1994. *Ethnicity, Identity and Music: The Musical Construction of Place*. Oxford: Berg.

Stokes, Martin. 2004. 'Music and the Global Order.' *Annual Review of Anthropology* 33:47–72.

Stokes, Martin. 2011. 'Migrant/Migrating Music and the Mediterranean.' In *Migrating Music*, edited by Jason Toynbee and Byron Dueck, 28–37. London: Routledge.

Sugarman, Jane C. 1997. *Engendering Song: Singing and Subjectivity at Prespa Albanian Weddings*. Chicago: University of Chicago Press.

Taylor, Timothy D. 1997. *Global Pop: World Music, World Markets*. New York: Routledge.

Taylor, Timothy D. 2001. *Strange Sounds: Music, Technology, and Culture*. New York: Routledge.

Ter Haar, Gerrie. 1998. *Halfway to Paradise: African Christians in Europe*. Fairwater: Cardiff Academic Press.

Tonah, Steve. 2007. 'Ghanaians Abroad and Their Ties Home: Cultural and Religious Dimensions of Transnational Migration.' In COMCAD Working Papers No. 25. Bielefeld: University of Bielefeld, Center on Migration, Citizenship and Development. Accessed January 9, 2013. http://www.uni-bielefeld.de/tdrc/ag_comcad/downloads/workingpaper_25_Tonah.pdf.

Toynbee, Jason, and Byron Dueck, eds. 2011. *Migrating Music*. London: Routledge.

Turino, Thomas. 1999. 'Signs of Imagination, Identity, and Experience: A Peircian Semiotic Theory for Music.' *Ethnomusicology* 43(2):221–25.

Turino, Thomas. 2008. *Music as Social Life: The Politics of Participation*. Chicago: University of Chicago Press.

Um, Hae-Kyung. 2000. 'Listening Patterns and Identity of the Korean Diaspora in the Former USSR.' *British Journal of Ethnomusicology* 9(2):121–42.

van Dijk, Rijk A. 1997. 'From Camp to Encompassment: Discourses of Transsubjectivity in the Ghanaian Pentecostal Diaspora.' *Journal of Religion in Africa* 27(2):135–59.

Zheng, Su. 2010. *Claiming Diaspora: Music, Transnationalism, and Cultural Politics in Asian/Chinese America*. Oxford: Oxford University Press.

12 Transnational Samba and the Construction of Diasporic Musicscapes

Natasha Pravaz

On a hot summer evening in 2008, I arrived at Toronto's Christie Pits Park to attend a *tambor de crioula* workshop, a unique opportunity as this traditional music/dance/play modality from northeastern Brazil is virtually unknown abroad.[1] While the workshop apparently had been canceled, several in attendance—like myself—had failed to be notified. Frustration gave way to opportunity, however, as conversation with other percussionists turned the occasion into fieldwork. One exchange was particularly informative: Jonathan Rothman (also known as J.R.), a cultural producer and freelance journalist in his early 30s I knew superficially, told us of his first encounter with Brazilian performance culture in Toronto about ten years earlier.[2] He and his friend Itay (Ty) Keshet (an emergency MD currently living in Pennsylvania) were walking down a busy street when they heard the spellbinding sounds of what they would later learn was a *berimbau*.[3] Shortly thereafter, they spotted a robust man executing elaborate acrobatics in a display of fitness and dexterity. Sighting a *capoeira* practice (the martial art derived from descendants of African slaves) turned out to be J.R.'s serendipitous introduction to what would become an endearing passion and occupy large portions of his free time: the Afro-Brazilian performing arts.[4] This typical story of love at first sight in the age of 'transnational soundscapes' (Lopes 2008) would not be all that remarkable if it were not for the fact that J.R. refers to himself tongue in cheek as a 'Born-Again-Brazilian'. For Jonathan, the drive to embody a Brazilian way of life is today significantly mediated by the practice of musicking (Small 1998), and he is not alone in this pursuit.[5]

Building upon my personal engagement with Toronto-based Brazilian percussion music players of diverse backgrounds, this chapter seeks to conceptualize the aesthetic practices of collective music making and active listening (Kun 2005; Stanyek 2004b) as sociopolitical interventions within global flows of people, goods, and ideas. I theorize here the formation of diasporic musicscapes by focusing on two interrelated empirical questions: (a) How does the circulation of Brazilian music and musicians enable the production of a diasporic space where both migrant and local Torontonians reshape their identities and find home by performing *samba*? and (b)

What are the wider sociocultural implications of transnational forms of collaboration that reconfigure embodied relations with sound and foster a horizontal pedagogy of intercultural transmission? These questions are approached through in-depth ethnographic exploration, so that a complex picture of the desires, worldviews, and social relations performed when Canadians join migrants to play Brazilian music may emerge.

Fundamentally, I argue that diasporic musical spaces include both those who hail from the same, foreign place of origin (i.e., Brazilian migrants to Canada) and those who have a particularly profound connection to cultural traditions not their own (including migrants from elsewhere as well as 'Canadian-Canadians' [Mackey 1999, emphasis in its original]).[6] My work is informed by scholars from a variety of disciplines (e.g., Aparicio and Jáquez 2003; Berríos-Miranda 2003; Corona and Madrid 2008b; Joseph 2008; Kun 2005; Magaldi 2008; Stanyek 2004a, 2004b) who seek to problematize straightforward understandings of cultural appropriation by emphasizing transnational connections and looking at instances of intercultural solidarity. In the first section, I situate *samba* as a consumer product in the context of World Music and speak to the ways in which the groups under study differ from their Brazilian counterparts, discussing the problem of perceived authenticity in *samba*'s transnational (re)production. Secondly, I turn to the internal dynamics of Toronto's ensembles, developing the concept of diasporic musicscape and discussing the differential access to choice inherent in affinity intercultures (Slobin 1993; Stanyek 2004a). Finally, I discuss the glocalization (Giulianotti and Robertson 2006) of Brazilian music by looking at *samba* as embodied practice.

Research for this chapter is based on ongoing fieldwork with several professional and amateur musicians of both foreign and local origins who are members of Brazilian percussion groups in Toronto. Ethnographic research methods used range from qualitative, in-depth interviews and long-term participant observation, to analysis of promotional materials (in print and Internet based) and video-recording of a variety of events and everyday life situations. My participation in the life of such bands has included attendance, practice and/or performance at rehearsals, concerts, festivals, meetings, friendly gatherings, and other group activities, as well as one-on-one engagements with band members of diverse backgrounds. I have been an active member in several ensembles across the city since 1998, and this participation has enhanced my ability to understand the key social and cultural themes surrounding group participation for both newcomers and Canadian-born participants. This participation has also made me aware of the richness of people's engagement with music, and of the minute inflections each and every subjectivity brings to this process. For this reason, the writing here intends to mirror the practice of deep, active listening (Kun 2005; Oliveros 2005; Stanyek 2004a, 2004b) that is fundamental to Brazilian music practices in Toronto, and this translates in a lot of room for participants' voices throughout the text. On a final note, I must mention my invested positionality as a diasporic subject (a White, middle-class Argentine who was raised in Brazil and resides in Canada) for whom the sounds of *samba* have indeed become a fundamental part of my sense of home.

THE INTERNATIONAL CIRCULATION OF BRAZILIAN MUSIC

The consumption of Brazilian sounds and dance moves across the globe is not a new phenomenon, dating back to at least the early 1900s, when the racy *maxixe* was adopted in Paris as the new dance craze. From the *chorinho* to the *bossa nova*, all the way through the transgressive songs of 1960s *tropicália* and other MPB (or Brazilian Popular Music) products, Brazilian music has become ubiquitous worldwide, as in the sonic presence of bass-heavy *batucada* drums like Timbalada's in nightclub remixes, for example. Today, a label such as Putumayo emphasizes 'tropical vibes' in its efforts to market the Brazilian Groove collection, a move Corona and Madrid (following Appadurai 1990) term 'the fetishization of geography' (2008a, 17). Such collection offers a combination of cultural Otherness and modern sameness in the form of retro *bossa nova* and *samba* mixed with electronically programmed beats (also known as *Bossatrônica*).

Yet today, more than ever, the exoticizing impulses of Westerners with musical appetite for palatable difference are wetted not only by CDs, the radio, or downloadable tracks, but also by experiences such as the ones provided by live performances of South American music and dance in Europe and North America (see, for example, Bingenho 2002; Desmond 1997; Mercier 2007–8; Savigliano 1995; Wong 2004). Alongside the pervasive, worldwide consumption of diverse forms of Brazilian music today, a new phenomenon has emerged in recent years, spearheaded by the massive exodus of the 1980s when mostly White, middle-class Brazilians began to flock to richer countries in search of a better life. Around that time, informal Brazilian percussion ensembles joining migrants and locals began to spring up everywhere in Europe, North America, and Australasia (Bendrups 2011; Eisentraut 2001; Stanyek 2004a), including the city of Toronto, to which I now turn.

My conversation with Jonathan Rothman that summer of 2008 at Christie Pits eventually veered toward my role as anthropology professor at a neighboring university. I commented that in one of my classes I had recently screened the classic B movie, *Only the Strong*, a 1990s 'good teacher turns troublesome inner-city kids around while defeating local drug lord' film. This action-piece of Latino stereotyping, which focuses on urban gangster culture, comes with a twist: The good guys defeat the bad guys at their own game by learning *capoeira* from the film's protagonist, a White, poster-boy schoolteacher (played by actor Mark Dacacous). I recounted the class discussion to J.R., detailing how we deconstructed the film for all the usual reasons: appropriation, geographic inaccuracies, racialized casting, sexism, etc. His reaction came as a surprise: 'That film is a huge point of reference for *capoeiristas* all over the world, and it actually got more than one person here in Canada into playing *capoeira*' (interview, Toronto, May 18, 2010). J.R. and I eventually came to know each other better as he joined the *samba* band I had been playing with, Batucada Carioca (Toronto's *samba* band with arguably the 'most Brazilian' musical feel, which is led by Rio's *escola de samba* master Maninho Costa). Since, I have come to deeply appreciate Jonathan's commitment to the advancement of Brazilian music in particular, as he took up a leadership role in Samba Elégua, self-described as 'Toronto's sexiest samba . . . con fusion' (Samba Elégua 2010), a group that supports anti-oppression causes through playing Brazilian music. Yet J.R.'s remarks about *Only the Strong* are indicative of a larger context that informs North American consumption of Brazilian culture. Such context needs to be addressed if one is to understand the complexity of the borrowings involved, borrowings which also diverge greatly regarding how close they remain to their inspiring traditions.

Samba ensembles around the world draw on the percussion-based rhythms of Rio de Janeiro's *escolas de samba* (*samba* schools; I use the terms *escola* and school interchangeably throughout this chapter), the cultural associations that come to life in the months leading up to carnaval and where people gather to play, sing, and dance the *samba* (see Bendrups 2011; Eisentraut 2001; Hosokawa 2005; Pravaz 2011). *Escolas de samba* parade in Rio's Sambódromo or *samba* stadium to compete for first place, and muster between 4,000 and 5,000 members each, who wear costumes representing their *escola*'s yearly theme song. *Escolas'* percussion wings or *baterias*, more specifically, have usually between 250 and 300 players and are a small, albeit central aspect of the carnaval organizations. Western-based ensembles, on the other hand, are a more modest affair, being often limited to a percussion ensemble, forfeiting dancers or costumes. Yet despite the differences in glamour and technical skill, the latter are just as committed to the drums as the most fervent of *escola de samba* percussionists in Brazil. But does this commitment mean the same thing?

The musicians of Brazilian *escolas de samba* are usually recruited at a very young age among neighborhood children to participate in a strenuous, demanding activity, highly esteemed by the local *samba* community. The vast majority of participants hail from the suburban, mostly Black working-class environments, which form the breeding ground for *escola de samba* activities. *Samba* largely defines the identities of such percussionists, and it permeates their activities providing an ongoing soundtrack for everyday life. In these environments, staying true to *samba* roots is a high stakes affair, as testified in *samba* lyrics such as 'Visual' by Neném e Pintado, and 'Argumento' by Paulinho da Viola.[7] This perceived authenticity is predicated upon variables such as what the music should sound like, what the dance should look like, which instruments should be involved, and what the visual outlook of *escolas* should be. As I discuss elsewhere (Pravaz 2002, 2008a, 2008b, 2012), the intensity of such disputes is fundamentally related to different understandings of the importance of Afro-Brazilian heritage in defining *samba* culture.

North American ensembles, on the other hand, are not as tied to tradition as Rio *escolas*, although perspectives toward how much fusion is palatable vary greatly across the board. While groups' positions along the tradition-fusion spectrum are usually an outcome of the background and commitments of band leaders, they are also informed by a generalized sense of what Western audiences expect and are able to appreciate. Catherine Mercier (2007–8) points out that in order to better appeal to consumers, Brazilian music bands in Toronto engage in autoexoticism or add specific elements to their music or self-presentation that make them appear more obviously Brazilian. For example:

> promotional materials used in the Toronto Brazilian music scene frequently employ images and buzz words that fit with stereotypical ideas of Brazilianness, such as 'heat,' 'drums,' 'Afro-,' 'roots,' 'raw,' 'traditional,' 'rhythms,' 'syncopated,' 'carnival,' 'dance,' 'movement,' 'energy,' 'party,' 'fun,' and 'colours'. (30)

Yet such appeals to the Canadian taste for exotica are not always a direct indication of the level of fidelity with which a group reproduces Rio's *samba* rhythms, which may draw migrants yearning for home or enthusiasts but not be as palatable to a broader audience.

As I have been able to observe throughout my long-term engagement with local groups, ensemble leaders of Brazilian origins have upon arrival to Canada at the turn of the 21st century tended to select or compose songs closer to musical forms readily identifiable as 'pure' or 'true to the roots' by Torontonians in-the-know. Joelson 'Maninho' Costa (a witty 40-year-old *samba* master and onetime construction worker), for example, used to take pride in the 'authentic' feel he was able to re-create in the sound of his band, Batucada Carioca. While Rio *samba*'s *cadência* (swing) is still his trademark (Pravaz 2011), intercultural engagements have led him to the recent incorporation of jazz and rap influences in the songs he chooses for the band to perform.

In the Canadian environment, Brazilian-influenced acts are certainly more popular than straight *escola de samba* rhythms as Layah Davis (a psychotherapist, yoga teacher and somatic therapist who has played percussion with several Toronto-based ensembles) once observed:

> In Brazil you have all those songs that are part of the carnaval, and the ones that win and everybody knows them and they're on CD and everybody sings them. But here, in the West, those songs are never going to become Top 40, so it's not the same thing. It's not like

people . . . the average person is not going to go to the CD store to buy traditional Brazilian *samba* music. But if it was inside a song that they were hearing on the radio, that would really freak them out. By freak them out, I mean really turn them on. (Interview, Toronto, November 24, 2008)

It is worth noting here, as Corona and Madrid (2008a, 10) do, the 'unavoidable relationship between economics and ethics in the process of music contact and hybridization.'[8] In keeping up with local preferences for hybridized cultural products, a group such as the Samba Squad (of which both J.R. and Layah are members) self-describes as follows: 'Based on the Brazilian tradition of Samba, the Squad takes you on an original dance-till-you-drop tour of global grooves' (Batuque 2000). By far the most successful Brazilian percussion ensemble in town, the Squad uses *escola de samba* instruments such as *surdos* (large bass drums), *caixas* (snares), *tamborins* (small hand drums without jingles played with a stick), and bells to play not only Brazilian, but also Funk, Cuban, and West African rhythms.

A household name in Toronto, the Samba Squad is directed by Rick Shadrach Lazar, a multitalented musician of Middle Eastern background who also leads Latin jazz ensemble Montuno Police, and has performed and recorded with the likes of Loreena McKennitt, Bruce Cockburn, and Barry White. In one of our interviews, he explained his approach to fusion thus:

If you grew up in North America, your concept as a percussionist, you are applying a mix of things, so the more knowledge you have, then you can have knowledge you can bring to a project. Which is the way my career kind of developed, if I'm playing with some pop singer, they don't want a real Cuban beat, they don't want a real Brazilian beat, you have to take your knowledge and make up something that works for them. They are not interested. 'Well, this is a Cuban beat'. They don't care. Just need whatever works for that song, right? . . . Or if I'm playing *tamborim* in a pop project, I might play it with a brush . . . not like a plastic stick 'cause it's like, you are adapting it for that. (Interview, Toronto, September 5, 2008)

His approach to the music produced by the Samba Squad is similar. While the word 'samba' is prominent in the band's name, the buzzword functions to attract North American audiences to a musical product better classified as World Music. While I will not attempt to provide a succinct definition of the term here (see Corona and Madrid 2008a; Feld 2000; Stanyek 2006, among others, for elaborate discussions), suffice it to say that I use 'World Music' to point to some of the hybridizations undergone by non-Western forms of popular music within the context of transnational borrowings. As

World Music has more chances to succeed if sung in English (Corona and Madrid 2008a, 10), several of the Squad's original compositions are indeed performed in this language.

On its part, Samba Elégua (the ensemble J.R. has codirected along with Ty Keshet and Jon Medow, among others), while inspired by the *samba* school *bateria* tradition of Rio de Janeiro, also 'mixes in the high-energy musical styles heard around us in our home city of Toronto, like reggae, funk and hip hop' (Samba Elégua 2010). Jon Medow (a public policy researcher originally from Detroit) talked about the group's repertoire as derived from the typical places you can find Brazilian music played for a Western public, such as Paul Simon's 'The Rhythm of the Saints'. In an interview, he stated that 'Samba Elégua plays on *samba* instruments but it is very much fusion . . ., it's a total extrapolation from *samba*, I guess' (Toronto, August 8, 2009).

Perhaps we could say that this embrace of Brazilian sounds by Canadians is informed in part by dominant narratives such as the ones presented in *Only the Strong*, where Others provide existential meaning and sensuality to emotionally drained and spiritually spent Western selves (see, among others, Desmond 1999; Hill 2008; Mackey 1999; Pravaz 2010, 2013; Savigliano 1995). A superficial look at non-Brazilian *samba* groups would want to chastise their borrowings along the lines of Lipsitz's (1994) critique of Paul Simon's *Graceland* project (i.e., as obscuring the power relations between Western artists and their sources of inspiration in the Global South). We may even argue that the international consumption of Brazilian music mirrors the internal appropriation of Afro-Brazilian cultural traditions by the Brazilian White elite, who in the 1930s embraced the promotion of hitherto banned *samba* as a nation-building strategy (see Pravaz 2002, 2003, 2008a). After all, are these new transnational configurations of *samba* not exercising power asymmetries by squeezing out its traditional counterparts?

Maybe so. As Corona and Madrid (2008a) and Stanyek (2006) have pointed out in discussions of World Music, however, it would be an oversimplification to deny that collaborative and third world productions associated with the genre do exist by characterizing it as a mere search of 'new sounds for a bored culture' (Corona and Madrid 2008a, 15). In fact, the marketing of World Music has not only given global exposure to subaltern musicians but also expanded their sphere of action at both the local and transnational levels. In terms of my ethnographic context, it is fundamental to note that unlike Simon's, Samba Elégua is a community-based ensemble where membership is free and open to all, from novices to experienced players, and participation is based first and foremost on the fun of playing, without any financial reward.[9] A nonprofit, volunteer-run musical group that 'supports a range of community-building, social justice and activist causes in the Toronto area' (Samba Elégua 2010), Samba Elégua embraces a horizontal pedagogy and members are very self-reflexive about their practices. As Jon revealed to me:

We've had discussions about cultural appropriation. We have discussions about should this be called *samba*, is that the right thing to do, or the wrong thing to do? Should we change our name? Or maybe it's right to change our name, but nobody will remember who we are, except everyone knows our name 'cause we've been around for ten years. So these conversations surface now and then, and you know, I've sort of thought about that a lot myself, and struggle with that a little bit. And I've sort of settled on the fact that it's like, someone in Russia playing rock 'n' roll. (Interview, Toronto, August 8, 2009)

The Samba Squad, in turn, has fostered the musical trajectories of transnational artists by collaborating with Toronto-based musicians such as Brazilian nationals Guiomar Campbell and Humberto Porto, as well as Venezuelan and Cuban singers Eliana Cuevas and Alberto Alberto, respectively. As importantly, the Squad is parent organization for Drum Artz Canada (DAC), a charity committed to making music and arts training accessible to all through educational programs that encourage creative expression, team building, youth leadership and self-esteem. According to their website (http://www.drumartz.com/content/programs), DAC expands Samba Squad's scope of practice by providing programs for Toronto's underserved and marginalized populations, adopting the Brazilian 'samba school' model as a vehicle to unite individuals, building cohesive groups in communities.[10]

Ultimately, while not sharing in the migrant condition, many Toronto-based Canadians identify with Brazilian music in ways that go beyond occasionally attending late-night shows at the Lula Lounge or the purchase of a Gilberto Gil CD in the World Music section of an HMV record store.[11] Moreover, my research suggests that collective music performance practices help both migrants and born-and-bred North Americans in their collaborative search for meaning and a sense of shared 'home', understood as 'an enacted space within which we try on and play out roles and relationships of both belonging and foreignness' (Angelika Bammer, cited in Harte 2003, 299). For Torontonians and fellow band members J.R. and Carlie Howell (a professional jazz bass player, educator and composer in her early 30s), for example, encountering the Brazilian expressive arts constituted a radical shift in referential perspective (marked by tears of joy in Carlie's case), whereby for the first time they felt their self-identities mirrored in collective cultural practices: 'I wept and wept. My friend was worried, and I just said, "this speaks to me so deeply."' (Carlie Howell, interview, Toronto, June 6, 2009) As Mark Slobin (1993, 64–65) himself stated in his seminal discussion of diasporic interculture, 'there is no simple relationship to a "homeland" [. . .] when the putative "homeland" has to be understood as a complex of locales, styles, and even families.' I explain in the next section that for my research participants, such relationship is facilitated both by specific social bonds formed within the contexts of music ensembles, and by symbolic associations generated through the aesthetic qualities of Brazilian music.

PERFORMING DIASPORIC MUSICAL IDENTITIES

In his discussion of Bossatrônica as a transnational soundscape, Lopes argues that a transnational affective community has been constituted that 'deterritorializes (on a national level) and reterritorializes (on a transnational level) discourses and cultural icons' (2008, 214) in ways that reject discourses about roots and essentialist notions of identity, authenticity, and cultural purity. Alternatively referred to as *frontera*/borderland (Anzaldúa 1987; Gómez-Peña 2002, 2006), globalization from below (Appadurai 2001), *hibridación*/hybridity (García-Canclini 1992; Bhabha 1994; Olson and Worsham1999), counterculture of modernity (Gilroy 1993), or glocalization (Giulianotti and Robertson 2006), among other conceptual developments, such reterritorializations present some unintended consequences to globalizing processes otherwise conceived of as monolithic and unidirectional, as extensively discussed in the literature (see Kearney 1995). While 'the transnational circulation of Bossa Nova is not the result of migratory movements but the consequence of its regulation via media and communications networks' (Lopes 2008, 215), the South–North flow of Brazilian percussion indeed is in large part built on the flesh and bone of recent migrants, who have left Brazil in an attempt to flee economic suffering. I consider here the implications of the transnational reterritorializations of music when migration processes are included in the mix, and expand on existing empirical examinations of the interplay between industrial, diasporic, and affinity intercultures (see, e.g., Farrell, Bhowmick, and Welch 2005; Slobin 1993, 1994, 2003; Stanyek 2004a, 2004b; Vélez 1994; Zheng 1994).

I am here first and foremost interested in how the complexity of transnational cultural flows affects collective processes of identity formation among Canadian and newcomer musicians from Brazil and elsewhere.[12] As Canadians readily associate with Brazilian masters and other migrants to develop the Brazilian music scene in Toronto, are we before another obvious case of appropriation by which North Americans use their connections to colorful migrants as a means to authenticate 'cool', 'exotic' self-fashionings? Or are we confronted here with an expanded version of Gilroy's Black Atlantic (1993, 202), where Euro-Canadian *aficionados* become unsuspecting bastions of diasporic Afro-Latin-American culture in their anti-modern embrace of the Brazilian syncope?[13] Personally, I have found approaching such questions with a 'both/and' perspective more fruitful than quick 'either/or' categorizations (see, for example, Pravaz 2010, 2011, 2013).

Music only comes into existence when it is being played, listened to, or otherwise enacted, and for this reason we may consider it a useful point of entry for thinking about the contingent character of identities common-sensically perceived as ontologically fixed. In its performative capacity, music mirrors identity practices such as gender, whose doing produces the illusion of an essential core through a discontinuous and stylized repetition of acts defined within compulsory systems of power (see Butler 1990). Indeed, identities based on national, ethnic, and racialized affiliations are just as performative as gender, except exercised on different—albeit inter-related—registers, as testified in the literature (Anderson 1983; Anzaldúa 1987; Bhabha 1994; Hall 1996; Nelson 1999; Povinelli 1997; Pravaz 2012; Savigliano 1995; Walters 2005). The relationship between such complex processes of identity formation and musical performance has been explored by a variety of authors with reference to realities as diverse as the Afro-Brazilian and Venezuelan expressive arts (Browning 1995 and Guss 2000, respectively), Puerto Rican *bomba* (Godreau 2002), Andean-Bolivian music (Bigenho 2002), Zimbabwean popular music (Turino 2003), and Mexican *mariachi* (Mulholand 2007), to name a few. Recently, the diasporic, transcultural, and/or postnational implications of these insights have been theorized by Aparicio and Jáquez (2003), Berríos-Miranda (2003), Corona and Madrid (2008a), Kun (1997, 2005), Pancini Hernández (2003), Pravaz (2010, 2011), Stanyek (2004a, 2004b), Stokes (1994), Um (2005a), and Wong (2004), among others. As Um has pointed out, the 'aesthetic traditions of homeland can be symbolically used as a basis of self and social identity of transnational community' (2005b, 6). For diasporic listeners, music is 'wired into the mobile body, forming earliest memories and later working deep-set emotions.' (Slobin 1994, 4)

My fieldwork experience suggests, however, that there is no easy answer to the question 'who are the diasporic?' in transnational contexts of production and consumption of Brazilian music. As I discuss elsewhere (Pravaz 2010, 2013), participation in Brazilian music ensembles enables Toronto migrants not only from Brazil, but from other Latin American countries in particular to have some of their cosmologies and kinesthetic dispositions partially reflected back through *samba* and *maracatu*'s resonance with, say, Afro-Cuban and Afro-Uruguayan music. This is possible because of the forms' emphasis on the offbeat, their polyrhythmic structures, and the group-oriented dances such musics are associated with. Participation in such ensembles, moreover, sustains the formation of pan-Latin(o) migrant communities in Toronto, which are commonly experienced as substitute families and foster mental health among recent newcomers (Pravaz 2010, 222–26).[14]

Yet, not only migrants but also Canadian nationals feel corporeally and symbolically connected to Brazil in profound ways through sonic, embodied practices. Playing in intercultural percussion ensembles such as the ones I study here assists nomad seekers of a broad range of backgrounds in sustaining links to both real and imagined places of origin. Music, after all, helps people 'stitch their lives together,' serving as 'a soundtrack for our consciousness' (Slobin 1993, 6–7). In fact, specific music forms may become 'homeland' not only to diasporic musicians from one or several locales of expulsion (see Slobin 2003, 290), but also to a motley crew of transregional migrants and host-national aficionados.

The diverse, intercultural membership and exchanges in Brazilian percussion groups (as with similar transnationally connected music groups worldwide) enable the creation of what I call diasporic musicscapes: spaces where symbolic and corporeal connections to real or imagined homelands are actualized through music, and where music and the forms of sociality associated with it may indeed become homeland themselves. In such spaces, belonging and identity are negotiated through sound, and the performative instance of group music making in particular may become an opportunity for experiencing new collective subjectivities that momentarily erase borders and establish unforeseen connections between 'us' and 'them'.

The concept of diasporic musicscapes, as I conceptualize it here, builds upon Avtar Brah's (1996) theorization of diaspora space as follows:

> 'Diaspora space' (as distinct from the concept of diaspora) is 'inhabited' not only by diasporic subjects but equally by those who are constructed and represented as 'indigenous'. As such, the concept of *diaspora space* foregrounds the entanglements of genealogies of dispersion with those of 'staying put'. (16; emphasis in the original)

The author argues that such entanglements decenter 'the subject position of "native," "immigrant," "migrant," the in/outsider, in such a way that the diasporian is as much a native as the native now becomes a diasporian' (238). The point is not whether Canadian nationals 'really' count as part of the Brazilian diaspora in socio-demographic terms by sheer virtue of their willful identification with Brazilian subjectivities (see Barbosa 2009 for empirical data on Brazilians in Canada). If we think of the diasporic stance 'not in substantialist terms as a bounded entity but rather as an idiom, a stance, a claim [. . .] a category of practice used to [. . .] articulate projects, to formulate expectations, to mobilize energies, to appeal to loyalties' (Brubaker 2005, 12), then we can begin to consider the implications of Canadians' involvement in Toronto's Brazilian music scene, including the contradictions, instabilities and multiplicities derived from their identificatory processes.

To the extent that old and new Canadians not originally from Brazil also become enamored with Brazilian music and genuinely seek to embody coveted kinesthetic dispositions and sound-producing abilities allegedly associated with Brazilian modes-of-being,[15] they become fundamental repositories of familiar traditions, which go beyond the musical, to Latin American migrants who join percussion ensembles as an answer to a longing for home. I am thinking here of musicians such as Alan Hetherington (a professional drum-kit player and percussionist originally from

Vancouver who leads the longest-standing *bateria* in Canada, the Escola de Samba de Toronto), Negin Bahrami (a Persian-Canadian graphic designer who has conquered *escola de samba* percussion instruments and manages Batucada Carioca with her husband, Maninho), Alex Bordokas (a Greek-Canadian anthropologist who leads *maracatu* ensemble Mar Aberto), Rick Lazar and Jonathan Rothman, among others, who have come to master not only portions of the Portuguese language but also Afro-Brazilian polyrhythms, and some of the *ginga* and *cadenciado* (sway and flair) necessary for honorary Brazilianness among Toronto's Brazilian music community, among other praised character traits considered typical of Brazilians vis-à-vis Westerners, such as informality and warmth (see Duarte 2005). The affinities between migrants and locals developed in the context of Brazilian music ensembles in Toronto are thus based upon a particular intercultural exchange: Brazilian and 'honorary Brazilian' *samba* masters offer their artistic expertise and, at times, the ability to embody highly praised personal qualities such as *malandragem* (mischievousness or rogue's wit; see Pravaz 2011), and other participants, whether Brazilian, Afro-Cuban, or Anglo-Canadian, offer their desire to engage in a highly demanding, often all-consuming practice.

Through the embodiment of sound, Brazilians and non-Brazilians create transnational spaces where migrants' and locals' ability to 'feel at home' is rearticulated in new surroundings. As Wendy Walters (2005) explains in her study of Black international writing, rather than bounded in 'a nostalgic exclusivity traditionally implied in the word home' (xvi), diasporic spaces may constitute home in themselves: homes that are not bounded, singular, or exclusionary, but rather multiple and plurilocal. A sense of home such as this has more to do then with a 'subjectivity of belonging' (Tölölyan, quoted in Walters 2005, xvii) harnessed by the 'familiarity and regularity of activities and structures of time' (Di Stefano 2002, 38) than with an original homeland. Within the context of the diasporic musics-capes I describe here, the 'familiarity and regularity of activities' at the basis of belonging are provided by attendance to rehearsals, gig, parties, and the like. Such activities are based upon the affectively charged, interactive practices of playing music and listening to others play that constitute border-crossing, identification-generating, hybrid musical spaces where subjectivities based on modern tropes such as the national, the ethnic, and the racial are disrupted.

Importantly, however, in the cases discussed here, physical travel to Brazil does indeed figure as a fundamental experience with a variety of functions. Rather than positing Brazilian citizenship and sojourners' return (or desire to return) to the putative homeland as analytically defining pieces of the diasporic, I will discuss symbolic and actual journeys to Brazil as practices used by both Brazilians and non-Brazilians to articulate specific claims and formulate specific identity projects and musical expectations. I also address this issue as a way to provide a more nuanced understanding of the internal social differentiations within diasporic spaces—which make them contested spaces- and as a segue into a discussion of the concrete, corporeal ways in which migrants' 'homing desire' (Brah 1996, 194) may indeed be successfully satiated in foreign surroundings (or not).

The non-migrant Canadians who choose to participate wholeheartedly in and devote a large part of their lives to Brazilian percussion groups in Toronto do not do so lightly, and, as I have just discussed, play a fundamental role in the creation of diasporic musicscapes. Yet what is at stake for them in such affairs is of a different order than the experience of voluntarily or involuntarily displaced participants (Pravaz 2010, 2011, 2013). As Appadurai (1990) pointed out in his landmark essay on the global cultural economy, the 'scapes' that he posits as dimensions of cultural flows are not objectively given relations, but perspectival constructs. More to the point, such scapes are constituted by the historically situated imaginations of persons and groups around the world (Appadurai 1990, 296–97). In diasporic spaces such as the musicscapes I discuss here, 'forms of belonging and otherness are appropriated and contested [and] cultural narratives of "difference" articulate specific formations of power' (Brah 1996, 241).

For Canadian nationals, the informal musical groupings I study are spaces where it is possible to experience relief from their own presentation of everyday self by trying on another self-presentation through the identification of a different identity projected by music (see Becker 2001). As Euro-North-Americans establish links to another culture, they participate in identity formations and expressions of sociability that carry social cachet. Anne Stadlmair, a music teacher and clarinetist who plays *surdo* in Batucada Carioca, self-consciously and tongue in cheek has referred to people like herself as 'Brazilian wannabes'. She discusses at length how important it has been for her to experience Brazilian culture in Toronto:

> So when you have another culture coming here, you have a bit of another country, in the city, and you know, you realize people do things differently. The music is one thing, the exchange of how you feel a beat, like as a musician, you know. And that's the reason for if you're in music and you have a curiosity and you wanna learn more, that's why you do it. Because the feel of the beat, when you do Brazilian music, you know just what is that. And then that expands into life philosophy. Like, I love the leader and it's so valuable to have somebody like that. And you can just step into it [...] you can just enter, enter that world. (Interview, Toronto, November 24, 2008)

I will address the 'life philosophy' Anne speaks of in further detail in the next section. For my purposes here, I want to point out to the fundamental difference that exists between the possibility of choosing to engage in a cultural tradition you did not grow up in and the engagements with the same traditions on the part of participants whose displacements put them at precarious junctures vis-à-vis immigration status, access to resources, the ability to reproduce collective identities, and the accessibility to familiar 'structures of feeling' (Williams 1977). As Jason Stanyek points out in his discussion of intercultural *capoeira*:

> Choice is never undifferentiated [. . .]. For people who choose their 'affinities' (as opposed to those who cannot choose) there are escape routes, lines of flight, available pretty much at any time [. . .]. The continued access to these 'hatches' is [. . .] what creates a kind of overlap between privileged participation in affinity groups and cultural tourism (which is premised on both the freedom to engage and the freedom to disengage). (2004a, 224)

It is easy for Canadian nationals who play in *samba* groups to 'step into' the Brazilian music world. It is also relatively easy (if you have the economic means to do so) for them to travel to Brazil for various lengths of time. Indeed, in many circles this counts as a sort of rite of passage, by which you come to see and hear firsthand what the music traditions you love look and sound like *in situ*. Other band members will harass you to buy instruments and other accoutrements for them, and you will feel compelled to regularly post pictures of your adventures on Facebook.

For Brazilians and other Latin American migrants, on the other hand, it is a different tune, pun intended. Considering that the Brazilian exodus of the 1980s and 1990s was primarily economically driven, it is fair to say that returns to the homeland are often prohibitively costly for most migrants. As a fellow band member stated on their Skype page: '*queria ser pobre um dia, porque todo dia tá foda*' (I would like to be poor one day, because every day is fucking hard). Immigration status is another important restriction, with people often waiting long months and even years for documents to be released, if indeed they are eligible according to governmental standards.

Band members' awareness of these power differentials varies across the board. Moreover, Canadians who spend considerable amounts of time in Brazil may be relatively aware that prolonged exposure to Brazilian proxemic rules and habitus (Bourdieu 1977) can reshape their musical abilities or characterological dispositions (see Downey 2005; Duarte 2005), yet their grasp of the extent to which changes such as these (whether effected by travel or sheer calisthenics) affect migrants' sense of homeliness and the very viability of diasporic music communities is limited at best, with a few exceptions:

> One time, I remember, I was playing with Maninho, and we fucked up something that was really basic, that we knew, and he just said afterwards: 'guys, when you make this mistake, this is the worst thing in my life.' And, everyone was laughing, like, hahaha, whatever. But he was so serious about that. It was liketelling a priest you don't believe in God

or something, it was like, you didn't love it and care about it enough to make sure you did it right, you know. (Jon Medow, interview, Toronto, August 8, 2009)

Several Canadian participants do, however, have a very sophisticated understanding of the role of collective creative processes in the production of community art:

Joining at that time was, if you were serious about going to rehearsals and learning something with enthusiasm, then you pretty much were joined. And it still is, and that's the thing about community music. I mean, coming from a background of community theatre, community theatre and community music are very similar in the sense that they're for the people. And really, being for the people means that they're used as inclusive, creative outlets, to bring people together to express not only energetic creativity, but also a form of collectivism. And I think I'm very drawn to those kinds of things, so naturally I was drawn to the idea of this big band of 20 people all playing rhythm together. (Layah Davis, interview, Toronto, May 5, 2009)

The draw of collectivism is a recurrent theme among members of the diasporic music communities in Toronto. A collaborative form of public art that engages participants in collective creative processes (Lowe 2000, 364), community art emphasizes face-to-face bonds and helps people feel included and accounted for, enhancing their sense of belonging.

When asked about feelings brought up while playing, Anne spoke about the importance of a Latin American connection (she lived in Venezuela until the age of 5 and returned on extended sojourns to visit her father and half-sister), and of being part of a group. She articulated how the joy of playing was linked to its function as an expression of belonging on multiple registers, from the imagined, transnational community to the face-to-face bonds with fellow *surdo* players, such as Negin Bahrami and Nyah (Christine) Evans (an ex-Batucada member currently living in Europe):

When we get something and it's really tight, you know, just the pleasure of that. And together as a group, because you can rejoice with each other, right. Alright we got it, right. So it really is very much a community thing . . . And then there is the community that I have like with Negin and Christine for when we're on the *surdos*, you know. (Anne Stadlmair, interview, Toronto, November 24, 2008)

Anne explained the importance of expressing joy not only in terms of rejoicing in collective musicking but also regarding the appreciation of each and everyone's individuality within the larger whole:

And if you have something, a talent to share, or something that you've been working at, like music, like in a band or a group, then you do that, you share that . . . You know, where you just are aware of everybody else's strengths and weaknesses and then as a group you create something that is only possible really as a group, right? You just come together and you make it work and you help each other. (Interview, Toronto, November 24, 2008)

The theme of inclusiveness is central in this understanding of collective musicking, where each individuality is celebrated and difference embraced as a rich component of diasporic musicscapes. While the celebration of diversity is an asset of such collectivities, the divergent subject positions of participants as I mentioned earlier, mean that the kinds of emotional, financial and/or existential needs brought into these spaces varies greatly across the board. The viability of diasporic, intercultural music communities, then, is predicated upon specific, embodied qualities which as I discuss below, are elusive and difficult to operationalize.

TU TU, TEE TEE, TU TUTU, TEE TEE, OR HUMBLING ONESELF TO THE SOUND OF BRAZILIAN MUSIC

Anne continued:

And I know I'm supported because I'm feeling that I'm still feeling my way around . . . So it's just that I feel 'Oh yeah, I'm supported. We're together.' You know? And we, through eye contact or through hearing that we get it together that, you know, all of these kind of things are on different levels. (Interview, Toronto, November 24, 2008)

I want to use the references in Anne's speech to point at the link between the production of intercultural communities and the centrality of the sensorium ('eye contact', 'hearing') through which the other is taken into account, taken in, embodied. There is a deep, active listening (Oliveros 2005; Stanyek 2004b) taking place here, in the sense of an expansion of consciousness of sound through active engagement with focused attention.

For example, Samba Squad's Rick Lazar thoroughly outlined for me the importance of listening to how others listen to sound in order to fully grasp their musical conceptions. It is worth quoting him at length here:

But the thing with percussion, just like anything with music is just lifelong, you know always, so then you see as you study more, how everything is related, you realize why it's Afro-Cuban music, traits, you know, concepts are all West African, right? Same with Brazilian stuff, when you sort of get into that. You hear the same bell patterns, but they start them in a different part of the bell pattern. Well the pattern for *ijexá, afoxé*. Teetee tu tutu, tee tee tu tu, teetee tu tutu, tee tee tu tu. Compare it to tu tu teetee, tu tutu tee tee, same bell pattern for *comparsa*, you start one way or the other, but it's the same bell pattern. So one is *ijexá, afoxé*, I mean, Ilesha that's an area in Nigeria, right? You see the root. I mean all over the funk, all the funk, rap grooves, they are really African bell patterns. . . . It's really the same . . . Cong, gek, cong cong cong, gek. You know, you see where the whole drum kit, tee teetee, tee teetee, tee teetee, you play like a be-bop thing, that's tch tchtch, tch tchtch. That's like the djembe patterns. So as you get into it more, you see the relations . . . Everything developed differently. (Interview, Toronto, September 5, 2008)

While Rick has been able to adapt his vast knowledge of West African rhythmic patterns to suit the needs of the Western musicians he has worked with, his personal engagement with these traditions is based on an ethics of listening that seeks to honor their context of production:

So, I mean, that's the thing about when you have like a discipline. So if you are playing Brazilian music, you have to go, *you always have to humble yourself* [added emphasis]. Because you will be learning it is different than Cuban music, because if you don't get into it, then you are playing Brazilian music and just playing [makes vocal sounds imitating rumba's clave pattern], which works in Cuba but doesn't sit right in the Brazilian vibe, you have to understand, even though the concepts, the root is the same, they develop in different ways, and have different ways. They sit within, so you gotta spend some time just learning the way they hear it there and the way they hear it in Cuba. (Rick Lazar, interview, Toronto, September 5, 2008)

The practice of humbling oneself in the process of deep listening is a profound experience at the heart of affinity intercultures, the global, political, highly musical networks that happen when musicians of different backgrounds get together to play (Stanyek 2004a, 93). This humbling has taken a very concrete shape in Toronto since the arrival of Maninho Costa to the scene. Undoubtedly the most accomplished and well-versed Brazilian *samba* percussionist in the area, he has persistently shared his skills with the Brazilian music community at large. This has included multiple jam sessions, guest appearances, and beginners' workshops, but the most significant way in which Maninho has been able to transmit his knowledge has been through a variety of workshops with members of the other *samba* bands in town, such as the Squad and Samba Elégua. The latest of such workshops at the time of writing had been held at a public park in downtown Toronto on Canada Day, July 1, 2010. Samba Elégua had recently acquired new equipment, such as heads for various drums (*repiques*—lead

and solo two-headed drums played alternating hand and stick strokes—
surdos, caixas and *tamborins*), and requested Maninho to show them how
to set them up, tune them, and take care of them. When I asked him why
he was doing it, he answered as follows:

> Trying to help another *samba* group in town, called Samba Elégua, and
> for a long long time I did this in Brazil with friends, and now this. It
> is very dedicated work, for, you know, to set up a snare, or *surdo*, or
> *repique*. So I try to help to have a good sound, and they all have good
> equipment, and they are here to get some information about how to
> deal with the *caixa*, how to deal with the *tamborim*, how to deal with
> the *repinique* (another word for *repique*), how to deal with the *surdos*.
> I already put all the *surdos* for them, and yeah, this to help. I feel very
> happy to help friends play *samba*. (Interview, Toronto, July 1, 2010)

Maninho's commitment is thoroughly appreciated by the *samba* community, as testified in Jon Medow's words:

> Maninho is a really amazing person. First of all, probably the most tal-
> ented percussionist I know, and he is also just incredibly modest about
> that. There's very few people who are as talented as him that are . . .
> He's not ash . . . you know like, he puts on a show, but he doesn't have
> the attitude of a front man. And he is an amazing person to be around
> because of that, he is just so dedicated to what he is doing, but it is not
> about being a star with him, at all, which I think is very unique. (Inter-
> view, Toronto, August 8, 2009)

This particular disposition is arguably common to *samba*'s *malandro* (rouge,
trickster) figure (see Pravaz 2011), whose main values revolve around group
vigor and the pleasure of playing together rather than individual success.
Maninho's humble and generous demeanors are expressions of a collective
mode of being-in-the-world that becomes transnational when he practices
his embodied pedagogy.

Layah once discussed the volunteerism aspect of collective music playing by saying: 'some people go to soup kitchens; I play music' (interview,
Toronto, May 5, 2009) She said she found it really cool that music gave
her the ability to affect someone's life in a way where they feel like they are
changed. When Maninho volunteers to share his tradition with Toronto's
fellow *samba* players, he affects them in a myriad of ways, from providing
sustenance to intercultural communities to alerting others to different possibilities of sound. In doing so, he is changing people's embodied relationship to their instruments, a fundamental aspect of musicking.

After the July 1 workshop at the park, Samba Elégua headed over to
Cherry Beach for Canada Day celebrations. While waiting to perform, J.R.,
who had coordinated the workshop, relayed some of the information to Ty

Keshet, another band leader (and original founder), who had not been able to attend. J.R. explained that because the drums had just been tuned, they had to be played with lower intensity. Ty wondered whether this meant playing closer to the drum's head, but J.R. emphasized that he should still lift his arm up (this is done to gather momentum and help with keeping the groove) while keeping the sound softer:

> It's like, it's part of the attack, I am talking about part of the attack, I am not talking about whether you bring up your hand or not. I am talking about the actual attack, instead of like, the louder, driving into it. (Jonathan Rothman, personal communication, Toronto, July 1, 2010)[16]

This fundamentally embodied practice is something that takes a lot of rehearsing to perfect, as Anne reported when describing the corporeality of rehearsing with the *surdo* at home:

> Like, sometimes being precise is a physical . . . you know you have to get the physicality of it. Of the actual thing, of your arm and that you want it swinging and how big the swing should be and how you want to do it. So that you are really trying, you know, you're as precise, you're where you want it to be. (interview, Toronto, November 24, 2008)

In relaying exactly how and why *surdo* players should raise their arms, Maninho is transmitting traditional knowledge across cultural borders. Interventions in the public politics of embodiment thus become an important contribution of Brazilian music masters to Toronto's cultural life. Back in Brazil such teachers are, in fact, commonly acknowledged as bearers of fundamental, valuable knowledge and referred to as *acadêmicos*, that is, 'scholars' (see Browning 1995). Maninho's scholarship has become a hallmark of Toronto's *samba* sound, transforming the ways locals listen and move to Brazilian music. His interventions participate in giving the diasporic musicscapes I discuss here an audiotopic quality.

Josh Kun (1997, 2005) coined the term 'audiotopia' to designate:

> sonic spaces of effective utopian longings where several sites normally deemed incompatible are brought together not only in the space of a particular piece of music itself, but in the production of social space and mapping of geographical space that music makes possible, [disrupting the] conventional mappings of the Americas. (1997, 290)

Canadian participants in percussion ensembles are part of a network of 'substitute kin' for migrants (Pravaz 2010, 222), and their ability to help recreate the necessary familiarity and regularity so that 'feeling included and accounted for becomes a means of defining a sense of belonging' (Di Stefano 2002, 38) is a high stakes affair for migrants, particularly for those who cannot return to their homelands because of immigration status or financial constraints, among other restraining factors. The intercultural sharing at the heart of diasporic musicscapes is not devoid of conflict, as the meanings associated with Brazilian percussion are contingent upon emerging contexts.

Maninho often tries to recreate a specific vibe, such as the euphoria experienced in Rio's *escolas de samba*. Much to his chagrin, however, we repeatedly fail to achieve this. He tells us about a particular *escola* tune: 'When you play this song in Brazil, people go crazy, they really love it,' as he points out how phony we look. It is painful and at times tragic for Maninho and others that we are unable to reproduce specific sonorities and the comportments traditionally associated with them: Our intercultural community as such, stands on shifting ground.

'AGONIZA MAS NÃO MORRE' (SAMBA AGONIZES BUT IT DOES NOT DIE)[17]

Audiotopias can create homeplaces within diasporic cultural formations (Kun 1997), and their disruption is particularly poignant for migrants. The audiotopic quality of diasporic musicscapes may begin to break down (at least for those finely tuned to the aesthetic fit between the 'here' and 'there'; see Slobin 1994, 245) when both the acoustic and physical dimensions of our practice fail to convey specific moods and longings. We may think about this failure in terms that go above and beyond issues such as technical ability, time devoted to training, or years of participation.

The ability for diasporic musicscapes to satisfy the homing desire of migrants rests greatly upon the successful recreation of a sound deemed authentic enough to evoke familiar feelings and emotions informed by a specific cultural habitus acquired in different contexts from the ones at hand. Such emotional worlds are largely associated with embodied dispositions and listening orientations whose transmission is often beyond the scope of Brazilian masters' pedagogical practice, regardless of how hard they may try. Yet, as Western *samba* players strive greatly to reproduce traditional sounds and perhaps even hope that the *malandro* informality and enthusiasm will become them, so are migrants changed both by interactions in the intimate spaces of group practice, and by the wider sociocultural context of the host country. The transnational circulation of *samba* and *sambistas*, thus, rather than a one-way street of North–South cultural appropriation or South–North migrants yearning for home, is effected by a wide array of peoples with different desires, personal histories, and corporeal outlooks. When they come together in informal gatherings, rehearsals, and performances, they produce diasporic musicscapes that are simultaneously fraught with perils and filled with possibilities. The kinesthetic and sonic communities at the heart of diasporic musicscapes exist only insofar as members orient toward music as a form of collective dialogue, a dialogue that reconfigures diasporic realities, transnational connections, and the pleasures of travel, imaginary or not. While most Toronto-based Latin-American migrants in general, and Brazilians in particular, may be technically classified as White, Afro-Brazilian music has become a central means for the articulation of a shared cultural identity in foreign surroundings.[18] If this appropriation of subaltern practices recreates deeply seated patterns of cultural appropriation by local elites in the Global South, it may simultaneously constitute a surreptitious way through which a counterculture of modernity (Gilroy 1993) makes its way into the heart of the Western metropolis.

NOTES

1. *Tambor de crioula* is an Afro-Brazilian percussion-based music and dance from northeastern Brazil characterized by its humorous, playful, and improvisational character. For a detailed discussion of the *tambor de crioula* workshops, see Pravaz (2013).
2. All names used here are real, at the request of my research participants. This procedure has been approved by the Research Ethics Board of my home university.
3. The *berimbau* is a single-string percussion instrument (a musical bow) from Brazil, which is used in the Afro-Brazilian martial art, *capoeira*.
4. For discussions of the place of Afro-Brazilian heritage in the transnational circulation of Brazilian aesthetic forms, see Pravaz (2011, 2013).
5. Evidently, the socially constructed, historically shifting, and context-specific notion of 'Brazilianness' is a highly charged idea with a very problematic, racialized past. Moreover, the role of Afro-Brazilian music in defining 'Brazilianness' is complex, and I do not have the space here to treat this topic in adequate depth, but see Pravaz (2002, 2003, 2008a).
6. See Eva Mackey (1999, 168) for a discussion of unmarked, White Canadianness and surrounding issues of political authority and nationalism.
7. Lyrics for the song 'Visual' (my translation): After visual appearance became a requisite / In the conception of these *sambeiros* (pej) / Samba lost its power / Since it bent to the circumstance / Imposed by money / And *samba*, which was born poor / Now dresses up as rich / In the carnaval parade / Where mercenarism / Imposes its will / And the sambista who doesn't have cash / Doesn't play anymore / Ah, how I miss / Satin costumes / *Samba* today is an imported luxury / Organdy, haute couture / With luxurious embroidery / And the sambista who lives hand to mouth / Doesn't even have the pleasure / Of watching the parade (*Depois que o visual virou quesito / Na concepção desses sambeiros / O samba perdeu a sua pujança / Ao curvar-se à circunstância / Imposta pelo dinheiro / E o samba que nasceu menino pobre / Agora se veste de nobre / No desfile principal / Onde o mercenarismo / Impõe a sua gana / E o sambista que não tem grana / Não brinca mais o carnaval / Ai que saudade que eu tenho / Das fantasias de cetim / O samba agora é luxo importado / Organdi, alta costura / Com luxuosos bordados / E o sambista / Que mal ganha pra viver / Até mesmo o desfile / Lhe tiraram o prazer de ver*) (Beth Carvalho, 1978).
   Lyrics for the song 'Argumento' (my translation): It's OK / I accept the reasoning / But please don't change *samba* so much / Pay attention because folks are missing / A *cavaco* (4–string small guitar), a *pandeiro* or a *tamborim*

(percussion instruments) / Without prejudice or longing for the past / Without supporting those who won't sail / Do like the old sailor / Who drives the ship slowly / Through the midst (*Tá legal / Tá legal, eu aceito o argumento / Mas não me altere o samba tanto assim / Olha que a rapaziada está sentindo a falta / De um cavaco, de um pandeiro ou de um tamborim / Sem preconceito ou mania de passado / Sem querer ficar do lado de quem não quer navegar / Faça como um velho marinheiro / Que durante o nevoeiro /Toca o barco devagar*) (Paulinho da Viola, 1975/2003).

8. For elaborations on the usefulness of the concept of hybridity for an understanding of the Afro-Brazilian performing arts, see Pravaz (2002, 2003, 2008a).

9. See Shelemay (2011) for a discussion of the concept of community in musicological studies.

10. In Rio de Janeiro, *samba* schools often have an outreach branch that provides educational and other social programming for the marginalized communities that form their home base.

11. According to its website, Lula Lounge is Canada's premiere live music venue for Latin, salsa, and World Music. Lula Lounge hosts the Lula Music and Arts Centre, a non-profit organization that, while supporting World Music from around the globe, 'has a strong focus on presenting work that draws on Afro-Latin-Brazilian forms as these evolve in a Canadian context' (Lula Lounge 2010).

12. I do not have the space here to treat the important issue of immigration status when considering the legal precariousness of non-Canadians.

13. On the Afro-Brazilian syncope as threat to Eurocentric aesthetic and philosophical values, see Sodré (1979) and Pravaz (2013). While some characterizations of local knowledge as non-modern are susceptible to accusations of neocolonial thinking, Mario Blaser's (2009) insightful analysis of political ontology makes it clear that this is not always the case. In fact, such characterizations may stem from a misguided understanding of modernity as single ontological matrix.

14. See Pravaz (2010) for an extended discussion of fictive family bonds among participants in Brazilian percussion ensembles, and Delgado and Muñoz (1997) for a discussion of the role of African traditions in the production of Latin/o identities through processes of migration and mass mediation.

15. See Pravaz (2009) for an elaboration on the role of corporeality in the ideological production of Brazilian and *Carioca* (from Rio) identities, and Joseph (2008) for a discussion of Brazilian-Canadian *capoeira* groups as kinesthetic communities.

16. J.R.'s comments were recorded during an informal exchange at Cherry Beach rather than in a formal interview.

17. 'Agoniza Mas Não Morre' is the title of a song by Chico Buarque (one of the foremost Brazilian MPB composers) about *samba*'s history of political persecution and eventual appropriation by the Brazilian elite, made popular by *samba*'s 'Godmother', Beth Carvalho (1978). Note that the verb *agonizar* in Portuguese makes specific reference to the suffering that precedes death.

18. See Bendrups (2011) for a discussion of the role of Latin American musicians in the migrant communities of Australasia.

REFERENCES

Anderson, Benedict. 1983. *Imagined Communities: Reflections on the Origin and Spread of Nationalism*. London: Verso.

Anzaldúa, Gloria. 1987. *Borderlands/La Frontera: The New Mestiza*. San Francisco: Aunt Lute Books.

Aparicio, Frances R., and Cándida Jáquez, eds. 2003. *Musical Migrations: Transnationalism and Cultural Hybridity in Latin/o America*. New York: Palgrave Macmillan.

Appadurai, Arjun. 1990. 'Disjuncture and Difference in the Global Cultural Economy.' *Theory, Culture and Society* 7:295–310.

Appadurai, Arjun. 2001. 'Grassroots Globalization and the Research Imagination.' In *Globalization*, edited by Arjun Appadurai, 1–21. Durham, NC: Duke University Press.

Barbosa, Rosana. 2009. 'Brazilian Immigration to Canada.' *Canadian Ethnic Studies* 41(1–2):215–25.

Becker, Judith. 2001. 'Anthropological Perspectives on Music and Emotion.' In *Music and Emotion: Theory and Research*, edited by Patrik N. Juslin and John A. Sloboda, 135–60. Oxford: Oxford University Press.

Bendrups, Dan. 2011. 'Latin Down Under: Latin American Migrant Musicians in Australia and New Zealand.' *Popular Music* 30(2):191–207.

Berríos-Miranda, Marisol. 2003. '"Con Sabor a Puerto Rico": The Reception and Influence of Puerto Rican Salsa in Venezuela.' In *Musical Migrations: Transnationalism and Cultural Hybridity in Latin/o America*, edited by Frances R. Aparicio and Cándida Jáquez, 47–67. New York: Palgrave Macmillan.

Bhabha, Homi. 1994. *The Location of Culture*. London: Routledge.

Bigenho, Michelle. 2002. *Sounding Indigenous: Authenticity in Bolivian Music Performance*. New York: Palgrave Macmillan.

Blaser, Mario. 2009. Political Ontology. *Cultural Studies* 23(5–6):873–896.

Bourdieu, Pierre. 1977. *Outline of a Theory of Practice*. Cambridge: Cambridge University Press.

Brah, Avtar. 1996. *Cartographies of Diaspora: Contesting Identities*. London: Routledge.

Browning, Barbara. 1995. *Samba: Resistance in Motion*. Indianapolis: Indiana University Press.

Brubaker, Rogers. 2005. 'The "Diaspora" Diaspora.' *Ethnic and Racial Studies* 28(1):1–19.

Butler, Judith. 1990. *Gender Trouble: Feminism and the Subversion of Identity*. New York: Routledge.

Corona, Ignacio, and Alejandro L. Madrid. 2008a. 'Introduction: The Postnational Turn in Music Scholarship and Music Marketing.' In *Postnational Musical Identities: Cultural Production, Distribution, and Consumption in a Globalized Scenario*, edited by Ignacio Corona and Alejandro L. Madrid, 3–22. Lanham, MD: Lexington Books.

Corona, Ignacio, and Alejandro L. Madrid, eds. 2008b. *Postnational Musical Identities: Cultural Production, Distribution, and Consumption in a Globalized Scenario*. Lanham, MD: Lexington Books.

Delgado, Celeste Fraser and José Esteban Muñoz, eds. 1997. *Every-night Life: Culture and Dance in Latin/o America*. Durham, NC: Duke University Press.

Desmond, Jane C. 1997. 'Embodying Difference: Issues in Dance and Cultural Studies.' In *Everynight Life: Culture and Dance in Latin/o America*, edited by Celeste Fraser Delgado and José Esteban Muñoz, 33–64. Durham, NC: Duke University Press.

Desmond, Jane C. 1999. *Staging Tourism: Bodies on Display from Waikiki to Sea World*. Chicago: University of Chicago Press.

Desmond, Jane C., and José Esteban Muñoz. 1997. 'Rebellions of Everynight Life.' In *Everynight Life: Culture and Dance in Latin/o America*, edited by Celeste Fraser Delgado and José Esteban Muñoz, 9–32. Durham, NC: Duke University Press.

Di Stefano, John. 2002. 'Moving Images of Home.' *Art Journal* 61(4):38–51.

Downey, Greg. 2005. *Learning Capoeira: Lessons in Cunning from an Afro-Brazilian Art*. Oxford: Oxford University Press.

Duarte, Fernanda. 2005. 'Living in "the Betweens": Diaspora Consciousness Formation and Identity among Brazilians in Australia.' *Journal of Intercultural Studies* 26(4):315–35.

Eisentraut, Jochen. 2001. 'Samba in Wales: Making Sense of Adopted Music.' *British Journal of Ethnomusicology* 10(1):85–105.

Farrell, Gerry, with Jayeeta Bhowmick and Graham Welch. 2005. 'South Asian Music in Britain.' In *Diasporas and Interculturalism in Asian Performing Arts: Translating Traditions*, edited by Hae-kyung Um, 104–28. London: Routledge Curzon.

Feld, Steven. 2000 'A Sweet Lullaby for World Music.' *Public Culture* 12(1):145–71.

García-Canclini, Néstor. 1992. *Culturas híbridas: Estrategias para entrar y salir de la modernidad*. Buenos Aires: Editorial Sudamericana.

Gilroy, Paul. 1993. *The Black Atlantic: Modernity and Double Consciousness*. Cambridge: Harvard University Press.

Giulianotti, Richard, and Roland Robertson. 2006. 'Glocalization, Globalization and Migration: The Case of Scottish Football Supporters in North America.' *International Sociology* 21(2):171–98.

Godreau, Isar. 2002. 'Changing Space, Making Race: Distance, Nostalgia, and the Folklorization of Blackness in Puerto Rico.' *Identities: Global Studies in Culture and Power* 9(3):281–304.

Gómez-Peña, Guillermo. 2002. *El Mexterminator: Antropología inversa de un performancero postmexicano*. Mexico City: Editorial Océano de México.

Gómez-Peña, Guillermo 2006. *Bitácora del cruce: Textos poéticos para accionar, ritos fronterizos, videografitis, y otras rolas y roles*. Mexico City: Fondo de Cultural Económica.

Guss, David M. 2000. *The Festive State: Race, Ethnicity and Nationalism as Cultural Performance*. Berkeley: University of California Press.

Hall, Stuart. 1996. 'Who Needs Identity.' In *Questions of Cultural Identity*, edited by Stuart Hall and Paul du Gay, 1–18. London: Sage.

Harte, Liam. 2003. '"Somewhere beyond England and Ireland": Narratives of "Home" in Second-Generation Irish Autobiography.' *Irish Studies Review* 11(3):293–305.

Hill, Michael. 2008. 'Inca of the Blood, Inca of the Soul: Embodiment, Emotion, and Racialization in the Peruvian Mystical Tourist Industry.' *Journal of the American Academy of Religion* 76(2):251–79.

Hosokawa, Shuei. 2005. 'Dancing in the Tomb of Samba: Japanese-Brazilian Presence/Absence in the São Paulo Carnival.' In *Diasporas and Interculturalism in Asian Performing Arts: Translating Traditions*, edited by Hae-kyung Um, 61–74. London: Routledge Curzon.

Joseph, Janelle. 2008. '"Going to Brazil": Transnational and Corporeal Movements of a Canadian-Brazilian Martial Arts Community.' *Global Networks* 8(2):194–213.

Kearney, Michael. 1995. 'The Local and the Global: The Anthropology of Globalization and Transnationalism.' *Annual Review of Anthropology* 24:547–65.

Kun, Josh. 1997. 'Against Easy Listening: Audiotopic Readings and Transnational Soundings.' In *Everynight Life: Culture and Dance in Latin/o America*, edited by Celeste Fraser Delgado and José Esteban Muñoz, 288–309. Durham, NC: Duke University Press.

Kun, Josh .2005. *Audiotopia: Music, Race, and America*. Berkeley: University of California Press.

Lipsitz, George. 1994. *Dangerous Crossroads: Popular Music, Postmodernism and the Poetics of Place*. London: Verso.

Lopes, Denilson. 2008. 'Transnational Soundscapes: Ambient Music and Bossatrônica.' In *Postnational Musical Identities: Cultural Production, Distribution, and Consumption in a Globalized Scenario*, edited by Ignacio Corona and Alejandro L. Madrid, 209–18. Lanham, MD: Lexington Books.

Lowe, Seana S. 2000. 'Creating Community: Art for Community Development.' *Journal of Contemporary Ethnography* 29(3):357–86.

Lula Lounge. 2010. Accessed August 25, 2010. http://www.lulalounge.ca/Lula-MAC.html.

Mackey, Eva. 1999. *The House of Difference: Cultural Politics and National Identity in Canada*. London: Routledge.

Magaldi, Cristina. 2008. 'Before and After Samba: Modernity, Cosmopolitanism, and Popular Music in Rio de Janeiro at the Beginning and End of the Twentieth Century.' In *Postnational Musical Identities: Cultural Production, Distribution, and Consumption in a Globalized Scenario*, edited by Ignacio Corona and Alejandro L. Madrid, 173–84. Lanham, MD: Lexington Books.

Mercier, Catherine. 2007/8. 'Interpreting Brazilianness: Musical Views of Brazil in Toronto.' *Musicultures* 34(35):26–46.

Mulholland, Mary-Lee. 2007. 'Mariachi and National Identity: Myths, Mestizaje and Mexicanidad.' *National Identities* 9(3):247–64.

Nelson, Diane. 1999. *A Finger in the Wound: Body Politics in Quincentennial Guatemala*. Berkeley: University of California Press.

Oliveros, Pauline. 2005. *Deep Listening: A Composer's Sound Practice*. Lincoln: Deep Listening Publications.

Olson, Gary A., and Lynn Worsham. 1999. 'Staging the Politics of Difference: Homi Bhabha's Critical Legacy.' In *Race, Rhetoric and the Postcolonial*, edited by Gary A. Olson and Lynn Worsham, 3–42. Albany: State University of New York.

Pacini Hernández, Deborah. 2003. 'Amalgamating Musics: Popular Music and Cultural Hybridity in the Americas.' In *Musical Migrations: Transnationalism and Cultural Hybridity in Latin/o America*, edited by Frances R. Aparicio and Cándida Jáquez, 13–32. New York: Palgrave Macmillan.

Povinelli, Elizabeth. 1997. 'Sex Acts and Sovereignty: Race and Sexuality in the Construction of the Australian Nation.' In *The Gender/Sexuality Reader: Culture, History, Political Economy*, edited by Roger Lancaster and Micaela di Leonardo, 513–30. New York: Routledge.

Pravaz, Natasha. 2002. 'Performing Mulatice: Hybridity as Identity in Brazil.' PhD diss., York University, Toronto.

Pravaz, Natasha. 2003. 'Brazilian Mulatice: Performing Mestiçagem in Rio de Janeiro.' *Journal of Latin American Anthropology* 8(1):116–46.

Pravaz, Natasha. 2008a. 'Hybridity Brazilian Style: Samba, Carnaval and the Myth of "Racial Democracy" in Rio de Janeiro.' *Identities: Global Studies in Culture and Power* 15(1):80–102.

Pravaz, Natasha. 2008b. 'Where is the Carnivalesque in Rio's Carnaval? Samba, Mulatas and Modernity.' *Visual Anthropology* 21(2):95–111.

Pravaz, Natasha. 2009. 'The Tan from Ipanema: Freyre, Morenidade, and the Cult of the Body in Rio de Janeiro.' *Canadian Journal of Latin American and Caribbean Studies* 34(67):79–104.

Pravaz, Natasha. 2010. 'The Well of Samba: On Playing Percussion and Feeling Good in Toronto.' *Canadian Ethnic Studies* 41(3):207–32.

Pravaz, Natasha. 2011. '"Na Cadência Bonita do Samba": Accomplishing Suíngue in Toronto.' *Critical Studies in Improvisation* 7(1). Accessed August 25, 2011. http://www.criticalimprov.com/article/view/1130/2058.

Pravaz, Natasha. 2012. 'Performing Mulata-ness: The Politics of Cultural Authenticity and Sexuality among Carioca Samba Dancers.' *Latin American Perspectives* 39(2):113–33.

Pravaz, Natasha. 2013. 'Tambor de Crioula in Strange Places: The Travels of an Afro-Brazilian Play Form.' *Anthropological Quarterly* 86(3):795–820.

Samba Elégua. 2010. Accessed July 19, 2010. http://www.sambaElégua.com/about.

Savigliano, Marta. 1995. *Tango and the Political Economy of Passion*. Boulder: Westview Press.

Shelemay, Kay Kaufman. 2011. 'Musical Communities: Rethinking the Collective in Music.' *Journal of the American Musicological Society* 64(2):349–90.

Slobin, Mark. 1993. *Subcultural Sounds: Micromusics of the West*. Hanover: Wesleyan University Press.

Slobin, Mark. 1994. 'Music in Diaspora: The View from Euro-America.' *Diaspora* 3(3):243–51.

Slobin, Mark. 2003. 'The Destiny of "Diaspora" in Ethnomusicology.' In *The Cultural Study of Music: A Critical Introduction*, edited by Martin Clayton, Trevor Herbert, and Richard Middleton, 284–96. London: Routledge.

Small, Christopher. 1998. *Musicking: The Meanings of Performing and Listening*. Hanover, CT: Wesleyan University Press.

Sodré, Muniz. 1979. *Samba: o dono do corpo*. Rio de Janeiro: Codecri.

Stanyek, Jason. 2004a. 'Diasporic Improvisation and the Articulation of Intercultural Music.' PhD diss., University of California at San Diego.

Stanyek, Jason 2004b. 'Transmissions of an Interculture: Pan-African Jazz and Intercultural Improvisation.' In *The Other Side of Nowhere: Jazz, Improvisation and Communities in Dialogue*, edited by Daniel Fishlin and Ajay Heble, 87–130. Middletown, CT: Wesleyan University Press.

Stanyek, Jason 2006. 'World Music.' In *Encyclopedia of Globalization*, edited by Roland Robertson and Jan Aart Scholte, 1292–97. London: Routledge.

Stokes, Martin. 1994. 'Place, Exchange and Meaning: Black Sea Musicians in the West of Ireland.' In *Ethnicity, Identity and Music: The Musical Construction of Place*, edited by Martin Stokes, 97–115. Oxford: Berg.

Turino, Thomas. 2003. 'Are We Global Yet? Globalist Discourse, Cultural Formations and the Study of Zimbabwean Popular Music.' *British Journal of Ethnomusicology* 12(2):51–79.

Um, Hae-kyung, ed. 2005a. *Diasporas and Interculturalism in Asian Performing Arts: Translating Traditions*. London: Routledge Curzon.

Um, Hae-kyung. 2005b. 'Introduction: Understanding Diaspora, Identity and Performance'. In *Diasporas and Interculturalism in Asian Performing Arts: Translating Traditions*, edited by Hae-kyung Um, 1–13. London: Routledge Curzon.

Vélez, María Teresa. 1994. 'Eya Aranla: Overlapping Perspectives on a Santería Group.' *Diaspora: A Journal of Transnational Studies* 3(3):289–304.

Walters, Wendy W. 2005. *At Home in Diaspora: Black International Writing*. Minneapolis: University of Minnesota Press.

Williams, Raymond. 1977. *Marxism and Literature*. Oxford: Oxford University Press.

Wong, Deborah. 2004. *Speak It Louder: Asian Americans Making Music*. New York: Routledge.

Zheng, Su. 1994. 'Music Making in Cultural Displacement: The Chinese-American Odyssey.' *Diaspora: A Journal of Transnational Studies* 3(3):273–88.

DISCOGRAPHY

Carvalho, Beth. 1978. *De Pé No Chão*. Rio de Janeiro. RCA.

Samba Squad. 2000. *Batuque*. Toronto: Indie Pool.

Viola, Paulinho da. 2003. *Meu Mundo É Hoje*. São Paulo: Biscoito Fino.

13 Music in Cyberspace

Transitions, Translations, and Adaptations on Romanian Diasporic Websites

Ruxandra Trandafoiu

In a globalized world, culture can become a hotly contested territory as it ceases to be the appanage of nation-states. Culture and music become the apparatus for contesting national realities and received identities, and for proposing instead transnational models and unfixed cultural spaces. In this chapter, I am using Romanian diasporic websites based in Italy, Spain, and the United Kingdom, countries that attracted significant Eastern European labor migration in the post-communist period, to study the online exchange and consumption of music by migrants. Music, and the way migrants relate to it, and reflect upon its significance and value becomes the conduit that channels their understanding of emerging diasporic culture and the diasporic condition. Through musical preferences that range from 1970s dissident rock and *Schlager* (the pop music of communism) to post-communist *turbo folk* (*manele*), digital migrants express their ambivalent relationship to the homeland and national culture as well as their aspirations toward a new spiritual *Heimat* anchored in the liquidity of migratory experiences. In his excellent and now classic analysis of music and identity, Simon Frith (1996, 109) postulates that music experiences can be defined as 'self-in-process' since identity is mobile. Diasporic voices best illustrate the process of being and becoming, which inherently produces disagreements and contradictions, but also offers the basis for contesting traditional understandings of culture.

The research was part of a larger project conducted over a period of two years, 2007 to 2009 (see Trandafoiu 2013). A total of six diasporic websites based in the three countries (Italy, Spain, and the UK) were monitored consistently.[1] Through them, I encountered several other websites, which became interesting for the purpose of this chapter. I conducted the project using the principles of netnography (Kozinets 2010). Like Ignacio (2005) and Nedelcu (2009), who have conducted online research with Filipinos and Romanians in the US and Canada, respectively, I saved relevant discussion threads, kept a research diary, coded, and analyzed emerging themes, situating them in the larger cultural and historical context.[2] I also posted messages about my research project, I invited people to comment online or e-mail me privately and I intervened occasionally in discussions, particularly to seek clarifications. I became therefore a participant-observer, avoiding to 'lurk', a practice now viewed critically in online research (Gaiser and Schreiner 2009, 133–34). Administrators, moderators, and users were both accommodating and unconcerned about issues of anonymity. Nonetheless, when quoting online voices, I modified the avatars (and occasionally the assumed gender) of the participants. This is considered to be a 'minimum cloaked' situation (Kozinets 2010, 154).[3]

FOLKLORE AND IDENTITY IN TRANSITION

After the fall of communism, in 1989, Romania embarked on a long process of identity reassessment and rewriting, an attempt to both rescue and reinterpret history and culture (Andreescu 1996, 41). This was not a new phenomenon, since Romanian culture (call it a minor culture, at the edge of 'civilization') has always been on the lookout for new models, as a result of three major fractures suffered over the past two centuries: the split from the Orient, as part of a process of Westernization led by elites in the 19th century; the enforced breakup with the West during communism; and the abrupt divorce from communism in 1989 (Boia 1997, 199).

While looking towards the West has remained a popular pursuit, many Romanians prefer to search for originality inside their own culture. This would not necessarily entail an outright rejection of the West; simply assigning Romanians a unique contribution to European history (through the 'bulwark of Europe' trope, for example) can help support claims of ancient tradition and continuity (Boia 1997, 2002). However, such a strategy can be easily high-jacked by nationalist extremists encamped on both wings of the political spectrum—the right, and also the neo-communist left. The result is a continuous and fierce debate between traditionalists and modernizers, nationalists and Europeanists (Andreescu 1996).

Nationalists continue to win battles, though not the war. According to Romanian political analyst Vladimir Tismăneanu, when communism became shipwrecked, Eastern Europeans were left downtrodden, having lived through a long period of injustice, lacking any achievement or justifications for national pride. Salvation mythologies and phantasmagoric recreations of the past (I call it 'nostalgism') were conveniently wheeled out to make up for their suffering (Tismăneanu 1999, 121 and 204). With elites also deploying populist nationalism as a means of staying in power (Tismăneanu 1999, 111), Eastern Europeans have remained tethered by nationalistic illusions.

Correspondingly, the West has seemed reluctant to welcome Easterners with open arms. After the short-lived enthusiasm of the democratization revolutions and the fall of the Berlin Wall, Westerners fell prey to old Orientalist, and occasionally Gothic, stereotypes that have abounded in Western writing since Voltaire (Wolff 2000, 127). While *Mitteleuropa* appeared, to some extent, culturally familiar, the East and especially the Balkans combined in the Western imagination the beauty and exoticism of landscapes with threatening experiences and primitive cultures (Wolff 2000, 162–63 and 248).

It is understandable why in this context, the music that Westerners seemed keen to rescue, was traditional Romani/Gypsy music. A good example is *Taraf de Haïdouks*, 'discovered' by Swiss and Belgian musicologists in 1990 and quickly promoted to European stardom. Their music had already been recorded in the 1980s by the Institute of Ethnography and Folklore in Bucharest, but Westerners found a better way to commercialize their exoticism. It is interesting therefore that although Roma folklore is very similar to Romanian folklore and many *taraf* are not only multiethnic but play a mixture of Gypsy and Romanian traditional songs (a fact also acknowledged by Silverman in this volume), the Roma displayed enough cultural distance to acquire exotic value in the process of commodification (Huggan 2001, 13), but were also familiar enough through their European presence and uninterrupted Othering to become appealing to Western tastes and the Western imagination.

Romanian folklore, on the other hand, remained difficult to sell. As part of European culture, it was supposed to sound somewhat familiar, but because of enforced cultural isolation during communism, its 'primitive' forms remained too alien to most audiences. Exoticization, in the current political context in which Romania has become a member of the European Union and claims its modernity, proved difficult. Instead, the Westernization of both music and musical performances was attempted with limited success.[4] Uncertain of the new value system to be applied to Romanian culture and confused by Western audiences' mixed responses, Romanians seem split between championing a return to the Golden Age of 'authentic' village traditions and the modernization/hybridization strategies. This dilemma appears clearly in the musical tastes displayed by Romanian migrants, as we shall see in the next sections. It is, however, important to discuss first why these apparently diverging stratagems—traditionalism versus Westernization—have emerged in the context of Romanian culture.

MODERNIZING TRADITION

Two main phenomena led to folklore becoming a symbol of Romanianness and an element of historical continuity—one belongs to elite culture, the other to popular culture.[5] As to the first, generations of Romanian intellectuals have extolled the virtues of rural life. In the 1930s the Transylvanian poet and philosopher Lucian Blaga found the essence of Romanian identity in the immutable landscapes that taught Romanians patience and endurance in the face of external aggression and historical upheavals (Blaga 1994). The village, embedded in this lasting geography, can thus be viewed as the 'repository of the national soul,' according to another philosopher (Noica 1996) who was writing in 1978. The reoccurrence of this theme is a sign of the undying belief that Romanian identity is defined by land and folklore (Boia 2001, 220). Such exaltations about rural life, often imbued with metaphysical considerations, became appealing to the communist regime, for whom references to an often imaginary Romania became a way of distracting attention from the effects of social engineering (Mungiu-Pippidi 2002, 169).

A second phenomenon appeared at grassroots level. Indirectly, it is an effect of the destruction that communism inflicted on the traditional Romanian village, first through collectivization and then through 'resystematization', which relocated the rural population to the factories and the urban high-rises. Dispossessed of land and economic opportunity, those who moved *en masse* to the cities took the village with them in the form of musical recordings. Continuing to consume traditional music suggested that despite uprooting and urbanization, some elements of the traditional community life were left intact (Connell and Gibson 2003, 37). Today, a large majority of this urban working class still enjoys folklore, as evidenced in the popularity of the television channels Favorit TV, Etno TV and Taraf TV,[6] and the key role played by this genre in virtually all media entertainment programs. The continuous popularity of Romanian folklore is a typical example of how popular music can rise from below but can also be superimposed from above (Manuel 1988, 8). However, audience tastes continue to change and today audiences enjoy both modern versions of traditional songs and hybrid subgenres, derivative of a process initiated during communism. I will now turn my attention to two such examples of 'modernization'.

During communism, *etno rock* became the ideologically acceptable, Romanian version of rock. Epitomized by the band Phoenix, who achieved almost a mythical status for the generations who grew up in the 1970s and 1980s, *etno rock* was somewhat tolerated by the communist regime. After all, though Western and capitalist in provenance, it used folkloric musical motifs, traditional instruments (such as the flute), and Romanian fables inspired the lyrics (the myth of master builder Manole, who sacrifices his wife in the foundations of the monastery he erects, or the ballad of Andri Popa, from the arsenal of famous haidouks or outlaws).[7] Phoenix returned to tour full stadia after 1989, helped by their earlier defection to Western Germany, which enshrined them in the popular imagination.

After 1989 *etno* became another favorite hybrid. Bands like Ro-mania sing folkloric music remixed with disco and techno. This fusion appeals to contemporary young audiences, the sons and daughters of those who moved from the village to the city during communism, but not only. Increasingly, a middle urbanite class craves the reconnection with a primordial and simple identity expressed by folklore. They reject their unsophisticated rustic roots, but buy into contemporary versions that seem to sell well on the

European party scene and make them feel part of a more cosmopolitan global audience.[8]

ONLINE IDENTITY NEGOTIATIONS

Because of the popularity of various versions of folklore, many websites that have been set up with the aim of catering for diasporic musical tastes have also included folkloric music as one of their main offerings,[9] and music, in general, and folklore, in particular, have started to play an increasingly important role in the diasporic Internet economy.[10] Folklore also channels the online discussions among diasporans interested in the evolution and modernization of the genre, its role in Romanian identity, its relevance for an emerging diasporic culture, and any insecurities held about the future of cultural tradition and authenticity.[11] The following examples showcase these debates.

On February 14, 2010, *Trăieşte româneşte!* (Live like a Romanian!), a website that champions Romanian traditions,[12] announced that the *doina* has been added to the UNESCO (United Nations Educational, Scientific, and Cultural Organization) intangible heritage list. According to UNESCO, the *doina*, a lyrical chant sung with or without orchestral accompaniment, was a justified choice, since it 'has been transmitted, mainly inside families, in many parts of Romania, where people regard it as part of their cultural heritage and their identity' (UNESCO website, http://www.unesco.org/culture/ich/index.php?RL=00192, accessed March 3, 2010). *Doina* thus joined the *Căluş Ritual*, a traditional Romanian male dance, which has been on UNESCO's 'list' since 2008. The event was celebrated on *Trăieşte româneşte!*, a website with similar aims to UNESCO's: the preservation of cultural products in an archetypal form, in order to help reconnect audiences with a way of life in danger of being extinguished. Ultimately, 'heritage' and 'tradition' sell national identity to tourists.

This case of diasporic nostalgia expressed by a virtual, imaginary return to some kind of golden age, which signifies sophistication through simplicity and purity, raises several issues around traditionalism and authenticity, modernization, and globalization. UNESCO's remit is an example of glocalization, although the idea that 'tradition', in itself an unstable term, can be artificially preserved and that choice elements of national culture can be treated as a given, as everlasting, used to be the appanage of nation-states, not international organizations. UNESCO's work, not to mention the harmless personal hobbies of people who set up websites with similar aims, also raises questions around how these elements of regional or national culture are experienced globally, when everybody knows that pickles and preserves never taste like the fresh produce. 'Freezing' only feeds exoticism, which traps rather than liberates identities (Connell and Gibson 2003, 44). During the discussions I observed online, some migrants also seemed to have some difficulty in adopting such a contrived view of authenticity (although there were also many who endorsed this view) and preferred to see music and their experience of it as a process of natural selection, survival of the fittest, and organic growth.

In the summer of 2009, for example, the *România Italia Net* forum started a well-attended discussion thread centered on Romanian folkloric music. The participants posted video clips of the songs, which were eagerly viewed and listened to, and exchanged views about the tunes, singers, and clips. One of the main themes to emerge was the importance of this genre to Romanian culture and identity. As Rozana pointed out, 'like it or not, Romanian folklore is a dominant aspect of Romanian culture' (Rozana, *România Italia Net*), while another participant added, 'I think that Gheorghe Zamfir's music would be most suited for the soundtrack of a film about Romania/Romanians' (Tulcic, *România Italia Net*). Zamfir, a diasporan himself during the communist regime, is mentioned as the exemplary master of *nai* (pan flute) interpretation of Romanian folklore. Tulcic sees Zamfir as an archetypal Romanian musician, playing archetypal Romanian music. However Zamfir, probably best known to Western audiences for 'The Lonely Shepherd' in Tarantino's *Kill Bill Vol. 1*, and his other contributions to *Karate Kid* and *Once Upon a Time in America*, is also a perfect example of cultural globalization, where traditional Romanian music, in a Westernized and highly cultivated form, is called upon to musically illustrate Hollywood action movies.[13]

Tulcic's comment also initiated another theme in the discussion, this time concerning quality, good versus bad music, old or 'classic' versus new and modern. This theme managed to split the participants. One of the clips prompted this reaction from Rozana: 'brothers, with all due respect to our cultural heritage, I have to tell you that I had such a good laugh, better than watching comedy [. . .] maybe Romanian folklore has become too alien to me in the past few years (it's been nine years since I left Romania), but it looked strange and hilarious. Don't you think?' (Rozana, *România Italia Net*). Floricica was quick to qualify Rozana's comments: 'You were referring to one of the contemporary ones; I do not take those into consideration, these new groups are made on a production line, like sexy groups in pop. The old ones, on the other hand, had their individuality and were singing true folklore, not "popular music". Take for example Maria Lătăreţu'[14] (Floricica, *România Italia Net*).

Floricica mocked the new styles as populist, while seeing long-gone performers like Maria Lătăreţu (whose recordings are still popular) as the yardstick of true Romanian folklore. Rozana, on the other hand, responded with: 'We cannot make "pure" folklore anymore; we do not represent people between fifty and one hundred years old who lived through its "primordial" forms [. . .]; we are who we are, young people who were given an inheritance which we have adapted to our new culture. Any musical genre evolves' (Rozana, *România Italia Net*).

Rozana contradicts here her earlier comments, in which she laughed at the new folkloric hits, which she now sees as being part of an 'evolution'. This change of heart is not unusual online, where in the heat of the debate many views quickly change under the pressure to win the argument. It is not uncommon for migrants in particular, who often display the tension between a nostalgic attachment for a cultural continuity abruptly cut by emigration and the cosmopolitan and often fluid capital acquired through immigration. This exchange is also indicative of the clash between what is considered to be an intrinsic part of identity, which in the good nationalist tradition is seen as immutable, and the natural aspiration to see one's own culture validated on the global stage, a process that brings both losses and gains.

The exchange between Rozana and Floricica continued, with Floricica sticking to her guns and referring to the new styles and performers as a decline: 'But there's an involution here, sadly . . . if we are talking about contemporary folklore, we could also include *manele*,[15] if we can call that evolution.' To which Rozana replied: 'Let's call it metamorphosis!'

I will turn to *manele* in the final section of this chapter, not before making the observation that online we can see the makings of a diasporic community through both a return to a familiar, and much missed, cultural territory, but also through rejection, conflict, and negotiation. The exchange between Rozana and Floricica can be viewed as a *mêlée* between a traditionalist and a modernizer, the nostalgic immigrant and the transcultural diasporan, displaying the usual vacillation between quality versus populism, genuineness versus imperfect copies. However, this online discussion also manages to bring the participants together as a 'diaspora'. 'It's incredible how much I appreciate folkloric music in comparison to when I was still living in Romania [. . .] I'm about to burst into tears' (Rodica, *România Italia Net*), reflected one participant, while another added 'yes, to this music . . . I had forgotten many of these songs' (Alun, *România Italia Net*). Through the consumption of folklore, the Romanian diaspora activates a shared sense of what it means to be Romanian in the global world today.

As Romanians, participants show an unsurprising concern with the survival of historic traditional life, and especially authenticity and purity: 'If some listen to *manele*, each to their own, but I got really upset when an Italian girl told me what fun she had had at a party with "traditional Romanian music" which "resembles Oriental music"' (Rodica, *România Italia Net*). Rodica's irritation does not allow for the inherent inauthenticity of the Western gaze, though in other contexts, as we shall see in further examples, the Westernization and commodification of music is commended for its ability to promote and ensure cultural survival. In another thread belonging to the *Români în UK* forum, where participants swapped songs and poems that reminded them of home, Maria exclaimed: 'A true Romanian, great folklorist and one of the few who are still hoarding and treasuring the true values of the Romanian village today: Grigore Leşe!' (Maria, *Români în UK*). Maria posted a couple of video clips of Leşe, a doctor in music, an associate professor, and a trained musician, who sings folkloric songs collected from the northern region of Maramureş. He is offered as an example of a genuine music lover who 'rescues' authentic folklore that, as Maria alludes, may be in danger of being lost. It reiterates the idea that when it comes to folklore many diasporans cling to authenticity because folkloric music defines Romanianness.

Nonetheless, as diasporans, some participants also feel their identity to be defined by the distance from the homeland. One contributor wrote: 'If you want to post something about Romania, why are you posting music for slitting the veins? Are you truly trying to represent Romania's real image?' (Toni, *România Italia Net*). In this post identity is expressed through the typically diasporic love-hate for the mother country, and so Romanian-ness is defined by a diasporic, adaptive, and transnational viewpoint, which erodes nationalist fixities. Such online debates are thus illustrative of the philosophy of being, becoming and contestation that characterizes diasporic cultures. Particularly for a relatively young diasporic commu-nity like the Romanian one, which is still in the process of establishment and self-definition, it is useful to observe the various models for a work-able diasporic culture being proposed. Of course, the main model still sees diasporic culture as an extension of the national one, but cultural adapta-tion and translation through emigration-immigration also influences the formation of a new model, defined by the aspiration to escape the inflexible rigors of national culture and elaborate a more liquid alternative, typical for cosmopolitan diasporas. Traces of this new model can also be found in some of the following examples.

DIASPORIC SEESAW

Diasporic theory recognizes the dialectic of looking back and looking for-ward that shapes life after emigration. Spatial metaphors such as 'third space' (Bhabha 1994), 'in-between' culture (Bhabha 1996), 'double con-sciousness' (Du Bois in Gilroy 1993), 'perpendicular' worlds (Ignacio 2005), and 'place-polygamy' (Georgiou 2006) all evoke the difficulty of 'locat-ing' the diaspora. Much of the classic diasporic literature (Cohen 2008; Safran 1991) emphasizes the importance of the home and implicit nostalgia (looking back). However, my own online research proved that diasporas also display a complementary premise, under which diasporans embrace a *Heimat* of a different kind,[16] which emerges from their specific migratory experiences (the looking ahead part of the 'looking back–looking forward' dialectic). In the following section I will explore both tendencies, starting with the 'looking back' one.

Recuperating some elements of the past remains an important charac-teristic of life in the diaspora. Romanian migrants show a real need for accessing online the music of their original home. The convergence of web, radio, and print into one product easily available to audiences means that 'brand Romania' can be consumed in various guises. Since 2007 *Români Online UK* has had its own web radio, *Radio Români Online*.[17] Its mission is 'to fill the void felt by Romanians abroad.' This is achieved by offering 'select music and the feeling that wherever you are, you are not alone. [. . .] We promote quality Romanian music, Romanian ideas and values. Our playlist contains 80s and 90s hits, but also today's hits. 25% of the music is purely Romanian' (http://www.romani-online.co.uk/radio, accessed March 2, 2010).[18] A short sample I listened to on March 2, 2010, included Fine Young Cannibals, the Beatles, Narcisa Suciu (a Romanian folk singer), Faithless, P.M. Dawn, and Holograf, a Romanian rock group. Folk, rock, R&B, old and new, coexisted and made for an interesting mix, although at the time (I listened at lunchtime), the radio had only ten other online listeners. Other times, though, the station seems to be more popular, with listeners concomitantly listening to the web radio and posting comments in the online forum.

One listener acknowledged that Romanian music was a conduit for reliving a place and time preserved by memory: 'I am listening to Hruşcă and suddenly I am missing home' (Ionica, *Români Online UK*).[19] 'True, Christmas is not Christmas without Hruşcă's *colinde* [carols]. Missing the snow' (Olivia, *Români Online UK*). 'Compact . . . reminds me of my youth!' (Remus, *Români Online UK*).[20] On another website and thread, Rada reflected: 'I miss my parents . . . The song *Prayer for parents* was just on and nostalgia is flooding me . . . ☹' (Rada, *Români în UK*).[21] The feelings expressed here are encapsulated in the Romanian word *dor*. Derived from the Latin for 'pain', *dor* does not have an equivalent in other neo-Latin languages, apart from the Portuguese *ter saudades*, which uses different words to express a similar feeling. It is a singular concept that condenses nostalgia, desire, longing, and loss, a sense of missing something or someone, of being incomplete. Andrei, one of the most active participants in the *Români în UK* forum, wrote: 'There, the first emotions [. . .] Here, where from time to time you wish you were There [. . .] Here where year after year you become more and more the memory of the person you were There. Between Here and There there's all this *dor* and your life' (Andrei, *Români în UK*; capitals in the original). Posted not long before Christmas, these reflections were met with approbation: 'You found the right place and time to share all these with us, I can only thank you ☺' (Victor, *Români în UK*).

On *Români Online UK*, Lara posted the lyrics belonging to 'Colindul celui fără de ţară' (Carol for Those without a Country), sung by Tudor Gheorghe, a well-known folk singer and composer.[22] The gesture received much praise from Ionela, Călin, and especially Babu, who wrote: 'We have so many cultural and spiritual values. Here I am in danger of losing myself, caught in the routine of material gains' (*Români Online UK*). Lara too commented: 'I'm fed up with living among strangers [. . .] when I think about how I used to dream . . . how impossible getting here seemed . . . and now I can't wait to escape from this island. [...] I miss Romania every second... I would love to listen to Sofia Vicoveanca, Tudor Gheorghe, Zoia Alecu, Semnal M in my home. [...] I feel empty here' (*Români Online UK*).[23]

Lara mentions artists and bands belonging to various musical genres, from folklore to rock, popular in the 1980s and early 1990s, in an attempt to salvage some continuity with a familiar past. Living through adversity, as migrants do, it is not unusual to regress to times when social bonds and friendships were readily available and strong. Online, they are free to lose themselves in *dor*, although something always brings them back to the here and now. In this case Laur reminds them that nostalgic attachments are for a time and place that has not survived but in memory: 'That Romania that some still dream of ... with good memories and wonderful landscapes, idyllic ... does not exist anymore' (Laur, *Români Online UK*). The loss expressed in migrants' musical choices may come from the inability to adapt, in its turn brought about by the 'fierce' attachment to the past (Rushdie 2009). Equally, it may be a sign of renunciation, of acknowledging that the past survives only as reminiscence and in the sharing of memories. These feelings echo some of those that we have seen expressed in the exchange between Floricica and Rozana in the previous section. However, it is now time to transit from the past into the future, by showing that diasporas are also well placed to look forward and elaborate a new cosmopolitan *Heimat*, inherently inspired by diasporic experiences of adaptation and cultural reelaborations.

In February 2010 *Români în UK* featured the arrival of Romanian gangsta rapper Puya for his concert at the Starlight Club in London. The online news section featured more than 100 photographs from the concert, posted by the webmaster. In addition, a feature article discussed Puya's consumption of Romanian food and wine at the Romanian restaurant *Amurg* (Twilight) in Leyton. Audiences were thus able to overindulge in 'brand Romania', constructed as it was on the web, through stories and photographs from the club and restaurant, as well as through YouTube video clips and advertising inviting diasporans to purchase Romanian products.[24]

Two superimposed phenomena thus emerged. On the one hand, audiences were enticed with nostalgic attachments and feelings of homeness. On the other hand, the structures that supported their nostalgic indulgences were typically global: a diasporic website, radio, and newspaper; a club with Romanian imported performers and a diasporic audience; Romanian food eaten in London. They are all part of the transnational structures of diasporic production and consumption. Puya himself is a symbol of this superimposition: a Romanian who sings gangsta rap in London. The concomitant 'here' and 'there', 'now' and 'then' in diasporic theory, achieved with the help of spatial metaphors that best describe 'in-betweenness,' are also suggested by the comments posted by diasporans: 'This technology's great! I'm in Bucharest, listening to a GB radio' (Iurie, *Români Online UK*). Reflecting on the merits of *Radio Români Online*, with its mix of

Romanian and global music, old and new, Marius commented: 'This is the second song I'm listening to. I am waiting for one of ours ... Very, very nice!!!!!' (Marius, *Români Online UK*). 'I like it, but I would prefer Romanian music only' (Spiru, *Români Online UK*). The mixture of nostalgic reminiscence and firm anchoring in the realities of migration was summarized by the DJ: 'We are trying to warm up our hearts when we feel nostalgic, alone, disoriented, or maybe we are looking for new friends among a million horizons' (DJ Radio, *Români Online*).

Although these are cautious beginnings, Puya's event and its online mediatization indicate the elaboration of a diasporic cosmopolitanism, which signals a partial decoupling from national culture. Although diasporic culture emerges in relation to national culture, its new *Heimat* is anchored in multiple potentialities. In the final section, I aim to expand my reflections on the nature of this diasporic *Heimat*.

TRANSITIONS, TRANSLATIONS, ADAPTATIONS

Some diasporic websites, such as *e-muzica*[25] and *Forum Romania Inedit*,[26] are entirely dedicated to music. The latter displays a diverse menu, taking users on a journey that includes *manele*, folkloric music, Romanian, and international pop hits. Similarly, *Marea unire, Spania* publicized on several occasions the diasporic website *xcoryxchat*, which is dedicated to Romanian chat, 'sexy girls', 'cool boys', and 'good music'.[27] Most of the music is in fact hosted through another link by the *mykhayl84* site.[28] The menu is extensive: Romanian *Schlager* or pop,[29] R&B, rock, and dance music, but also Romanian Christmas carols, music *de inimă albastră*,[30] and *etno*.[31] Romanian clips are interspersed with international offerings. Ashanti and Ce'cile mix with Romanian *Schlager* singers popular in the communist era, like Corina Chiriac and Dan Spătaru. The Bangles feature on the same page as 50 Cent, Romanian dance singer Inna, and Dan Bălan, a Moldovan pop singer and songwriter. The website endeavors to cater to eclectic musical tastes. There are recommendations in the form of the 'clip of the day' and music tops. Users can search by genre or singer, but a continuous strip of miscellaneous clips is automatically offered.

Some diasporic websites specialize further, catering to the younger demographics, interested in the club scene. *Pagina Românilor din Barcelona* (The Online Page of Romanians in Barcelona) offers videos featuring disco/house Global Club gigs in Spain, but also Romanian dance clips, like *Nu* (No) by DJ Project featuring Giulia or *Samba* by Andreea Bănică featuring Dony.[32] The first is sung in Romanian, the second in English, with some interspersed Spanish. The Barcelona-based website is very similar to websites hosted in the US also dedicated to the Romanian club scene, like *RomNights, Romanian Nights in New York*,[33] and *RoNights, chefurile românești din Chicago* (Romanian parties in Chicago).[34]

A few websites, like *Italia România*, also dedicate entire sections in the forum to music-related discussions. Here, too, the choice is eclectic, reflecting various user interests. Romanian folklore chosen to induce a good time atmosphere blends with international music in the form of classic hits, new trends, and enticing video clips. Participants seem to be interested above all in quality and relevance. On one such thread, Floricica asked: 'What does GOOD music mean?' (emphasis in the original). Referring to singer Sophia,[35] Arina answered: 'It's subjective . . . if we invite a *manelist* [*manele* lover] here, he would post the best *manele* [. . .] this is an easy song with a nice tune, Occidental video clip and one of the few girls not singing in her knickers.' 'Has a voice,' Arina added (*România Italia Net*). Mentioning the group Urma,[36] Arina described them as 'one of the best Romanian groups, almost impeccable English and the lyrics at least mean SOMETHING' (*România Italia Net*, emphasis in the original).

While folklore is readily associated with identity and tradition, as we have seen, pop music is more difficult to interpret within the same paradigm. Participants are tempted to judge its quality according to Western standards. Many video clips are shot and produced according to Western criteria and the lyrics are sung in English, opening thus the door to global exposure. Romanianness needs to be adapted through Westernization in order to become attractive to the Western gaze and palatable to Western tastes. The music is packaged accordingly. Sophia's video, shot mainly in black-and-white contrasts, is reminiscent of Kate Bush or Madonna in her Frozen period. Urma's minimalist videos—smoky, sepia, playing with light and darkness—are much reminiscent of the 1990s MTV. The moody singing and the acoustic guitar loosely recall Badly Drawn Boy or David Gray. It is debatable whether this is a form of adaptation or mimetism, but participants do not seem to be concerned about issues of originality. On the contrary, they apply positive readings to what they see and hear, an indication that their taste is constructed from a Westernized and transnational viewpoint.

Another interesting example at the confluence between political transition, cultural adaptation, and global translation is the *manele* musical genre, already mentioned previously. The Romanian equivalent of *turbo folk* or *chalga*, popular throughout the Balkans (for a further discussion of this genre in other countries, see Buchanan 2007; Silverman 2012), is a post-communist hybrid of American hip-hop mixed with Turkish and Gypsy rhythms. *Manele* seem to baffle online diasporans, whose opinions are often divided.[37] This is clearly a culturally globalized product, yet it has also achieved national status. On the one hand, it is 'original', since it depicts a way of life and a value system characteristic of post-communist Romanian society. On the other hand, it is 'inauthentic,' because of its Oriental musical undertones and Roma associations. The genre was first promoted by Roma performers, like Adrian Minune (Adrian Wonder), but later embraced by Romanian singers, like Costi Ioniță, formerly with the pop boy band Valahia.[38]

Manele depict life after communism, the increasing importance of riches in a society obsessed with consumption and brands, the growth of a new social class (the *nouveau riche*), and the opportunity for escapism, through make believe. The repetitive but catchy melody is the carrier of stories about achievement and its palpable proof—the lifestyle, the girl, the luxury car, the jewelry, and the booze (preferably Western and thus expensive). *Manele* video clips are miniature soap operas that stem from former Eastern communist fantasies about Western opulence. They glamorize post-communist gangster lifestyles, which are far removed from the pains of the social transition. Music and partying thus become palliative devices.[39] The idealized exoticism and the success story contained within tell Romanians that if the Roma can make the transition from racialized underclass to successful *nouveau riche*, anybody can do it. In many ways *manele* provide a somewhat ironic and therefore postmodern commentary on social realities.

Though incredibly popular,[40] *manele* also elicit a strong elitist rejection based on the fear of kitsch saturation in a culture that seems, to many, to have lost its way. Being a *manelist* (a *manele* lover) has thus come to signify becoming part of 'anticulture', removed from mainstream and usual norms or tastes (I am appropriating here a term from Nettl 2006, 423). In a previous online discussion between Rozana and Floricica, we have seen that some diasporans comment, in fact, on the differences between true folklore and *manele*, good music and *manele*. Dismissal is also encouraged by widespread anti-Roma attitudes stemming from the difficulties of socially 'managing' the Roma community (Cesereanu 2003, 11).

A similar example is Romania's presence in the 2012 Eurovision Song Contest. Initially, Mandinga's *manele* inspired 'Zaleilah' received positive endorsements. However, when it only came in at number 12 in the final, both the press and viewers posting online accused it of being no more than 'kitsch', representing 'the Roma and the Romanian political class,' but not Romanian culture (www.hotnews.ro, accessed May 27, 2012).

Manele are a classic example of music that is constructed as different in order to maintain hierarchies of power (according to Nettl, following Derrida, 2006, 419–30).[41] Thus the success of *manele* (as guilty pleasure) has not led to improvements in the status of the Roma community or dismantled negative stereotypes, nor has the financial success of Roma *manele* performers affected positively the poverty in which most of the community lives.[42]

This does not stop the obsession with *manele* in popular discourse, in an attempt to ascertain their role in Romanian post-communist culture and identity. At the beginning of 2010, on the *România Italia Net* website, user Adi posted an assertion by Romanian's president, Traian Băsescu, according to whom *manele* is now a genre appreciated by the large majority of Romanians, proof that the social rejection of the Roma is no longer a reality. Quoting from a news story published by the Romanian news agency *Mediafax*, Adi positively referred to the comments of Nicolae Guţă, a Roma musician, who explained that more than 90 percent of Romanians now enjoy listening to *manele*, songs that may be written by Roma without education but that provide a reflection of daily life as it happens, in a language that people find accessible (http://www.mediafax.ro/life-inedit/nicolae-guta-cred-ca-domnul-presedinte-s-a-aliniat-majoritatii-5603433, accessed March 3, 2010). Through *manele*, the Roma, the suppressed and repeatedly racialized minority, have found a way into mainstream culture.

Nonetheless, the ethnic aspect of *manele* is causing unease, especially as because of the magnitude of *manele*'s popularity, they cannot be ignored, in the same way Gypsy music's contribution to Romanian folklore has been. The Roma have been constructed as quintessential musicians, which is the case for many ethnic minorities (Nettl 2005, 423), but their music has been subsumed into Romanian folklore to a certain extent. Still, music has provided the Roma with an acceptable status and the only public recognition available to them (see also Silverman's chapter in this volume). The president seemed to acknowledge that music could be integrative in minority–majority situations (Nettl 2006, 426), but the underlying debate and some of the comments made by diasporans online seem still to suggest that *manele* remain a type of 'deviant' music (to use Nettl's term) that puts the listener 'in league with the Devil' (Nettl 2006, 423). The following online post seems to suggest this.

'Do we equate ethnic music with *manele*, or does ethnic music have its own value and can be enjoyed as such?' asked Rodica, an immigrant in Italy (*România Italia Net*). She was reflecting on a news story about Nino D'Angelo's failure to qualify for the San Remo Song Festival in 2010. The Italian press had been speculating that his failure was due to D'Angelo singing in the Neapolitan dialect. Rodica was asking whether the *canzonetta napolitana* is a type of *manele* or not. Rodica's confusion is understandable in the Italian context, where people from the south are often stereotyped as lazier and worse educated but friendly and musically gifted. This replicates, to some extent, the situation of the Roma, who have historically been excluded from all levels of society, apart from the musical scene.[43] Rodica seemed to imply that the *canzonetta napolitana* is similar to *manele*, and therefore culturally irrelevant, unsuitable for a prestigious competition promoting 'national' music. Not wishing to speculate on the multifarious nature of Italian national identity and its tensions with equally strong regional identities, this online discussion thread alluded again to issues of quality and authenticity in national music.

If we return to the previously mentioned exchange between Rozana and Floricica and their implied question 'What is GOOD music?' we can attempt to provide the 'correct' (according to some diasporans) answer: 'An easy song, a nice tune, a Western video clip, a girl not singing in her knickers.' *Manele* are excluded from this classification. They may represent a form of glocalization best described as global provincialism, in that the local is displayed on the global stage, but only to limited and mostly

Romanian audiences, but audiences have ambivalent feelings about the ethnic and geographic origins of the genre. Because these audiences are diasporic, their frame for interpreting pecuniary and social success is the Western context in which they try to forge their existence. They do not warm up to music that draws inspiration from the tribulations and opportunities of the post-communist social transition (though some seem to appreciate the ironic commentary). Instead, their taste is forged by the need to conform to Western tastes, in the same way they have to mimic Western integration as immigrants. Westernized Romanian pop (both the sound and its aesthetics) is preferred because it tells of an existence amid multiple anchorings, in various cultural realities. It may not always appear so, but this phenomenon speaks of the attempt to look forward by integrating an already ambivalent national identity into a new life that is more liquid, cosmopolitan, and transnational.

CONCLUSION

Diasporic cosmopolitanism is rooted in the migrants' experiences as cultural insiders (Romanians who grew up with Romanian values, sounds, and styles), but also outsiders (removed from Romanian culture as it is presently lived and experienced by Romanians back home). Their views are instead influenced by another double positioning: as witnesses and participants in another Western culture, which nevertheless they experience as foreigners. As cultural insiders they reveal how Romanian culture sees itself (Nettl 2006, 153) while as cultural tourists they place themselves at the crossroads between *flânerie* and *chora* (Wearing, Stevenson, and Young 2010, 6–10), between being and becoming, distant gaze but also meaningful experience.

Positioning oneself across shifting spaces is not a particularly unique position, but now normal practice of globalization. Romanian diasporans express this liquidity (to use Bauman 2005) in complementary terms, by looking back towards tradition and authenticity, controversial concepts to interpret outside nation-state nationalism, and by looking forward, towards what comes after national culture, what comes after the 'loss'.

What comes after, from the point of view of diasporic culture, is a new *Heimat* that defies traditional understandings of homeness, with all its assumed fixity and permanence. It is a liquid cultural *Heimat*, stemming from the mobile condition of migrants who elaborate culture outside national confines making use of their 'transnational capital' (Meinhof and Tryandafillidou 2006). The unfixed nature of 'becoming' that defines diasporic practices enables migrants to continuously interrogate our understanding of tradition and authenticity in a globalized world. The loss suffered through emigration is thus supplanted by a gain in the form of cultural transitions, translations, and adaptations.

NOTES

1. The selection was based on key word searches and user recommendations, a commonly used method (Graham and Khosravi 2002; Hiller and Franz 2004; Siapera 2006) and included *Români în UK* (Romanians in the UK) and *Români Online UK* (Romanians Online UK); *Marea unire Spania* (Great Union Spain) and *Spania românească* (Romanian Spain); *România Italia Net* (Romania Italy net) and *Italia România* (Italy Romania).

2. The final sample amounted to hundreds of discussion threads.

3. Online pseudonyms are altered, but the name of the online community is mentioned and direct quotes are used. However, I left aside the titles of the discussion threads and the exact date of the exchanges to increase the 'cloaking'. My translation from Romanian further reduces the opportunity to trace the participants.

4. Moldova's entry in the Eurovision Song Contest in 2005, 'Grandma Is Playing the Drums', is a typical example of Westernization. The archetypal Romanian grandmother dressed in traditional costume is on the stage playing traditional drums. The folkloric tune kicks in midway supplanting the otherwise pop song. The band Zdob şi Zdub is dressed and acts like Aerosmith, with the exception of a traditionally inspired 'ethnic' pinny strategically placed.

5. In Romanian, folklore (*folclor*) denotes not just the music, but also the associated cultural practices like performance and dance, community events and religious fetes, traditional costumes and occupations. The more commonly used expression (for music alone) is 'popular music' (*muzică populară*). This is a genre associated with rural oral culture, often produced anonymously and transmitted through generations from musician to musician. Musicians perform in traditional costumes accompanied by traditional Romanian instruments (*nai* or panpipes; accordions; *ţambal*, a form of xylophone; *fluier*, a type of flute; *ceteră* or violin; *goarnă*, a type of bugle; *zongoră*, a type of guitar; and *dobă*, a percussion instrument. *Muzică populară* is different from 'folk music'. The term *folc* suggests in Romania a modern ballad usually sung by a singer/composer who accompanies herself with a guitar.

6. Etno TV specializes in Romanian folkloric music, while Taraf TV broadcasts mainly Romani music. They have the same owner. Favorit TV also specializes in folklore, but also hybrids (folklore and pop). There are additional locally based channels (e.g., Hora) broadcasting similar music: Romanian folklore, Gypsy music, and *manele* (for *manele*, see below).

7. In Romanian *baladă*, a poem or song with unknown authors, orally transmitted.

8. The short-lived Romanian boy trio O-zone, originally from the Republic of Moldova, whose hit *Dragostea din tei* (or Mai Ya Hee) was a global MTV and Eurochart Hot 100 success in 2004, is an example of this subgenre.

9. Most diasporic websites are based abroad; however, increasingly diasporic websites are set up in Romania, in order to capture a considerable diasporic audience and cater to its nostalgic attachment to the homeland.

10. The survival of these websites depends on diasporans returning to consume various diasporic 'products': music, language, companionship, shared experiences, and aspirations.

11. In this chapter I use the terms 'diasporan' and 'migrant' interchangeably. The Romanian diaspora is relatively young and the great majority of diasporans have experienced firsthand emigration and immigration. The newness of this community does not invalidate their presence and behavior as diaspora:

diasporans come together as a group to reconnect to familiar notions of Romanianness, but also elaborate new identities and new claims, within new symbolic cultural and political spaces.

12. *Trăieşte româneşte!* was set up with the aim to 'recreate virtually the Romania of the legends told by grandparents, of the inherited traditions, childhood holidays spent in the village, remembered dishes enjoyed with strong and aromatic beverages, the Romania of skilful craftsmen and ingenious inventors ... therefore an authentic Romania' (http://www.traiesteromaneste. ro/despre.php, accessed March 9, 2010). Such claims raise the issue of the relationship between virtual recreations of reminisced history and claimed 'authenticity'.

13. This is a perfect example of cultural globalization, if there ever was one: Traditional Romanian music, in its Westernized form, is called upon to musically illustrate Hollywood action movies inspired by Chinese *kung fu* and Japanese Samurai films. Not to mention that 'The Lonely Shepherd' was actually composed by a German calling himself James Last (not his real name).

14. Maria Lătăreţu is a folkloric singer, part of the great generation of artists in the first half of the 20th century that made folkloric music accessible through recordings.

15. Romanian *turbo-folk. Manele* is the plural and it is generally how this genre is known. The singular is *manea*, but this is rarely used.

16. I use the word *Heimat* to talk about a homeland with porous boundaries, continually being remade in the image of multiple and concomitant departures, journeys, and settlements. As far as homelands go, this one is symbolic, imbued with the power of imagination and longing for a safe and illusory home.

17. See http://www.romani-online.co.uk/radio (accessed March 2, 2010).

18. What can percentages say about musical tastes and musical consumption? Initially, 25 percent output set aside for 'purely Romanian' music may seem slim for a diasporic website; however, we have to understand nostalgia as only a facet of diasporic expression. Even more than non-diasporic audiences, diasporas naturally acquire eclectic tastes. Though they might turn to diasporic radio to taste 'home' primarily, it is only natural that homeness soon makes way for diversity.

19. Romanian folk singer, popular in the 1980s and 1990s, who also recorded traditional Christmas carols.

20. Romanian rock band very popular in the 1980s.

21. One of Hruşcă's best-known songs.

22. The lyrics are by Adrian Păunescu, Nicolae Ceauşescu's court poet and left-wing nationalist politician in the post-communist period, but the online participants seem to extract relevance from the performance, not the ideological implications, which are simply ignored.

23. Sofia Vicoveanca is a folkloric singer; Zoia Alecu is a Romanian folk singer and composer; Semnal M is a rock band established in 1977.

24. This website also has a web radio, *Radio Ciocârlia* (Skylark, named after a popular folkloric song).

25. See http://www.e-muzica.net/ (accessed March 2, 2010).

26. See http://romania-inedit.3xforum.ro/ (accessed March 2, 2010).

27. See http://www.xcoryxchat.com/ (accessed March 2, 2010).

28. See http://www.mykhayl84.com/ (accessed March 2, 2010).

29. Not much different from the 'ballads' one often hears in the Eurovision Song Contest.

30. This Romanian genre is dedicated to aching or longing 'blue hearts'. It resembles *chansonette*-style music.
31. *Etno* is Romanian folkloric music turned into dance music with techno overtones (the group Ro-mania) or techno music, which incorporates folkloric sounds or traditional instruments (the group Akcent).
32. See http://romanii.ning.com/ (accessed March 2, 2010).
33. See http://www.romnights.com/ (accessed March 17, 2010).
34. See http://www.ronights.com/ (accessed March 17, 2010).
35. Former participant in the 2009 Romanian Eurovision preselection.
36. Romanian alternative band.
37. Recently I have come across the word *manelizare* (manelization) in the Romanian press. It seems to describe the phenomenon of dumbing down, of poor quality, disorganized or Balkanized. *Manele* seem to be considered an inferior type of music, but altogether accepted as a by-product of both the region's multiculturalism and its post-communist political context.
38. Non-Romani musicians have colonized the genre, once it became popular and thus lucrative.
39. See, for example, *Chef de chef*, sung by Adrian Minune (available on YouTube at http://www.youtube.com/watch?v=DMEbr8v8PXI , accessed January 9, 2013) *Chef the chef* is a popular slang expression, coined in recent years. It can be loosely translated as 'in the mood for partying' or 'partying to party' and it is to be found on many diasporic websites catering for younger demographics like *RomNights, Romanian nights in New York, RoNights, chefurile românești din Chicago*, and *Români în UK*. In the context of the recommended video clip, it signifies the fun-loving aspect of Roma culture, which is to some extent an internalized cliché.
40. A trip to the market would be accompanied by the familiar sounds of *manele*, the latest hits being available for purchase, together with free-range eggs and organically grown vegetables.
41. It should be noted that *manele* are sung from an exclusively male perspective and both the lyrics and video clips are incredibly sexist.
42. However, *manele* success has translated into increased visibility for the minority. It may not transform marginality into resistance, contestation, and empowerment (Huggan 2001, 20), but it may offer Roma musicians a platform for future political negotiations.
43. The widespread belief is that the Roma are lazy but musically talented and therefore becoming a musician is possibly the only acceptable career available to them.

REFERENCES

Andreescu, Gabriel. 1996. *Naționaliști și antinaționaliști . . . O polemică în publicistica românească*. Iași: Polirom.
Bauman, Zygmund. 2005. *Liquid Life*. Cambridge: Polity.
Bhabha, Homi K. 1994. *The Location of Culture*. London: Routledge.
Bhabha, Homi K. 1996. 'Culture's In-Between.' In *Questions of Cultural Identity*, edited by Stuart Hall and Paul du Gay, 53–60. London: Sage.
Blaga, Lucian. 1994. *Spațiul mioritic*. Bucharest: Humanitas.
Boia, Lucian. 1997. *Istorie și mit în conștiința românească*. Bucharest: Humanitas.
Boia, Lucian. 2001. *Romania*. London: Reaktion Books.

Boia, Lucian. 2002. *Jocul cu trecutul. Istoria între adevăr și ficțiune.* Bucharest: Humanitas: Bucharest.

Buchanan, Donna A. 2007. *Balkan Popular Culture and the Ottoman Ecumene: Music, Image, and Regional Political Discourse.* Lanham, MD: Scarecrow Press.

Cesereanu, Ruxandra. 2003. *Imaginarul violent al Românilor.* Bucharest: Humanitas.

Cohen, Robin. 2008. *Global Diasporas. An Introduction.* London: Routledge.

Connell, John, and Chris Gibson. 2003. *Sound Tracks: Popular Music Identity and Place.* London: Routledge.

Frith, Simon. 1996. 'Music and Identity.' In *Questions of Cultural Identity*, edited by Stuart Hall and Paul du Gay, 108–27. London: Sage.

Gaiser, Ted J., and Anthony E. Schreiner. 2009. *A Guide to Conducting Online Research.* London: Sage.

Georgiou, Myria. 2006. *Diaspora, Identity and the Media. Diasporic Transnationalism and Mediated Spatialities.* Cresskill, NJ: Hampton Press.

Gilroy, Paul. 1993. *The Black Atlantic. Modernity and Double Consciousness.* London: Verso.

Graham, Mark, and Shakram Khosravi. 2002. 'Reordering Public and Private in Iranian Cyberspace: Identity, Politics and Mobilization.' *Identities: Global Studies in Culture and Power* 9(2):219–46.

Hiller, Harry H., and Tara M. Franz. 2004. 'New Ties, Old Ties and Lost Ties: The Use of the Internet in Diaspora.' *New Media and Society* 6(6):731–52.

Huggan, Graham. 2001. *The Postcolonial Exotic: Marketing the Margins.* London: Routledge.

Ignacio, Emily N. 2005. *Building Diaspora. Filipino Cultural Community Formation on the Internet.* New Brunswick, NJ: Rutgers University Press.

Kozinets, Robert V. 2010. *Netnography: Doing Ethnographic Research Online.* London: Sage.

Manuel, Peter. 1988. *Popular Musics of the Non-Western World: An Introductory Survey.* Oxford: Oxford University Press.

Meinhof, Ulrike H., and Anna Triandafyllidou, eds. 2006. *Transcultural Europe. Cultural Policy in a Changing Europe.* Basingstoke: Palgrave Macmillan.

Mungiu-Pippidi, Adriana. 2002. *Politica după communism.* Bucharest: Humanitas.

Nedelcu, Mihaela. 2009. *Le migrant online. Nouveaux Modèles Migratoires à l'ère du Numérique.* Paris: L'Harmattan.

Nettl, Bruno. 2006. *The Study of Ethnomusicology: Thirty-One Issues and Concepts.* Baltimore: University of Illinois Press.

Noica, Constantin. 1996. *Sentimentul românesc al ființei.* Bucharest: Humanitas.

Rushdie, Salman. 2009. 'A Fine Pickle.' *Guardian Review*, February 28.

Safran, William. 1991. 'Diasporas in Modern Societies: Myths of Homeland and Return.' *Diaspora* 1(1):83–99.

Siapera, Eugenia. 2006. 'Multiculturalism Online. The Internet and the Dilemmas of Multicultural Politics.' *Cultural Studies* 9(1):5–24.

Silverman, Carol. 2012. *Romani Routes. Cultural Politics and Balkan Music in Diaspora.* Oxford: Oxford University Press.

Tismăneanu, Vladimir. 1999. *Fantasmele salvării. Democrație, naționalism și mit în Europa post-comunistă.* Iași: Polirom.

Trandafoiu, Ruxandra. 2013. *Diaspora Online. Identity Politics and Romanian Migrants.* Oxford: Berghahn.

Wearing, Stephen, Deborah Stevenson, and Tamara Young. 2010. *Tourist Cultures: Identity, Place and the Traveller.* London: Sage.

Wolff, Larry. 2000. *Inventarea Europei de Est. Harta civilizației în epoca luminilor.* Bucharest: Humanitas.

WEBSITES

e-muzica: http://www.e-muzica.net/, accessed March 2, 2010.
Forum Romania Inedit: http://romania-inedit.3xforum.ro/, accessed March 2, 2010.
Italia România: http://www.italiaromania.com/, accessed January 9, 2013.
Marea unire, Spania: http://www.mareaunire.com/spania/, accessed January 9, 2013.
Mediafax: http://www.mediafax.ro/, accessed January 9, 2013.
mykhayl84: http://www.mykhayl84.com/, accessed March 2, 2010.
Pagina Românilor din Barcelona: http://www.romaniadinbarcelona.es/2012/03/inceput-emisia-radio-buzz-radioul.html, accessed January 9, 2013.
Români în UK: http://romani.co.uk/, accessed January 9, 2013.
România Italia Net: http://romaniaitalia.net/, accessed March 2, 2010.
Români Online UK: http://www.romani-online.co.uk , accessed January 9, 2013.
RomNights, Romanian nights in New York: http://www.romnights.com/, accessed March 17, 2010.
RoNights, chefurile româneşti din Chicago: http://www.ronights.com/, accessed March 17, 2010.
Spania Românească: http://www.spaniaromaneasca.com/, accessed January 9, 2013.
Trăieşte româneşte!: http://www.traiesteromaneste.ro/, accessed January 9, 2013.
UNESCO: http://www.unesco.org/new/en/, accessed January 9, 2013.
Xcoryxchat: http://www.xcoryxchat.com/, accessed March 2, 2010.

Afterword

Identities and Tourisms in Globalized Neoliberal Capitalism

Timothy D. Taylor

This interesting and provocative volume could just as accurately be titled *Identities in Transit* given the ubiquity of the theme of identity, which appears in almost all the chapters in one way or another.

So, let's talk about identity. As Timothy Rice has noted (2007), identity has exploded as a theme in the ethnomusicological literature in the last few decades (at least as represented in the journal *Ethnomusicology*, the focus of his study), though it has scarcely been treated theoretically or reflexively. But even without Rice's careful study, anecdotally, it is just as clear that identity has become perhaps the main theme in a wide range of writings by people in all corners of music studies and beyond. Professional meetings offer papers on it, graduate and undergraduate term papers tackle it, dissertations thematize it. And so do countless articles and books such as this one.

The problem is, identity is almost never theorized (although it could be, and has been by many people outside of music studies, e.g., Castells 1997; Friedman 1994; Giddens 1991; McCracken 1997, 2008; and many others). Identity is a concept that is used to explain people's behavior, and is rarely analyzed itself. But to say that a particular social actor or social group does something because of his/her/their identity explains very little, unless identity is theorized and situated in the history and culture and social world of the social actor(s) involved. That is to say, to invoke 'identity' is not the same thing as offering an explanation of something; it is a placeholder for an explanation, and as such needs to be put into productive dialogue with the history and culture of the social actors whose identity-making practices are the subject of analysis.

Accordingly, let me ask, where does our—and I include myself—where does our concern for identity come from? It seems to me that our interest in identity, and that of our subjects (when they mention it), is a symptom of today's neoliberal capitalism, not a natural category. That is, our concern for our ethnographic subjects' or interlocutors' 'identity' is really our concern for our own identity, a concern that we frequently project onto those we study.

Let me talk about this concern. For centuries, Western culture has possessed a notion of a unique, autonomous self, whether stemming from

René Descartes or another Enlightenment thinker. Of course, in the grand scheme of things, few people actually read (or read) Descartes, but that doesn't mean that high philosophical ideas didn't gain traction in the culture more generally, or (more correctly, I think) that Descartes's and others' ideas about selfhood were symptoms rather than causes of broader shifts in Western culture as a result of the rise of capitalism, Protestantism, literacy, and other such historical transformations that slowly emphasized the importance of the individual over the group, paving the way for our current fascination for identity.

At the same time, however, there have been what one could call 'folk' conceptions of selfhood that have operated alongside this 'higher', more philosophical and abstract conception of the autonomous subject. In the US, for example, the dominant folk conception during the Victorian era was 'character'—it was the possession of character, in whatever degree, that defined the individual. Warren Susman has written interestingly and influentially of how, in the early 20th century, conceptions of character began to give way to a notion of 'personality'. The self was something that could be worked on using self-help books, books that were supposed to help one improve one's personality (Susman 1984). This conception lasted at least until the 1970s.

Today, the dominant folk conception is identity, and, like its predecessor, it is something that our culture believes can be made, worked on. More than that, it can be constructed, chosen, even consumed. Anthropologist Grant McCracken has written of the explosion of self-conceptions in the last few decades. He examines the personal ads in the *Village Voice* and notices how much more complex they became, with 'woman seeking man' eclipsed by terms such as 'BiSWM', 'Pre-op TS', and more (McCracken 1997, 33). Similarly, I remember the rise of queer theory and gay and lesbian studies, which then became LGB studies, which then became LGBT studies, which then became LGBTQ studies, which then became LGBTQI studies.

In a later book, McCracken (2008) calls this sort of thing an 'expansionary individualism'. That is, it is commonplace in Western culture today for individual subjects to define themselves not only in more complex ways than in the past, but in more numerous ways, with 'identity' as the main descriptive ideology of this expansionary individualism. McCracken doesn't make a point about the consumption of other identities (which is odd, given his influential work on the subject of consumption), but I would certainly make the point that part of the reason for the proliferation of possible identities is that, like everything else, they are available to be consumed: One can consume different sorts of clothes and try on being part of a different subculture or social group, listen to different music, eat different cuisines, and so forth.

As I say, these are *our* conceptions of identity, those of us in the global North. But they, like many other ideologies from here, have traveled. Identity—whether individual (Pravaz), national (Oldfield, Trandafoiu), national-cultural

(Cohen and Roberts), social (Carl), ethnic (Amico, Silverman), local (Connell and Gibson, Krüger), musical (Muir), or more—is a powerful concept. It can feel liberating since, as I will discuss in a moment, it is something that can be worked on, perfected. But it can also be divisive, separating us from others with whom we might have something else in common.

Here it would probably be useful to say something about positionality and identity, for they are often confused, or conflated. I would argue (as I have elsewhere, in Taylor, forthcoming) simply that positionality makes us, but we make identity. That is, if one is, say, a lower-middle-class, small-town Midwestern Irish (Protestant)/Swedish American straight male born in the 1960s (me), all of these things, to a large extent, make me who I am, even though today I am an upper-middle-class urban professional. It is perfectly possible that I could choose a particular positionality to work on, to make: I could take up, say, Irish traditional music as a way of getting in touch with my ethnic roots, or hanging out with other Irish and Irish Americans. And, after living in Northern Ireland, the land of my father's forebears as a fellowship/exchange student at Queen's University of Belfast in the late 1980s, I did.

There are many chapters in this volume that raise the specter of identity and it's now time to consider them. I will sort them by type as a modest beginning to what I hope will be a contribution to deepening the theorization of identity through ethnography. I would first propose that we understand conceptions of identity as additive (as does McCracken 2008): An older form, such as national identity, does not disappear as newer forms such as individual or personal identity emerge. And, as some of these chapters show, identity-forms such as national identity can take on a new life or urgency as empires fall and/or as national boundaries are redrawn. And national or other group identity-forms can become personalized, individualized, through diasporic or other experiences.

On to the chapters collected in this volume. The first I'll mention tackles the question of positionality. Jonathan McIntosh's useful contribution on tourism and child performers in Bali draws on Dean MacCannell's classic work on tourism to chronicle his own shifting positionality from a tourist to ethnographer with access to the 'backstage' lives of child performers.

Anna Oldfield's contribution tackles the complex problem of national or cultural identity in a postimperial nation, in this case, Azerbaijan, showing that in today's neoliberalizing world, something as seemingly straightforward as 'national' identity might be a historical relic, for this identity today is too easily caught up in others. The problem of identity in Oldfield's case is made even more complex by the fact that the Republic of Azerbaijan, like many, contains different ethnic groups, so there are many tensions over which cultural forms will be permitted to represent the nation. Oldfield writes of the *ashiq* tradition of music and storytelling, which serves that role, even during the Soviet period when stories told reflected the Soviet celebration of the worker. *Ashiq* practitioners, writes Oldfield, were able through their traveling to celebrate the locality of their tradition even while spreading it throughout the nation, which, she writes, offers a different model of a national cultural symbol than the (Benedict Andersonian) norm of imagined communities through national publications.

A couple of chapters considers the question of identity in diaspora. Ruxandra Trandafoiu's chapter addresses the use of websites devoted to music that help diasporic Romanians maintain contact with home. 'Romanianness' itself is not a monolithic idea, as she points out, and thus, constructing it while abroad is not a straightforward endeavor, with long-standing debates between 'traditionalists and modernizers, nationalists and Europeanists', debates that continue online among diasporic Romanians. And, Trandafoiu writes, being a diasporic subject also contributes to these Romanians' complex of identities.

Another study of a diaspora, Florian Carl's contribution on music and the Ghanaian diaspora in Germany, argues that German-Ghanaians' participation in music 'constitutes an integral part of the negotiation of social identity', which is also a status game. Diasporic Ghanaians can accumulate a form of capital by becoming an immigrant, which results in greater economic capital, creating respect at home. Status, it seems, is all about money; as one of Carl's interlocutors said, 'Money is what constitutes a man. If you have little money in this world, your word counts little.'

Carol Silverman's chapter doesn't much consider identity, though there are plenty of notions of selfhood circulating in it that are worth commenting on in my continuing consideration of identity as it runs through the book. To begin, there is the question of 'authentic' Roma music, 'hybrid' Roma music, and those who 'pass' as Roma but who actually aren't. Silverman's discussion of hybridity draws on John Hutnyk's (2000) useful work, in which he argues that the concept of hybridity is a marketing term used to promote world music. True enough, but that is not all the work that the concept of hybridity does, for, as I have written elsewhere (Taylor 2007), hybridity is a softer, gentler way of marketing Otherness to western consumers who might find more 'authentic' musics too exotic, too foreign (Silverman comes to this conclusion later). 'Gypsies' are destigmatized to some extent through hearings of their music as 'hybrid', which might explain why some of the most famous Roma musicians (e.g., Goran Bregović) who are not Roma at all have been willing to pass as Roma. Silverman's chapter shows how complexly positionality (as Roma) and identity (as a Roma positing a public self, or a 'Gypsy') can become intertwined, and how processes of the commodification and circulation of music can dislodge a particular identity-form, making it available for others to adopt.

Unique among these chapters is Marta Amico's contribution, which discusses both Tuareg identity and that of tourists who visit the annual Festival au Désert in Mali. Tuaregs stage aspects of their culture in ways that are not always true to that culture but that satisfy tourists seeking to see and hear authentic Tuareg music and culture in the Sahara. Amico carefully constructs a reciprocal model of complex dialogical encounters between Tuareg people and Western tourists, each of whom accomplishes some identity-work in the process: The 'Tuareg culture' displayed at the festival 'is dialogically built through an interactive game engaging the festival actors (musicians, audience, organizers, local and national institutions, journalists) in specific cultural and identities and contexts.' Tuaregs are agents in their own representations, which contributes to their display of Tuareg identity, a display to which tourists (whose conceptions of identity aren't really addressed in this chapter), presumably seeking experiences of others' identities, seek to consume as a way of defining themselves by travel and the consumption of cultural commodities such as world music.

John Connell and Chris Gibson describe a much different presentation of local conceptions of identity in their chapter on a small-city music festival in Australia. Such festivals seem to be more common in Europe and Australia than the US, which means that communities that host festivals in Australia and elsewhere must create a branded identity in order to attract tourists and festival participants. This created some tension, as Connell and Gibson relate, between people of different class positionalities—farming and rural versus more cosmopolitan and urban, a positionality held by transplants. The latter was allowed to adopt its conception of the festival town's identity in order to attract tourists. Connell and Gibson's story shows how a town's changing sense of itself slowly becomes imbricated in residents' conceptions of their identity as small-town but cosmopolitan Australians in Bermagui.

Probably the most problematic form of 'identity' that I regularly encounter is the concept of 'musical identity', problematic because for virtually everyone in the so-called developed countries, music is an object of consumption. One fashions oneself in part with what one consumes; if one accepts that there is such a thing as 'musical identity', then one must also consider, say, sneaker identity, haircut identity, clothing identity, cell phone identity, and so forth. If the object of study is musicians who are in the midst of choosing a style or styles of music to perform, then we are in the realm of a field of cultural production in which musicians (or other cultural producers) are choosing what positions to take in a field of possibles (Bourdieu 1993). Stephen Muir's discussion of the Jewish community in Cape Town, South Africa, particularly the Marais Road congregation, shows how this group adopts various popular music styles for its own use, then through YouTube sends their versions back out to the world. Muir shows how diasporic Jews negotiate musics and each others' positionalities.

Last, I will consider the question of individual identity fashioning among cosmopolitan urbanites. Natasha Pravaz's consideration of individual identity describes what is by now a fairly commonplace occurrence: urban cosmopolitans partaking in music and dance activities that originate with an ethnic group other than their own. Pravaz supposes that Torontonians who play Brazilian music 'experience relief from their own presentation of everyday self by trying on another self-presentation through the identification of a different identity projected by music.' While I wouldn't agree that music 'projects' identity, or that these Canadians are necessarily trying on different selves, I do agree that the participation in various activities, musical or otherwise, can shape one's perception of oneself and become an important component of one's self-identity. The affective, and, in some cases, as Pravaz discusses, political relationship that one can form with a particular cultural activity can be quite powerful.

It may seem that the other main theme that emerges from this book, tourism, is far from the question of identity. But we have already seen how in a few cases, especially Amico's chapter, and Connell and Gibson's contribution, that identity making and identity consuming are deeply caught up in touristic practices; and other chapters show how tourism and conceptions of identity are intertwined. Further, if we understand concerns over identity not to be 'natural', but cultural, and that they have a history, we can see that the rise of concerns for identity occurred at the same moment of the rise of neoliberal capitalism and the shift toward postmodernity, or whatever one would like to label the ramifications of this shift in terms of cultural production. Scott Lash and John Urry (1994) have usefully argued for the importance of tourism in Western culture, even suggesting that the capitalism of the 20th century commonly referred to as 'Fordism' would be better described as 'Cookism' for Thomas Cook, the 19th-century British travel agent (Lash and Urry 1994, 261).

Sara Cohen and Les Roberts's chapter visits London and the UK not just as sites where tourists pay homage to the Beatles, but as part of a nation-wide campaign to attract tourists to music sites in Great Britain, capitalizing on perceptions of the UK as a major producer of important musicians. They also note, interestingly, the new Conservative government's emphasis on the importance of tourism to the UK economy. They conclude that the web-based interactive and smartphone maps produced for tourists in some sense 'perform' the nation as well as rehearsing or characterizing the state of the nation as a way of producing a national-cultural identity.

Coeditor Simone Krüger's chapter on the touristification of Liverpool offers a useful case study of how a medium-size city, once a major imperial centre, rebrands itself as a musical city worthy of fans' pilgrimages. This contribution is particularly illuminating for it shows the central role that branding has assumed in today's neoliberal capitalism, a role that uses every tool in the advertiser and marketer's handbook to infiltrate products into consumers' consciousnesses so that those products take on the personal qualities of an old friend. Branding has become a potent means of selling, a powerful way that today's capitalism can wrap itself in the culture in order to infiltrate the culture ever more effectively (see Banet-Weiser 2012; Lash and Lury 2007; Lury 2004; and Taylor, forthcoming).

It was good to revisit the Goa or psytrance scene in Graham St John's chapter, since I studied this scene in 1999 in New York City (Taylor 2001). St John's chapter perhaps best represents the extremely complex ways that tourism and identity-making or identity-supporting activities can contribute to each other. Global flows of music can encourage tourism, at least to Goa (and the Sahara and Bermagui and, of course, many other places). This music, which has engendered scenes all over the world, not just in Goa, has inspired what St John calls a 'traveler dance music culture'. Through drugs and music, Goa/psytrance events (or 'parties' as they were known in New York City when I did my research), 'evolved as an epic journey in an exotic location removed from routine domestic life,' writes St John—traveling without going away.

David Cashman and Philip Hayward's chapter examines music on cruise ships, providing a useful overview of the industry and the role played by music on cruise ships, which is partly about entertainment, partly about controlling passengers' interactions with the world outside the ship, and partly about encouraging passengers to consume more. These travelers do go away, though their encounters with potential Others is carefully controlled.

Taken as a whole, these richly ethnographic chapters demonstrate in various ways the complexity of 'identity', the complicated contestations over it, and fabrications of it, as well as the ways that various identity-forms can conflict or coexist or overlap. 'Identity' has become a commonplace discourse, so commonplace that it all too frequently has escaped critical attention. These chapters usefully help bring questions of identity—and tourism—to the fore in ways that identity, and ways of being a touristic subject, have proliferated in today's neoliberal capitalist world.

REFERENCES

Banet-Weiser, S. 2012. *Authentic™: The Politics of Ambivalence in a Brand Culture*. New York: New York University Press.

Bourdieu, Pierre. 1993. *The Field of Cultural Production*. Edited by Randal Johnson. New York: Columbia University Press.

Brubaker, Rogers, and Frederick Cooper. 2005. 'Identity.' In *Frederick Cooper, Colonialism in Question: Theory, Knowledge, History*. Berkeley: University of California Press.

Castells, Manuel. 1997. *The Power of Identity*. Volume 2. *The Information Age: Economy, Society and Culture*. Malden, MA: Blackwell.

Friedman, Jonathan, ed. 1994. *Consumption and Identity*. Chur, Switzerland: Harwood Academic Publishers.

Giddens, Anthony. 1991. *Modernity and Self-Identity: Self and Society in the Late Modern Age*. Stanford: Stanford University Press.

Hutnyk, John. 2000. *Critique of Exotica: Music, Politics, and the Culture Industry*. London: Pluto.

Lash, Scott, and Celia Lury. 2007. *Global Cultural Industry: The Mediation of Things*. Malden, MA: Polity.

Lash, Scott, and John Urry. 1994. *Economies of Signs and Space*. Newbury Park, CA: Sage.

Lury, Celia. 2004. *Brands: The Logos of the Global Economy*. Abingdon, UK: Routledge.

McCracken, Grant. 1997. *Plenitude*. Toronto: Periph.: Fluide.

McCracken, Grant. 2008. *Transformations: Identity Construction in Contemporary Culture*. Bloomington: Indiana University Press.

Rice, Timothy. 2007. 'Reflections on Music and Identity.' *Musicology* 7:17–38.

Susman, Warren I. 1984. *Culture as History: The Transformation of American Society in the Twentieth Century*. New York: Pantheon.

Taylor, Timothy D. 2001. *Strange Sounds: Music, Technology and Culture*. New York: Routledge.

Taylor, Timothy D. 2007. *Beyond Exoticism: Western Music and the World*. Durham, NC: Duke University Press.

Taylor, Timothy D. Forthcoming. *Commercializing Culture: Capitalism, Music, and Social Theory after Adorno*. Chicago: University of Chicago Press.

Contributors

Marta Amico holds a PhD in Anthropology and Music at the École des Hautes Études en Sciences Sociales, Paris, France. Her PhD research focuses on the new expressions of Tuareg music on the world music scene, examining the impact of music on the changing meaning of identity, territory, and performance. She has presented papers on Tuareg music, cultural staging, and ritual at conferences in France, Germany, Portugal, Switzerland, Italy, and the United Kingdom. She is also a violinist.

Florian Carl is a Senior Lecturer in the Department of Music and Dance at the University of Cape Coast, Ghana. He studied ethnomusicology at the University of Cologne, Germany, and the University of Chicago, and received his PhD from the University of Music, Drama, and Media Hanover, Germany. He is author of *Was Bedeutet uns Afrika? Zur Darstellung Afrikanischer Musik im Deutschsprachigen Diskurs des 19. und frühen 20. Jahrhunderts* [What Does Africa Mean to Us? On the Representation of African Music in German Literature of the 19th and Early 20th Century] (LIT 2004) and *Berlin/Accra. Music, Travel, and the Production of Space* (LIT 2009). An article on 'The Representation and Performance of African Music in German Popular Culture' appeared in the *Yearbook for Traditional Music* 43 (2011). His major research interest currently is in music and popular culture in Ghana and its diaspora.

David Cashman is an Adjunct Senior Lecturer at Southern Cross University. He has an ongoing research interest in music on passenger shipping and other research interests that include popular music studies and music and fashion. David worked as a pianist on cruise ships between 2004 and 2007, and performs and records still in Sydney.

Sara Cohen is a Professor at the School of Music at the University of Liverpool and Director of the Institute of Popular Music. She has a DPhil in Social Anthropology from Oxford University and is author of *Rock Culture in Liverpool: Popular Music in the Making* (Oxford University

Press 1991) and *Decline, Renewal and the City in Popular Music Culture: Beyond The Beatles* (Ashgate 2007).

John Connell is a Professor of Human Geography in the School of Geosciences, University of Sydney. He has written three books on geography, music, festivals, and tourism, all jointly with Chris Gibson, and more than 20 other books, mainly on development issues in small island states. These include *The Last Colonies* (with R. Aldrich, Cambridge 1998); *Urbanisation in the Island Pacific. Towards Sustainable Development* (with J. Lea, Routledge 2002); *The Global Health Care Chain. From the Pacific to the World* (Routledge 2009); *Migration and the Globalisation of Health Care* (Edward Elgar 2010); *Medical Tourism* (CABI 2011); and *Islands at Risk* (Edward Elgar 2013). When he is not engaged in these loosely academic activities, he plays football in the Eastern Suburbs (Sydney) Over 45s League—without great success.

Chris Gibson is a Professor of Human Geography at the University of Wollongong. He holds a BA (hons) and PhD in Geography from the University of Sydney. His books include *Sound Tracks: Popular Music, Identity and Place* (Routledge 2003), *Music and Tourism* (Channel View 2005), and *Music Festivals and Regional Development in Australia* (Ashgate 2012), all cowritten with John Connell, and *Deadly Sounds, Deadly Places: Contemporary Aboriginal Music in Australia* (UNSW Press 2004), cowritten with Peter Dunbar-Hall. His most recent edited collection is *Creativity in Peripheral Places: Redefining the Creative Industries* (Routledge 2012).

Philip Hayward is Deputy Pro Vice Chancellor (Research) at Southern Cross University and an active researcher in Island Studies. He is coeditor of *Shima: The International Journal of Research into Island Cultures* and is also international network convenor of *SICRI: The Small Island Cultures Research Initiative*. He has published books, journal articles, and book chapters on various aspects of island cultures, and he has ongoing research projects in the Amami and Tokara islands of southern Japan and in the southeastern Pacific. Professor Hayward has previously received two Australia Research Council Discovery grants and is a Chief Investigator on an ARC Collaborative Grant team led by Professor Huib Schippers (Griffith University Conservatorium of Music) researching Sustainable Musical Futures (2009–2014). His most recent research has concerned tourism and local culture in Hainan Island, China (fieldwork undertaken in April 2009) and on tourism, local culture, and salmon aquaculture on Chiloe Island, Chile (fieldwork undertaken in January 2010). Outside of academe, he is actively involved in rainforest reforestation in the Northern Rivers area of northern New South Wales.

Simone Krüger is a Programme Leader in Popular Music Studies at Liverpool John Moores University, UK, with research interests in ethnomusicology and world music pedagogy, music education (ethnography education and employability), popular music and cultural studies, globalization, and the music of Paraguay. She is the author of *Experiencing Ethnomusicology: Teaching and Learning in European Universities* (Ashgate 2009) and *Popular Musics in World Perspective* (Polity forthcoming), guest editor of *Ethnomusicology in the Academy: International Perspectives* (*The World of Music* 2009), coeditor of *Ethnomusicology Forum* (Routledge), and editor of the *Journal of World Popular Music* (Equinox).

Jonathan McIntosh is an Assistant Professor of Ethnomusicology in the School of Music at The University of Western Australia. His 2006 PhD dissertation (Queen's University of Belfast) focused on children's practice and performance of dance music and song in Bali, Indonesia. He has published articles on Balinese music and dance, music pedagogy, applied ethnomusicology, and the Indonesian diaspora in Western Australia.

Stephen P.K. Muir is a Senior Lecturer in Music at the University of Leeds, specializing in Russian and East European music, Jewish liturgical music, and critical editing of music. He is also an active freelance singer and conductor/musical director. Recent publications include a chapter on Rimsky-Korsakov's opera *Pan Voyevoda* in a volume of essays in honor of Julian Rushton, an article for Music and Letters on the 19th-century English reception of Rimsky-Korsakov, and conference papers on Jewish liturgical music. He has coedited a collection of essays *Wagner in Russia, Poland and the Czech Lands* (Ashgate 2013). He has conducted fieldwork in synagogues in Leeds, Liverpool, and Cape Town, and in February 2013 was awarded an international research collaboration grant by the Worldwide Universities Network for his project 'Music, Memory and Migration in the Post-Holocaust Experience,' working with colleagues from the UK, US, South Africa, Australia, and Israel. He is associated with the Leeds University Centres for Opera Studies, Jewish Studies, and African Studies.

Anna Oldfield is an Assistant Professor at Coastal Carolina University, where she teaches World Literatures and Cultures. She specializes in the written and oral literature of the former Soviet Union, primarily Central and Western Asia. Oldfield has published on Turkic literatures, epics, and singers, including her book on Azerbaijani women bards, *Azerbaijani Women Poet-Minstrels: Women Ashiqs from the Eighteenth Century to the Present* (Edwin Mellen 2008) and a chapter in *Resounding Pasts: Essays in Literature, Music, and Cultural Memory* (Cambridge 2008). She is currently working on a co-translation of the Kazakh Koroglu epic and an edited volume of Uzbek short stories. She is especially interested in how narrative poetics intersect with and transform real and imaginary times and places. Oldfield is active in cultural exchange initiatives, including with the British Library Endangered Archives Programme and the Smithsonian Folkways Music of Central Asia Series.

Natasha Pravaz is an Associate Professor of Anthropology at Wilfrid Laurier University, Canada, where she teaches on performance theory, postcoloniality, embodiment, and popular culture. Her research interests revolve around the performative production of social identities, focusing both on the racialization of gender and on transnational exchange in Latin American dance and music. She has published several articles on Brazilian samba and mestiçagem, discussing their links to the sexualized figure of the 'mulata', the myth of 'racial democracy' as national identity in Brazil, and the normalization of carnivalesque practices under modernity. Pravaz's current research among local and diasporic sambistas in the city of Toronto (where she plays the tamborim) addresses the complexities of intercultural pedagogy, the production of emotional well-being through community bonds, and the magnetism of exotica in the West.

Les Roberts is a Lecturer in Digital Cultures in the Department of Communication and Media at the University of Liverpool. His research interests are in the cultural production of space, place, and mobility, with a particular focus on film and popular music cultures. He is author of *Film, Mobility and Urban Space: A Cinematic Geography of Liverpool* (University of Liverpool Press 2012), editor of *Mapping Cultures: Place, Practice, Performance* (Palgrave 2012), and coeditor of *Liminal Landscapes: Travel, Experience and Spaces In-Between* (Routlegde 2012) and *The City and the Moving Image: Urban Projections* (Palgrave 2010).

Carol Silverman is a cultural anthropologist and folklorist who has been involved with Balkan music and culture for over 30 years as a researcher, teacher, activist, and performer. Her book *Romani Routes: Cultural Politics and Balkan Music in Diaspora* was released in 2012 with Oxford University Press with an extensive accompanying website. Her research has been supported by Guggenheim, IREX, NEH, ACLS, and NCSEER. Among her many articles and book chapters about Balkan folklore and Romani (Gypsy) communities in the US and abroad are: 'Trafficking in the Exotic with "Gypsy" Music: Balkan Roma, Cosmopolitanism, and "World Music" Festivals,' in Donna Buchanan, ed., *Balkan Popular Culture and the Ottoman Ecumene: Music, Image, and Regional Political Discourse* (Scarecrow Press 2007); and 'Education, Agency, and Power among Macedonian Muslim Romani Women in New York City,' *Signs: Journal of Women in Culture and Society (Symposium on*

Romani Feminisms) 38(1) (2012). In 1996, Silverman was the recipient of a university award for distinguished teaching. She teaches courses on the Balkans, Jewish folklore, ethnography, feminism, and performative theories of culture.

Graham St John is a pioneering researcher of electronic dance music cultures, festivals, and movements. He has held postdoctoral fellowships in three countries, including an SSRC Research Fellowship at the School for Advanced Research, Santa Fe, New Mexico, and is currently Adjunct Research Fellow at the Griffith Centre for Cultural Research, Griffith University. Graham's latest book is *Global Tribe: Technology, Spirituality and Psytrance* (Equinox 2012). His previous books include *Technomad: Global Raving Countercultures* (Equinox 2009) and the edited collections *The Local Scenes and Global Culture of Psytrance* (Routledge 2010); *Victor Turner and Contemporary Cultural Performance* (Berghahn 2008); *Rave Culture and Religion* (Routledge 2004); and *FreeNRG: Notes from the Edge of the Dance Floor* (Commonground 2001). Graham is Executive Editor of *Dancecult: Journal of Electronic Dance Music Culture.*

Timothy D. Taylor is a Professor in the Departments of Ethnomusicology and Musicology at the University of California, Los Angeles. He is the author of *Global Pop: World Music, World Markets* (Routledge 1997); *Strange Sounds: Music, Technology and Culture* (Routledge 2001); *Beyond Exoticism: Western Music and the World* (Duke 2007); *The Sounds of Capitalism: Advertising, Music, and the Conquest of Culture* (University of Chicago 2012); and *Music, Sound, and Technology in America: A Documentary History of Early Phonograph, Cinema, and Radio* (Duke 2012), coedited with Mark Katz and Tony Grajeda, and numerous articles on various popular musics, classical musics, and social/cultural theory. He is currently writing a book about music in today's capitalism.

Ruxandra Trandafoiu is a Reader in Communication at Edge Hill University, UK. Her areas of research are: nationalism and migration, social media and online communication, European Union politics, and the Eastern European postcommunist transition. She is the author of *Diaspora Online: Identity Politics and Romanian Migrants* (Berghahn 2013).

Index

An environmentally friendly book printed and bound in England by www.printondemand-worldwide.com

#0027 - 200314 - C0 - 229/152/19 [21] - CB